THE ECCLESIASTICAL POLITY OF THE NEW TESTAMENT.

THE

ECCLESIASTICAL POLITY

OF

THE NEW TESTAMENT.

A STUDY FOR THE PRESENT CRISIS IN THE CHURCH OF ENGLAND.

BY THE

REV. G. A. JACOB, D.D,

LATE HEAD-MASTER OF CHRIST'S HOSPITAL.

NEW-YORK:
T. WHITTAKER,
No. 2 BIBLE HOUSE.
1872.

St. Johnland Stereotype Foundry,
SUFFOLK COUNTY, N. Y.

PREFACE.

THE following pages were written as a course of Lectures; which, however, were not delivered. They are now presented to the public in their original form and arrangement, though with some alterations in the substance of their contents, in the belief that a review of the organization and outward life of the Christian Church, as exhibited in the New Testament, and compared with the Church in the post-apostolic times, especially in what is termed the Nicene period, will suggest some useful thoughts for the Church of England in the crisis through which it is now passing.

The words which M. de Pressensé wrote a few years ago in the Preface of his 'Church History' have lost none of their force and truth at the present time. "Il n'est pas un seul parti religieux qui n'éprouve le besoin ou de se raffermir ou de se transformer. Les Eglises nées du grand mouvement du seizième siècle sont toutes engagées dans une crise sérieuse."

Whether this crisis shall in our case issue in good, or in evil, is almost identical with the question whether the English Church has sufficient wisdom to see what ought to be done, and sufficient courage to do it.

The object of these Lectures is not to advocate the views or opinions of any Church party, or theological school; but to present to thoughtful men a view of the Christian religion in its original form; to mark some of the differences between Scripture truth and Church tradition, between the primitive state of Christianity as it came from the Apostles, and what it became in the hands of uninspired men; and from thence to point out some obvious suggestions for our consideration at the present time.

It has been thought desirable in almost every case, instead of merely giving references to quote the words of the authorities appealed to; and to these the attention of the reader is especially requested.

TWICKENHAM,
May, 1871.

CONTENTS.

CONTENTS.

LECTURE I.

THE APOSTLES AND THE CHRISTIAN CHURCH.

I.

THE APOSTLES AND THE CHRISTIAN CHURCH.

THERE are in the New Testament several names and titles given to Christians as individual men, each one in and for himself believing in Christ, and guided by His Spirit: and many doctrines and preceptive instructions are addressed to them in this character, with a view to their personal edification, and their progress in the Christian life.

But however true it may be that this individual Christianity is the first and most important;—and that his own particular religious state is the first and most important consideration for each human soul;—it is evident that it was from the beginning the intention of the Divine Founder of our religion that there should be societies or communities of His disciples, acting together as united members of a corporate body, with mutual relations to each other as well as to Himself, and with mutual duties connected with this union.

Different names are accordingly given to them,—some with a figurative, and others with a more literal meaning,—descriptive of this religious incorporation, and exhibiting different aspects of its nature and design.

As therefore the subject which I propose to consider embraces the Ecclesiastical Polity of the Apostles of Christ—or the organization and outward life of the Apostolic Church as it appears in the New Testament—it may be well first of all to notice, briefly, the most prominent of these descriptive names, and the manner in which the apostolic office and work are set forth in connection with them.

I.—*Christians represented as a temple.*

One of the most striking figures, by which the corporate life of Christians is described represents them as a magnificent and sacred building—a temple of God wherein He spiritually dwells. In this figure each Christian is one of the stones built up into the gradually rising structure;—the apostles are sometimes the *foundation*, or stones first laid in the building, sometimes themselves the *builders* of the temple;—and Jesus Christ is in one aspect the *builder*, in another the *foundation*, and in another the *chief corner-stone*. Thus our Lord said to Peter, "Thou art Peter, and upon this rock I will build my Church." St. Paul wrote to the Ephesians, "Ye are built upon the foundation of the apostles and prophets, Jesus Christ Himself being the chief corner-stone, in whom all the building fitly framed together groweth unto a holy temple in the Lord; in whom ye also are builded together for a habitation of God through the Spirit." And to the Corinthians, "Ye are God's building;—as a wise master-builder I have laid the foundation, and another buildeth thereon;—other foundation can no man lay than that which is laid, which is Jesus Christ." And St. Peter, in similar terms, "To whom coming as unto a living stone, disallowed indeed of men, but chosen of God and precious, ye also as living stones are built up a spiritual house."

2.—*Christians represented as the body of Christ.*

Another figure which frequently occurs in the Pauline Epistles,—a figure more simple and familiar, but more rich in spiritual sympathies, and in the view which it displays of the Christian's life, strength, health, and joy, in his union with the Saviour,—describes the whole number of Christian people as a *body*—the body of Christ;—Christ Himself being the head, and each Christian one of the members,—so that the whole together are even said to be "Christ." Thus to the Corinthians it is written, "For as the body is one and hath many members, and all the members of that one body, being many, are one body, so also is Christ; for by one spirit we are all baptized into one body." The Ephesians are exhorted to "grow up into Him in all things which is the head, even Christ; from whom the whole body, fitly joined together, and compacted by that which every joint supplieth, according to the effectual working in the measure of every part, maketh increase of the body unto the edifying of itself in love." In a similar manner the bringing in of Christians indiscriminately from all nations is spoken of as "the mystery," or once hidden truth, "that the Gentiles should be fellow-heirs, and of the same body, and partakers of His promise in Christ by the Gospel." The various Church ministrations, to which the different gifts of grace gave birth, are said to have been designed "For the perfecting of the saints, for the work of the ministry, for the edifying of the body of Christ." And those who departed from essential Christian truth are described as "not holding the head, from which all the body by joints and bands having nourishment ministered and knit together increaseth with the increase of God."

But of far more frequent occurrence than either of these figurative appellations are the two names of a "Kingdom," and a "Church;" which represent not by way of similitude, but as a matter of fact, the united state and position of Christ's disciples;—the former expression appearing most frequently in the Gospel narratives, as commonly used by Jesus Himself in his public life among the Jewish nation; while the latter occurs more often, though not exclusively, in the Acts and Epistles, as employed by the Apostles in their ministrations in the world at large.

3.—*Christians the subjects of a kingdom.*

In the very beginning of the Gospel it was declared

that the mission of Jesus was to establish in the world a kingdom—the kingdom of heaven or of God—of which He was Himself to be the king. John the Baptist, as His forerunner, proclaimed, "The kingdom of heaven is at hand." Jesus Himself, at the first commencement of His ministry, published the same announcement. He called His public teaching, "preaching the kingdom of God;" He told those who rejected Him that "the kingdom of God had come upon them before they were aware"—ἔφθασεν ἐφ' ὑμᾶς: and in the "good confession" which He witnessed before Pilate, He acknowledged Himself to be a King—not indeed of this world's kingdoms, but of a kingdom founded on divine truth, and containing the lovers of truth as its subjects.

The Apostles of Christ were heralds sent forth to proclaim this kingdom, and to invite men into it. They preached "the Gospel of the kingdom." Those who assisted them in their ministrations were styled their "fellow-workers unto the kingdom of God." Those who listened to their proclamation, and joined themselves to their company, were assured that they were "no longer strangers and foreigners, but fellow-citizens with the saints;"—they were "called into God's kingdom;"—"translated into the kingdom of his dear Son."

4—*Christians formed into a church*—ἐκκλησία.

The word "Church"—ἐκκλησία—signified primarily any number of men possessing common privileges, and called out (ἔκκλητοι), or summoned, to meet together for the exercise of some common or united functions. And in the New Testament it is used especially of Christian men in their collective capacity, having been called by God's grace out of the darkness of sin and condemnation into the light and liberty of the Gospel covenant; and in Christ, as citizens of His kingdom, enjoying common privileges, and entitled to united action as a lawfully constituted community.

The word thus used is found in the New Testament with either a comprehensive or a restricted meaning—in the singular or the plural number—the Church, a Church, or Churches.

(*a.*) In its highest and most comprehensive signification it denotes all real Christians, who have been, are, or will be, on earth, and who will be united in Christ's kingdom of glory. It is in this sense that St. Paul speaks of "the general assembly and Church of the first-born which are written in heaven." In this sense the Church is the true body of Christ, "the fulness of Him that filleth all in all;" in which the glory of God will be displayed "throughout all ages world without end."

(*b.*) It is also used to signify the "Visible Catholic Church," *i. e.*, all professing Christians living at any given time upon earth: in which sense, "The Lord added to the Church daily those who were being saved;" and St. Paul exhorted the Corinthians to "give none offence, neither to the Jews, nor to the Gentiles, nor to the Church of God."

(*c.*) But this word is much more frequently used with

a restricted meaning to denote a distinct Christian community in a particular place; in which connection it should be observed that in the apostolic writings it is never said of a *country* or *nation*. It is always the Church in a city or town. Neither is it ever said to be the Church *of* any given town;[1] but always *in* or *at* the place,—or else the Church of the inhabitants, *i.e.* the *Christian* inhabitants of the town; as "the Church which was at Jerusalem;" "the Church that was in Antioch;" "the Church of the Laodiceans." Whenever the Christians of a country or nation are spoken of collectively, the word is always in the plural number; as, "The Churches of Galatia;" "The Churches of Judea." There is no example of a "National Church" in the New Testament.[2]

(d.) And lastly, in its most restricted meaning, the word is applied to a congregation assembling in one place for Christian worship; as, "The Church that is in their house;" "When ye come together in the Church,"

---

[1] An *apparent*, but not a real, exception is found in Rev. ii. 1, "Unto the angel of the Church *of* Ephesus;" but this is an error, for the words are, *τῷ ἀγγέλῳ τῆς Ἐφεσίνης ἐκκλησίας*, not *Ἐφέσου*; not to mention that *τῷ ἐν Ἐφέσῳ* is a preferable reading.

[2] From the very circumstances of the case there could be no such thing as a "National Church" in the apostolic period. National Churches, however justifiable and desirable in certain periods of national life, are not divine or apostolic institutions. Their propriety rests altogether on the ground of general expediency and public advantage; and to attempt to furnish them with a higher sanction by arguments drawn from the theocratic government of the Jewish people seems to me to savour but little of sound reasoning, and to confound together some of the distinctive characteristics of two widely different dispensations.

i.e. in your assembly as a Christian congregation;—and, "if the whole Church be come together into one place."

But the word is never used in the New Testament to signify a *building* or a *place of worship*:[1] nor does it ever mean Christian ministers as distinguished from the general body of Christians. On the contrary, in two instances, it is found to signify the Laity or general body as distinguished from the Apostles and Elders; thus, "they were received of the Church, and of the Apostles and Elders, and it pleased the Apostles and Elders with the whole Church," who are afterwards in the same chapter designated as "the Apostles, and the Elders, and the Brethren."[2]

---

[1] The word Church in 1 Cor. xi. 18–22, is sometimes represented as meaning a building; but no reason can be assigned for this, except the puerile one (which would justify any amount of erroneous translation), that such a rendering *will make sense* in this particular passage. There is no good example of *ἐκκλησία* meaning a building earlier than the third century.

[2] It is by no means an unnecessary or trivial thing to mark these different significations of the word Church. What may justly be affirmed of the Church in one sense, may be a fatal delusion when applied to it in another. And the want of clearly distinguishing between such differences has been at the root of many evils in the course of ecclesiastical history. Thus, in the third century, both Novatian and his orthodox opponents fell into the same fundamental error of confounding the visible with the invisible Church, though they differed in the application of their mistaken notion. Throughout the Nicene period, the same unfortunate mistake wrought incalculable mischief in doctrine and in practice. It is needless to say that it has dominated in the Church of Rome. And even now there are those amongst ourselves who to this ancient misapprehension join the additional error of confounding their own particular Church platform with that of the whole Catholic Church, to the great detriment of Christian feeling, and the encouragement of a blind and uncharitable bigotry.

"Inextricable confusion and dangerous error must arise, unless we keep distinct two things—abso-

Of this Gospel Church in its highest and most comprehensive meaning our Lord Jesus Christ is declared to be the Head ;—the source of life to each member of this His body ;—the chief shepherd of this flock and fold. But while all true Christians are thus united to Him. and have in Him a common life, the Church, in this sense, being at present altogether a spiritual body, has no visible form or organization, in the regulation of which man has anything to do, however human instrumentality may be employed in bringing men, one after another, into it. The place and time of its manifestation in its completeness as an organized community,— or what St. Paul terms a *πολίτευμα*,—is not on earth or in the existing gospel dispensation.

The Church which the Apostles were sent forth to constitute and establish in the world, though possessing spiritual blessings, and containing within it those who have an inner spiritual life in Christ, is yet a visible body, Catholic or one in nature, privilege, doctrine, and position, so far as any portion of it succeeds in realising

lutely different in themselves, and yet too often regarded as one and the same—I mean, on the one hand, *visible Christianity*, or the system of Christian doctrines and practices existing or established in this and that country, sometimes giving direction to the course of events on the great stage of affairs, sometimes depressed and confined within the narrowest limits ; and, on the other hand, the *True Church* [the portion of the invisible Catholic Church] on earth, or the aggregate of individuals, whether scattered or congregated, whose hearts have been quickened from above, and whose dispositions and conduct are actually governed by the genuine motives of the Gospel ; in a word, the children of God, of whatever name or communion."—'Ancient Christianity,' p. 433.

its professed character and state; but including any number of Christian societies, which, as far as human authority is concerned, are independent of each other. It is this visible Catholic Church,—as a community,—or number of communities, of professedly Christian men,—in the regulation of which human agency has in all ages had a part to take and a duty to perform; and the polity of which as instituted by the Apostles we have now to consider.

The two names of a Kingdom and a Church, although sometimes apparently used as synonymous and interchangeable, yet represent the Christian body under different aspects, and correspond respectively with the *moral* and the *religious* position of Christ's disciples. And, in connection with this distinction, it may be observed, that the *kingdom of God,* with Jesus as its king, began during the Saviour's life upon earth; but the *Church* was not brought into existence until after He had left the world.

Jesus Himself commenced his kingdom; and those who attached themselves to Him became its citizens. Jesus Himself made known the great moral principles which were to regulate His subjects; as may be seen in a condensed form in the Sermon on the Mount, and more diffusively in other portions of the Gospel narratives.[1] He shewed plainly in the course of His instruc-

[1] Some rationalistic writers have unfairly seized on this circumstance to represent that Jesus was only a moral Rabbinical teacher introducing a purified Judaism without adding a single doctrine to

tions that the moral life, or citizenship, in His kingdom was not a mere enforced subjection to the yoke of law, or an outward conformity with the letter of commandments; but a life proceeding from an inward powei imparted by His spirit to those who were united to Him, as fruitful branches of the living vine;—a life acting through the influence of love, and not of a slavish fear, producing a happy, spiritual, and enlarged obedience to His will, and extending to every particular of the Christian character. And all that was left for His Apostles, in this portion of their work, was to proclaim and inculcate what Christ Himself had taught,—to teach men that "the law of the spirit of life in Christ Jesus made His subjects free from the law of sin and death" (Rom. viii. 2), in order that they might live the new life unto God;—and to exhort them to walk in a manner worthy of the vocation wherewith they had been called, —the heavenly citizenship to which they had been admitted.

But the Church was not begun until after the descent of the Holy Spirit upon the Apostles on the day of Pentecost; and it is never mentioned, except prospectively, before that time. Men could be admitted into the kingdom of Christ, as soon as they were willing to

---

the older religion. They ignore the important facts that Christianity, *as a religion, could not exist* until after the death of Christ; and also that, although the Christian life in its moral aspect is the more prominent in the Gospels, yet the great Christian doctrines are also alluded to; and, above all, the historical foundation of those doctrines is most distinctly recorded.

submit to His authority, and to conform to the life which He lived and taught; but they could not be formed into a Church, until they believed in Him as the Son of God,—the Saviour of those who received Him, by the justifying righteousness of His life and the atoning sacrifice of His death,—and the imparter of the Holy Spirit, and the future judge of man ; and this could not be, until after His work on earth was done, and He had risen again, and ascended into heaven.

The Apostles, therefore, were the founders of the Christian Church. They were its divinely appointed and infallible teachers and legislators. They were its supreme authorities on earth, to declare its doctrines and to prescribe its form and polity,—to admit into it and exclude from it,—to bind and to loose,—to remit and to retain sins. They were in short to organize the Church as a regular society possessed of a definite character, with its own especial rights, privileges, and objects. They were to rule in it as long as they lived; and it rested with them to leave such instructions for its future guidance, as they might consider necessary for its continuance and welfare, as a permanent institution in the world.

To qualify them for this high office and important work the Apostles received a divine *authority* and *power*, from the commission of Christ, and the inspiration of the Holy Spirit. The authority was given them by Christ Himself, when He said to them, as recorded by St. Matthew, "Go ye therefore and teach—or rather *μαθητεύσατε*, make disciples of—all nations, baptizing them in the name of the Father, and of the Son, and of the Holy Ghost; teaching them to observe all things, whatsoever I have commanded you; and lo! I am with you always, even unto the end of the world." And when, as related by St. John, He declared to them, "As my Father hath sent me, even so send I you;" and, "Whosesoever sins ye remit, they are remitted unto them, and whosesoever sins ye retain, they are retained." And a divine *power* was given to them by the coming of the Holy Spirit, of whom Jesus had told them beforehand, that when He was gone they should receive another Comforter, to abide with them forever—even the Holy Ghost, who would teach them all things, and bring all things to their remembrance, whatsoever He had said unto them; and who, as the Spirit of truth, would "guide them into all the truth," *πᾶσαν τὴν ἀλήθειαν*,—which they were to proclaim to men. This was "the power from on high," for which, after His ascension, they were "to tarry at Jerusalem." This power, as the last words of Jesus informed them, "they would receive, when the Holy Spirit came upon them," and thus fitted them to be His witnesses and ambassadors, throughout the world.

And this power and authority *were both combined* in those words, so often, as I venture to think, misinterpreted and misapplied, which Jesus addressed to Peter—certainly not to the exclusion of the other Apostles—"Thou art Peter, and on this rock I will build my

Church;[1] and I will give unto thee the keys of the kingdom of heaven; and whatsoever thou shalt bind on earth shall be bound in heaven, and whatsoever thou shalt loose on earth shall be loosed in heaven"[2] (Matt.

---

[1] I am unable to see that the "rock" in this verse can mean anything but Peter himself; nor do I believe that any Christian scholar reading the original text would assign to it any other meaning, if he had no special opinion which he was determined to maintain. Some Protestant interpreters in their zeal against popery have rejected this obvious meaning. But it is a very dangerous practice, whatever be the motive, to make the sense of Scripture conform itself to our opinions, instead of making our opinions conform themselves to it. It is, moreover, difficult to see why Peter should not be called the "foundation" in this verse, as well as the Apostles in general in Eph. ii. 10. See also Rev. xxi. 14. The ancient fathers are but little to be relied on as interpreters of Scripture; and they differ from each other in their interpretation of this verse. Augustin once held the common-sense view, and afterwards changed his opinion. But his second thoughts were not always the best, seeing that he inveighed against the superstitions of his time, and then gave the weight of his authority to support them. Ambrose also held that Peter was the "rock," as Augustin acknowledges. "Dixi," he says, "in quodam loco de Apostolo Petro, quod in illo, tanquam in petra, fundata sit ecclesia; qui sensus etiam cantatur ore multorum in versibus beatissimi Ambrosii, ubi de gallo gallinaceo ait:

Hoc ipsa petra ecclesiæ
Canente culpam diluit."

Aug. lib. i. Retract. xxi.

So Cyprian, a century earlier, says, "Petrus tamen, super quem ædificata ab eodem domino fuerat ecclesia, unus pro omnibus loquens et ecclesiæ voce respondens, ait, domine, ad quem ibimus?—Epist. 55, ad Cornelium.

[2] The words of this apostolic commission, "I will give thee the keys," &c., have been a favourite text with Papal despotism, and have given occasion to some very gross delusions.

Protestant divines, rejecting these, have yet too often entangled themselves and their readers in unprofitable speculations on these simple words. Romanists are, at any rate, *consistent* in their error when they use this text as a foundation for the pretended infallibility of their church; for the words addressed to Peter do distinctly speak of an infallible authority; and if they applied to successive ages of the Church, they would justify ecclesiastical claims of the

xvi. 19)—words both of *power* and of *authority*, for he who has the keys given to him is both *able* and *authorised* to admit and to shut out; while the last part of this commission declares this authority to be infallible, and makes the Apostle's words of command or solemn instruction the *Word of God* to men.[1]

The INWARD *and* OUTWARD *aspect of the Church.*

This Church of the apostolic times, as in every other period of its history, presents an *inward* and an *outward* aspect. To the former belong the doctrines which the Apostles taught: the latter is exhibited in its apostolic form,—its institutions and laws. These two are, indeed, intimately connected together; for "the form of the Church, at any period, is a result primarily of its doctrine. Its external phase in constitution and worship is,

papal type. But Protestants are *inconsistent* when, denying the claims of Rome, they deduce for themselves from this verse a divinely-given church authority, which they call the "power of the keys."

Every Church, as a lawfully constituted body sanctioned by Christ, has, in accordance with his will, a legitimate authority over its members, just as all other voluntary communities have over those who join them; but it does not depend upon such texts as these. The words will justly apply to Peter and the other apostles alone. To them alone could it be said with truth, that "Whatsoever they should bind or loose upon earth, would be bound and loosed in heaven."

[1] As Peter was specially mentioned by name in this giving of the keys, so he is specially named when the keys were first used on the day of Pentecost to admit the believing Jews into the Church. It was also Peter who, with these keys, opened the door of entrance to Cornelius and his friends, the first-fruits of Gentile Christianity. With the same keys, again, Peter and John shut out Simon of Samaria from the Church, when his real character was discovered.

for the most part, the necessary fruit and effect of the inner principle of doctrine and creed." (Guericke.) And conversely the outward form and constitution of a Church,—the laws or customs which regulate its worship and discipline,—the functions assigned to its officers,—the ritual observed in its devotions,—and its whole action as a visible Christian body,—re-act with great force upon its inner life,—upon the doctrines which it most prominently teaches,—the manner in which those doctrines are received and held by its individual members, and the whole of their religious character and state. Neither can such outward forms be lightly passed by on the ground that the real strength and essence of such a religion as ours is the invisible spirit of its inner life. For every religion, however spiritual in its nature, must have some outward exhibition of its truths and principles, —must have a visible organization, through which its inner life may act and be maintained, and its power duly exercised among men. Without these external things no visible Church could be gathered together or continue to exist,—no Christian community—and, possibly, no individual Christian—could long preserve his religion unimpaired. The importance, therefore, of the external action in any Christian Church, though it must be confined to its own proper sphere, can hardly, within that sphere, be exaggerated, or too highly placed. Outward forms and ordinances are not, indeed, the life, yet they are necessary as means and instruments of the life's powers and influences. They stand related to the real life and spirit of a Christian Church nearly as the organs of the human body do to the soul,—dead and powerless by themselves, yet requisite for the soul's contact with the material world. And as in the man, considered as a creature of this world, his best and soundest condition is when his body, healthy and complete in every limb, subserves and exhibits the action of a healthy mental state;—so *that* is the best and soundest condition of a Church on earth, when an external organization, healthy and complete in all its parts, most freely and fully displays the working of a divine life within;—neither by an *excess* of laws and ceremonies, causing the true spirit to be lost sight of in adherence to the form;—nor by an opposite *defect* and want of forms preventing the spirit, from its very spirituality, from being apprehended by ordinary men;—nor by unauthorised, unsound, or questionable observances and rules giving erroneous views of Christian doctrine—hindering the healthy action of Christian feeling—unduly fettering Christian liberty—or distorting the fair proportions of Christian truth, which it is the office of the Church to cherish and make known.

Hence in every Church a due attention to its outward organization,—its regulations, ceremonial, government, and polity in general,—is intimately connected with its most vital interests, and can never with safety be omitted, or regarded as a matter of slight and trivial concern.[1]

---

[1] With regard to our own Church, surely there never was a time since the reign of Queen Elizabeth, when it was more imperatively called to a large and scriptural consideration of such questions with

For this reason the outward aspect and constitution of the apostolic Church, as it is exhibited in the New Testament, has seemed to me a subject not likely to be unprofitable, even when handled with no more power than I can hope to bring to it, and to no wider an extent than the limits of these lectures will allow. And in dwelling upon this subject I purpose at the same time to wander so far into the regions of the post-apostolic Church, as to compare, in certain striking respects, the institutions and practices of the apostolic age with those of the three following centuries,—especially that latter portion of them which is commonly called the Nicene period.

It seems to me the more important to take this double view of the subject, because there is so very much in the aspect of Church thought and action at the present time, which demands from true and earnest Christian men an impartial and unshrinking consideration not only of the teaching of the New Testament, but also of the real teaching of the Nicene Church, and of the authority supposed to be attached to it. Notwithstanding the still generally acknowledged supremacy of Holy Scripture

all earnestness and gravity. The dangers which hung over the Church of England at the beginning of the seventeenth century may seem to us now more alarming than those of the present day ; but the Churchmen of those times made light of the storm, until it burst upon their heads. With less violent elements, perhaps, on the surface, but with deeper grounds of apprehension underneath, the national Church, endangered from within and from without, is still, unfortunately, shrinking from that which alone, humanly speaking, could ensure its safety.

amongst us, the main current of Church opinion on all questions of polity and practice (to say nothing here of doctrines) has for a very considerable time been setting strongly towards the ecclesiastical system of the third and fourth centuries, to the neglect, in this respect, of the New Testament; and many are carried quietly along with the tide, knowing little or nothing of the shore to which it is wafting them. The movement, which was commenced in our Church nearly forty years ago, and which has gradually extended its influence under various forms and phases, until it is now felt throughout our ecclesiastical life, was begun and carried on by men, who diligently and perseveringly brought to bear upon the public mind their stores of learning, gathered, not from the Apostles, but from the post-apostolic Fathers; not from the divinely taught Church of the New Testament, but from the humanly deteriorated Church of a later time. The opponents of this Oxford school of theology cried out against what seemed to be the Romanistic nature of its teaching;—a considerable number of its teachers and disciples ended their career in the Church of Rome;—and Romanizing predilections and practices are still plainly seen in some of its adherents. Yet it was a mistake to suppose that Rome was the proposed object of the Oxford Tractarians' aims or wishes. The accomplished leaders of that movement were no doubt perfectly sincere, when at an early period of their course they denied the charge of Rome-ward tendencies which was brought against them. It was not into conformity with the Church of Rome, but into conformity with the Church of the fourth century, that they desired to bring us. It was only at a later time that some of them, discovering the end to which their accepted principles naturally led, but which they had not at first perceived, honestly went over to the Romish communion. And even now, after the long, and for the most part triumphant, career which this Church party has pursued, it is only the very advanced members of it who distinctly hold Romanistic tenets, and long for an actual re-union with the Papal See. The greater number, the more moderate and less deeply imbued portion of the High Church or Anglo-Catholic school, who do not denounce the English Reformation as a blunder and a crime, desire still, with a consciousness more or less indistinct, to draw as near as they can, in doctrine and in practice, to the model of the Church, as it existed before the supposed commencement of the Papacy;—or at any rate they entertain a great reverence for the Nicene period, as if the true Christian system had then reached its perfection, and as if the doctrines and practices then in force, were in some way or other binding upon Christians now. Yes, and even with some, who do not by any means belong to the High Church school, there may be found a vague feeling that the Nicene period enjoys a kind of authority in the Church of England beyond that of any other time. And so when "Church authority" or "Church principles," instead of the teaching, or as supplemental to the teaching, of the New Testament, are urged upon our acceptance under the penalty of our being considered untrue to the Catholic Church, if we reject them, the Church as it was in the fourth century is intended.

And all the while there is frequently a profound ignorance of what the Church system at that time really was, and of the extent to which it had departed from the simplicity of the apostolic age and truth.

In the following pages therefore some particulars of that Church system will be noticed in connection with the apostolic practices, with which they are contrasted; and in the meanwhile I would observe in general terms respecting it, that it is not at all surprising if modern Anglo-Catholicism, while following the Nicene Church, has been popularly accused of Romish tendencies; or if some of the leaders or promoters of this theology have joined themselves to the Papal Church. Nor is it by any means so extraordinary or outrageous a thing, as it might at first sight be deemed, when clergymen of the Church of England,—a Church which protests against Romish errors,—seem to conform their ministrations as nearly as possible to the rites and ceremonies of Rome. For almost all the doctrines and practices which characterize modern Romanism, are to be found only a little less intensified in times long before the date of what is considered the commencement of the Papal system; beginning, indeed, at the end of the second century,—making large growth, and gaining strength and development in the third and fourth,—and numbering among its adherents, expositors, and supporters, the greatest names in patristic divinity.[1] And consequently a reverent and admiring study of those times, pursued to any length, must exert a powerful, if not an irresistible, influence in this direction,—an influence which naturally and necessarily lands the captivated student in something scarcely distinguishable from full-grown Romanism,—unless the New Testament is placed high and alone above all other authorities in his mind, and the words and deeds of the best and most honoured of men and Churches, are constantly brought to the test of the inspired record, and of the apostolic teaching in the really primitive Church. And as long as the Church of the third and fourth cen-

---

[1] Full and irrefragable proofs of this assertion, which may seem strange and incredible to some worthy men, are to be found in the ecclesiastical writers of the period. Our Church histories are, in this respect, of very little use. Bingham's 'Antiquities' (if it be an edition in which the original authorities are quoted at length) supplies many useful materials for forming a sound judgment on some particulars; but he passes too lightly over many points which are the most necessary for the discovery of the truth; and his explanations and inferences are often too *innocent* to be of any value.

A large amount of most valuable information, with authorities quoted or referred to, is contained in 'Ancient Christianity,' by Isaac Taylor, first published thirty years ago—an unanswerable book, which deserves more attention than it has received from English Churchmen; and which may be studied with advantage by all who wish to know the source and end of modern Anglo-Catholicism.

Mede's learned work on 'The Apostacy of the Latter Times,' may also be read with advantage in connection with this subject.

In Appendix A. I have endeavoured to give, within a short compass, a synopsis of the doctrines and practices which are sometimes thought to be exclusively Romanistic, but which were maintained by the Christian Church before or at the end of the fourth century. The attention of the reader is specially requested to the proofs which are there given for every statement.

turies is regarded with especial reverence, and its authority over us is even partially admitted, it will be possible for our clergy, who desire to reproduce its system, to draw through it quite close to Romanism, without being self-convicted of unfaithfulness or dishonesty,—but on the contrary having many pleas wherewith to satisfy their own conscience, and to excuse, if not to justify, their proceedings. Such Anglo-Catholics often seem to feel that they need not go over to Rome, because they can thus make a Rome for themselves where they are, without the painfulness and scandal of a secession.

But the opinion that we are bound dutifully to submit to the authority, and ought to be guided by the practice and example, of the Church as it was in the first three, four, or any other centuries, however prevalent and plausible, is delusive and ensnaring. The Church of the apostolic period is the only Church in which there is found an authority justly claiming the acknowledgment of Christian bodies in other times. And such authority is found in this Church,—not because it was possessed of a truer catholicity, or a purer constitution, or a more primitive antiquity, than belong to succeeding ages; for neither antiquity, nor purity of form, nor catholicity, confers any right to govern or command; but because it was under the immediate rule and guidance of the Apostles; and it is their infallible judgment alone, as exhibited in this Church, which has a legitimate claim to our submission.[1]

[1] Pressensé says of the apostolic age in his forcible language, "Il est toutefois une période de son histoire, qu'il importe de distinguer

Of the Church of no other period can the same be said, because the Apostles had no successors in their office.[1] They stand alone. They stand alone as the

des autres ; c'est l'âge apostolique. Sa mission spéciale fut de conserver au monde le souvenir vivant du Christ. L'Eglise primitive est l'intermédiaire obligé entre nous et lui ; elle seule nous le fait connaître ; elle est pour nous comme le canal qui nous apporte l'eau de la source. Aussi a-t-elle reçu les dons nécessaires à l'accomplissement de sa mission. Il en est deux surtout qui lui sont particuliers. Elle est l'Eglise de l'Apostolat, et l'Eglise de l'Inspiration. D'une part, elle est le temoin immédiat du Christ, et de l'autre elle a reçu l'esprit de Dieu dans une mesure extraordinaire, afin de poser solidement le fondement, sur lequel l'Eglise de tous les temps devait être assise."—'Histoire des Trois Premiers Siècles,' vol. i. p. 350.

[1] "Ipsius Apostolatus nulla successio. Finitur enim legatio cum legato, nec ad successores ipsius transit." 'Staple,' quoted by Hooker (Eccl. Pol. vii. § 4), who remarks upon it, "Such as deny Apostles to have any successors at all in the office of their Apostleship, may hold that opinion without contradiction to this of ours, if they will explain themselves in declaring what truly and properly Apostleship is. In some things every presbyter, in some things only bishops, in some things neither the one nor the other are the Apostles' successors."

It might with equal truth and force be added that in some things *every Christian man* is a successor of the Apostles. The Apostles ordained presbyters, and so do bishops ; the Apostles preached Christ, and so do presbyters ; the Apostles believed in Jesus, and so do Christian men ; but all this has really nothing to do with the question whether the Apostles had any successors *in their Apostleship.* In all the essential powers and authority of the Apostles' office they had, and could have, none to succeed them. And the question is not fairly met and argued by Hooker.

Indeed, in spite of the high estimation in which Hooker has always been justly held, in spite of his great and admirable qualities—his genius, learning, eloquence, and piety—a thoughtful and unprejudiced man will hardly read through the whole of his 'Ecclesiastical Polity' (which I suspect very few of our modern divinity students do), without once and again feeling that he is listening to an advocate bent upon saying all that can be said on one side, and not always having the best of the argument, rather than a fair investigator of the truth ; and regretting that never since his time has an

divinely inspired teachers, legislators, and rulers in Christ's Church and kingdom. They stand alone as men appointed and commissioned by Christ Himself, and not by man; whereas all Christian ministers since their time, of whatsoever order or degree, have been fallible men, and have been appointed and commissioned by man,—by the authority of the particular Church in which they were to minister.

The promise of our Lord, that He would be with the Apostles even to the end of the world, as it did not secure to them a continuance on earth beyond their own generation, so neither did it engage or imply that others with a similar power and authority should succeed them. With faithful preachers of Christ, and sound teachers of His word and doctrine, and diligent pastors of His flock, their divine Master has in all ages been present by His Spirit. But no Christian ministers having received the commission or inspiration of the Apostles, none of them could inherit the apostolic office, nor could they individually or in any collective body ever possess the apostolic authority. And as no Church ministers, so neither the Church itself of any post-apostolic time, (in whatever mode we may suppose it to have uttered a united voice), has ever had any apostolic or divine authority to which after-ages owed submission.

The opinion that such submission is due to the Church

---

authoritative and impartial judge summed up the case between Hooker and his Puritan opponents, and obtained a just verdict in the cause.

of any given period, can be justified only on the supposition that the Church of that period was infallible: that in fact our Lord was then so present with the visible Church, as to miraculously exempt it from error in the exercise of its legislative and administrative functions, in doctrine and in practice. But if so, is there any ground whatever for rejecting the claims of infallibility such as are persistently and consistently put forward by the Church of Rome? Is there any ground whatever for ascribing this divine sanction to the Nicene period, and denying it to the modern Papacy? For surely it is impossible with any show of reason or truth, to draw the line at any one place in the history of the Church, after the Apostles had been withdrawn; and to say, before this the Church was divinely preserved from error,—after this it was fallible and erred.

Nor can the *nearness* of the early Church to the Apostles' time be with any effect pleaded in behalf of its authority. For it is not being *near* to truth and wisdom that makes men true and wise. And there is unquestionable evidence that soon after the Apostles disappeared, the Church was no longer always guided by the spirit of truth and wisdom; but, on the contrary, gradually yielded to the seductions of error,—was corrupted by its contact with Judaism, Gnosticism, and Heathenism, and advanced more and more along the downward road of superstition and formality.

The only deference, therefore, which we owe to Church antiquity, as distinguished from the inspired authority of the Apostles, is this,—that whenever good men, either singly or unitedly, have said or done what is right and good, we should love to listen to them, and to tread in their steps—to follow them as they followed Christ. But we must use our own judgment, guided by Scripture, reason, and experience, in deciding what is right or wrong in their words or deeds.

I appeal, therefore, from the Nicene Fathers to the Apostles of Christ; from patristic literature to the New Testament; from ecclesiastical authorities and practices of post-apostolic centuries to the primitive Church of the apostolic age. To go back to that time, and to endeavour, as far as possible, to reproduce the Church of the New Testament, is most needful for us now, if we would preserve a faithful and distinct acknowledgment of Christian truth amongst our people. By realizing as far as we may the ideal of that Church in our own community, we shall best maintain its liberty and purity—we shall best meet the peculiar dangers of the present time, and prepare for the future which is at hand.[1]

---

[1] The following words of Pressensé are well worthy of the attention of English Churchmen at the present time: "Pour quiconque admet la divinité du Christianisme, l'Eglise de l'avenir a son type et son idéal dans ce grand passé qui remonte non pas à trois siècles, mais à dix-huit siècles en arrière. Le connaître toujour mieux pour le reproduire toujours plus fidèlement, telle est la tâche de l'Eglise contemporaine. C'est dans cette voie qu'elle trouvera la liberté et la sainteté, ces deux attributs si etroitement liés et qui lui sont si nécessaires pour s'élever à la hauteur de sa vocation actuelle. C'est dans cette voie qu'elle accomplira aussi dans sa théologie ce progrès, que tout prépare, et que tout conseille, et qui ne séra qu'une appropriation plus profonde de la doctrine apostolique. . . . . . .

But in considering the constitution of the apostolic Church of the New Testament, it will be necessary to remark with as much precision as we can, and to bear in mind, throughout our investigations, the following distinctions :—

1. What, according to the apostolic record, is *necessary* and of perpetual obligation in the Church.

2. What is *non-essential* and *discretionary*, being allowable and under certain circumstances the best, but not necessary or at all times right or desirable.

3. What is *excluded*, and expressly or virtually forbidden, as unsuitable to the Christian dispensation, or inconsistent with its essential character and design.

From the *first* and the *last* of these expressions of the apostolic judgment no Church ought ever to deviate. It is the duty and the wisdom of all Christian communities carefully to retain, and to embody in their ecclesiastical regulations, whatever the inspired teachers and rulers of the original Church regarded as essential; and with equal care to avoid in practice, and to exclude from their ordinances and polity, whatever is shown on the same authority to be alien to the Gospel principles or plan. On the other hand all non-essential things, which in the New Testament are not commanded or for-

---

Puisse-t-elle y reussir de nos jours moins imparfaitement que par le passé, et remonter dans son dogme, comme dans son organisation, par delà toutes les obscurités et toutes les entraves humaines jusqu'au type apostolique. Rien ne lui est plus nécessaire pour les luttes solennelles qui l'attendent."—'Histoire des Trois Premiers Siècles,'—Preface.

bidden, or for which no obligatory form or mode has been prescribed, even where in *some* form or mode they must have a place, and must have had a place, in the practical life of every Church,—all these are left to the discretion and judgment of each Christian community. Every such community is fully authorized to retain, change, or discontinue any ordinance or practice of this nature. It is wise and good for non-essentials to be always distinguished from things of perpetual obligation, and to be altered when changes, or time, or circumstance require such change of ministration. It is wise and good for every Church from time to time to revise its formularies, and to consider with all gravity, but with all Christian freedom, whether any such alterations be required or no. It is very unwise, unapostolic, and un-Christian to bind fast what the Apostles left unbound, and for one Church to condemn another for differences of judgment in such questions. It is very unwise and hostile to the best interests of a Church to regard its regulations, its liturgy, or its other formularies, as fixed for ever, and virtually unalterable, as if they were the embodiment of a divine inspiration or of an express commandment, and so to refuse all change, until at last what was a harmless practice becomes a hurtful superstition, or what was once believed to be a bond of union and strength becomes a source of division, weakness, or disruption. It is a valuable remark of Richard Hooker that, "The superstition that riseth voluntarily and by degrees which are hardly discerned, mingling itself with the rites even of very divine service done to the on y true God, must be considered of as a creeping and encroaching evil—an evil the first beginnings whereof are commonly harmless, so that it proveth only then to be an evil, when some further accident doth grow unto it, or itself come unto further growth . . . This might be exemplified even by heaps of rites and customs, now superstitions in the greatest part of the Christian world, which in their first original beginnings, when the strength of virtuous, devout, or charitable affection bloomed them, no man could justly have condemned as evil." (Eccl. Pol. v. 3.)

Furthermore, in endeavouring to arrive at just conclusions respecting the mind and will of the Apostles on all such questions, it will be necessary to observe not only what they commanded, practised, or allowed, but also whether these commands and practices were of lasting obligation, or were only of a temporary or non-essential character. And it will be necessary also to notice some things *not* commanded or practised in the Apostolic Church—the *Omissions* in the New Testament.[1] Such omissions always prove as much as this—that the matter in question was left to the discretion of future Churches to adopt or to decline it; but there are cases in which they lead us much further than this, and warrant—nay, enforce—the conclusion that what is omitted is in effect forbidden.

---

[1] See 'Essays on the Omissions in the New Testament,' by Archbishop Whately, especially portions of them quoted in his 'Kingdom of Christ Delineated.'

This negative argument from the omissions of Holy Writ may doubtless be rashly and illegitimately used, as it was most notably by the Puritans in the latter part of the sixteenth century; but it ought not on that account to be neglected. For although many truths may be rightly believed, many actions in life be justly done, and many rites and practices in the Church be wisely adopted, without their being expressly sanctioned, or even mentioned, in Holy Scripture, yet in all questions of which we know nothing except by divine revelation, or by the express direction of Christ or His Apostles, the negative argument is conclusive; and the omissions of the New Testament are in all such cases equivalent to authoritative prohibitions.

I desire to bear in mind these considerations, as general principles of thought and argument, in all that I may have to say about the apostolic administration of the Church, and its bearing upon the times and questions of our own day. And as it is desirable in so wide a field, and one admitting of such various aspects, to select certain prominent points of view, and by dwelling on them to make our investigation as systematic and connected as we may, I purpose to consider the whole subject under the following heads, each of which will be comprised in a separate lecture.

The First Organization of the Church, with the officers who ministered in it.

The Origin of the Form of the Church Ministry, with a further consideration of its nature and functions.

The Laity, or Church body at large, with their position and duties.

The Places of Christian Worship, and the manner in which the public devotions were conducted.

The Sacrament of Baptism.

The Sacrament of the Lord's Supper.

And lastly—

A review of the whole subject, with special reference to the application of it to our own time and Church.

LECTURE II.

THE FIRST ORGANIZATION OF THE CHURCH.

II.

THE FIRST ORGANIZATION OF THE CHURCH.

ON the very day that the Apostles received their full power from on high, and the divine seal and sanction was affixed to their authority, they began to organize the Christian Church. The three thousand converts of the Day of Pentecost, without reckoning those who were daily added to them, must at once have required some system of administration; some regulations for their orderly guidance as the professed disciples of Christ; some provision for their instruction in Christian doctrine and practice; some arrangements for their meeting together as a united body, and for their common worship as a religious community. We could have had no reasonable doubt that these wants were supplied without delay, even if the sacred historian had not given us, as he has done in immediate connection with the first ingathering of disciples into the Church, a detailed, though very brief, account of their public or social religious life.

But the moment that we look at the Apostles as the organizers and legislators of the primitive Church, and enquire how they exercised these important offices, we are met at once by a very remarkable circumstance, presenting us with a striking characteristic of the Christian dispensation in the form which it was to assume as a new religion; and with an equally striking contrast to the divinely constituted form of the elder dispensation, which was now to be superseded and pass away. The Jewish Church, as instituted and settled by the Mosaic Law, exhibited from the first an elaborate code of ordinances and regulations, prescribed by divine authority even in their minute details. Their priesthood was not only expressly appointed by a divine selection, but arranged for all their future generations in a course from which no man was to presume to deviate. The modes in which their highest religious worship was to be conducted were marked out with an unalterable precision. Their whole ritual with all its ceremonies was given to them for their invariable use, without an authority being vested anywhere in their Church to change or interfere with it. And all these ordinances and statutes were at once recorded in a written document, that they might be preserved in their integrity to guide and bind succeeding ages.

But the Apostles, habituated as they were to a religion thus formed and ordered, adopted no such plan in the institution of the Christian Church. They issued no such orders for regulating the form of Christ's religion. There is no Leviticus in the New Testament. There are no "Apostolic constitutions"[1] *truly* so named. In all that relates to the outward life and polity of the Church the Apostles did not begin with promulgating a code of laws, and then shape the new community into a conformity with them. Still less did they record a series of fixed rules for the Church Government or ceremonial of future times. On the contrary, they began with the formation of Christian communities; necessarily giving them such directions as each case immediately required, but enforcing, as of general or permanent obligation, only a few principles or obvious truths, which admitted of great variety in their practical application; and leaving each community to exercise a large amount of independent discretion, and to develope its organization from within itself, if any further development should be needful. And they showed themselves throughout their whole course on earth much more solicitous to inculcate and cherish sound doctrine among Christian men, than to enjoin a precise ritual; more concerned to maintain a unanimity of kindly feeling and mutual

---

[1] The so-called 'Constitutiones Apostolicæ' are a compilation of ecclesiastical formularies and regulations of various dates, from the second to the fourth or fifth century, some of which are very good, and might with advantage be adopted by our own Church; but none of them are of apostolic origin or authority.

forbearance, than to require a uniformity of opinion in non-essentials, or of observance in outward forms.

This remarkable feature in the original constitution of the Church ought never to have been, as it often has been, overlooked or disregarded by later times, exhibiting, as it does, the *liberty*, the *duty*, and the *responsibility*, which Christian societies should recognise in dealing with ecclesiastical questions; remembering that every particular Church in its present visible development is a *human institution*, formed and continued by man's authority and laws, and by man's authority and laws to be, when necessary, altered and reformed.[1]

It is very desirable, however, to know and mark what the Apostles ordered or sanctioned in the Church of their own time; because whatever they appointed (whether designed to be perpetual or not) we may be confident was the very best for the time then being, and for the

[1] Grave and lamentable errors and mischiefs have arisen, and must arise, from men's confounding together, sometimes unconsciously, what is divine and what is human, in their conception of a Church — a confusion which tends most effectually to aggravate abuses, and to prevent their removal.

It may be well maintained that "The Church" is a divine institution, in accordance with the will and command of Christ, and upheld by His power and promises; but each particular Church, whether national or otherwise—however it may embrace a portion of this divine element, so far as it is faithful to Christ and Christian truth—is, nevertheless, in its special form, and in all the individualities of its regulations and observances, a work of men. "All the Church's constitutions," it is well observed by Hooker, "are of the nature of a human law" (Eccl. Pol. iii. 9), savouring therefore of man's imperfection; his wisdom, or folly; his perception of truth or entanglement in error; his passion, pride, and perversity, it may be, as well as his sound judgment, piety, and discretion.

circumstances of those days and people. And just so far as the present time and the circumstances in which we are placed resemble them—to the same extent we may be equally confident that the apostolic form and order are the very best for us. And so far as there are wants in the Church which belong to every time and people, so far the manner in which these wants were met by apostolic injunctions is the best for the Church in every age.

And even where our position differs from that of the primitive Church, and needs a different mode of treatment the more effectually to encounter new difficulties and forms of evil, and to bring old Christian truths to bear with renewed force upon modern life and manners, a consideration of what the Apostles ordered, or did not order,—of their way of dealing with their own times and difficulties, or their silence respecting the course which they pursued,—may greatly assist us, either by the analogies of cases which differ, or by way of suggestion, caution, and warning, or even by showing us that our liberty in Christ is not restrained from meeting new requirements with new forms of Christian policy, and from regulating Church practices in accordance with the specialities of our own age. Moreover, as the Church is now the Church of history as well as of revelation, linked with the past centuries, and inheriting portions of their tradition, it can never be unprofitable to go back further still to the original source of all Christian truth, and to see whether even long-cherished and inveterate usages are conformed as much as they might be to the example of apostolic authority.

A knowledge then of the mind and judgment of the Apostles, in matters of Church order and associated life, must be gained by considering what the New Testament has recorded respecting the prescribed or permitted practice of the apostolic Church. And a consideration of the Christian ministry of that time will serve as a starting point in our enquiry to give us some insight into the general character of the ecclesiastical body and its common action as a Church.

Now leaving out of view the apostolic office, which stands alone and separate from every other, the Christian ministry appears in the New Testament in two distinct forms. One of these had, at any rate, in some places, an earlier existence than the other, though both for a while stood as it were side by side, and acted contemporaneously together, until the former gradually disappeared, leaving the other still in force to become a permanent institution in the Church.

These two forms of the Christian ministry may be called "the Ministry of Gifts," and "the Ministry of Orders."

The Ministry of Gifts comes first. It belonged to apostolic times alone, when præternatural or spiritual gifts, *Χαρίσματα*, usually by imposition of the Apostles' hands, were abundantly shed abroad in the Church.

In the earliest part of this period it was exercised the most extensively, and probably in some places exclusively, before the ministry of the other form was sufficiently matured.

Some of the spiritual gifts then bestowed were specially adapted for congregational use, and the edification of religious assemblies. The gift of a spirit and utterance of prayer, the gifts of the "word of wisdom" and the "word of knowledge," the gift of prophecy, *i.e.*, not of *fore*-telling future events, but *forth*-telling solemn truths—explaining and enforcing with fervid words the lessons of Scripture, and Christian doctrine practically applied—seem to have been bestowed for the express purpose of supplying what must have been a pressing want—sound instruction, impressive exhortation, and fervent but enlightened prayers—in the newly gathered Christian congregations.

It is evident from the circumstances mentioned by St. Paul in connection with the Church at Corinth (1 Cor. xi.–xiv.) that the public worship there was not conducted by one or two ministers expressly chosen and appointed to the office; but any one, who possessed a spiritual gift available for general edification, was permitted either to pray or prophesy; to address words of exhortation, instruction, or encouragement; to lead the devotional singing with psalms or hymns of his own selection; to speak in a foreign language,[1] if either he himself

[2] The difficulties connected with some of St. Paul's remarks about the "gift of tongues" in 1 Cor. xiv. have never, as far as I am aware, been satisfactorily explained, owing probably to the want of fuller contemporary information. Those, however, who would represent these "tongues" to have been, not foreign languages, but ecstatic

or some one else interpreted his words; and in short to exercise his peculiar gifts with the full sanction of apostolic authority, and without any other restraint than a conformity to such wholesome general admonitions as, "Let all things be done unto edifying," "Let all things be done decently and in order."

This picture of the mode of conducting public worship at Corinth comes before us only incidentally, and is given as in consequence of certain disorders in that Church, which St. Paul found it necessary to reprove. But we can have no reasonable doubt that a similar mode prevailed in other Churches of the time; seeing that the same spiritual gifts were very widely diffused, and there is no intimation in St. Paul's words that the custom of the Corinthians was at all confined to *them*.

The ministrations of this nature were of great ad-

---

and almost incoherent utterances, seem to reverse the order of sound interpretation, and to explain away what is clear and plain by that which is obscure. The account of these "tongues" in Acts ii. makes it evident that they were foreign languages, quite intelligible to the natives of their respective countries. In this chapter they are not called simply "tongues," γλώσσας, but "other tongues," ἑτέραις γλώσσαις, *i. e. different* languages, *different* from what they usually spoke. Those who heard them remarked, "We hear every man in our own tongue," τῇ ἰδίᾳ διαλέκτῳ; and, "We do hear them speak in our tongues," ἡμετέραις γλώσσαις; where γλῶσσα and διάλεκτος are used as synonymous, and must mean a real and distinct language. And even in 1 Cor. xii. 10, "divers kinds of tongues," γένη γλωσσῶν, intimates the same thing, although there is no word for "divers" in the original; for γένη must imply an orderly diversity—different kinds. It surely cannot be right to set aside this positive evidence, because there is something in St. Paul's brief allusions to the Corinthian gifts which we cannot clearly understand.

vantage to the infant Church. For, although at Jerusalem, while the Apostles were all there, a large number of congregations might have been supplied with the very best ministerial services at the hands of the twelve, and other experienced disciples of Christ; yet, as soon as Churches began to be multipled in other and more distant places, it would often have been difficult to find competent and trustworthy men to lead their public devotions, if this providential supply of spiritually-gifted persons had not been given to the Church.

The possessors of these spiritual gifts were not, as far as we are informed, ordained or specially appointed to their office by any ceremony; and hence their functions have been sometimes represented as merely one phase of the operation of that universal priesthood which belongs to all Christians; or as the absence of all ministry in those times, when, as it is alleged, "all Christians were allowed, before the Church was fully settled, to preach, baptize, and expound the Scriptures in the Church." But that this was really an acknowledged and authorized ministry attached to the possessors of such gifts, and exercised because of this possession, and not merely a liberty indulged in from the absence of all rule, appears still more plainly from its not being confined to edifying ministrations in social worship, but extended to other spheres of labour also. For among the possessors of spiritual gifts are enumerated not only such as those already named, but also "Teachers, helps, and governments, evangelists and pastors," who are expressly declared (Eph. iv. 12) to be "for the work of the ministry;" and all of whom could find employment for their gifts only in addressing themselves to the general life of Church-members, or in endeavouring to bring in fresh accessions to the flock, and thus exercising just such a superintendence or influence over Christian communities, as we commonly include in the idea of a well-ordered parish under clerical supervision among ourselves.[1]

A due consideration of this "Ministry of Gifts" in the earliest days of Christianity,—"those times of high and sanctified spiritual freedom"—both shows and justifies the custom of the public ministration of women at that time in the Church. The very ground and title of this ministry being the acknowledged possession of some spiritual gift—and such gifts being bestowed on women as well as men—the former as well as the latter were allowed to use them in the Christian assemblies. This seems to me quite evident from St. Paul's words in 1 Cor. xi. 5, where he strongly condemns the practice of women "praying or prophesying" *with the head unveiled,* without expressing the least objection to this

[1] It does not fall within the scope of these Lectures to dwell upon the special nature and uses of the different spiritual gifts, the fact only that they formed the basis and supplied the materials of the earliest Christian ministry being sufficient for our present purpose. A full and learned discussion of these different χαρίσματα in their various forms, and in their probable relations to the more permanent Ministry of Orders, may be found in the works of Neander, particularly in his 'History of the Planting and Training of the Christian Church by the Apostles.'

public ministration on their part, but only finding fault with what was considered an unseemly attire for women thus publicly engaged.

The injunction contained in this same Epistle (1 Cor. xiv. 34), "Let your women keep silence in the Churches, for it is not permitted unto them to speak," refers, as the context shows, not to prophesying or praying in the congregation, but to making remarks, and asking questions about the words of others. The directions given to Timothy at a later period (1 Tim. ii. 11, 12), and forbidding "a woman to teach or to usurp authority over the man," seem also to have no reference to spiritual gifts, and therefore to be no contradiction to what had been before allowed.

This "Ministry of Gifts" was, from its very nature, only for a time. It was liable to obvious abuses; and it did not contain the elements of order and sobriety in sufficient strength to make it suitable for a permanent institution. The gifts moreover not being conferred by any hands but those of Apostles, the ministrations which depended on them must have gradually passed away. And long before they disappeared, the other form of the Christian ministry was introduced and extended generally throughout the Church. As this became more and more fully established, it was not unnatural that the "Ministry of Gifts"—once the glory, and, it may be said, the *pride*, of Christian congregations—should suffer some disparagement, and possibly should at times be regarded as an irregularity, or an interference with established order. And I think there are traces of this to be found in the New Testament. The warnings given by St. Paul (1 Thess. v. 19), "Quench not the spirit," and "Despise not prophesyings," probably point to this tendency, and express the Apostle's desire that the possessors of such gifts might still be allowed to use them for the benefit of their several Churches, and receive a becoming attention from their hearers.

The attempts of some Christian sects and associations of a recent date to re-establish this ancient form as their ordinary and only ministry, seem to show that they had forgotten the proverbial hopelessness and uselessness of reviving the obsolete practices of a by-gone age not founded on any abiding and living principle; and that they ignored the fact, that what made these ministrations necessary, possible, and right, in the infant Church, is no longer in existence now. At the same time, since natural gifts in an extraordinary degree, and of a kind most available for extensive good, are sometimes found even now in Christian men and women, it would seem that Churches might still advantageously imitate the example of the apostolic age, by employing such powers to supplement, though not supplant, their more regular ministrations.

The "Ministry of Orders," which gradually superseded the more free and unrestricted form of Church administration, was exercised by men especially selected for this purpose, and ordained, or solemnly appointed by ecclesiastical authority, to minister in their respective congregations. This ministry may possibly in some localities, as at Jerusalem, have been contemporary with the earliest labours of the Apostles; in other places it was introduced, or at any rate brought into full operation, at a later date. But, if we may judge from recorded instances of St. Paul's practice, the Apostles ordained "Elders" in the Churches which they founded, as soon as intelligent and suitable men could be found for this purpose;[1] and long before the end of the apostolic

[1] The account of the apostolical journey of Paul and Barnabas in Acts xiii., xiv. throws some light upon this subject. As they passed through the different towns on their way, they gathered together many converts, *μαθητεύσαντες ἱκανούς*, on whom, doubtless, as in other cases, they conferred "spiritual gifts," which were at once available for the edification of the newly-formed societies. But when Paul and Barnabas visited these towns again on their return towards Antioch, besides encouraging the disciples by exhortations "to continue in the faith," they ordained them elders for each Church or congregation, *χειροτονήσαντες αὐτοῖς πρεσβυτέρους κατ' ἐκκλησίαν*, to whom the general charge of each community was committed.

The difficulty of finding men fit for the ordained ministry among bodies of Christians recently gathered from Gentile populations, and only just reclaimed from the debasing principles and practices of their gross idolatry, must, humanly speaking, have been very great, not to say insuperable. St. Paul cautions Timothy against ordaining "a novice;" and, in modern missions, it is found necessary to prove converts from heathenism for a long time before any of them can be safely admitted as candidates for ordination. There was, however, at that period, in many of the towns throughout the Roman empire, a class of men, prepared by divine providence, and better fitted than all others for supplying this need of the Gentile Churches.

Educated and thinking men among the Greeks and Romans had for some time felt the hollowness and worthlessness of their old religions; and the dispersion of the Jews in "every nation under heaven," with the Greek translation of their Scriptures, had brought to the conviction of such men that there was a higher and purer knowledge of God to be obtained, than was afforded by their own poetical but effete mythology. Hence many

age, the "Ministry of Orders" had become a generally re-

---

of them renounced polytheism and idolatry; and, although they did not become Jews, they acknowledged and worshipped the one true God, joined in the services of the Jewish synagogue, and were commonly regarded by the Jews with a friendly feeling, though they were still to the Jewish mind essentially Gentiles, and Jews would not enter their houses or eat with them.

These intelligent and earnest religionists are often mentioned in the Acts of the Apostles—Cornelius, the Roman "officer and gentleman," and the first Gentile Christian, being an eminent example of the class. They have been sometimes called "proselytes of the gate," to distinguish them from the Gentiles who became Jews, and were called "proselytes of righteousness." In the Acts they are designated by various names, significative of their religious position. Thus Cornelius (Acts x.) is said to have been *εὐσεβής*, not "devout," as in our English Bible, but, as the word literally means, "worshipping aright," and *φοβούμενος τὸν Θεὸν*, "fearing the [true] God." Hence a mixed congregation of Jews and these religious Gentiles at Antioch, in Pisidia, was addressed by St. Paul as, "Men of Israel, and ye that fear God," *οἱ φοβούμενοι τὸν Θεόν* (Acts xiii. 16); and again, in verse 26, "Men and brethren, children of the stock of Abraham, and whosoever among you feareth God," *οἱ ἐν ὑμῖν φοβούμενοι τὸν Θεόν*. In verse 43 of the same chap. such persons are termed "religious proselytes," *σεβόμενοι προσήλυται*, *i. e.* proselytes, as far as their *worshipping* was concerned, though still called Gentiles in the preceding verse. So also the "honourable women" of this class, whom the Jews stirred up against Paul and Barnabas are *τὰς σεβομένας γυναῖκας* in verse 50.

Now such men were usually those who most readily and heartily welcomed the Gospel doctrines which the Apostles proclaimed. They had the religious knowledge of Jews, without their narrow-mindedness, formality, and prejudices; they were often men of good education. They had given proof of their love of truth, their earnestness and sincerity. They had already renounced the gross vices of heathenism. These, therefore, both became the first-fruits of the Apostles' labours in Gentile lands, and also among these they would find some who might almost immediately be entrusted with the ministerial charge of Christian congregations. And with this agree the words of Clement, when he writes to the Corinthians that the Apostles appointed their first converts to be "bishops and deacons": *κατὰ χώρας καὶ πόλεις κηρύσσοντες, καθίσταναν τὰς ἀπαρχὰς αὐτῶν, δοκιμάσαντες τῷ πνεύματι, εἰς ἐπισκόπους καὶ διακόνους τῶν μελλόντων πιστεύειν*.—'Clem. ad Cor.' § 42.

ceived and ordinary institution throughout the Churches. And, as doubtless many of those who were thus formally ordained were also possessors of spiritual gifts, the earlier ministrations, which these gifts supplied, must commonly have passed into the later form without difficulty or any painful change, until at last they were quietly merged in its permanent establishment.

In the mean time, while both these forms of the ministry were in operation together, those who had gifts of "teaching," and of "prophecy," and other χαρίσματα of a similar nature were subject to the general superintendence and control of the ordained officers, who always acted as rulers or overseers—ἐπίσκοποι—of the Christian communities, whether they themselves took a prominent part or not in the instructions, prayers, and other services of their religious assemblies. And, as might be expected, several different phases of the working of this double system might be seen in different Churches, and at different times, during the period embraced by the New Testament, and before the final disappearance of the "Ministry of Gifts" as a distinct ordinance in the Church.[1]

---

[1] Different phases of the double ministry:

1. In the Corinthian Church the χαρίσματα are seen in full operation, and, it may apparently be said, in uncontrolled exercise. If there were presbyters in authority among the Christians at Corinth, when St. Paul wrote his first epistle to them, they do not seem to have made any attempt to prevent or restrain even the gravest disorders. St. Paul, indeed (1 Cor. xvi. 15), speaks of the house of Stephanas as having "addicted themselves to the ministry of the Saints," and beseeches the brethren, "Submit yourselves unto such, and to every

It is one of the marked and significative *omissions* in the New Testament, that no account is given of the first appointment of ordained men to minister in Church offices. But after a time the two orders of Presbyters (πρεσβύτεροι), and Deacons (διάκονοι), appear as well-known titles; and in the later books of the New Testa-

---

one that helpeth with us, and laboureth." But the expressions here used are peculiar: εἰς διακονίαν τοῖς ἁγίοις ἔταξαν ἑαυτούς, "they appointed, or set, *themselves* to minister"—words which do not necessarily imply anything more than a devoted exercise of some χαρίσματα for the general good. If they were ordained presbyters, their authority was here at the weakest.

2. In Thessalonica, at a rather earlier date, both forms may be traced (1 Thess. v. 12, and 19, 20); but the possessors of spiritual gifts seem to have been losing their influence more rapidly than St. Paul thought desirable.

3. In Ephesus, at the time referred to in Acts xx., a united body, or council, of presbyters had the complete charge of the Church, and no others are alluded to by St. Paul in his solemn address to them as the overseers, ἐπίσκοποι, of the flock. Yet there must have been men there with spiritual gifts; and several years later than this (1 Tim. v. 17), there is a notice of presbyters at Ephesus "who *ruled* well," οἱ καλῶς προεστῶτες πρεσβύτεροι, as distinguished from those who also "laboured in the work and doctrine," the duties of the former class being supplemented, as we may well conclude, by men who had χαρίσματα for teaching and exhortation.

4. Timothy, however, at Ephesus, and Titus in Crete, are directed, in choosing presbyters for the future, to take care that they be "apt to teach;" the time being now come when it was desirable that the "Ministry of Orders" should be carried out in its completeness.

"At this later period, when the pure Gospel had to combat with manifold errors which threatened to corrupt it—as was especially the case during the latter portion of St. Paul's ministry — at this critical period, it was thought necessary to unite more closely the offices of teachers and overseers, and with that view to take care that overseers (ἐπίσκοποι) should be appointed, who should be able by their public instructions to protect the Church from the infection of false doctrine, to establish others in purity of faith, and to convince the gainsayers." —Neander, 'The Planting of the Christian Church,' Bk. iii. 5.

ment their functions are alluded to as already familiar in the Church.

The first occasion on which Christian Elders, or Presbyters, are mentioned is in Acts xi. 30, when the collection made for the relief of the Christians in Judea, against the predicted famine, was "sent to the elders by the hands of Barnabas and Saul." Not long after this the same Paul and Barnabas, on their first apostolic journey in Asia Minor, are recorded to have ordained presbyters in the different Churches which they established in those countries; and the office is frequently referred to in other parts of the New Testament.

The first mention of deacons by name as a distinct order in the ministry is found in St. Paul's Epistle to the Philippians; and the title only occurs again in the same Apostle's Pastoral injunctions in his first Epistle to Timothy. That the order of deacons is so seldom expressly named is perhaps owing to the circumstance that the title of Presbyter, or Elder, is sometimes used as a general appellation for Church officers, including the inferior order of deacons, as it sometimes did the higher office of the Apostles. Thus St. Paul gives directions to Timothy for ordaining presbyters and deacons, while in his similar directions to Titus he names presbyters only.

Whether deacons are alluded to at a much earlier period, is a question which cannot be decided with any positive certainty. The seven, who were selected to superintend the daily ministration of the tables spread for the poorer Christians, were generally looked upon as deacons by the early post-apostolic Church, which considered their appointment as the first institution of the diaconate. And from the number of those who were appointed on this occasion, some Churches—for example, the Church of Rome in the third century—confined themselves to seven deacons; and when a larger number was required the later office of Sub-deacon supplied the want. And the council of Neo-Cæsarea (A.D. 315) affirmed that this number ought to be always maintained, even if the Church was very large, on the ground that it had been so ordered in the history of their institution.[1]

But it must be observed that these seven officers are never called deacons in the New Testament; that they were selected entirely from the Hellenistic Jews, to look after the interest of that body, in consequence of some alleged neglect; and that, if they are to be regarded as deacons, it must be concluded that Hebrew deacons had been appointed before.

It is very probable that "the young men" who buried Ananias and Sapphira, held the office of deacon, although they are not designated by this name. They appear, at any rate, in an official character, and when first mentioned they are called *οἱ νεώτεροι*,[2] the word

[1] *Διάκονοι ἑπτα ὀφειλοῦσιν εἶναι κατὰ τὸν κανόνα, κἂν πάνυ μεγάλη εἰη ἡ πόλις· πεισθήσῃ δὲ ἀπὸ τῆς βίβλου τῶν πράξεων.*—'Conc. Neo. Cæs.' Can. 15.

[2] All officers in the early Church were *Διάκονοι*; and the two orders of ministers instituted by the Apostles seem to have been at first distinguished as *Διάκονοι πρεσβύτεροι*, and *Διάκονοι νεώτεροι*, the *elder* and the *younger* ministers. Then, after a time, the

apparently used for deacons by St. Peter in 1 Pet. v. 5, and by St. Paul in 1 Tim. v. 1. If this be so, it will carry back the institution of the diaconate to the very earliest times.

The duties which belonged to these ministerial offices are nowhere formally laid down in the New Testament; but in the case of the presbyters in particular they may be gathered in some detail from the scattered notices which here and there occur.

As men appointed by the Apostles under divine direction, and holding a sacred office approved by the divine Head of the Church, they were charged, "to feed the flock over which the Holy Ghost had made them overseers" Hence it was their duty to exercise a general superintendence in religious things over the body of Christians amongst whom they ministered, and whom they were to tend after the similitude of a shepherd's care. In this their pastoral office therefore, they had an authority given to them—not as lords or masters of their respective congregations,[1] but as those who were to be

superior order were called by their specific name, *πρεσβύτεροι*, presbyters, while the inferior order kept the generic term, *Διάκονοι*, deacons.

[1] The words used in the New Testament to describe the position and authority of Christian presbyters are very significative, and contrast strongly with the titles and assumptions of the clerical office, even in the third century. Besides *ἐπίσκοποι*, bishops *i. e.* "overseers," no higher terms are used in the apostolic writings, [than *προϊστάμενοι* and *ἡγούμενοι*; and presbyters are expressly forbidden to be *κατακυριεύοντες τῶν κλήρων* (1 Pet. v. 3). The word *ἡγούμενοι* is employed in the same manner by Clement, in his Epistle to the Corinthians; and Justin Martyr, in the middle of the second century, has no higher title than *ὁ προεστὼς* for the chief minister in his Church.

their guides and leaders, their pattern and example; and who, without interfering with the Christian liberty of all Church-members, were by their position and influence to prevent that liberty from degenerating into disorder, and preserve, as much as possible, among the faithful, a godly unanimity in creed and life. They were, therefore, themselves to hold fast, and to admonish all others to hold fast, the divine truths of their religion;—to warn or rebuke the unruly—to support the weak—to bring back the wandering—to build up the faithful—and to animate and encourage all in godliness of living. During the time that the "Ministry of Gifts" continued in operation, the presbyters did not necessarily take the lead in the public prayers and praises of Christian worshippers, or in the public instruction of the people by those expository addresses and practical exhortations which were comprised under the name of prophesying, and were the originals of our modern sermons.

These duties might be performed by those who, without ordination, had the "gifts" which were suitable for such ministrations; though, doubtless, it was within the province of the presbyter to see to the orderly performance of the whole service, and to make regulations to this effect. Hence some presbyters might "rule well," though they did not "labour in the word and doctrine."[1]

[1] "Let the elders that rule well be counted worthy of double honor, especially they who labour in the Word and doctrine," 1 Tim. v. 17. On the supposed authority of this one text, some Churches have built their favourite institution of "lay-elders," or "ruling elders," as distinct from the ordained presbyters, who were to teach and preach. But

But as the "Ministry of Orders" gradually prevailed over the earlier system, it more and more devolved on the presbyters to undertake the duties of religious teaching, of conducting the devotions of the people,

this is claiming a great deal for what is, at the most, only an obscure allusion, while there is in the New Testament no other trace of any such distinction between one elder and another, as that above alluded to. Neither is there anything in the records of the sub-apostolic Church which gives the least countenance to such a theory: while, after the end of the second century, the sacerdotalism which universally prevailed made it utterly impossible that such an institution should find a place in the ecclesiastical system.

The *seniores plebis*, or *seniores ecclesiæ*, in the African Church, mentioned by Optatus and Augustin, were evidently nothing like the lay-elders in the modern sense; nor were they ruling elders in that Church, but only persons of rank or respectability, who were of note and influence in their congregations, and to whom the care and custody of Church property was sometimes entrusted.—See 'Bingham,' B. II. xix., 19, and his authorities.

The passage in 'Hilary' (Ambrosiaster), Com. in 1 Tim. v. 1, "Apud omnes utique gentes honorabilis est Senectus; unde et synagoga et postea ecclesia seniores habuit, quorum sine consilio nihil agebatur in ecclesia. Quod qua negligentia obsoleverit nescio, nisi forte doctorum desidia aut magis superbia," is sometimes quoted in support of the supposed antiquity of lay-elders; and Guericke, in his "Manual of Church Antiquities" (i. 2, 8), seems doubtful what to make of it. But the testimony of a Church writer of the fourth century, about an apostolic practice no longer, as he acknowledges, in existence, would not be worth much if this *were* Hilary's meaning. And, moreover, the comment is not made on the 17th, but on the 1st verse of this chapter, which speaks of *πρεσβύτεροι* merely, and this the commentator takes to mean simply "old Christian men," as modern commentators often do; and his remark is quite correct, so far as this,—that not only old laymen, but the laity in general, were in the apostolic and following times much consulted, and had great influence in Church matters, until priestly pretensions, and pride (as he honestly admits), had pushed them aside.

Lay, or ruling-elders, may be a very lawful institution, sufficiently maintainable on the authority of the Church which uses it. It may also have been, and may still be, very useful for preventing or restraining the growth of hierarchical propensities; but it need not, and must not, claim for itself an Apostolic antiquity.

and of administering all Church ordinances for the edification of the Church at large. And, before the death of St. Paul, it was required that they should be men well instructed in the Christian faith,—apt to teach, and able to exhort their flocks with sound doctrine, as also to convince or refute opposers of the truth, and to stop the mouths of those who were already beginning to mislead individual Christians, and whole congregations, by dangerous errors plausibly put forth. It is therefore at this completed and fully developed form that we must look, in order to view the office of the Christian presbyter as it was designed and established by the Apostles, and bequeathed by them to the future Church.

The duties of deacons, which are, however, very scantily noticed in the New Testament, appear to have been to render a general assistance to the presbyters in a subordinate capacity; and to perform such services as were needful in a well-ordered Christian community, without being immediately connected with religious teaching or divine ordinances. At the same time, since deacons were required to be men "holding the mystery of the faith in a pure conscience," and by using the office well "acquired great boldness—or rather freedom of speech—παρρησίαν—in the faith which is in Christ Jesus," we may infer that they also took some part in the work of instruction and propagation of Christian doctrine.

If the seven, mentioned in Acts vi., were really deacons, it would follow that the special duty of this order was to attend to the wants of the poor, and to superintend the application of the contributions for their relief. And in post-apostolic times this was generally considered to be the case, and thus deacons are called by Jerome, "Attendants on tables and widows." In these times also (especially after the third century), it was their duty to look after the morals and behaviour of the people, reporting particular cases to the presbyter or bishop. And in connection with public worship, they had charge of the sacred vessels used in administering the Lord's Supper; and at the celebration of this sacrament they received the offerings of the congregation, and presented them to the officiating minister.

In the second century, as mentioned by Justin Martyr, they distributed the bread and wine to the communicants; but at a later period they were not allowed to do so. On some occasions the deacon appears to have been a special or confidential attendant on the bishop; not only acting as his sub-almoner and his medium of communication with the people, but being even sent to represent him at councils when the bishop himself was unable to attend. There is no intimation of any such duties as these being discharged by deacons in the New Testament; but in the absence of express injunctions of apostolic authority it was competent for any Church at any time to alter or add to the functions of these or any other officers in its service.[1]

---

[1] Hooker, who takes it for granted that "the seven," in Acts vi., were the original deacons, gives the following account of the functions of this order:

"Deacons were stewards of the

In our own Communion the duties of the diaconate are *in theory* not very different from those which were most usually attached to it in the early Church; as appears from the description of them in our ordinal. But, *in practice*, at the present time the services of a deacon differ in nothing from those of a presbyter, except that he does not consecrate the elements at the celebration of the Lord's Supper, or read "the Absolution" in the Liturgy.[1] He now but seldom retains the office for more than one year, regarding it as a mere stepping stone to the higher order. And thus the diaconate is stripped of its distinctive character, and rendered almost useless in our Church.

Church, unto whom at the first was committed the distribution of Church goods, the care of providing therewith for the poor, and the charge to see that things of expense might be religiously and faithfully dealt in. A part also of their office was attendance on their presbyters at the time of divine service. For which cause Ignatius, to set forth the dignity of their calling, saith that they are in such case to the bishop as if angelical powers did serve him. These only being the uses for which deacons were first made, if the Church have since then extended their ministry farther than the circuit of their labours at the first was drawn, we are not herein to think the ordinance of Scripture violated, except there appear some prohibition, which hath abridged the Church of that liberty.—'Eccl. Hol.' v. 78.

[1] Why these two ministerial acts, and these alone, should be denied to our deacons, it seems impossible with any consistency to give a reason. A deacon may, and often does, consecrate the water for baptism; then why not the bread and wine for the other sacrament? A deacon may preach, and is often licensed to do so, and in so doing he may, and ought, to declare that "God pardons and absolves all them that truly repent, and unfeignedly believe His holy Gospel;" then why may he not read the very same declaration from the prayer book in the morning or evening service? Such inconsistent prohibitions, authorized neither by Scripture, Church antiquity, nor common sense, necessarily tend to foster superstition.

It was very different in the Church of ancient times. Not only were the deacon's functions quite distinct from those of the presbyter, but he continued in his office for a much longer period, or it might be even for life. Indeed, deacons, from their immediate contact with their bishops, and from many matters of order and discipline being entrusted to them, together with other incidental circumstances in particular Churches, sometimes became persons of great importance, and looked down upon presbyters as beneath them. That this was not so very uncommon an occurrence may be inferred from the decree of the Council of Nice (and other Councils) against it, as well as from Jerome's sharp remonstrance half a century later against certain deacons at Rome. And, although such conduct was an abuse of their privileges, it shows plainly that it was by no means the custom then for deacons to regard their office as a merely temporary step to a higher ministry. And the same thing is further indicated by the circumstance, also mentioned by Jerome, that deacons chose one of their number and made him an *Archdeacon*—an office then, as well as now, considered superior to an ordinary presbyter.[1]

---

[1] The Council of Nice decreed, *'Εμμενέτωσαν οἱ διάκονοι ἐν τοῖς ἰδιόις μέτροις, εἰδότες, ὅτι τοῦ μὲν ἐπισκόπου ὑπηρέται εἰσὶ, τῶν δὲ πρεσβυτέρων ἐλάττους τυγχανουσιν.*—Can. 18 'Labbé Concil.' vol. ii. p. 676.

Jerome at the beginning of his Epistle to Evagrius, says, "Audio quendam in tantam erupisse vecordiam, ut diaconos presbyteris id est episcopis, anteferret. Nam quum Apostolus perspicue doceat eosdem esse presbyteros quos episcopos, quid patitur mensarum et viduarum minister, ut supra eos se

So distinct, indeed, and complete in itself was each one of these three orders of Deacon, Presbyter, and Bishop, in the earliest ages of the Church, that it was by no means without example for a layman to be at once made a presbyter, or even a bishop, as Ambrose of Milan was, and Nectarius, the predecessor of Chrysostom at Constantinople. In the fourth century, however, this was considered irregular. Decrees of councils and other directions were issued to restrain the practice, to the existence of which, however, they clearly testify. And by the end of that century it had become the established rule that the clergy should pass through the inferior orders to the diaconate, and so to the higher offices. Yet even then it seems not to have been considered very strange for a deacon to be at once made a bishop.[1]

---

tumidus efferat, ad quorum preces Christi corpus et sanguis conficitur !"

And in this same Epistle, "Quo modo si exercitus imperatorem faciat, aut diaconi de se quem industrium noverint, et Archidiaconum vocent."

[1] A Council at Rome, under the Bishop Silvester I. A. D. 324, directed that no layman should be ordained except through the regular degrees of lector, exorcist, acolyth, subdeacon, &c.—cap. xi. 'Labbé Concil.' vol. ii. p. 627. "Ut nullus ex laïca persona ad honorem acolythus usque ad Episcopatum sublevarctur, nisi prius fuisset lector annis triginta, deinde uno die exorcista," &c.

The Council of Sardica (A. D. 347) ordered that no one should be made bishop without having been a presbyter, or, at least, a deacon; and that no layman should be at once ordained deacon, or presbyter.—'Labbé Concil.' vol. iii. p. 35. "Episcopus non prius ordinetur, nisi ante ex lectoris munere, et officio diaconi et presbyter fuerit perfunctus," &c.

Siricius, Bishop of Rome (A. D. 384), directed that the clergy should pass regularly through all the orders, inferior and superior; though even he seems not to have objected

And so in the New Testament there is no appearance of the offices of deacon and presbyter being linked together in any necessary or indispensable succession; nor is any instance mentioned of a promotion from one to the other. St. Paul, indeed, observes that, "they who have used the office of a deacon well purchase to themselves a good degree"—βαθμὸν ἑαυτοῖς καλὸν περιποιοῦνται,[1] *i.e.*, gain an honourable standing or position—"and great boldness in the faith;" but he does not intimate that they were, or ought to be, selected as presbyters.

In Churches which, like our own, have retained the

to a bishopric being conferred upon a deacon; while condemning the practice of making laymen presbyters. Siricius says:

"One who has devoted himself to the Church *from his infancy*, ante pubertatis annos baptizari et *lectorum* debet ministerio sociari; then when he is thirty years of age *acolythus* et *sub-diaconus* esse debebit; post quæ ad *diaconii* gradum. . . . accedat; ubi si ultra quinque annos laudabiliter ministrarit congrue *presbyterium* consequatur. Et inde post decennium *Episcopalem* cathedram poterit adipisci."

"If any one entered the ministry when more advanced in life, jam ætate grandævus; he was still to be made first of all *lector* aut *exorcista*; then *acolythus* et *subdiaconus* fiat, et sic ad *diaconatum*, si per hæc tempora dignus judicatus fuerit, provehatur. Exinde jam accessu temporam *presbyterium* vel *Episcopatum*. . . . . . sortietur.—'Ep. ad Himerium I, Labbé Concil.' vol. iii. p. 669.

[1] It should however be noticed that at a later period βαθμὸς, as used in this text, seems to have been taken to mean a *degree or step in the way of promotion*, since the prayer at the ordination of a deacon, given in the 'Constitutiones Apostolicæ,' ends with the words, καταξίωσον αὐτὸν εὐαρέστως λειτουργήσαντα τὴν ἐγχειρισθεῖσαν αὐτῷ διακονίαν ἀτρέστως, ἀμέμπτως, ἀνεγκλήτως, μείζονος ἀξιωθῆναι βαθμοῦ "to be thought worthy of a higher degree or step" in the ministry—*i.e.*, I presume, to be made a presbyter. In St. Paul's words, however, there is no comparison used to correspond with μείζονος.

three orders, it surely is desirable that each one of them should have a special character and service of its own. At the present time, if our diaconate were made a real office instead of a name—if it were understood that it would not, as a matter of course, or even usually, lead to any higher ecclesiastical position, and if our Church would decide, as it has full authority to do, that deacon's orders at any rate should not be indelible, or incompatible with secular occupations—perhaps the wants of extensive parishes might be more easily met, and the spiritual destitution of our populous towns be encountered with more hopefulness.

Our view of the ancient diaconate will not be complete without noticing that it included women as well as men. As deacons are not often expressly named in the New Testament, it is not surprising that deaconesses are still more rarely mentioned. Yet one distinct instance at any rate occurs, not obvious, indeed, in our English version, but evident in the original. Phœbe, who in Rom. xvi. 1, is termed "a servant of the Church in Cenchrea," was a deaconess—διάκονος. And if a place comparatively so unimportant as Cenchrea had a deaconess to minister in its Church, it can hardly be possible that other more populous towns, with larger Christian communities, should not also have been supplied with the same female ministry. And is it not highly probable that "Tryphœna and Tryphosa" with "the beloved Persis," who are named in this same chapter as labouring in the Lord, just as presbyters in 1 Tim. v. 17 are said to "labour in the word and doctrine," were regularly appointed ministers in their Church?[1]

In the post-apostolic Church the office of deaconess was for a long time continued, especially in the Eastern portion of it, where the greater seclusion of the female sex, which ordinarily prevailed, made the ministrations of women more requisite than in the Western populations. The deaconesses at first were commonly widows past middle age; indeed by Tertullian and others their office is called "the Widowhood" (*viduatus*), and the Church at that time seems to have regarded the widows mentioned in 1 Tim. v. as deaconesses, and to have acted according to the directions there given in their appointment. In the early times the deaconesses were formally ordained by imposition of hands; but after the middle of the fourth century this was thought undesirable; after which the office appears to have received less consideration than formerly, and was gradually laid aside altogether, disappearing in Western Europe earlier than in the Greek Church, where deaconesses were still found at the end of the 12th century.

---

[1] Whether "the elder women," and "the younger," πρεσβυτέρας and νεωτέρας, in 1 Tim. v. 2, may be considered female *ministers*, corresponding with presbyters and deacons, is at the best too uncertain for this passage to be adduced in evidence. For, in the first place, it is doubtful whether πρεσβυτέρῳ, and νεωτέρους in the preceding verse, are used in an official sense; and, secondly, in the parallel passage of Titus ii. 2, 3, the non-official words πρεσβύτας, πρεσβύτιδας, and νέας, seem to decide the question in the negative.

The "Pastor of Hermas" probably alludes to a deaconess, when a woman named Grapté is mentioned; καὶ Γραπτη μὲν νουθετήσει τὰς χήρας καὶ τοὺς ὀρφανούς.—Book i. Vis. ii. 4.

This ancient institution has in later times been revived in an analogous form by the Moravian brethren; and very recently in our own Church the proved value of ministering women has in some few instances led to a similar revival. This practice, if carried out with judgment and an unostentatious simplicity, may in some places be productive of good. But in general the reasons for discontinuing this office are equally valid against restoring it; and what is needed in order to meet the crying wants of the present age is not so much an increase in Church officials, as in the sound and self-denying unofficial ministrations of Christian men and women.

The offices of sub-deacon, acolyth, and other inferior orders of the clergy, which began to appear in the third century, were added one after another, as the ecclesiastical system became more complicated and formal; but these had no place in the Church of the New Testament, —their services, so far as they were needed, being performed by the deacons or by lay members of the congregations.

In order to obtain a correct conception of the Christian ministry in its primitive state, it is necessary to distinguish clearly between what the Apostles themselves established in the Church, and what was afterwards found to be expedient as a further development of their polity. That which may justly claim to be a legitimate and beneficial extension of apostolic order must not on that account be confounded with ordinances of apostolic institution. I have, therefore, thought it necessary to omit all notice of Episcopacy in considering the offices of presbyters and deacons. These were established in the Churches by the Apostles themselves; while the episcopate, in the modern acceptation of the term, and as a distinct clerical order, does not appear in the New Testament, but was gradually introduced and extended throughout the Church at a later period.

That it was perfectly lawful for the post-apostolic Church to adopt the episcopal form of ecclesiastical government can be reasonably doubted by no one who believes the Church itself to be a lawful, not to say a divine, institution. That the establishment of episcopacy was proved to be a good thing in its effects and influence, and may therefore so far be said to be of divine origin, because, in the words of Richard Hooker, "Of all good things God Himself is the author," and "All things are of God which are well done," cannot justly be questioned. That, our Lord having directed that His disciples should be gathered into religious societies, and His apostles having carried out His directions, all lawful exercise of the powers of such societies is sanctioned by Christ Himself, as well as by His Apostles—is a position which may be indisputably maintained.

But, unfortunately, not contented with such indisputable, just, and reasonable sanctions, writers on Church matters in all ages have too often evinced a tendency to represent the regulations of their own time as precisely those which were made at the beginning;[1] and to insist upon referring to the actual institution of the Apostles, or even the personal appointment of Christ Himself, all the existing ordinances of their own Churches. And thus after the general establishment of episcopacy, it was often assumed and asserted that this ordinance emanated immediately from these sources; and the more the powers of bishops were enlarged beyond all that savoured of the apostolic age, the more boldly was a direct apostolic constitution claimed for their position and authority.

Such assertions put forth in the early centuries of Christianity have often been repeated even by learned men in later times without any sufficient examination of their correctness, and of the evidence—or the lack of evidence—on which they rest;[2] and the unlearned, if they have indulged in any thought on the subject, have com-

---

1 Bingham, in the Preface to his learned 'Antiquities,' justly reprobates this tendency of Church writers; without, unfortunately, in his following pages being altogether free from its influence himself.

2 Bingham, and others, sometimes take the assertions of men who lived one, two, three, or more centuries after the Apostles' time —assertions made without any proof at all—as if they sufficiently substantiated any statement respecting apostolic practices or commands.

Thus Bingham informs us that, "The ancient writers of the Church derive the original of bishops from divine authority and apostolical constitution," and quotes their assertions to this effect without the least investigation of their correctness: whereas the accounts given of the first century by men who lived in the third or fourth were always more or less affected by the then prevailing notions and practices, and often merely prove that their authors took for granted that what was established and acknowledged in their own time had been so also in the apostolic age.

monly taken it for granted that such assertions have been fully proved, and that there is no reasonable doubt whatever to be entertained respecting them. The assertions themselves, however, as they appear in writers at the end of the second and in the following centuries, are sometimes obviously incorrect in matters of fact recorded in the New Testament; sometimes mere suppositions more or less extravagant of their respective authors, or vague traditions current at the time; and the only attempted *proof* is a reference to lists of bishops in different Churches, beginning with the names of those who were said to have been settled there and consecrated by the Apostles, and reaching down to some later date. But these lists are of little or no historical value, and cannot be relied upon for the earliest names, which alone are of any importance. If any one Church had possessed an authentic and trustworthy catalogue of this nature, we might justly expect to find it in so important a Church as that of Rome. But the catalogue of the earliest Roman bishops exhibits so many variations and contradictions, as it is recorded by different authors, that it is evidently of no authority whatever. Indeed, the only authentic accounts of successive bishops, which anywhere existed, were those which were recorded by their contemporaries in the Church books, called Diptychs, and kept for such purposes. But there is no mention of such books before the fourth century, and the Archives of Churches, supposed to have been kept from the very beginning, were nothing but oral traditions, most doubtful, when most confidently affirmed.[1]

---

[1] The following are some examples of the testimony of the early Fathers respecting the apostolic or divine institution of episcopacy.

Irenæus (about A. D. 180), the earliest of the authorities cited, says that *bishops* and presbyters from Ephesus *and the neighbouring cities* came to meet St. Paul at Miletus. "In Mileto convocatis *Episcopis* et Presbyteris qui erant ab Epheso et *reliquis proximis civitatibus*."—Lib. iii. 1. Although it is evident, from Acts xx. that they were presbyters only; and nothing is said about "other cities." Irenæus, however, inserts these because a number of bishops, in his sense of the word, could not have come from Ephesus alone.

For the evidence of Tertullian and Clemens Alexandrinus, see Note, page 71.

The great reverence entertained by the Church at Jerusalem for Jâmes, the Lord's brother, and the eminence which he evidently held there, naturally led those, who fondly painted the past with the colours of the present, to assert that he was the first Bishop of Jerusalem ; but even this is not enough for the Fathers of the fourth century ; thus Epiphanius (about A. D. 370) declares that St. James was not only the first Bishop, but that *Christ committed to him his own throne upon earth; πρῶτος οὗτος εἴληφε τὴν καθέδραν τῆς ἐπισκοπῆς ᾧ πεπίστευκε Κύριος τὸν θρόνον αὐτοῦ ἐπὶ τῆς γῆς πρώτῳ.* 'Hæres,' 78, § 7.

Chrysostom also affirms that St. James was made Bishop of Jerusalem *by Christ himself; ἔπειτα ὤφθη Ἰακώβῳ, ἐμοὶ δοκεῖ, τῷ ἀδελφῷ ἑαυτοῦ, αὐτὸς γὰρ αὐτὸν λέγεται κεχειροτονηκέναι, και ἐπίσκοπον ἐν Ἱεροσολύμοις πεποιηκέναι πρῶτον.*—'Hom.' 78, in 1 Cor. xv.

Chrysostom further asserts, that the presbytery which laid hands on Timothy must have been bishops. Why so? Because Timothy was a bishop, and therefore could not have been ordained by presbyters! *οὐ γὰρ ἂν δὴ πρεσβύτεροι ἐπίσκοπον ἐχειροτόνησαν.*—'Com.' in Phil. i. ; also, referring again to the same circumstance, he says, *οὐ περὶ πρεσβυτέρων φησὶν ἔνταυθα, ἀλλὰ περὶ ἐπισκόπων, οὐ γὰρ δὴ πρεσβύτεροι τὸν ἐπίσκοπον ἐχειροτόνουν*—'Com.' in 1 Tim. v. 14 ; 'Hom.' 13—perverting the words of St. Paul to suit the ideas of his own time.

The same tendency to thrust the Church usages of later times upon the apostolic age, without regard to the facts of the case, is seen in the assertions made by several writers, that the Apostles John and James (the Lord's brother), and even St. Mark were made Jewish high priests, the title of high priests hav-

The argument put forward in more modern times for proving the episcopate to be an apostolic or divine

---

ing been given to bishops from the beginning of the third century. Thus Eusebius, quoting from Polycrates, who lived at the very end of the second century, says, Ἰωάννης . . . ὃς ἐγενήθη ἱερεὺς τὸ πέταλον πεφορεκὼς, καὶ μάρτυς καὶ διδάσκαλος, 'H. E.' v. 24, the πέταλον being the gold plate on the high priest's mitre. Epiphanius also says of St. James, οὗτος Ἰάκωβος καὶ πέταλον ἐπὶ τῆς κεφαλῆς ἐφόρει, Hæres, 78, § 14. For the story about St. Mark, see 'Bingham,' ii. 9, 5.

What then is the value of any amount of testimony of such a character as the foregoing?

The following are the lists of the first bishops of Rome, given by—

Irenæus.	*Tertullian.*	*Augustin.*
1. Peter.	1. Peter.	1. Peter.
2. Linus.	2. Clemens.	2. Linus.
3. Anacletus.	3. Linus.	3. Clemens.
4. Clemens.	4. Anacletus.	4. Anacletus.

Eusebius gives the same list as Irenæus; and, living much later than he, when the traditions had gathered accretions by time, and the ignorance of those who handed them down was greater, he undertakes to give the exact dates of their episcopates, thus—

1. Peter	to	68 A. D.
2. Linus	from 68 "	80 "
3. Anacletus	" 80 "	92 "
4. Clemens	" 92 "	101 "

Thus, to say nothing of St. Peter at the head of the list, even so well-known a name as Clemens is placed in three different positions in different accounts, appearing as second, third, and fourth. Bingham remarks upon this discrepancy, that "it is easily reconciled by learned men, who make it appear that Linus and Anacletus died, while St. Peter lived, and that Clemens was ordained their successor by St. Peter also" (ii. 1, 4.) It is a very easy expedient in a story to kill off personages who are in the way, but in this case the explanation is worthless, besides its being a mere conjecture of modern date; for the lists must be still equally due to varying and erroneous traditions; and the date of Clemens in Eusebius is quite irreconcileable with it. Was St. Peter living in A. D. 92?

An ingenious explanation of the confusion in these lists of the early bishops of Rome solves the discrepancies, at the same time that it

institution, from the Apostles themselves having been (as it is alleged) the first bishops, has more appearance of truth and validity, but in reality helps to establish the very opposite conclusion. For as the Apostles exercised all, and more than all, the authority which legitimately belonged to the episcopal office in after-ages, there were not only no bishops then, but not even any need or room for their appointment.

But if we turn from such questionable arguments, to take our stand upon more solid ground, I venture to think that the following conclusions are supported by as strong historical evidence as such a subject can well demand.

1. Firstly, the only bishops mentioned in the New Testament were simple presbyters; the same person being a "bishop"—ἐπίσκοπος, *i.e.*, a superintendent or "overseer," from his "taking an oversight" of his congregation, as is distinctly shewn by Acts xx. and other passages; and a presbyter—πρεσβύτερος or elder, from the reverence due to age. It may, however, be observed that the office of elder is of Hebrew origin; while the

---

utterly destroys the value of this catalogue as an evidence of episcopacy. It is suggested that Clement, Linus, and Anacletus were all presbyters together, and were therefore bishops only in the New Testament sense; that Clement survived his two colleagues, and, from having been the companion of St. Paul, had a moral authority in the Church above the other elders.

Thus Pressensé says "Clement a partagé la direction de l'Eglise avec Linus et Anaclet, qui ont été évêques ou anciens en même temps que lui. Après la mort de ses collègues, il demeura le seul ancien de l'époque apostolique, et fut par conséquent investi d'une autorité morale toute particulière."—Vol. ii. p. 387.

term "bishop"—ἐπίσκοπος—is Hellenic, and is applied in the New Testament only to the officers of Gentile Churches, though it did not supersede the use of the word presbyter among them.[1]

2. Secondly, Timothy at Ephesus, and Titus in Crete, were delegated by St. Paul to perform for him what we might call episcopal functions, in ordaining, superintending, reproving, or encouraging the ministers of those Churches, as well as endeavouring to promote the general well-being of the Christian communities there. But they are never called "bishops," or any other name which might indicate a special order or ecclesiastical office. Their commission was evidently an exceptional and temporary charge, to meet some peculiar wants in those places during the necessary absence of St. Paul; and there is no intimation of any kind that such appointments were of general necessity—no intimation that they were needed; or that they were made, or ought to be made, in any other Churches of the time. Nevertheless, the authority thus delegated to Timothy and Titus may justly be considered the embryo of the episcopacy of the following age, or the pattern which the Churches probably followed when it was found desirable to establish an order superior to that of the presbyters, and which may have suggested the nature

[1] The word ἐπίσκοπος was well known in classical Greek. It signified in particular the civil officer sent by the Athenians to exercise a superintending authority in cities of their "subject-allies," and corresponded with the Lacedæmonian term ἁρμοστής.

and measure of the functions and authority which were committed to their bishops at the first.

And if it be thought that this in fact supplies an apostolic origin to the episcopal order, the admission may be so far made in this limited sense—an Apostle having suggested the idea, and the Churches afterwards on their own authority having adopted and embodied it in their ministry.

3. Thirdly, the tradition alluded to by Tertullian, and more strongly noticed by Clement of Alexandria,[1] that St. John after his release from Patmos established bishops in the different Churches around Ephesus, suggests a very interesting step in the rise and progress of episcopacy,

---

[1] The reference in Tertullian is very brief, "Ordo Episcoporum ad originem recensus in Johannem stabit auctorem."—'Adv. Marcion,' iv. 5.

Clemens Alexand. writes more at length: *ἐπειδὴ, τοῦ τυράννου τελευτήσαντος, ἀπὸ τῆς Πάτμου τῆς νήσου μετῆθεν ἐπὶ τὴν 'Εφεσον, ἀπῄει παρακαλούμενος καὶ ἐπὶ τὰ πλησιόχωρα τῶν ἐθνῶν, ὅπου μεν ἐπισκόπους καταστήσων, ὅπου δέ ὅλας ἐκκλησίας ἁρμόσων, ὅπου δέ κλῆρον, ἕνα τέ τινα κληρώσων ὑπὸ τοῦ Πνεῦματος σημαινομένων.*—'Quis Dives Salvetur,' § 42.

The words are part of a story which Clement honestly says has been handed down only by tradition, and which he fears may be regarded as fabulous. He introduces it with *ἄκουσον μῦθον οἰ' μῦθον ἀλλὰ ὄντα λόγον περι 'Ιωάννου τοῦ ἀποστόλου παραδεδομένον καὶ μνήμῃ πεφυλαγμένον.* And the quotation above given is followed by the story of a youth, whom St. John commended to the care of one of these bishops, and who afterwards became a robber. St. John, however, went to him to reclaim him; and, with very questionable theology, assures him, that there is still hope for him. "For I," said he, "will account to Christ for thee; I will bear thy death for thee, as the Lord did for us:" *ἐγὼ Χριστῷ δώσω λόγον ὑπὲρ σοῦ ἂν δέῃ, τὸν σὸν θάνατον ἑκὼν ὑπομενῶ, ὡς ὁ Κύριος τὸν ὑπὲρ ἡμῶν· ὑπὲρ σοῦ τὴν ψυχὴν ἀντιδώσω τὴν ἐμήν.*

and its relations to the earlier polity. And it may probably have had a basis of truth. For the Churches in Asia Minor seem to have been the first to exhibit the episcopal form of Church government; and the state of things at that time may naturally have led St. John to repeat, and perhaps enlarge, what St. Paul had done many years before at Ephesus and Crete. But this tradition indicates that at any rate at the end of the apostolic age, when St. John was probably the only surviving Apostle, the order of bishops had not previously been called into existence. The tradition itself appears for the first time a hundred years or more after the alleged events, and is too brief and obscure for anything more than historical conjectures. Moreover, whatever St. John may have found it desirable to do, he did not think it necessary to record or refer to it in any of his canonical writings, nor is there any reason to suppose that he gave any general instructions on the subject to the Church at large.

4. Fourthly, there is evidence of the most satisfactory kind, because unintentional, to the effect that episcopacy was established in different Churches *after the decease* of the Apostles who founded them, and at different times;—some Churches being considerably later than others in adopting this form of government. Thus there was evidently no bishop over the Church at Corinth, when Clement wrote his Epistle to the Corinthians[1] some

[1] Clement wrote his Epistle to the Corinthians on account of the disorders in that Church; and his special complaint against them is

time after the death of St. Paul. In the time of Ignatius, at the beginning of the second century, there were several Asiatic bishoprics; Ignatius himself being Bishop of Antioch, while Onesimus of Ephesus, and

---

their conduct to their presbyters. They had got up factious parties (*στάσεις*) against their presbyters (§ 47): they had even dismissed from their office presbyters, who had been regularly appointed, and who had blamelessly discharged their duties (44); he exhorts them to live at peace with their presbyters (54); and to submit to their presbyters (57). And not only does he say nothing about a bishop, or any one officer in authority over the presbyters, but if there had been a bishop in the Corinthian Church, it is impossible that the people could have acted as they did, without the bishop's authority being utterly set at nought, and a still graver cause of complaint being created, which Clement must have noticed.

Clement mentions the two orders of Presbyters and Deacons, sometimes calling the former *ἐπίσκοποι* (§ 42) after the manner of the New Testament; and he seems to know of no other.

Those, indeed, who are determined to find "bishops" in the apostolic age, profess to find them hidden under the words *ἡγούμενοι* and *προηγούμενοι* in two passages of this Epistle; namely—

'*Τοῖς νομίμοις τοῦ Θεοῦ ἐπορεύεσθε, ὑποτασσόμενοι τοῖς ἡγουμένοις ὑμῶν, καὶ τιμὴν τὴν καθήκουσαν ἀπονέμοντες τοῖς παρ' ὑμῖν πρεσβυτέροις, νέοις τε μέτρια καὶ σεμνὰ νοεῖν ἐπετρέπετε, γυναιξίν τε ἐν ἀμώμῳ καὶ σεμνῇ καὶ ἁγνῇ συνειδήσει πάντα ἐπιτελεῖν παρηγγέλλετε.* § 1. And *Τὸν Κύριον Ἰησοῦν Χριστὸν, οὗ τὸ αἷμα ὑπὲρ ἡμῶν ἐδόθη, ἐντραπῶμεν, τοὺς προηγουμένους ἡμῶν αἰδεσθῶμεν, τοὺς πρεσβυτέρους ἡμῶν τιμήσωμεν, τοὺς νέους παιδεύσωμεν τὴν παιδείαν τοῦ φόβου τοῦ Θεοῦ, τὰς γυναῖκας ἡμῶν ἐπὶ τὸ ἀγαθὸν διορθωσώμεθα.* § 21.

But it must be observed that both these passages, so similar to each other, evidently refer to the common relative duties of life; duties owing to persons in authority,—to our elders—to our children and wives: and they may be compared with 1 Tim. v. 1, 2, and Titus ii. 2–6.

If Church authorities are here alluded to at all, they are not bishops, but presbyters, called *ἡγουμενοι*, as they are in the New Testament.

To say that *ἡγουμενοι*, being plural, means a series of Corinthian bishops, past and present, is a mere contrivance to prop up a preconceived opinion.

Polycarp of Smyrna, are mentioned by name in his genuine epistles. But some years later, when Polycarp wrote his Epistle to the Philippians, there was no bishop over the Church at Philippi.[1] And, later still, in Justin Martyr's account of Christian worship in his time only two orders of ministers are seen, with no allusion to any other, even under circumstances which a century or less later would necessarily have introduced the services of a bishop.[2]

---

[1] The proof from Polycarp's Epistle to the Philippians, is similar to that from Clement to the Corinthians; namely, that under the circumstances, it is morally impossible that the bishop should have been unmentioned, if there had then been one in that Church.

Polycarp addresses exhortations to the people, to the deacons, and to the presbyters. In particular he urges the Philippians to submit themselves to the presbyters and deacons—*ὑποτασσομένους τοῖς πρεσβυτέροις καὶ διακόνοις; ὡς Θεῷ καὶ Χριστῷ*—but he mentions no bishop. Was no obedience due to him, if he had been there?

The learned Hefele, in his edition of the 'Patres Apostolici,' has a curiously characteristic note on these words, namely, "Policarpus episcopi non facit mentionem, quippe qui verecundia impeditus eum nollet cohortari!" But, however great his *verecundia,* would it have been any mark of disrespect to the bishop to *exhort the people to obey him?* Ignatius had thought it no disrespect to Polycarp to write *τῷ ἐπισκόπῳ προσέχετε ἵνα καὶ ὁ Θεὸς ὑμῖν;* and *ἀντίψυχον ἐγω τῶν ὑποτασσομένων τῷ ἐπισκόπῳ, πρεσβυτέροις, διακόνοις.*

[2] Justin Martyr mentions only two kinds of ministers; and in particular in the account of the celebration of the Lord's Supper, he introduces only *ὁ προεστὼς* and *οἱ διάκονοι;* thus, *προσφέρεται τῷ προεστῶτι τῶν ἀδελφῶν ἄρτος καὶ ποτήριον ὕδατος καὶ κράματος, . . εὐχαριστήσαντος δὲ τοῦ προεστῶτος, . . . οἱ καλούμενοι παρ' ἡμῖν διάκονοι διδόασιν ἑκάστῳ τῶν παρόντων μεταλαβεῖν ἀπὸ τοῦ εὐχαριστηθέντος ἄρτου, καὶ οἴνου καὶ ὕδατος.*—'Apol.' i. § 85, also 87.

If it be contended that *ὁ προεστὼς* here is a bishop, then the presbyters are entirely omitted. Were there none of them in Justin's time?

The author of the 'Hermæ Pastor,' who probably lived after the middle of the second century, knew only the two orders of presbyters and deacons; though he alludes, with disapprobation, to a tendency then existing towards episcopacy, or a pre-eminence among presbyters. The "bishops" whom he mentions, like those in the New Testament, were only presbyters taking the oversight of Churches.[1]

Before the end of the second century, however, the episcopal form was probably established by general consent in all the churches of the Roman empire.

The causes of this change, or rather development, of the apostolic form of the Christian ministry are not doubtful, or far to seek. The want of united action among the different presbyters of the same Church, when they were all of equal authority, and there was no official superior to control or direct them; the dis-

---

Or was there ever a Church with a bishop and no presbyters?

[1] In the 'Hermæ Pastor' occur such expressions as *σὺ δι ἀναγγελεῖς τοῖς πρεσβυτέροις τῆς ἐκκλησίας*, or in the Latin, senioribus, qui præsunt ecclesiæ.—Lib. i. 2, 4. Episcopi, id est præsides ecclesiarum—and then, qui præsides sunt ministeriorum qui et inopes et viduas protexerunt. Lib. iii. 9, 27: a description of Presbyters and Deacons.

The words Apostoli, et Episcopi, et doctores et ministri, in Lib. i. 3, 5, are taken by Romanists to allude to bishops as distinguished from presbyters; but *doctores* is not an appropriate word for presbyters, and if there were then bishops superior to and presiding over presbyters, he would not have blamed them for seeking a pre-eminence; as, Nunc itaque vobis dico qui præestis ecclesiæ, et amatis primos consessus.—Lib. i. 3, 9. And again, Verum omnes hujusmodi insipientes sunt et fatui, qui habent inter se æmulationem de principatu, &c.—Lib. iii. 8, 7.

putes and divisions which consequently arose similar to those which disturbed the Corinthian Church in the lifetime of St. Paul, and which, checked for a while by him, broke out again after his removal; the need which must have been felt more and more of a centre of union and of religious teaching and action, to bind together in one harmonious body the different members of each Christian community, and to facilitate their communication with other Churches—led naturally, after the departure of the Apostles, to the wise and wholesome practice of appointing one presbyter to have a superiority over the rest in every Church; and then the name of bishop, which before was common to them all, was restricted to the superior authority.[1]

This origin of episcopacy is expressly acknowledged by patristic testimony even in the fourth century, when there was so strong a tendency to magnify the bishop's

[1] As in the case of the Jewish Synagogues, so in the earliest Christian Churches, there was usually, if not always, a body or "College" of presbyters at the head of each society. At any rate, in the New Testament, presbyters, in the plural, are expressly mentioned in connection with the Churches at Jerusalem, at Ephesus, and even at Philippi, where probably the Church was not large. While, on the other hand, there is no recorded instance of a single presbyter superintending any congregation. With this associated authority, it would doubtless happen that one of the number by mutual arrangement would, either in rotation or otherwise, act as the President or Chairman of their meetings, or—to use an ecclesiastical term—their "Consistories." To make such a presidency a permanent office, and to invest it exclusively with certain portions of the ministerial authority once common to all the presbyters, is all that was needed to originate the primitive episcopate, and thereby to secure a united action, without any violent innovation.

office. It is acknowledged that Churches were at first governed by the common advice of presbyters; that schisms and contentions among them made it necessary to place one over the others; and that the custom of the Church, rather than any ordinance of the Lord, made bishops greater than the rest.[1]

The causes above mentioned might, under any circumstances, have had sufficient force to produce such a change; but the gravity of the crisis, which marked the last years of the first century, immensely increased the urgency of their operation. At that time the growing dissensions between the Jewish and Gentile Christians—the destruction of Jerusalem with the entire breaking up of the Church in that city which had been the source and centre, the strength and example, of the whole Christian body—the appearance of the Gnostic heresy with its delusive, pernicious, and widely spreading doctrines—the impending and already commenced collision of Christianity with the power of the Roman empire, which was to test the faith, and patience, and

1 Let Jerome's unmistakeable words be a sufficient evidence of this—

"Idem est ergo Presbyter qui Episcopus; et antequam diaboli instinctu studia in religione fierent, et diceretur in populis, Ego sum Pauli, Ego Apollo, Ego autem Cephæ, communi presbyterorum concilio ecclesiæ gubernabantur. Postquam vero unusquisque eos, quos baptizaverat, suos putabat esse, non Christi, in toto orbe decretum est, ut unus de presbyteris electus superponeretur cæteris, ad quem omnis ecclesiæ cura pertineret....... Sicut ergo presbyteri sciunt se ex ecclesiæ consuetudine ei qui sibi præpositus fuerit, esse subjectos,—ita Episcopi noverint se magis consuetudine, quam dispositionis dominicæ, veritate, presbyteris esse majores."—'Comm. in Titus.' i.

courage of the Churches with a fiery trial—all created a pressing need of some organization to meet the accumulating dangers of the time, and to cement together the diverse elements of Christian society thus threatened with dissolution.

The establishment of episcopacy saved the Church; whatever mischiefs were afterwards wrought by the abuse and perversion of the system.

The episcopal office in its original institution was one of simple priority among the other ministers, rather than a superior order in the Church. Every town had its bishop with a body of presbyters and deacons under him; the Church often consisting of a single congregation assembling in one place of worship, and the bishop himself performing all the duties of a presbyter among them, and having a personal acquaintance with every member of his flock.[1] So that the condition of each

[1] Lord King, in his "Enquiry into the Constitution of the Primitive Church,' declares that during the first three centuries each bishop's diocese,—or rather his "parish," for it was then called παροικία,—contained only one Church, *i. e.*, one congregation meeting in a single place of worship. This, however, is too sweeping an assertion. Many large towns must even from the earliest times have had several places, where different congregations of Christians met, as Jerusalem and Ephesus are in the Acts of the Apostles expressly said to have had. Yet, on the other hand, many παροικίαι had doubtless only one Church; and consequently the number of such primitive bishoprics in the course of time became very great. Thus, in Augustin's days, there were nearly 500 bishoprics in the African Church, and 400 in Asia Minor. And Ignatius, in his Epistle to Polycarp, bids him not only to let nothing be done in his Church without his concurrence, μηδὲν ἄνευ γνώμης σου γινέσθω; but to be able to enquire after every member of his flock by name, ἐξ ὀνόματος πάντας ζήτει; which could not possibly

diocese, and the relations of its ministers to each other, were very much like what is now seen in one of our parishes in the charge of an incumbent with several curates working under him and with him in it. But as the numbers of Christians increased, and were spread abroad more widely, separate congregations were necessarily formed and multiplied, and bishops appointed presbyters to take charge of them; until by degrees the episcopal office was fully occupied with the ordination and general superintendence of the clergy and other special duties, without any longer taking an active part in the parochial ministrations. And thus the episcopate became quite distinct from the office of the presbyters, and was naturally regarded, as indeed it then was, a separate order in the ministry.

It is not necessary for our present subject to trace in any detail the progress of events and changes, in the course of which the episcopate gradually rose from its originally simple position of priority, to the culmination of its authority as a dominant power in the Church. A very interesting account of the successive advances, which were thus made in the second and third centuries, is given by Professor Lightfoot in his treatise on the Christian ministry appended to his edition of the Epistle to the Philippians. He there points out that the development of the episcopal authority was marked by

---

have been done if the see of Smyrna had been an extensive district with a number of congregations separate from each other, and superintended by their own distinct pastors respectively.

three distinct stages of progress, which were connected respectively with the names of Ignatius, Irenæus, and Cyprian. In the time of Ignatius, the bishop, then only *primus inter pares* among his co-presbyters, was regarded as a *centre of unity;* in the time of Irenæus, he was looked upon as the *depositary of primitive truth;* and with Cyprian, the bishop was the *absolute vicegerent of Christ* in things spiritual in the Church.

This great change was fully confirmed and established in the following century, in spite of some struggles on the part of the presbyters to maintain their original position. But this exaltation of the bishop's power was not the only thing which marked the contrast between the hierarchy of the Nicene period, and the ministry of the apostolic age. That contrast was completed by the contemporaneous introduction and expansion of the sacerdotal element, which will be noticed in the following Lecture.

LECTURE III.

A FURTHER CONSIDERATION OF THE CHRISTIAN MINISTRY,

WITH A SPECIAL REFERENCE TO THE QUESTION WHETHER IT IS RIGHTLY REGARDED AS A PRIESTHOOD.

III.

A FURTHER CONSIDERATION OF THE CHRISTIAN MINISTRY,

WITH A SPECIAL REFERENCE TO THE QUESTION WHETHER IT IS RIGHTLY REGARDED AS A PRIESTHOOD.

THE Christian Ministry in its two Orders instituted by the Apostles, and in its subsequent episcopal development, has been so far considered, as it appears in the New Testament, and in the period immediately ensuing; but there still remain some particulars connected with it, some questions respecting its nature and functions, too important to be omitted.

The simple account of the public services of Christian ministers, which is given by Justin Martyr,[1] towards the middle of the second century, shows that very little deviation from the apostolic practice had then taken place; and from the testimony of other Christian authors, together with the taunts of Pagan adversaries, it appears

[1] See Justin Martyr 'Apol.' i. § 85, 86.

probable that during the course of this century the essential character of the original office continued to be preserved. By the commencement of the third century, however, this apostolic simplicity had begun to be greatly marred by the assumption of a more ostentatious style of ministration, and a more imposing authority. The Christian ministry was now changed into a *Priesthood* after the model of the Levitical Law.[1] Bishops, presbyters, and deacons, became high-priests, priests, and Levites, and were gradually more and more regarded as a mediating, sacrificing, and absolving order, standing between God and the general body of Christian men. Before this the reproach cast by Pagans against the Christian Church that it had no temples, altars, priests, or sacrifices, had been its praise and glory; for its temple was the whole world, or wherever two or three were gathered together in the Saviour's name; its altar was the Cross; its priest the Lord Jesus Christ, at once the Priest and the all-sufficient sacrifice. And the only earthly priesthood was confined to no sacerdotal cast, or tribe, or separated order; but was co-extensive with the whole community of the faithful, who in a figurative or spiritual meaning were kings and

[1] Jerome expressly says that the scheme of a priesthood in the Christian Church was taken from the Old Testament. "Et ut sciamus traditiones apostolicas sumptas de veteri testamento, quod Aaron, et filii ejus, atque Levitæ in templo fuerunt, hoc sibi Episcopi, et Presbyteri, et Diaconi vindicent in Ecclesia." —'Epist. ad Evagrium,' *the end.*

Accordingly a bishop was then often called Ἀρχιερεύς or *Summus Sacerdos*, a presbyter Ἱερεύς or *Sacerdos*, and a deacon Λευίτης or *Levita.*

priests unto God in Christ. But now the leaven of Jewish and of Pagan influences,[1] which from the first

[1] Professor Lightfoot—('Epistle to the Philippians,' p. 258)—ascribes the origin of the Christian sacerdotalism to Pagan influences exclusively, though he admits that its *form* was taken from the Jewish priesthood of the Old Testament. Pagan influences, in the midst of which the Christian Churches were located, contributed doubtless in some measure to this effect; but I think that Judaism also furnished a large contribution in the same direction. The Professor's arguments do not appear to me conclusive. The absence of sacerdotalism up to this time may be due to the *strength* of the Church's hold upon apostolic truth rather than to the *weakness* of Jewish influences; and the following considerations appear to me to have great weight.

1. After the destruction of Jerusalem, and the utter overthrow of the Jewish nation, Judaism was no longer formidable to the Church as an enemy attacking it *from without*, but this did not hinder it from being even more dangerous as an evil influence *within* the Christian body. It was the Judæo-Christianity of Church-members which wrought the greatest mischief.

2. The victory which the Church had gained over Judaism as an open antagonist, made it only the more formidable as an insidious influence. By a strange law the conquered almost always in the end exercise an influence over their conquerors; and vanquished Judaism, being no longer watched and guarded against, was enabled to work its way with more security, and with a more deadly effect.

3. The prevalence of Judæo-Christianity in the Church was proved by the breaking out of the heresies of the Nazarenes and the Ebionites in the second century, these sects being formed out of the two parties into which the Judaizing Christians split themselves when they became openly separated from the Church.

4. The existence of Judaizing tendencies in the Church is also indicated by the *reaction* against them which gave occasion to such heresies as those of Marcion, who by his eager and enthusiastic spirit was hurried into opposite extremes in combating the Judæo-Christianity of those times. And again, the Church, while encountering these heresies, was led too strongly in the direction of the Jewish Law.

5. The Canon of the New Testament was not yet fully formed, at least in many Churches; the Old Testament was still the sacred Book; and there were in the second century no divinely inspired men to teach the Christian body how to

had been working insidiously in the Church, although the religious systems from which they sprang were formally renounced and resisted, began to make itself felt and seen; and as the inner life of the Church declined in spirituality, and lost its firm hold of apostolic truth, its outward form and show became more prominent and presuming, and challenged more attention from the world.

Tertullian[1] is the first Christian author by whom the Church ministry is directly asserted to be a priesthood. By Cyprian an undisguised sacerdotalism is maintained; and in the fourth century the sacerdotal system took deep root in the Church, and grew and flourished, until it culminated at last in the overbearing pretensions of the priesthood in the later Church of Rome.

In our own Church the attempt was made at the Reformation to bring back the presbyter's office as nearly as might be to the apostolic model, without making

---

distinguish in it the abiding truth from the obsolete form.

See some admirable remarks on all these points in Pressensé's 'Hist. des Trois Prem. Siècles,' vol. ii.

[1] This change had been gradually approaching, but distinctly appears first at the beginning of the third century. Thus Tertullian, "Dandi baptismum quidem jus habet *summus Sacerdos*, qui est *Episcopus*." 'De Bapt.' 17.

"Vani erimus si putaverimus, quod *sacerdotibus* non liceat, Laïcis licere."—'Exhort. Cast.' 7.

The system, once introduced, soon developed itself in strength and pretensions. Cyprian in his time contributed greatly to establish the sacerdotal position and power in the Church. "Vel eligendi dignos *sacerdotes*, vel indignos recusandi. . . . . ut *sacerdos*, plebe presente, sub omnium oculis deligatur."—Cyp. 'Ep.' 68.

"Utique ille *sacerdos vice Christi vere fungitur.*" *Ep.* 63, *ad Cœcilium.*

See further, Appendix A.

more violent and sudden changes than were absolutely necessary. The noble-minded Reformers in the reign of Edward VI. in this, as in other portions of their work, faithfully followed the light of the New Testament, as far as that light gradually shone in upon their minds with increasing clearness; but they did not continue long enough to complete their labours. And their efforts never having been subsequently followed up in a similar spirit, some blemishes, which they failed to notice, or could not then remove,—some expressions which savour more of the Romish errors which they desired to eliminate, than of the apostolic truth which it was their object to restore,—have not yet disappeared from our formularies.[1]

In order, therefore, to a right appreciation of the true nature of the ministerial offices in the Christian Church, and of the ministrations essentially belonging to them, it is necessary to enquire more particularly what the Apostles really intended their Church officers to be, and

[1] The Reformers of Edward VI.'s time evidently proposed to themselves the noble object of bringing their Church into as close a conformity as possible with Scripture truth; and they endeavoured quietly but honestly to make our Church formularies accord with that truth, so far as they were enabled themselves to perceive it. But all the subsequent revisions of our Liturgy and ecclesiastical system, were undertaken in a very different spirit, and for very different purposes. At the beginning of Elizabeth's reign the spirit of compromise prevailed. In the time of James I., the leading object was to assimilate us to Rome without submitting to the Roman Pope. And at the "Restoration" the violent reactionary feeling against the Puritans carried the day, and influenced the whole proceedings.

Since then—what has been done during more than two hundred years?

to do; and what they purposely and altogether excluded from the sphere of their authority and duties; and so to arrive at a just and sober judgment respecting the claims and assertions of post-apostolic times.

And herein, with a view to bringing the question in as distinct and clear a manner as possible before those who may be inclined to give it a careful consideration, I will at once state that the proposition which I undertake to prove from the New Testament, and from the teaching and practice of the Apostles there recorded, is that, according to Scripture truth, the *Christian ministry* is *not* a *priesthood,* and Christian ministers are not *priests,* are not invested with any sacerdotal powers, and have no sacerdotal functions to perform.

The English word "priest" is indeed only the word "presbyter" abbreviated in its passage into our modern language; and were it not for the equivocal meaning of the term, and the consequent confusion of thought, and the excuse for erroneous teaching, which it favours, there could be no objection to our thus using it to designate the truly apostolic office of the presbyter, or elder, of the New Testament.[1] But I here use the words

---

[1] The word "presbyters" became "prester;" then in Norman French "prestre;" and from this the modern French "prêtre," and the English "prest," afterwards "priest."

The circumstance that this word is used to denote the Jewish and Pagan sacrificers, as well as Christian ministers, indicates that the nations which thus use it were Christianized after sacerdotalism had gained a settled place in the Church.

The word "priest" from its equivocal meaning, is still employed amongst ourselves to prove by an argument,—weak indeed and illo-

priest and priesthood only in the other and more common meaning, as the equivalents of the Greek ἱερεὺς

gical, yet not without its influence on weak and illogical minds,—that the Church of England retains all the sacerdotalism of the older Church. Thus, the Church of England declares certain of her ministers to be "priests;" a priest must offer sacrifices (Heb. viii. 3, x. 11), and must have an altar whereon to offer them; the altar in our churches must be the Communion Table, and the Lord's Supper the sacrifice; and then any amount of sacerdotal and sacramental superstitions can be introduced *ad libitum*, in direct opposition to our Prayer-Book's teaching. It is most desirable, therefore, that this equivocal word should be avoided, and the honest, original "presbyter" be restored to its place.

It is much to be lamented that good and learned men, while acknowledging that a Christian minister is not a sacrificing priest,—a ἱερεὺς or *sacerdos*—but an Elder, a πρεσβύτερος or *presbyter*—should yet have countenanced the continued use of the word "priest;" thus giving a handle to those who well know how to use it for evil.

Thus Hooker, long ago, admitted that, "in truth, the word *Presbyter* doth seem more fit, and in propriety of speech more agreeable, than *Priest*, with the drift of the whole Gospel of Jesus Christ." And "What better title could there be given them than the reverend name of *Presbyters*, or fatherly guides? The Holy Ghost throughout the body of the New Testament, making so much mention of them, doth not anywhere call them Priests."—'Eccles. Polit.' v. 78. Yet he says, that after all it makes no difference; and he will make no concession of the name.

And very recently indeed Professor Lightfoot, in his valuable *Excursus* on the Christian ministry, appended to his edition of the 'Epistle to the Philippians,' declares "as broadly as possible," that "the Kingdom of Christ has no sacerdotal system;" that in the Christian Church "for communicating instruction, and for preserving public order, for conducting religious worship, and dispensing of social charities, it became necessary to appoint special officers. But the priestly functions and privileges of the Christian people are never regarded as transferred or even delegated to these officers. They are called stewards, or messengers of God, servants or ministers of the Church, and the like; but the sacerdotal title is never once conferred upon them." He declares that the idea of a priesthood was brought into the Church at the end of the second century, by the influence of Paganism, and took its form from the Levitical law; that Christian ministers are not priests in the sense of offering sacrifices for sin, or

and ἱερατεία, and as they are used throughout our English Bible. A priest in this acceptation of the word is one whose office it is to act as a mediator, or medium of acceptable communication, between God and man in sacred things, to offer acceptable sacrifices to God for the people, and to impart to them by the power of his official acts the grace or blessing which God is ready to bestow, especially the absolution or forgiveness of their sins, when they have confessed, and repented of them. And in this sense it is that I undertake to prove that the Christian ministry is not a priesthood.

1. The first evidence, which I adduce in proof of this proposition, is supplied by a consideration of the source from whence the form and shape (so to speak) of the Christian ministry was derived; the model which the Apostles saw fit to imitate in the offices which they instituted in the Church.

As the Christian religion rose up out of the very depth and essence of Judaism, following it as its fore-

---

making an atonement. Yet he asserts that they may be so called, "if the word be taken in a wider and looser acceptation." And this is quite enough for those, who desire it, to cite him as an authority for asserting that the Christian presbyter is a "priest," and, therefore, that all priestly acts and functions may be predicated of him.

It is in vain that Professor Lightfoot adds, "Only in this case the meaning of the term should be clearly apprehended ; and it might have been better, if the later Christian vocabulary had conformed to the silence of the apostolic writers ; so that the possibility of confusion would have been avoided." This undecided protest is of no avail. As far as the Professor is concerned the mischief is to go on, and his name is, and will be, used to support the very sacerdotalism against which he so forcibly declaims.

ordained end and consummation, it might reasonably be expected, that such forms and regulations of the Jewish Church, as were not inconsistent with the principles of the Gospel Dispensation, would be retained and adapted to its use. And the Apostles being men deeply imbued with Jewish feelings, and (it may even be said) with Jewish prejudices, must have been inclined to deviate no further from the customary observances of their law, than their Divine Instructor taught them to be absolutely required. And they must have felt that it was wise to give their new religious life and worship as little innovation and strangeness to Jewish minds as possible, by continuing whatever could consistently be continued of their accustomed ceremonial.

But when we proceed to trace how far these anticipations were realized in the apostolic ordering of the Christian societies, we meet with a peculiarity in the Jews' religion, which must be clearly apprehended before the retention or rejection of Jewish ordinances can be rightly understood; but which, when clearly apprehended, throws great light not only on the origin of the Christian ministry, but also on all the powers and functions which were assigned to it at the first, or which it could ever afterwards legitimately claim.

The religious life of the Jews in its outward practice and operation at the commencement of the Christian era, and for at least several centuries before it, exhibited a remarkable *Dualism*,—a two-fold system,—each part of which was quite independent of the other, though their operation and effects were harmoniously combined. These two parts were respectively centred in

The Temple and *The Synagogue.*

The religious system of the Temple was altogether of divine appointment, and all its services divinely ordered, even in their minute details, without an authority being vested anywhere on earth for altering any of the regulations originally prescribed.

The religious system of the Synagogue was of man's appointment, its services being ordered by no divine law, but originating in the wisdom of man, and by man's authority and discretion regulated and maintained.

In the Temple was the priest consecrated according to a precise regulation, and a sacerdotal succession laid down by God Himself, with the altar and its sacrifices at which he officiated, the incense which he burned, the holy places into which none might enter, but those to whom it was especially assigned.

In the Synagogue was the reader of the Scriptures, the preacher or expounder of religious and moral truth, the leader of the common devotions of the people, unconsecrated by any special rites, and unrestricted by any rule of succession; with a reading-desk or pulpit at which he stood, but with no altar, sacrifices, or incense, and no part of the building more holy than the rest.

And without attempting now to dwell upon all the remarkable contrasts thus displayed, it may suffice to say that the Temple exhibited in a grand combination of typical places, persons, and actions, God dwelling with man, reconciling the world unto Himself in the person and work of Christ; and pardoning, justifying, and graciously receiving those who come to Him through the appointed Saviour: while the Synagogue exhibited a congregation of men, already reconciled to God, assembled as devout worshippers for prayer and praise, for instruction in divine knowledge, and edification in righteous living. And the two systems,—the one divine, the other human,—the one gorgeous and typical, the other simple and real,—in the one, God drawing near to man, in the other, man drawing near to God,—never clashed or interfered with each other: were never intermingled or confounded together. "In the Temple there was no pulpit, in the Synagogue there was no altar."

Now it was the Temple system with its imposing æsthetic services, its associations of awe and mystery, and not the simple unexciting worship of the Synagogue, that naturally appealed to the imagination and feelings of men. And accordingly, from the beginning of the third century, portions of this system began, and continued increasingly, to be introduced into the Church; and in particular the idea of the Temple service was imported into the worship of Christian congregations; the Christian ministry, as already mentioned, was represented to be a Hierarchy; the form and arrangements of the buildings for public devotions were assimilated as much as possible to those of the Hebrew sanctuary; and a system of sacerdotalism grew up, and became so inveterate in the Church, that it still lingers and revives even amongst ourselves, purified indeed from its grosser superstitions, but not altogether removed by the happy influence of the Reformation.

Not so, however, was it in the Apostles' days, or with any of their ordinances and institutions. They retained and adapted to Christian use some Jewish forms and regulations; but they were taken altogether, not from the Temple, but from the Synagogue. The offices which they appointed in the Church, and the duties and authority which they attached to them, together with the regulations which they made for Christian worship, bore no resemblance in name or in nature to the services of the priesthood in the Temple. The Apostles had been divinely taught that those priests and services were typical forms and shadows, which were all centred, and fulfilled, and done away, in Christ: and to reinstate them in the Christian Church would have been in their judgment to go back to the bondage of "weak and beggarly elements" from the liberty, strength, and rich completeness, of the Gospel Dispensation. They saw that as the ordinances of the Temple represented the work of God wrought out for man, not man's work for God, to continue them, after that work was finished in the life and death of Jesus, would be in effect so far to deny the efficacy of the Saviour's mission, and to thrust in the miserable performances of men to fill up an imagined imperfection in the Son of God.

The Apostles therefore took nothing from the Temple

system for the machinery of their Church government; but the offices which they appointed, and the duties and authority which they attached to them, together with the regulations which they made for Christian worship, corresponded in a remarkable and unmistakeable manner with the whole system of the Jewish synagogue.

It would be too long to enumerate here all the particulars of this similarity. They may be found at length, with the whole subject exhaustively discussed in a spirit of great fairness in Vitringa's treatise 'On the Synagogue.'[1] It will be sufficient for our present purpose to observe that a Jewish synagogue was governed by a body of elders, some of whom acted especially as rulers or judges, others were the public religious ministers, and led the prayers of the people, and took care of the

---

[1] The agreement of the Christian Church with the Synagogue, and its disagreement with the Temple system, are specially seen in the following particulars :

1. The *names of the office-bearers* in the Church, before the third century, were those of the Synagogue, not of the Temple.

2. The *places of worship*—only one Temple, but Synagogues anywhere ; so Churches.

3. No *different degrees of sanctity* in the Synagogues—or in the Churches.

4. The *services* in the Synagogue, but not in the Temple, corresponded with those of Christians.

5. *Vestments* were necessary for priests in the Temple ; but no particular dress was used in the Synagogue, nor in Christian Churches.

6. No *restriction of persons* to a particular tribe or class in the Synagogue ; but any fit person might be appointed to minister there ; so also in Christian Churches.

7. No *fixed rule about the age* of those who officiated in the Synagogue ; nor in the Christian Churches.

8. No *exclusion* on the ground of *bodily defects* in the Synagogue ; or in the Christian Church.

9. The Synagogue had a *raised desk or pulpit* for the reader, but no altar ; so Churches had only an *Ambo* or *pulpitum* of the same kind.

reading of the law; and such an officer was called the angel of the Church, and the *chazan* or bishop of the congregation. There were also deacons or almoners, on whom the care of the poor devolved. And these offices with their ministrations the Apostles transferred to the Christian Churches.[1] Nor is it an unreasonable supposition that "whenever a Jewish synagogue existed which

---

[1] "In a Synagogue, three have the magistracy, and were called *the Bench of Three;* whose office it was to decide the differences arising between members, and to take care of other matters of the Synagogue. These judged concerning money matters, thefts, losses, &c. These were properly and with good reason called ἀρχισυνάγωγοι, rulers of the Synagogue, because on them lay the chief care of things, and the chief power.

"Besides these, there was the *Public Minister of the Synagogue,* who prayed publicly, and took care about the reading of the Law, and sometimes preached, if there were not some other to discharge this office. This person was called the *Angel of the Church,* and *Chazan* or *Bishop of the Congregation.* . . . . . . The Public Minister of the Synagogue himself read not the Law publicly; but every Sabbath he called out seven of the Synagogue (on other days fewer), whom he judged fit to read. He stood by him that read, with great care observing that he read nothing either falsely, or improperly, and calling him back and correcting him, if he had failed in anything. And hence he was called *Chazan,* that is ἐπίσκοπος, or Overseer. Certainly, the signification of the word *Bishop,* or *Angel of the Church,* had been determined with less noise, if recourse had been had to the proper fountains, and men had not vainly disputed about the signification of words, taken I know not from whence.

"The service and worship of the Temple being abolished as being ceremonial, God transplanted the worship and public adoration of God used in the Synagogues, which was moral, into the Christian Church; to wit, the public ministry, the public prayers, reading God's word, and preaching, &c. Hence the names of the ministers of the Gospel were the very same, *the Angel of the Church,* and the *Bishop,* which belonged to the ministers in the Synagogue.

"There were also three Deacons, or Almoners, on whom was the care of the poor; and these were called *Parnasim,* or Pastors."—Lightfoot, 'Heb. and Talmud. Exercit. on Matth.' iv. 23.

was brought, the whole or the chief part of it, to embrace the gospel, the Apostles did not there so much *form* a Christian Church (or congregation, ἐκκλησία), as *make an existing congregation Christian*, by introducing the Christian sacraments and worship, and establishing whatever regulations were requisite for the newly adopted faith; leaving the machinery (if I may so speak) of government unchanged, the rulers of synagogues, elders, and other officers (whether spiritual or ecclesiastical, or both) being already provided in the existing institution."[1] That such was sometimes the case in Jerusalem and other Jewish towns is highly probable; and this possibly is the reason why St. James calls the place where Christians met for public worship, or the congregation itself, their Synagogue,[2] as he does in his epistle addressed especially to Hebrew disciples.

The Apostles, therefore, having adopted the official arrangements of the synagogue, and discarded those of the Temple, in the institution of Church offices, plainly showed by this circumstance that no priestly powers or duties were attached to their ministrations.

2. Another argument which lands us in the same con-

---

[1] Archbishop Whately—'Kingdom of Christ Delineated,' p. 108.

[2] Epist. of James, ii. 2. "If there come into your assembly," εἰς τὴν συναγωγὴν ὑμῶν.

"Christian congregations in Palestine long continued to be designated by this name of Synagogue. With the Synagogue itself they would naturally, if not necessarily, adopt the normal government of a Synagogue; and a body of elders or presbyters would be chosen to direct the religious worship, and partly also to watch over the temporal well-being of the society."—Professor Lightfoot, 'Ep. Philip.' p. 190.

clusion is deduced from the condition of the lay members of the Church as it appears in the New Testament, and the equality of privilege or standing-ground in Christ which Christians of all orders or degrees possessed. The way of access to God being open to all without distinction through the priesthood of Christ, there was nothing for a priest to do—no sacerdotal work or office for him to undertake. But the substance of this argument, being specially connected with the position of the Christian laity, will be more fully considered in the following Lecture.

3. A third distinct proof that the office-bearers in the Church of the Apostles were not, and could not be, priests, or perform any sacerdotal duties, is seen in a condensed form in the Epistle to the Hebrews, and is found at large in the whole of the Old and New Testaments, of which that Epistle, as far as its subject reaches, is so valuable an epitome. We there learn that from the very nature of the priestly office, it is necessary for those who hold it to be specially called and appointed by God, either personally by name, or according to a divinely instituted order of succession; and that, since the patriarchal dispensation, only two orders of priesthood have ever had this necessary divine sanction granted to them. These two orders are the *Order of Aaron* and the *Order of Melchizedec.* The priests of the former Order belonged to the Jewish dispensation only, and have indisputably passed away. The only priest after the Order of Melchizedec, ever mentioned

in the Bible, is our Lord Jesus Christ,—the "Priest upon His throne," without a successor, as He had none before Him, in the everlasting priesthood of His mediatorial reign. This argument appears to me to be conclusive. It appears to me that the Epistle to the Hebrews shuts out the possibility of there being any other priest in the Christian Church besides Christ Himself. But this does not so appear to a large number of our clergy. Bishops, as far back as the third century, claimed to be successors or vicegerents of Christ on earth;[1] and our presbyters now do not hesitate to declare that they are *Priests after the order of Melchizedec.* To my mind and feeling this is an impious claim; but countenanced as they are by

[1] In the estimation of Cyprian, in the middle of the third century, the Bishop was the absolute vicegerent of Christ upon earth in spiritual things.

"Nam si Jesus Christus Dominus et Deus noster ipse est summus sacerdos Dei patris, et sacrificium patri se ipsum primus obtulit, et hoc fieri in sui commemorationem præcipit, utique ille sacerdos *vice Christi vere* fungitur."—'Cyp. Ep.' 63, *ad Cæcilium.*

And again, "Neque enim aliunde hæreses obortæ sunt, aut nata sunt schismata, quam inde quod sacerdoti Dei non obtemperatur; nec unus in ecclesia ad tempus sacerdos et ad tempus judex *vice Christi* cogitatur."—'Cyp. Ep.' 65, ad *Cornelium.*

These pretensions were not diminished in the fourth century, for which the testimony of Ambrose will be sufficient. He declares that a Bishop *performs the part of Christ* in the Church, and is the *vicegerent of the Lord.*

"In ecclesia propter reverentiam Episcopalem non habeat caput liberum, sed velamine tectum; nec habeat potestatem loquendi; quia *Episcopus personam habet Christi.* Quasi ergo ante judicem, sic ante Episcopum, quia *vicarius Domini est,* propter reatus originem subjecta debet videri."—'Ambros. Com.' in 1 Cor. xi. 10.

The interpolator of the Ignatian epistles, whatever was his date, "had used almost the highest possible language about Episcopacy;" but from Cyprian's time and onwards, the addition of sacerdotalism raised it to a higher level.

numberless past and present examples, good men are not conscious of impiety in making it. But then it is necessary to ask these "priests" for their *credentials*. Where is the record of their divine appointment to the sacerdotal office? In what part of the New Testament, and in what form of words, is the institution of such priests, and the manner of their succession, to be found? And to such inquiries no satisfactory answer has been or can be given.

But there is still another way in which the priestly claims of the Christian ministry are presented, and which is thought to be less arrogant in its pretensions than the one just noticed. Christian priests, it is urged, are representatives of the whole Christian body; even as under the Jewish law the priestly tribe held their position as representatives of the whole people, who were "a kingdom of priests—a holy nation." And since in a secondary and spiritual sense all those who are in Christ are "kings and priests unto God"—"a holy nation, a royal priesthood,"—the clergy as a representative order, and delegates from the whole Christian community, have a priestly office in the Church.

But if this were so, then the Christian minister, as such a representative priest, could at any rate only exercise the powers of the body which he represented; he could therefore offer only spiritual sacrifices, without any material altar or material sacrifice to put upon it,—only such sacrifices as that of praise and thanksgiving, which every individual Christian is to give; and for this purpose a separate order of priests is useless.[1] Besides this the idea of the spiritual priesthood of each individual Christian being delegated to the clerical order is only a fond imagination, put forward to support a favourite claim. There is no ground for supposing that the priestly functions and privileges of the Christian people ever were or can be thus transferred or delegated. Although the Jewish people were a nation of priests, it was only by a divine command expressly and distinctly given that one tribe was selected to minister for the nation in sacred things, and one family out of this tribe was appointed for the priesthood. No such divine selection or appointment for a priesthood in the Christian Church is anywhere to be found; and the want of this, plead what we will, is absolutely destructive to all priestly claims.

4. And this brings us to a fourth and conclusive proof of my proposition, to be found among the remarkable

[1] "The sacrifice of praise," is a Scriptural expression, and our Communion Service speaks of "this our sacrifice of praise and thanksgiving." Such spiritual sacrifices are offered up by all and each of the faithful from the altar of the heart; and there is no place for any other priest, besides the worshippers themselves, in such a sacrifice. This is the old Christian view before sacerdotalism infected the Church. Justin Martyr (A. D. 155), says that *prayers and thanksgivings* are the *only* acceptable sacrifices, and that they are offered by Christians (not by a priest or minister), in the memorial of the bread and wine, in which they remember what Christ suffered for them. *Ὅτι μὲν οὖν καὶ εὐχαὶ καὶ εὐχαριστίαι, ὑπὸ τῶν ἀξίων γενόμεναι, τέλειαι μόναι καὶ εὐαρεστοί εἰσι τῷ Θεῷ θυσίαι, καὶ αὐτός Φημι, ταῦτα γὰρ μόνα καὶ Χριστιανοὶ παρέλαβον ποιεῖν, καὶ ἐπ' ἀναμνήσει δὲ τῆς τροφῆς αὐτῶν ξηρᾶς τε καὶ ὑγρᾶς, ἐν ῇ, καὶ τοῦ πάθους, ὃ πέπονθε δι' αὐτοὺς ὁ υἱὸς τοῦ Θεοῦ, μέμνηνται.*—'Justin M. Dial. c. Tryph.' § 117.

omissions of Holy Writ. In nothing is the speaking silence of the New Testament more complete and significant, than in the fact that never *there* are Christian ministers of any degree called priests. Neither the Apostles themselves, nor any office-bearers whom they appointed, are ever spoken of as having sacerdotal powers, or sacerdotal duties, committed to them. In *no single instance* is any one of the words, which describe the priesthood and its work, assigned to the office of the Christian ministry or to its ministrations.[1] Familiar as

[1] Such words as ἱερεύς, ἱερατεία, ἱεράτευμα, ἱερουργέω, θύω, θυσία, θυσιαστήριον, or any others of sacerdotal meaning, are never so much as once in the New Testament spoken of the ministerial services in the Christian Church.

They are used when speaking of the priesthood of Jesus Christ; and the following obviously *figurative* expressions are found applied to Christians in general,—not Christian ministers. Thus—

θυσία, a *sacrifice*. "Present your bodies a living sacrifice."—θυσίαν ζῶσαν. Rom. xii. 1.

The contribution sent by the Philippians to St. Paul is called "a sacrifice (θυσίαν) acceptable, well-pleasing to God." (Phil. iv. 18.)

"The sacrifice (θυσίαν) of praise:" and "to do good and to distribute forget not, for with such sacrifices (θυσίαις) God is well pleased." (Heb. xiii. 15, 16.)

"To offer up spiritual sacrifices" θυσίας πνευματικάς. (1 Pet. ii. 5.)

Ἱερεύς and ἱεράτευμα *priest* and *priesthood*,—said of all Christians. "Ye are a holy priesthood"—ἱεράτευμα:—and "a royal priesthood" ἱεράτευμα. (1 Pet. ii 5, 9.)

"Hath made us kings and priests (ἱερεῖς) unto God." (Rev. i. 6). and also in Rev. v. 10, xx. 6.

St. Paul on one occasion, in a very grand figure of speech, represents the whole body of Gentile Christians as a great *sacrifice* offered up to God, and himself as a *priest* ministering at it; thus "That I should be the minister (λειτουργόν, not a sacerdotal word) of Jesus Christ to the Gentiles, *ministering* the Gospel of God." (Ἱερουργοῦντα τὸ εὐαγγέλιον—acting as a priest with respect to the Gospel) "that the *offering up* of the Gentiles" (προσφορὰ τῶν ἐθνῶν) "might be acceptable." Rom. xv. 16.

He also uses a similar metaphor in writing to the Philippians, "And if I *be offered* (σπένδομαι, am poured out as a libation or drink offering),

the Apostles were with the striking ceremonial of the Temple worship, and sometimes deriving from it a figurative language of the greatest force, they never employ terms of priestly import in any manner which countenances the supposition that they, or the presbyters of their Churches, were acting as Priests in the congregations of Christian people.

This omission is acknowledged by High Churchmen to be a "difficulty;" but it is far more than a difficulty, it is an *insuperable bar* to all sacerdotal assumptions. For when it is considered that before the Apostles' times neither they, nor any one else, had even so much as ever heard of a religion without a visible priesthood, and its necessary accompaniments; and that after the Apostles were gone the Church turned back to this conspicuous element of all other religions; when it is considered also that a priesthood requires not merely a non-prohibition, but *a positive and express appointment of divine authority*, I am justified in affirming that this negative argument from the omissions of the New Testament proves as strongly as any historic evidence can demonstrate, that in the Christianity which the Apostles preached and taught, there was no priesthood or priestly ministrations, but those of Jesus Christ Himself,—the

---

upon the *sacrifice* (θυσία) and service of your faith." (Phil. ii. 17.)

And he uses the word σπένδομαι in the same sense in 2. Tim. iv. 6, "I am ready to be offered" ἤδη σπένδομαι.

These are all the instances in which words occur in connection with Christians, except in Heb. xiii. 10, for which see Note (p), and Lecture vii.

one great and sufficient High-priest of the whole Church of God.[1]

I am well aware that a single expression in the Epistle to the Hebrews—"We have an altar"—is sometimes put forward as opposed to what has been here advanced. The "altar" is then taken to mean the communion table, the Eucharistic elements laid upon it are declared to be a sacrifice, and the officiating minister necessarily becomes a priest. But such an interpretation is inconsistent with the context, and is on all grounds, altogether indefensible.[2] Indeed, these words, "We have an altar"

---

[1] The office and work of a "priest" is one which so absolutely requires a divine appointment, that nothing short of an *express and positive declaration* to this effect in the New Testament could justify our calling the Christian ministry a priesthood. The Jewish priests could point to a distinct and unmistakeable ordinance of God in their Law, instituting their order and assigning to them their powers and duties. Those who claim to be Christian Priests, must be called upon to show an equally distinct appointment of *their* order in the New Testament. This they are utterly unable to do: and nothing can supply the absence of it. No pleas of "antecedent probability," or analogies between the Jewish and Christian dispensations, or other similar arguments, can be of any avail in such a case. Until a distinct divine institution of a priesthood for the Christian ministry can be produced, it must be affirmed that the New Testament and the Apostolic Church repudiate such claims; and their only support must be sought for in the later time, when "the mystery of iniquity" was doing its work, and the predicted apostacy had already begun.

The arguments commonly put forward to support the allegation that the Christian ministry is a priesthood,—when they are not simply borrowed from the unscriptural practices of the third and following centuries,—are marked by the fallacy technically called *ignoratio elenchi*, or irrelevant conclusion; being such as do not tend to *prove* the existence of this priesthood, but *assuming* its existence, proceed to account for it, or to explain the nature and mode of its operation.

[2] These words, "We have an altar," are more fully considered in

when rightly understood, confirm instead of invalidating the preceding argument.

And these four proofs, each one by itself complete, must be taken together in their accumulative force, in considering the question whether the Christian ministry is a priesthood or not.[1]

But this is not all. There is other collateral or secondary evidence by no means void of weight, though not bearing so directly on the subject as the preceding testimony. Thus it is a significant fact that neither presbyters nor deacons were *anointed,* like the Jewish priests, to consecrate them for their ministerial work; but they were admitted to their sacred offices by a solemn but simple form of *ordination.* And a brief consideration of the nature of this ordination,—of the persons from whom it was received,—and what was conferred by it,—will still further illustrate the design and character of the Christian ministry in the apostolic Church.

1. There are no rules prescribed, nor any precise directions given in the New Testament, as to the form or manner in which ministers were to be ordained. But

---

Lecture VII. in connection with the Sacrament of the Lord's Supper. See Note, p. 306.

[1] Another proof still,—or at any rate, an indirect confirmation of the foregoing proofs—is seen in the fact that the Apostles continued to attend the Temple services and the ministrations of the Jewish priesthood at the temple altar: since it would have been utterly alien and repulsive to their ideas and principles as faithful Jews, to have set up other priests and altars, either to rival or to co-operate with those of the Temple. After the overthrow of the Jewish polity, there is no indication anywhere that any apostolic authority then established a priesthood which they had not previously instituted.

in Acts xiii. it is recorded that Paul and Barnabas were ordained to the office of Apostles by the imposition of hands, accompanied with prayer and fasting.[1] And doubtless this simple ceremonial, which sufficed for assigning the highest place of dignity in the Church, was used with appropriate variations in the ordination of presbyters and deacons. So that when St. Paul warned Timothy at Ephesus "to lay hands suddenly on no man," these words had become a well-known expression for ordaining to a sacred office. And this mode continued to be used in the post-apostolic Church, as is evidenced by the directions and the forms of prayer for ordinations in what are called "the Apostolic constitutions."

2. The persons who ordained Christian ministers were at first naturally and necessarily the Apostles, as the founders and chief rulers of the Church. Thus Paul and

[1] It may possibly be objected that this ceremony was not an Ordination to the Apostleship, inasmuch as St. Paul declares in his Epistle to the Galatians, that he was "an Apostle not of man neither by man." This objection does not seem to me to have much force; because St. Paul was directly chosen and appointed by Jesus Christ; whether any ecclesiastical ceremony was afterwards added or not. However this may be, the argument in the present case is not affected; since, if the transaction recorded in this chapter was only a solemn Church sanction given to the particular mission, which Paul and Barnabas then undertook, it was at any rate considered sufficient to entitle them to exercise apostolic powers and authority in that mission, by ordaining presbyters, and regulating Churches, as well as preaching Christ.

It is further to be noticed that St. Paul seems not to have preached to the gentiles, until he had been thus formally sent to do so by the direct call of the Spirit, and this imposition of hands at Antioch.

"Jusqu'au moment où il reçut la délégation de l'Eglise d'Antioche, Saul s'était borné à annoncer l'Evangile aux Juifs et aux proselytes."—Pressensé, 'Histoire des Trois Premiers Siècles,' vol. i. p. 447.

Barnabas having gathered together Christian converts at different places in Asia Minor, "ordained them elders in every Church." And Clement of Rome remarks of the Apostles generally, what he had probably himself witnessed in some instances, that they appointed some of their earliest converts—the first-fruits of their Apostleship—as ministers in their several congregations.[1] But when fresh ministers were ordained in an already constituted Church, the presbyters there present took part in an Apostle's ordination by laying their hands with him on those who were ordained; a custom which was preserved in the later Church, and has been retained even to the present day, in some slight respect, in our own.

But it was evidently not by an Apostle's hands alone that sacred orders could be conferred. The authority to appoint Church officers was inherent in every duly constituted Church, as the natural right of a lawful and well organized society. And as presbyters might be joined with an Apostle in ordaining, so might they without an Apostle, give this sanction of ecclesiastical authority in the ordination of any minister in their Church. And thus not only Timothy and Titus, who were specially delegated by St. Paul, ordained presbyters and deacons in the Churches of Ephesus and Crete; but "certain prophets and teachers" at Antioch, without any

---

[1] *Κατὰ χώρας οὖν καὶ πόλεις κηρύσσοντες καθίσταναν τὰς ἀπαρχὰς αὐτῶν, δοκιμάσαντες τῷ Πνεύματι, εἰς ἐπισκόπους καὶ διακόνους τῶν μελλόντων πιστεύειν.*—'Clem. Rom. ep. ad Cor.' i. 52.

such apostolic delegation, were competent to ordain an Apostle.

When Episcopacy was fully established in the Church it became the rule that Bishops only should ordain the presbyters and deacons; but this was not owing to any divine law or apostolic prescription.[1] And the Article

[1] Jerome expressly affirms that it was ecclesiastical custom, and the desire to prevent disputes, and not any divine law, that caused the distinction between Bishops and Presbyters—see Lecture II. note (c) p. 79. This distinction, according to him, consisting principally, if not solely, in the authority to "Ordain."

Long after the general establishment of Episcopacy, and reaching even into the 4th century, traces are to be found of presbyterian ordinations still retaining their place in the Church.

Professor Lightfoot (Ep. Phil. p. 231), quotes a decree of the Council of Ancyra (A.D. 314), to the effect that neither the country bishops nor the *city presbyters* were to give ordination without permission from the Bishop of the diocese in writing.

χωρεπισκόποις μὴ ἐξεῖναι πρεσβυτέρους ἢ διακόνους χειροτονεῖν, ἀλλὰ μηδὲ πρεσβυτεροις πόλεως χωρὶς τοῦ ἐπιτραπῆναι ὑπὸ τοῦ ἐπισκόπου μετὰ γραμμάτων ἐν ἑκαστῃ παροικίᾳ.

"Thus, while restraining the existing license, the framers of the decree still allow very considerable latitude. And it is especially important to observe that they lay more stress on Episcopal *sanction*, than on Episcopal *ordination*."

See also the Professor's remarks about the origin and position of the Chorepiscopal office.

Another remarkable testimony to the existence and long continuance of presbyterian ordination is given by Eutychius, a Patriarch of Alexandria. He represents that from the very foundation of the Church at Alexandria by St. Mark, down to the time of the Council of Nice (A. D. 325), the Bishop of that Church was always chosen by and out of the twelve presbyters, and was by them consecrated as their Bishop by the imposition of their hands. The eleven presbyters then chose another to fill up their number, and made him a co-presbyter with themselves.

"Constituit item Marcus Evangelista duodecim presbyteros cum Hanania, qui nempe manerent cum patriarcha [*i.e.* Episcopo], adeo ut, quum vacaret patriarchatus, eligerent unum e duodecim presbyteris, *cujus capiti reliqui undecim manus imponerent, eumque benedicerent, et patriarcham crearent;* et dein *virum aliquem insignem eligerent, eumque*

of our own Church is most scriptural, when, without any allusion to bishops, it declares those to be lawfully ordained, "who are chosen and called by men who have public authority given unto them in the congregation to call and send ministers into the Lord's vineyard." A priest, indeed, whose office is to stand between God and man, must be specially called by God; and as far as he is authorized by man at all, he must be authorized precisely in the way of God's own prescription; but a pastor and teacher and administrator of sacred things in a congregation of Christian men, who have access to

---

presbyterum secum constituerent loco ejus qui sic factus est patriarcha."—Eutychius. 'Origines Ecclesiæ Alexandrinæ,' translated from the Arabic by Selden; who reckons the date of Eutychius to have been A. D. 876.

Eutychius adds that the custom which he describes continued to the time of Alexander, the Bishop of Alexandria, who was one of the 318 bishops at the Council of Nice.

This distinct testimony of Eutychius is confirmed by Jerome, who lived so close to the time when the Alexandrian practice was still in force. "Nam et Alexandriæ a Marco Evangelista usque ad Heracleam et Dionysium Episcopos, presbyteri semper unum ex se electum, in excelsiori gradu collocatum, Episcopum nominabant; quo modo si exercitus imperatorem faciat, aut diaconi eligant de se quem industrium noverint et archidiaconum vocent."—'Ep. ad Evagrium.'

And so Richard Hooker, though an uncompromising opponent of Presbyterianism, was too honest and too learned a man not to admit the validity of Presbyterian orders. "Now whereas," he writes, "some do infer that no ordination can stand, but only such as is made by Bishops, which have had their ordination likewise by other Bishops before them, till we come to the very Apostles of Christ themselves; to this we answer that there may be sometimes very just and sufficient reason to allow ordination made without a Bishop. The whole Church visible being the true original subject of all power, it hath not ordinarily allowed any other than Bishops alone to ordain; howbeit, as the ordinary course is ordinarily in all things to be observed, so it may be in some cases not unnecessary that we decline from the ordinary ways."—'Eccles. Polit.,' vii. 14.

God through the priesthood of Jesus Christ—whatever inward call he may require—needs no other outward appointment to his office than the authority of the Church in which he ministers. And the visible Church, "as the true original subject of all power" in such matters, may make such appointments in any mode which may be deemed most expedient; amenable only to the general law of decency and order.[1]

The Churches, which like our own have retained the

[1] "They [the Authorities of a Christian Church] have an undoubted right . . . . to appoint such orders of Christian ministers, and to allot to each such functions as they judge most conducive to the great ends of the society: they may assign to *the whole*, or to *a portion*, of these, the office of ordaining others as their successors; they may appoint *one* superintendent of the rest, or *several*, under the title of Patriarch, Archbishop, Bishop, Moderator, or any other that they may prefer; they may make the appointment of them for life, or for a limited period, by election, or by rotation, with a greater or a less extensive jurisdiction: and they have a similar discretionary power with respect to liturgies, festivals, ceremonies, and whatever else is left at large in the Scriptures." "The bodies of Christians we have been speaking of [*i.e.*, the Reformed Churches] had full power [*i.e.*, authority] to retain, or to restore, or to originate, whatever form of Church government they, in their deliberate and cautious judgment, might deem best for the time, and country, and persons, they had to deal with; whether exactly similar or not to those introduced by the Apostles; provided nothing were done contrary to Gospel precepts and principles. They were, therefore, perfectly at liberty to appoint Bishops, *even if they had none* that joined in the Reformation; or to discontinue the appointment, *even if they had:* whichever they were convinced was the most conducive, under existing circumstances, to the great object of all Church government. And though their decision on this point ought to have been greatly influenced by their belief as to what were the forms adopted by the Apostles (which must have been not only wise, but the very wisest, *for those times and persons*), they had no reason to hold themselves *absolutely bound* to adhere always and everywhere to those original models."—Archbishop Whately, 'Kingdom of Christ Delineated,' pp. 248, 252.

Episcopate and Episcopal ordination, may reasonably prefer this form of government; and justly consider that it is one of all but apostolic antiquity,—and one, which having been found desirable, or even necessary, after the departure of the Apostles,—and having been well tried by long experience,—should never lightly be given up. But on the other hand, the government and the ordinations of Presbyterian Churches are just as valid, scriptural, and apostolic as our own; and when circumstances made it necessary or expedient, it was quite lawful for them to adopt this form of Church polity, and, having found it effective, to retain it.

3. What is conferred upon a Christian minister by his ordination has generally been said to be a certain *power*, —a power ecclesiastical or spiritual, or both,—communicated by divine appointment through the hands of him from whom the orders are received. And this power has been variously interpreted in a wider or more restricted sense, according to the respective tenets of individuals, or of Churches. It has been declared to be the same power which was given to the Apostles, continued and handed down in the Church; it has been called the power of forgiving sins, or of conferring the grace of absolution: of effectually administering the sacraments, or of making the body and blood of Christ in the Eucharist; or generally and vaguely the power of acting as a Christian priest, whatever that may be held to mean.

But with all due respect to the antiquity of such opinions, and to the Churches and theologians who have held them, I must, with the New Testament in my hands, venture to affirm that, according to its divine teaching, it cannot be shown that ordination confers *any power at all;* and from what we can gather from its pages respecting the nature and work of the ministry to which men are ordained, it may be confidently and reasonably concluded that ordination confers, not *power*, but ecclesiastical *authority*, to perform the duties of the clerical office.

The words "power" and "authority," though very distinct in meaning, have often been confounded together, and much confusion of thought and language has thereby ensued. When the distinction between them is borne in mind, and the erroneous notion of the ministry being a priesthood is eliminated, there will not be much difficulty in seeing that *authority* and not *power* is given by ordination.

1. To assist in substantiating this assertion I appeal to the words used in the New Testament to denote ordination; and I ask what inference may be deduced from them? The word "ordain" occurs very often in our English version, and is used for any kind of appointment or regulation, being applied indifferently to persons and to things. It is given as the translation of no less than *twelve* Greek words of very different force and meaning, but all implying some kind of causation, appointment, or selection.[1] Of these twelve words six are

[1] The word "Ordination" does not occur in our version of the Bible; nor is there in the New Testament any word of the original language corresponding to it.

The verb "to ordain" occurs

used of persons appointed to some office; but only two of these, καθίστημι and χειροτονέω, are spoken of the ordination of Christian presbyters. The former of these two words, καθίστημι, is one of very wide and general meaning, and signifies "to set up," "constitute," or "place in a position," in any way, or for any purpose whatever. The other word, χειροτονέω, with its kindred substantive χειροτονία, was the word commonly employed in post-apostolic times for ordination, in the strictly ecclesiastical sense; but as in two of the three places, where it is found in the New Testament, it means simply selected, chosen, or appointed; as, in Acts x. 41, to be witnesses of Christ's resurrection; and in 2 Cor. viii. 19, to convey the contributions of the Gentile Churches to Jerusalem; there is no ground for supposing that it has any other special or different meaning in Acts xiv. 23,

very often; and the following are the twelve Greek words of which it is the translation:—

γίγνομαι—Acts i. 22, "must one *be ordained to be*," &c.

γράφω—Jude 4, "before of old *ordained* to this," &c.

διατάσσω—1 Cor. viii. 17, "so *ordain* I." Also 1 Cor. ix. 14. Gal. iii. 19.

ἑτοιμάζω—Eph. ii. 10, "hath before *ordained*," &c.

καθίστημι—Tit. i. 5, "and *ordain* Elders." Also Heb. v. 1.

κατασκευάζω—Heb. ix. 6, "these things were thus *ordained*."

κρίνω—Acts xvi. 4, "the decrees that were *ordained*."

ὁρίζω—Acts xvii. 31, "by that man whom he hath *ordained*." Also Acts x. 42, 1 Cor. ii. 7.

ποιέω—Mark iii. 14, "he *ordained* twelve."

τάσσω—Acts xiii. 48, "were *ordained* to eternal life."

τίθημι—1 Tim. ii. 7, "I am *ordained* a preacher." John xv. 16.

χειροτονέω — Acts xiv. 23, "When they had *ordained* them Elders."

In one passage, Rom. vii. 10, the English word "ordained" has nothing to correspond with it in the original,—ἐντολὴ ἡ εἰς ζωήν.

Of these twelve, the six words γίγνομαι, καθίστημι, ὁρίζω, ποιέω, τίθημι, and χειροτονέω, refer to persons appointed to office.

when applied to the ordination of presbyters. Neither of these words, therefore, implies anything more than that presbyters and deacons were in a regular, orderly, and becoming manner appointed to their offices; and were authorized to act as ministers in their respective Churches; without expressing, or in any way intimating, that any special *powers* were thereby given, or anything conveyed to them, except the *lawful authority* which office-bearers in a well regulated community of any kind must be expected to possess.

2. I further observe, that all spiritual power is a gift from God. And power of various kinds was thus given in the apostolic age; and usually through the Apostles' hands in the spiritual gifts, or χαρίσματα, which characterized that period. But these gifts were bestowed upon men and women without any connection with sacred orders; and there is no intimation that ordination conferred them. Doubtless some of these spiritual gifts, and the powers which they imparted, were possessed in those days by ordained men; and it is quite possible that such gifts were sometimes given them at the time of their ordination; but it was not *by their ordination* that they received them, but by the same means as at other times. The only passage in the New Testament which seems to countenance the contrary supposition is the well-known verse in 1 Tim. iv. 14,—"Neglect not the gift that is in thee, which was given thee by prophecy with the laying on of the hands of the presbytery." This gift, no doubt, was a spiritual power. But this was given to him

by prophecy, *i.e.* by express divine direction; and although it was probably given at the time of his ordination, yet it was given not *by* the laying on of the hands of the presbytery, but *with*, i.e. *together with* this imposition of hands,—μετὰ τῆς ἐπιθέσεως τῶν χειρῶν;—the presbyters joining in the ordination, but the gift being bestowed by the hands of Paul, as in other cases,—a fact which he himself mentions in his second Epistle (2 Tim. i. 6), when he says, "Wherefore I put thee in remembrance that thou stir up the gift of God which is in thee *by* the putting on of *my* hands"—διὰ τῆς ἐπιθέσεως τῶν χειρῶν μου. It is indeed indubitable that such powers were given only by the Apostles, and therefore if they did accompany *their* ordinations, they must have ceased to do so when the Apostles were no more; and as to any power specially imparted by the act of ordination, independently of such gifts, there is not in the New Testament the slightest trace of its existence, much less of its continuation from age to age.

We are therefore brought again to the conclusion that ordination gave, and still gives, *ministerial authority*, and not *power*,—authority to use gifts or powers for the benefit of the Church, as its recognized office-bearers, but not itself conferring them. Richard Hooker indeed has said, that "No man's gifts or qualities can make him a minister in holy things, unless ordination do give him power." But gifts and qualities *do give power*: what they do *not* give is *authority* to minister in the congregation, which authority ordination supplies.

And so again, on looking at ordination in the present time, either amongst ourselves, or in other Churches, it is not seen that it bestows any power upon those who receive it. Authority it gives, according to the order and constitution of each Church, but no other power than men possessed before, or afterwards by whatsoever means obtain. The power of preaching the word, of bringing God's truth home to men's hearts, of winning souls, converting sinners, building up believers, reclaiming the backsliding, supporting the weak, and comforting the sorrowful,—these and all other such powers are evidently not given in or by ordination, however abundantly some ordained men may possess them. Those therefore amongst ourselves who contend that spiritual power is given by the act of ordaining, if they are not merely misunderstanding the word, and using it in a sense which does not belong to it, are brought to the assumption (which, to say the truth, they are usually not backward to acknowledge), that this power is not anything like what has just been mentioned,—a power producing effects which are seen and felt in the hearts and lives of men,—but one much more secret and unappreciable in its working,—the power, as it is alleged, of conferring divine grace through the sacraments,—of giving absolution to those who repent,—of rendering men's prayers and services acceptable to God;—thus making the effect of the sacraments to depend upon something in the administrator, instead of the ordinance of Christ; and consciously or unconsciously adopting the notion of a priestly office, which the Apostles, as before shown, did not institute in the Church. Indeed the real ground of all that has been held and taught respecting such ministerial power from the third century to the present day; the true reason which underlies all the arguments used to justify the claims to such powers, is the original assumption that Christian ministers are priests to mediate between God and men, to make intercession for them, to offer sacrifices, to remit sins, and to do all that a priesthood has to do.

It is this conception of the Christian ministry that has given birth, among other things, to all the questions of ancient or modern times respecting the confession of sins, and the absolution of those who confess them. A large page in Church history is filled with such questions, and their practical results; a long catalogue of Church scandals and crimes is supplied by them, and the confessional, penance, and priestly absolution, have been made powerful engines of sacerdotal tyranny and debasing superstition. But the apostolic record by its very silence testifies aloud that all these are the doctrines and doings of men, opposed to the word of God, and the practice of the primitive Church. The Apostles commanded no man to confess his sins to them, or to the presbyters of his Church; though it might at times be desirable for Christians to "confess their faults to one another;" and converts might naturally sometimes think it right publicly to confess and show their former evil deeds, in order to declare more distinctly their renunciation of them. It may still at times be good for a perplexed or burdened conscience to seek relief or guidance by making known its secret troubles to some experienced and sympathizing Christian brother; and such a one a Christian minister may well in many cases be:—but such confession is in no case commanded or required; nor is there any advantage in making it to a presbyter, rather than to any other prudent Christian friend.

As to the "grace of absolution" presumed to be given by Christian ministers to those who confess their sins, there is not the least appearance of it in the New Testament. The Apostles indeed proclaimed most plainly forgiveness of sins to all who would receive their word—to all who had "repentance towards God, and faith towards our Lord Jesus Christ." It was the office and duty of the presbyters to do the same. It is still the duty and the privilege of Church ministers "to declare and pronounce unto Christ's people that God pardoneth and absolveth all them that truly repent and unfeignedly believe His holy gospel." But neither Apostle nor presbyter in the primitive Church, as far as we know, pronounced absolution upon those who had confessed their sins for the purpose of conveying to them a grace from God, which otherwise they would not have had; nor is there anything in the New Testament to show that the declaration of God's forgiveness has any greater efficacy from the mouth of an ordained presbyter, than from that of any ordinary Christian. The doctrine of ministerial absolution had no existence in the Church until after it had so far departed from apostolic truth, as to suppose the Christian presbyter to be invested with sacerdotal powers; and not even then, until the lapse of several centuries had sunk it deeper still in superstitious error.[1]

The clergy, then, not being a priestly caste, or a mediating, sacrificing, absolving order, but Church officers appointed for the maintenance of due religious solemnity, the devout exercise of Christian worship, the instruction of the people in divine truth, and their general edification in righteous living,—are the acting representatives of the Church of which they belong, and derive their ministerial authority from it. In the words of Archbishop Whately, "the clergy are merely the functionaries of the particular Church to which they are members; it is in that capacity only that they derive their station and power from Christ, by virtue of the sanction given by Him to Christian communities; their authority, therefore, comes direct from the society so constituted, in whose name and behalf they act as its representatives, just to that extent to which it has empowered and directed them to act."[2]

And I venture now, with all respect, to commend the arguments, which in the preceding pages I have endeavoured to set forth in conformity with the teaching of the New Testament, to the serious consideration of our clergy at the present time. For "the clergy," writes the archbishop just quoted, "are under a peculiar temptation

[1] See Appendix C. on "Confession," &c.

[2] See Appendix D. on 'The Apostolical Succession.'

to lean too favourably, and with too little of rigorous examination, towards a system which confers the more elevation and grandeur on *them,* in proportion as it detracts from the claims of the entire community," and which "derives our Church's authority rather from *them,* than theirs from *it.*" Far better, however, is it for us to exalt Christ alone, and to seek no other place in His service than He has appointed for us. And when stripped of the false glare of sacerdotal pretensions, and restored to its apostolic simplicity, though less imposing then in the eyes of men, how truly dignified is the office, how solemnly important is the work of the Christian minister! How great is the honour laid upon him, that he should be a fellow-worker with God Himself in the world,—an ambassador of Christ to men,—a dispenser of divine truth to His people! And when grace and wisdom, earnestly sought and freely given, have enabled him effectually to do the work of his ministry by the words which he speaks, by the ordinances which he administers, and by the life which he lives,—how immeasurable is the joy and blessing which crown his successful ministrations!

Several other particulars, not without their interest, but of less vital importance, in connection with the ministry of the Church, can only be just alluded to here, when even the gravest questions have been but lightly touched. Of this kind are the social condition of the clergy,—their connection with secular pursuits,—the sources of their maintenance,—and the indelibility of their orders.

1. The Apostles evidently intended the ministers of the Churches which they formed, to be *of* and *with* their people,—to be united with them in all the social ties, the relationships and sympathies, of common life. And accordingly among the very first of the directions given by St. Paul, in his Pastoral Epistles, for their ordination, appears the injunction that a presbyter and a deacon should each be "the husband of one wife." Whatever points of dispute may be raised upon these words, it is clear that a Christian minister was expected to be a married man. The honour given by the apostolic religion to married and domestic life, and the responsibility assigned to the Christian family, as the wholesome fountain from whence sound piety and moral purity were to flow forth into the whole Church, were to be especially exemplified in the office-bearers of the community. The contrary rule of a later age took its origin from the perverse one-sided asceticism which the wide diffusion of Gnostic principles had introduced. The Gnostic doctrines respecting the material world and animal life began very early to infect the Church, and produced a general sentiment that celibacy was a much higher and holier state than married life,—that it brought men nearer to God, and fitted them for receiving and imparting the Holy Spirit. Such false sentiments, encouraged and strengthened by the extravagant manner in which Church authorities extolled the celestial virtues

of a single life, very naturally attached themselves to the prevalent idea of a priestly caste, pre-eminently consecrated to God. The state which was the holiest upon earth ought surely to belong to those who ministered in the holiest mysteries. And by the end of the third century a strong feeling had grown up in the Church that its ministers ought to be unmarried men. This unscriptural opinion, as is often the case with religious errors, originated with the general body of the people, who however only carried out to its legitimate effects the teaching which they had received. Married priests began to be looked upon, in the popular estimation, as degraded. Some persons refused to accept their ministrations; and although synodal decrees at first reproved this objection, the popular prejudice prevailed, and by the end of the fourth century the celibacy of the clergy was enforced; and a married presbyter became a *criminal*. So directly was the apostolic rule contradicted, and that brand of the predicted apostacy, "forbidding to marry," was stamped upon the Church, to its lasting injury.[1]

[1] The sentiments which led to the enforcement of celibacy in the clergy, began to show themselves at the beginning of the 3rd century, when we see an expression of them in Tertullian's indignant remonstrance against a presbyter, who should have committed the offence of marrying a second time. "What!" he exclaims, "do you, a twice-married man, venture to baptize, and to offer the oblation! *Digamus tingis! Digamus offers!*" These false notions of holiness went on infecting the Church more and more throughout this century; and by the end of it another stage had been reached. It was then considered a discreditable thing for a presbyter to be a married man at all; and some of the clergy were constrained to cast off their wives with a view to greater piety.

The *Canones Apostolici* indeed condemn this practice, and order that any one who did so, should be

2. In the primitive Church it was not thought unworthy, even of an Apostle, to engage in the work of a manual art, and to support himself, as St. Paul often did, by the labour of his hands. And to do this for his own sustenance, or to raise funds for religious and benevolent purposes, was long after still thought not unbecoming to the ministerial office. No rule, however, is given in the New Testament for such cases. The matter was left to each one's own judgment; but presbyters and deacons who heartily devoted themselves to their Christian work, would, through want of time, if from no other cause, be increasingly withdrawn from secular occupations. And when in any Church a permanent maintenance for its officers is provided, it is clearly to the advantage of the community at large that they should be unencumbered with secular cares. Whether this should be enforced by law or not, is a question for each community to decide for itself; but it should be remembered that it is a question unrestricted by any divine or apostolic command; and is open to the free consideration of every Church, to be decided as times and circumstances may suggest.

3. That it was a divine appointment inculcated by the Apostles, "that those who preach the gospel should live

deposed from his office. Ἐπίσκοπος, ἢ πρεσβύτερος, ἢ διάκονος, μὴ τὴν ἑαυτοῦ γυναῖκα ἐκβαλλέτω προφάσει εὐλαβείας ἐὰν δὲ ἐκβαλῇ, ἀφοριζέσθω, ἐπιμένων δὲ, καθαιρείσθω.—(Can. v.)

And the Council of Gangra as late as A.D. 324, condemned those who went so far as to refuse the ministrations of a "married priest," as some persons had done: but the Church authorities soon gave their sanction to the popular feeling which they had themselves created.

For further particulars, see Appendix A. No. xi.

of the gospel," is repeatedly recorded in the New Testament; and it would appear that very early in the Church payments were made to the clergy according to some scale of proportionate remuneration. For the words in 1 Tim. v. 17, "Let the Elders that rule well be counted worthy of double honour," when taken with the context, can scarcely refer to anything but a salary,—a money payment, or its equivalent,—which might be increased, when special care or labour had been bestowed. And further, it would possibly not be too much to infer from this text that Church officers at that time partly supported themselves by their own means; and that when they gave up to the Church in godly ministrations the time and labour which they might have employed for themselves, it was thought that they should be remunerated by an additional income from the church treasury.

The source from whence such funds were supplied was at first the liberal contributions of Christians, such as those mentioned at the very beginning of the apostolic history. These were afterwards reduced to a more systematic liberality. Oblations were given every week for clerical and ecclesiastical purposes; and sometimes, as mentioned by Tertullian, certain *monthly* contributions were collected.[1] Before the end of the third century

[1] Justin Martyr mentions that these voluntary contributions were made every *Sunday*—*τῇ τοῦ ἡλίου λεγομένῃ ἡμέρᾳ*—and were placed in the hands of the presiding minister—*Οἱ εὐποροῦντες δὲ καὶ βουλόμενοι κατὰ προαίρεσιν ἕκαστος τὴν ἑαυτοῦ, ὃ βούλεται δίδωσι· καὶ τὸ συλλεγόμενον παρὰ τῷ προεστῶτι αποτίθεται.*—'Apol.' § 88.

Tertullian says of the monthly contribution, "Modicam unusquisque stipem *menstrua die*, vel quum

houses and lands had been occasionally given or left by will, and Christian emperors having sanctioned such acquisitions, Church property rapidly increased. Before this the practice of giving tithes to the Church had been voluntarily begun; and men of influence, such as Origen, and afterwards Jerome and Augustin, endeavoured to create a conviction that the Jewish law of tithes was obligatory upon Christians. In the fourth century, tithes were irregularly and uncertainly paid; and it is not clear when laws were first made to enforce them.

In the fourth century it was the custom in some Churches for the bishop and his clergy to live together in one house, and eat at the same table—like fellows in a college—their expenses being taken from a common purse. But from the manner in which such instances are mentioned it would seem that this was not the usual practice.[1] In general each one of the clergy had his portion of the church revenues and oblations, which were managed by the bishop, distributed to him; and

---

velit, et si modo velit, et si modo possit, apponit."—'Apol.' § 39.

Not only money was given in these contributions, bnt sometimes *fruit*, *fowls*, *beasts*, &c., as mentioned in the 'Canones Apostolici,' which direct that such things should not be presented at the "altar," but taken to the Bishop's house—See Can. iii. iv.

For a full account of the sources and the increase of clerical revenues, see Bingham.

[1] That Augustin lived in this manner with his clergy at Hippo, is mentioned by his biographer, Possidius—"Cum ipso semper Clerici una etiam domo ac mensa sumptibusque communibus alebantur et vestiebantur." — 'Vita August.' § 25.

And Sozomen says the same thing of the Church of Rhinocorura on the borders of Palestine and Egypt. κοινῆ δέ ἔστι τοῖς αὐτόθι Κληρικοῖς οἴκησίς τε καί τράπεζα, καί τἄλλα πάντα.—'Eccl. Hist.' vi. 1.

Cyprian mentions that in his Church such distributions were made every month.[1] The beginning of the more modern system of parochial endowments may be traced to the middle of the fifth century, when it is said that it was first ordered that the clergy of each congregation should receive the revenues of their own Church.

Questions connected with the endowments of a national Church, and the right of the national government to interfere with them, which have lately acquired so serious an importance, and may possibly ere long be agitated with a still deeper interest, cannot be determined by appeals to Scripture. There is nothing about them in the New Testament; and the laws and principles of the Jewish Theocracy cannot be justly applied to such cases. They are matters very grave indeed, and involving the gravest issues; but they belong to the domain of *politics*, in the highest and noblest meaning of the word, and must be determined by reason, sound expediency, and a careful consideration of the nation's truest good.

4. There is not in the New Testament the slightest intimation that any peculiar or official dress was worn by Church officers in their public ministrations, or in private life. The vestments of the Jewish priests belonged, like the rest of their prescribed distinctions, to that Temple service, which the Apostles did not imitate; and there was no peculiar dress worn by those who offi-

---

1 "Cæterum presbyterii honorem designasse nos illis jam sciatis, ut et sportulis iisdem cum presbyteris honorentur, et *divisiones mensurnas* æquatis quantitatibus partiantur." —Cyprian 'Ep.' 34, end.

ciated in the synagogues. The *pallium*, or cloak, a more simple garment than the Roman toga, was usually worn by Christians, or at any rate by those who were the more strict and austere in their mode of life; and no mention is made of the use of any other for Church purposes until after the third century. When the Church was fostered, instead of being persecuted, by the imperial power, and began to exhibit more of ornament and display, a white garment, the original of the modern surplice, was worn by the officiating clergy in the administration of the sacraments.[1] More splendid vestments, such as that presented by Constantine to Macarius, Bishop of Jerusalem, were gradually introduced in conformity with the rest of the sacerdotal system already established in the Church.

5. The indelibility of Church Orders is a subject about which nothing is said in Holy Writ; but it is an opinion of long standing, encouraged by Rome, and not rejected by our own Church, that a man once ordained cannot

---

[1] The use of the simple *pallium* by Christians, gave occasion to the sarcastic proverb used against them by the pagans, *A toga ad pallium.*

The white dress is mentioned by Jerome, "Si Episcopus, presbyter, diaconus, et reliquus ordo ecclesiasticus, in administratione sacramentorum *candida veste* processerit."—'Cont. Pelag.' Lib. i. And also by Chrysostom.

At a later period, distinguishing vestments and other insignia marked the different orders. The Council of Toledo (A.D. 633), mentions that all the three superior orders then wore the *Orarium*, a stole or scarf, while a Bishop had a ring and staff *(annulus et baculus)*; a Presbyter, the *planeta*, or chasuble; and a Deacon, the *alba*, i.e., *tunica alba*, an albe—or surplice.

The mitre *(mitra* or *infula)* began to be worn by Bishops about the 10th century.

either voluntarily, or by compulsion, give up the commission which he has received, and return to the ranks of the laity again. Accordingly, ordination has been described as "the grant of a peculiar commission and power, which remains indelible in the person to whom it is committed, and can never be obliterated or rased out, except the person himself cause it by his heresy, apostacy, or most extremely gross and scandalous impiety." But such a description is founded on the unwarranted supposition that a certain special grace or supernatural power is imparted by the act of ordination, mysteriously handed down by a succession from the Apostles; and that this therefore cannot be removed, unless it be sinned away by the recipient. But the power which gives a commission can also take it away. When therefore it is acknowledged, and so far as it is acknowledged, that ordination is the act of a Church giving its officers authority to minister in its behalf, it will follow that the same Church can revoke what it has thus given. In the absence, therefore, of all scriptural direction, the indelibility of clerical orders is a question of expediency which every Church is at liberty to decide for itself. It may generally be advisable that the solemn engagement of the Christian ministry, especially in the case of a presbyter, should be for the whole of life; but there is nothing in the office itself, as there is nothing in the New Testament, to justify its being regarded, as some worthy men have regarded it, as a profane or monstrous thing for a Church to allow its orders to be rescinded.

LECTURE IV.

THE LAITY, OR CHURCH BODY AT LARGE,

WITH THEIR POSITION AND DUTIES.

IV.

THE LAITY, OR CHURCH BODY AT LARGE,

WITH THEIR POSITION AND DUTIES.

IN endeavouring to give an outline of the ecclesiastical polity of the Apostles, it seemed expedient to exhibit first the ministry, which they established in their Churches, as presenting some of the most characteristic features of these societies. But the laity, or Church at large, must now be considered. After which some particulars respecting the relations subsisting between these two parts of the general body, and some notice of their discipline, government, and social life so far as it was affected by Church influences, will naturally follow in their place.

I know not how it may appear to other minds, but for my part the first thing which strikes me in the general body of the apostolic Church, is the marvellous *equality* which sprung up—or rather, it may be said, *burst forth*—

so suddenly did it at once appear in full completeness, on the very first day that the Church began.

This equality, in the enthusiasm which seized the hearts of those who were baptized on the day of Pentecost, produced at the moment a *holy communism.* The new converts were so closely united, that they formed, as far as possible, one great family together—with a common life, and a community of goods—or, if not exactly what is now meant by a community of goods, at any rate such an overflowing liberality of heart and hand, that each one used his property as readily for others, as for himself. "They that believed were together, and had all things common; and sold their possessions and goods, and parted them to all men, as every man had need."[1]

---

[1] There is great reason to doubt whether what is commonly called a community of goods—amounting to a renunciation of all private or individual property—ever existed in the apostolic Church, even at the very beginning. The following considerations, at any rate, go far to establish the contrary conclusion.

1. In the first place, it is evident that no such custom was in existence at a somewhat later period, when rich and poor found their place in Christian societies, and when, as is often seen in St. Paul's epistles, men were exhorted to care for others as well as for themselves, and to give to those who were in need, each according to his ability.

2. But much earlier than this, even at the time when self-denying men were selling their possessions for the benefit of the poorer Christians, the case of Ananias and Sapphira shows that the owners of property were under no obligation to give it up, but might give it or keep it in whole or in part, just as they were disposed to do. "Whilst it remained, was it not thine own; and after it was sold, was it not in thine own power?"

3. Neither is this all. For Acts iv. 32–35, one of the passages which records that "they had all things common," contains intimations which show that even in those early days these words must not be

It was thought by Chrysostom that this community of life and property existed only among the three

taken too literally, or pressed into the meaning of an absolute communism. For we are here informed that no one "said that aught of the things which he possessed was his own." There were still then "things which he possessed," τῶν ὑπαρχόντων αὐτῷ, only he did not say that any part of them "was his own," ἴδιον εἶναι, to be kept exclusively for his own use. And, further, when the lands or houses of such benefactors were sold the proceeds were not given indiscriminately to all, but went to a fund entrusted to the Apostles, out of which, as occasion required, distribution was made, ἑκάστῳ καθότι ἄν τις χρείαν εἶχεν, "according as any one had need." This was, no doubt, liberally done; but this was not in the modern sense "a community of goods."

4. But if this be so in Acts iv., can the circumstances have been very different in that earliest instance related in Acts ii. 44? Even in this case, there is the same expression καθότι ἄν τις χρείαν εἶχεν; and if in the former instance "having all things common" did *not* preclude the possession of private property, must we say that it did so in the latter case?

The only circumstance which marks a difference in the alleged communism of Acts ii. is that "all that believed were together." Probably, therefore, they took their meals—or the principal meal—in social parties arranged for that purpose, since their numbers were too great for all to meet in one room; and the requisite expenditure for these Christian συσσίτια was taken from a common purse.

Besides these considerations, derived from the expressions used in the history, another argument is supplied by the known sentiments and practice of the Apostles, bearing directly upon this subject. It is an elementary and indisputable principle in Economics, "that a community of goods, *as a permanent ordinance*, is totally impracticable, except on one condition, namely, the abrogation of marriage in one of the two modes in which it may be abrogated; that is to say, either by admitting a community of wives, or by the renunciation altogether of the sexual relationship. . . . . . It cannot be necessary to prove that the family economy—the sacredness of the matrimonial connection, and the consequent dependence of children upon their parents—must very speedily break up any scheme intended to perpetuate the non-property principle."—('Ancient Christianity,' p. 521.) The Essenes among the Jews, and the monks in the Christian Church kept up a communism among them, because celibacy was an essential part of their system. And, on the other hand, the honour assigned by the

thousand who first joined themselves to the Apostles; and that *they* all took their meals together, as well as possessed all that they had in common. However this may have been, although the practice of thus living together—never commanded, and unsuitable as it was for general adoption—did not long continue, yet the same mutual feeling of equality and close union manifested itself as strongly as ever, when with increased and increasing numbers "the multitude of them that believed were of one heart and one soul; neither said any of them, that ought of the things which he possessed was his own, but they had all things common: neither was there any among them that lacked; for as many as were possessors of lands or houses sold them, and brought the prices of the things that were sold, and laid them down at the Apostles' feet; and distribution was made to every man according as he had need."

And later still, indeed throughout the apostolic age, and far beyond it, the same thing was plainly visible, however the expression of it varied in form and manner with varieties of time and place; "the brother of low degree rejoicing in that he was exalted, and the rich in that he was brought low." The names of "brother," and "friend," by which they usually called each other; the form of the Christian salutation; and the spontaneous acts of loving-kindness, which abounded everywhere,

Apostles to married life and family religion [see the last part of this Lecture] is conclusive against the possibility of a community of goods having, or being intended to have, any lasting existence in their polity.

testified that it was no mere short-lived unnatural excitement, but a deep-rooted and abiding principle which animated Christian men—an influence which might begin with enthusiasm, but could not end with it; a flame flashing out at first with dazzling brilliancy to settle down into a steady unwavering light.

This equality observable in the early Church was as unlike as possible the dishonest, selfish, rapacious schemes of modern equalities and socialisms. *They* are born of a desire to seize and take away; but this of a desire to impart and give. It was essentially an equality of heart and feeling; and it was only incidentally, and by an easy and natural consequence, that it affected (as far as it did affect) men's possessions and goods. It sprung up from a community of great and absorbing interests, and from the common possession of advantages of incalculable worth.

How often is it seen even in secular things that the pursuit of some interesting object—some literary or scientific study, or a fondness for some pleasing art—produces, as far as its influence can reach, a wholesome equality and communion between men of the most widely differing rank and social position; raising up the low, and bringing down the high, to the same level without unduly exalting the one or degrading the other! How strongly too can a common danger, or the enjoyment of a common benefit, bind men together who otherwise would have been separated and estranged! But the religion of Christ presented objects of pursuit and interest infinitely more attractive and sublime than those of any secular art or study. It often associated in the greatest dangers those who had embraced it. It bestowed advantages, and conferred an elevation upon them, in comparison with which all earthly rank and wealth are trivial and poor. And thus it united men of all degrees together in mind and heart; and by actually making them equal in the highest things led them to regard their inequalities in less important matters as comparatively of little moment.

Besides this, even now, in spite of the very artificial state of modern civilization, and the consequently wider dissociation of ranks and classes, genuine Christianity still produces a great effect in smoothing down the sharp distinctions between man and man; subduing pride and superciliousness in the rich and great; and softening the roughness of speech and manners in the low-born and illiterate, and supplementing often in a marvellous degree their want of culture and education. Such influences in a more simple state of society must have operated with a still greater force.

But there is another peculiarity which specially marked the general body of the Christian Church, lying deeper beneath the surface than the equality just mentioned, and therefore not meeting the enquirer's view so obviously at first, while it is still more deserving of his attention as a most essential property of the whole community—a most distinctive characteristic of its nature and position—the very cause of its being what it was.

This peculiarity indeed itself took the form of an equality, since it belonged equally to every member of the body—an equality of privilege or standing-ground in Christ, the divine Head of all and each one in the Church, in contradistinction to the equality of social intercourse, or property, or kindly feeling, exhibited visibly in the Christian life. But its own distinguishing character, and that from which it most justly takes its name, is *Liberty*.[1] In Christ every Christian was delivered from bondage, and made free—free from the bondage of sin, the bondage of condemnation, the bondage of fear and superstition, the bondage of ordinances, and rites, and burdensome ceremonial laws—from the bondage of all law, so far as he was led by the Spirit of life. And just as the Christian equality of self-denying kindness was utterly different from the selfish and rapacious equality which has usurped its name; so this Christian freedom was as opposite as possible to that lawless licence by which, when misnamed liberty, ignorant and unprincipled men have sometimes been deceived. The Christian man had liberty in Christ, not in Satan; in godliness, not in sin. It was the glorious liberty of the children of God, not the licentiousness of evil men.

It was a truth clearly proclaimed by the Apostles, and

[1] How needful St. Paul felt it to watch and guard this liberty, is shown by his strong and earnest language in his Epistle to the Galatians. In his time the Christian liberty was in danger, not from an excessive assumption of ministerial authority, but from the entanglement of ceremonial observances. Both of these, however, since his time have too soon and too long wrought mischief in the Church.

received with undoubting and joyful confidence by the Church in those days, however it has been often unfortunately obscured or kept out of sight in later times, that every believer had himself an unrestricted access to Christ, and through Him unto the Father, without the intervention of any other person or thing whatever. That Jesus and His finished work, Jesus the Son of God, and the Son of Man, with His atoning blood and justifying righteousness, Jesus born into the world, dying, rising again, ascending into heaven, sitting at the right hand of the Father, and ever living to make intercession for us, was all that any man required for coming boldly, so to speak, into the presence of God, to receive the fulness of His favour and blessing;—all that he needed to break down the barrier which sin had placed between him and the Holy One, to entitle him to be enrolled as a free citizen of Christ's kingdom, a son in God's family, an heir of the heavenly inheritance.

And as Jesus, the Christ, was the sole author and all-sufficient security of this heavenly freedom; so besides Him there was no more need, or place, for any priest, or altar, or sacrifice, or mediator, or any one of whatsoever office, name, or service to stand between any man and God, to present his prayers at the throne of Grace, or to bring back a blessing from above. The rent veil of the Temple at the death of Jesus indicated that the "holiest of all" was no longer to be hidden or closed against the approach of men, but "opened to all believers." Instead of needing the priestly ministrations of another, each Christian was to be himself a priest, called and consecrated to a holy priesthood, to offer spiritual sacrifices acceptable to God—even the living sacrifice of himself, his soul and body—the sacrifices also of praise and thanksgiving, of self-denying kindness to others, and godliness of living for Christ's sake. "That which the priesthood before Christ had only typified and prefigured was now accomplished for all; and the duty of constantly realizing it by the oblation of his own heart became the priestly duty of each individual Christian."[1]

Such then being the condition of the Christian community with its most essential characteristics—a personal, spiritual *liberty* in Christ, and a social, loving *equality* in the Church—the whole polity of the apostolic times was necessarily adapted to it; and may even be said to have grown out of this condition, as a natural organism of the common Christian life. From this the true relations subsisting between the general body of the laity on the one hand, and the clergy or Church officers on the other, unfold themselves distinctly to our view. And the position which the laity occupied, and the part which they were expected to perform in the Church, is seen to be quite in harmony with this their normal and recognized *status* in it.

It was a necessary consequence of this *status* that the Christian ministry instituted by the Apostles could not

---

1 Guericke's 'Manual of the Antiquities of the Church,' i. 1, 7.

be a priesthood. In the preceding Lecture arguments were adduced to prove that the Christian ministers of the New Testament *were* not priests; but a consideration of the standing held by the lay-members of the apostolic Church shows that they *could* not have been so. It would have been quite at variance with the whole character of that Church, and inconsistent with the fundamental principles of its formation and coherence, that a literal, objective, separated priesthood should be established in it. The Christian ministry was requisite, not on account of any spiritual functions, which could not otherwise have been lawfully discharged; but for the sake of the solemnity and regularity which are essential in a religious and permanent society. There was no spiritual act which in itself was of such a nature that it might have been done by every individual Christian;[1] but the general well-being

[1] There are positively no sacred rites or acts which it is declared in the New Testament *must* be administered by men ordained, or in any way separated from the general body of Christians. The two sacraments are justly considered the most solemn of Christian ordinances; but even for *them* such administration is nowhere commanded.

With regard to baptism, the Apostles evidently did not care to baptize with their own hands, but directed others to perform the rite. See Acts x. 48; 1 Cor. i. 14. And lay baptism has always been considered valid, even in the most sacerdotal periods of the Church. Thus Jerome, "Unde venit ut sine chrismate et episcopi jussu neque presbyter neque diaconus jus habeant baptizandi; quod frequenter, si tamen necessitas cogit, scimus etiam licere laicis."—'Ep. adv. Luciferianos.'

The celebration of the Eucharist at first included an actual supper, in imitation of the scene at its institution. And as at the Jewish Passover any person might preside, usually the master of the house—this was probably the case in the

and healthy action of the whole body, required that known and responsible officers should be charged with certain religious duties in the midst of it. There were no mysteries or rites of any kind too sacred to be touched by ordinary Christian hands, and demanding a separated caste of holier men for their pious celebration; but it was absolutely necessary that all things should "be done decently and in order," and that provision for this should be uninterruptedly secured.

It was again a necessary consequence of the acknowledged *status* of the whole Christian body, that the Church government ordered or sanctioned by the Apostles was not and could not be oppressive or overbearing, or such

---

earliest times in the Christian Church also.

And so Pressensé remarks that the words of St. Paul to the Corinthians imply that all Christians might break the bread and bless the cup at the Lord's Supper, and not an officiating minister only; for he says, "the bread which *we* break," and "the cup of blessing which *we* bless." "Pour ce qui concerne la Cène, Paul atttribue à tous les Chrétiens la bénédiction de la coupe, et la fraction du pain. La coupe de bénédiction que *nous bénissons*, . . . le pain que *nous rompons*."—Vol. ii. p. 224.

The view given in the text is in accordance with the following passage from a commentary on Eph. iv. 11, by the author whose writings are appended to those of Ambrose, and who is therefore called the Ambrosiaster. "Postquam omnibus locis ecclesiæ sunt constitutæ et officia ordinata, aliter composita res est, quam cœperat. Primum enim omnes docebant, et omnes baptizabant, quibuscunque diebus vel temporibus fuisset occasio. . . Ut ergo cresceret plebs et multiplicaretur omnibus inter initia concessum est, et evangelizare, et baptizare, et scripturas in ecclesia explanare. At ubi autem omnia loca complexa est ecclesia, conventicula constituta sunt et rectores, et cætera officia in ecclesiis sunt ordinata, ut nullus de clericis auderet, qui ordinatus non esset, præsumere officium, quod sciret non sibi creditum vel concessum. Et cœpit alio ordine et providentia gubernari ecclesia, quia si omnes eadem possent et vulgaris res et vilissima videretur."

10

as to paralyze, or crush out the active and wholesome influence of popular thought and feeling. The Christian, individually set free from the moral and spiritual bondage of sin, was kept socially free from all ecclesiastical bondage of priestcraft and ministerial domination.

Though the whole Church might be termed a spiritual monarchy under Christ its King, each Christian community was a republic. The clergy were its representative and responsible officers; and as such were invested with official authority, were entitled to due respect and submission, and "had the right to rebuke and repress the extravagances of individual fancy or of congregational caprice and self-will." But on the other hand the laity possessed and exercised a large amount of power and influence, not only as the original earthly source and fountain of ecclesiastical authority, or on the occurrence of momentous emergencies; but also in the ordinary affairs of Church life. And to trace the nature of this power and influence as they are seen in operation during the apostolic and sub-apostolic period is especially interesting in the present day, when one of the greatest questions of the time is, What ought to be the place and voice of the laity in the government and administration of our Church?

With the strictly official, or what may be termed the professional acts of the clergy, in conducting public worship or administering religious ordinances, the laity of course did not interfere, as soon as order had been taken for their regulation; such duties having been then committed to their ministers for the express purpose of confining them to their hands. But in all other Church matters; (i.) in the appointment and removal of the ministers themselves; (ii.) in the general edification and discipline of the Church; and (iii.) in questions of doctrine and dogmatic teaching, the laity had a voice, and were able to make it heard.

I. The people took part in the selection and appointment of Church officers. For although presbyters and deacons were ordained, and afterwards bishops were consecrated, by the hands of the ministry; yet as soon as any regular Church was formed, the popular voice elected or approved of them; and might on the other hand disallow and reject them, or might (as it would seem) with sufficient and reasonable cause depose or remove them from their office. It is true that the only clear and decided instance of such popular selection in the New Testament is in the case of the seven officers mentioned in Acts vi., and usually, but not indisputably, called deacons. And there are in St. Paul's pastoral Epistles no directions as to the manner in which presbyters and deacons should be chosen. Clement, however, a contemporary and friend of St. Paul, speaks in his Epistle to the Corinthians of presbyters ordained by the Apostles, or after them by other men of high repute, *with the common assent and approbation*[1] *of the*

---

[1] Τοὺς οὖν κατασταθέντας ὑπ' ἐκείνων, ἢ μεταξὺ ὑφ' ἑτέρων ἐλλογίμων ἀνδρῶν, συνευδοκησάσης τῆς ἐκκλησίας πάσης.—Clem. 'ad Cor.' § 44.

whole Church; so that the omission of such directions in the Epistles to Timothy and Titus may be due to the fact that the apostolic practice was then fully established and well-known. And for several centuries afterwards, although the tendency of the times was rather to silence the voice of the laity than to make it more distinctly heard, it is evident that a popular election or approval was considered requisite both for presbyters and bishops; and was looked upon as a regulation of apostolic authority.[1]

---

1 The people continued to have a voice and vote in the choice of bishops and presbyters, and to have the right that none should be forced upon them against their will, until at least the middle of the sixth century. And, notwithstanding the increasing power of the episcopate, the bishops seem to have made no attempt to deprive them of this right.

Eusebius ('H. E.' vi. 29), in his account of the election of Fabian as Bishop of Rome, (A. D. 236) says, *τῶν γὰρ ἀδελφῶν ἁπάντων, χειροτονίας ἕνεκεν τῆς τοῦ μέλλοντος διαδέξασθαι τὴν ἐπισκοπὴν, ἐπὶ τῆς ἐκκλησίας συγκεκροτημένων*, when Fabian, who had not previously been thought of, was unanimously chosen from a dove having alighted on his head.

Cyprian (A. D. 250) frequently testifics to this effect; thus—

"In ordinationibus clericis, fratres carissimi, *solemus vos ante consulere*, et mores ac merita singulorum *communi consillio* ponderare."—Epist. 33, addressed to the clergy and laity at Carthage.

"Factus est Cornelius Episcopus de Dei et Christi ejus judicio, de clericorum pene omnium testimonio, *de plebis* quæ tunc adfuit *suffragio*, et de sacerdotum antiquorum et bonorum virorum collegio."—Epist. 52.

Cyprian also asserts that this custom was derived "de traditione divina, et apostolica observatione," and that in his time "apud nos quoque et fere per provincias universas tenetur."—Epist. 68.

Siricius, Bishop of Rome (A. D. 384) says that one, having worthily filled the office of deacon, "exinde jam accessu temporum presbyterium vel episcopatum, si eum *cleri ac plebis evocaverit electio*, non immerito sortietur."—'Epist. ad Himerium,' i. 10; in Labbé 'Concil.' vol. iii. p. 660, ed. 1769.

Chrysostom was chosen to be

It would further appear from Clement's Epistle that Church-members might depose their presbyters. For whereas he wrote to the Corinthians expressly on account of the disorders in that Church, in which presbyters had been deposed, he blames them, not simply for so doing, as if it were an unlawful assumption of power on their part, but only for acting thus in the case of those who had blamelessly, quietly, and without arrogance discharged their sacred duties. He seems therefore to admit that for a just and reasonable cause a presbyter might be deprived of his office by the popular judgment of the Church in which he ministered. And at a much later time it was distinctly acknowledged that no Church ought to submit to the ministrations of a presbyter or bishop of scandalous life, or who had

---

Bishop of Constantinople ψηφίσματι κοινῷ ὁμοῦ πάντων, κλήρου τε φημὶ καὶ τοῦ λαοῦ.—Socrat. 'Hist.' vi. 2.

Leo, Bishop of Rome (A. D. 440), writes, "Quum de summi sacerdotis electione tractabitur, ille omnibus præponatur quem *cleri plebisque consensus* concorditer postularit."—Epist. 14. 5, Labbé 'Conc.' vol. v. p. 1276.

And Liberatus (A. D. 533), "Ut *omnium civium voluntate eligerent ordinandum Episcopum . . . collecti sunt ergo nobiles civitatis* ut eum, qui esset vita et sermone pontificatu dignus, eligerent."—'Breviar.' 14; Labbé 'Concil.' vol. ix. p. 690.

At these clerical elections disorders sometimes took place, and the emperors occasionally interposed their authority. By the laws of Justinian the elections were confined to the Optimates, which seems to be alluded to in the quotation from Liberatus, though he says the election was to be *omnium civium voluntate*. On the breaking up of the Roman empire, kings (especially in France and Spain) had a voice in these appointments; and, afterwards, "the interests of the people was secured (says Bingham) by their consent in parliaments; and by such consent the nomination of bishops was reserved to princes, and the patronage of livings to particular persons."—Bing. iv. 2, 1.

himself departed from the essentials of the Christian faith; but that on the contrary it was bound to desert such an offender, and to choose another in his stead.[1]

When Christian communities felt themselves obliged to adopt such strong measures, they naturally desired to justify their conduct in the eyes of other Churches; and hence the practice gradually arose of referring such cases to the consideration of some synod or council; until as the Church system became more and more concentrated and consolidated throughout the Roman empire, the power of deposition at last slipped away from the hands of the people.

II. In the exercise of the Church discipline and government, which were thought requisite in the apostolic age, the influence and action of the whole Church body may be very plainly traced. Although the authority of the ministerial office is distinctly acknowledged in the New Testament, and Christians are admonished "to obey them that have the rule over them, and to submit themselves;" yet the right and duty of the whole congregation to take a sensible, and indeed a prominent, part in the maintenance of necessary discipline is equally enforced. If the very design of the

---

[1] Cyprian declares distinctly, that the people ought to separate themselves from heretical bishops or presbyters. Referring to the command of Moses, "Depart, I pray you, from the tents of these wicked men," he adds, "Propter quod plebs obsequens præceptis dominicis, et Deum metuens, a peccatore præposito separare se debet, nec se ad sacrilegi sacerdotis sacrificia miscere; quando ipsa maxime habeat potestatem vel eligendi dignos sacerdotes, vel indignos recusandi."—Epist. 68.

Christian ministry is "the edifying of the body of Christ," Christian laymen are also bidden to "edify one another." If Christian ministers are "to reprove, rebuke, and exhort with all long-suffering and doctrine," Christian laymen are also "to admonish one another," and "to warn the unruly" and disobedient. And, as if to show beyond dispute that official ministerial functions and unofficial popular influence were quite compatible, and ought to be in active and harmonious exercise together in the Church, the two are united in a remarkable manner in a single utterance by St. Paul when he writes thus to the Thessalonians, "Wherefore comfort yourselves together [or exhort each other, παρακαλεῖτε ἀλλήλου], and edify one another, even as also ye do. And we beseech you, brethren, to know them which labour among you, and are over you in the Lord, and admonish [νουθετοῦντας] you; and to esteem them very highly in love for their work's sake; and be at peace among yourselves. Now we exhort you, brethren, warn [νουθετεῖτε] them that are unruly, comfort the feeble-minded, support the weak, be patient towards all men." (1 Thess. v. 11–14.) Where the brethren in general are exhorted to do what is also expressly spoken of as a ministerial duty; and such exhortations are placed in close combination with directions to esteem the ministry very highly for its work's sake.

Nothing can be more distinct than this testimony from St. Paul to the Thessalonians; but this view of the ministerial and popular duties in the Church is not confined to this one passage. The Epistles in the New Testament addressed to Christian communities again and again present the authority and work of the ministerial office, and of the whole company of faithful people, in a similar light; sometimes one, and sometimes the other, being pressed on the attention of the reader.

Nowhere in them is the position of presbyters so exalted as to leave little or no power to be exercised by the people; but with impartial faithfulness, the ministry is duly honoured while the authority of the whole Christian body is unhesitatingly maintained. There can hardly be a greater contrast than that which appears between the relative position of ministers and people as it is seen in the New Testament, and as it is displayed in the spurious or interpolated Epistles of Ignatius, which exhibit the ideas and practice of a later age when episcopacy had enlarged its powers, and a dominant hierarchy was growing up in the Church.[1]

---

1 The manner in which the ministers of the Church are dealt with in the Epistles of the New Testament is remarkable, and, one would think, must sometimes have surprised Churchmen of the Nicene period, as it surely must their modern admirers and imitators; who think that the only privilege of the laity in Church matters is, "to hear and to obey."

In some of the Epistles, Churches are addressed and admonished without any notice at all being taken of their ministers, who remain undistinguished in the general body, as in Romans and Galatians. In some, the presence of ministers is acknowledged, but with only a passing allusion, if any, to the nature of their office, as in Ephesians and Philippians. In one, a message is sent to a minister, *through the Church*, bidding him "take heed to his ministry, that he fulfil it," as in Colossians. In another, presbyters are warned not to assume too high an authority,

Nor is it only on a general view that the action of the laity is discerned. If the particulars of Church discipline are marked in more detail, the popular element is still more clearly seen.

Church discipline, so far as it was concerned with the infliction of rebuke or punishment, exhibits in the New Testament three different degrees of severity, corresponding pretty accurately with the different forms of the "ecclesiastical censures" of the third and fourth centuries, which were called "admonitions," "the lesser excommunication," and "the greater excommunication," or expulsion from the Church. And in all these in the apostolic age the whole Christian body took an authoritative part.

(*a*.) With regard to the first of these, "the admonition," it has been already noticed that it was the duty of Christian laymen, as well as of the clergy, to warn and admonish the unruly.

(*b*.) In the infliction of "the lesser excommunication," which was a breaking off of friendly association or communion with an offender for a time, while still regarding him as a member of the Church, the Christian brethren in general, and not the presbyters merely by

by lording it over their people, as in the First of Peter. Yet all this is not without a distinct acknowledgment of the respect which was due to them. For Churches are expressly bidden to revere and obey them; and in the pastoral epistles Timothy and Titus are strongly urged to assert their authority.

A careful consideration of what is due from the clergy to the laity, and from the laity to the clergy, would not be unprofitable at the present time.

special virtue of their office, are bidden thus to mark their disapprobation of wrong-doing, and to vindicate the purity and healthy life of their society. Thus the Christians at Rome are bidden "to mark them which cause divisions and offences, and to avoid them." And the Thessalonians are urged "to withdraw themselves from every brother that walketh disorderly." And "if any man obey not the Apostle's word to note that man, and to have no company with him that he may be ashamed."

(*c*.) And in the case of some grievous offence which demanded expulsion from the Church, while an inspired Apostle, as a divinely appointed ruler in the Church, might by his own authority excommunicate the offender, as we may perhaps say that Peter and John did to Simon of Samaria, and as Paul did to Hymenæus and Alexander; yet no minister of lower rank in the Apostles' times appears to have had authority to do this. But so serious a punishment—the highest which the Church as a voluntary association,[1] and as a Christian community[2] could inflict—required the united action of

---

[1] Political communities, not being altogether voluntary, exercise an absolutely coercive power. But in a purely *voluntary community*, such as the Christian Church, the ultimate penalty must be expulsion; all others short of this being submitted to as the alternative.—Archbp. Whately's 'Kingdom of Christ Delineated,' p. 90.

[2] The Jewish dispensation being divinely founded on temporal sanctions, and wrought into the civil polity of the nation, used forcible penalties, and coerced religious offences with the sword. But the Christian dispensation rests only on spiritual sanctions, and its true power is entirely independent of civil laws. It therefore does not

the whole society, solemnly assembled together, to consider the offence, and to impose the penalty: the same general assembly having authority also to remit the punishment, and, when satisfied of the offender's repentance, to receive him again into the Church. (See 1 Cor. v. 4, and 2 Cor. ii. 6.)

In the exercise of ecclesiastical discipline, however, there is no mention whatever in the apostolic age of the imposition of *penance*, or subjecting a repentant offender to some painful infliction, or a long course of abasement and exclusion. Even in the case of the gravest sins such usages had not then been introduced; nor could they plead with truth any apostolic sanction, when at a later date they so extensively prevailed. In the fourth century an offender such as he who was excommunicated at Corinth by St. Paul's command, would have been subject to long years of humiliating penance, before he was re-admitted into the Church; but St. Paul directed that he should be restored as soon as he had repented; and that without any forms of degradation or abasement. Different times and circumstances might indeed recommend different regulations for such cases, which it was competent for any Church in its discretion to adopt; but the departures from the simple discipline of the Apostles, which soon began after they were gone, savoured little of simplicity or discretion.

---

authorize the punishment of religious offences by any positive inflictions; but unworthy members of a Church may be expelled.

It is not necessary here to dwell at any length on the remarkable expression twice used by St. Paul as descriptive of a judicial expulsion from the Church, when he terms it, "the delivering of the offender to Satan." Little light is thrown upon the precise meaning of these words by any powers or practices of the later Church. But that it involved some temporal or corporal suffering designed to bring the offender to a sense of his sin, seems evident from St. Paul's remark that it was done "for the destruction of the flesh, that the spirit may be saved in the day of the Lord Jesus." The power of imposing this infliction was confined to the apostolic age, and probably to the Apostles themselves. For even in the case of the Corinthian offender, though he was excommunicated by the whole Church, yet St. Paul says, "I have determined already . . . to deliver such an one unto Satan." And this is rendered the more probable by the fact that later Church authorities, though not apt to be over-scrupulous in their assumptions, very seldom ventured to use this formula in their ecclesiastical sentences; nor is there, I believe, any instance of its adoption by them, when they did use it, being followed by any peculiar effects.[1] Instead of

---

[1] There seems to be some reason for believing that in the early apostolic age Christians were to a certain extent placed under a peculiar providence, or divine discipline; and that not only did some bodily or temporal suffering come upon those who were excommunicated by an Apostle, but also that, without any Church censures, sickness or other painful visitations came upon them as warnings and chastisements on account of their sins. Thus, St. Paul distinctly tells the

being contented with ordinary and lawful weapons, when this extraordinary power had ceased, the Church in an evil hour employed the aid of the civil magistrate to inflict punishment on ecclesiastical offenders; and thus from the time of Constantine, forgetful of its true mission and policy, it was gradually led on to those atrocious persecutions which afterwards disgraced its history, and made it often a curse, instead of a blessing, to the nations of the earth. But there is nothing in the New Testament, nor in any recorded apostolic command or practice, which can justify such a departure from the will and mind of Christ,—such a contradiction to His assertion, "My kingdom is not of this world."[1]

Corinthians that "many were weak and sickly among them, and many had died," because of their disorderly and profane behaviour; and that these inflictions were intended to recall them from their wrong-doings, 1 Cor. xi. 30.

St. James also seems to allude to something of the same kind, when, referring to the case of a Christian restored to health after a dangerous illness, he says that "the prayer of faith shall save the sick, and the Lord shall raise him up, and *if he have committed sins, they shall be forgiven him.*"—James v. 15.

[1] The emphatic declaration of Jesus before Pilate respecting the nature of His kingdom, and the means by which it was to be sustained, ought for ever to have settled the question for His disciples, and to have taught them that His religion was not to be propped up with civil penalties, or enforced by persecution. More especially when the whole conduct of Jesus Himself, and His words on other occasions—the example of His Apostles, their directions for encountering grave errors and heresies, the manner in which they dealt with offenders in their own time, the whole temper and spirit of their teaching—all show that throughout the New Testament there is nothing to justify the use of force and compulsion for promoting the cause of Christianity.

"Yet no sooner had the Church obtained civil power under Constantine, than the general principle of coercion was admitted and acted upon against the Jews, the heretics, and the pagans." The Christians in the fourth and fifth centuries—

III. Having thus seen the influential position assigned by the Apostles to the law element in preserving and

---

like the puritans in the seventeenth—began to persecute others when they ceased to be persecuted themselves. The New Testament refused to sanction such conduct; but having long before gone to the Old Testament for the sacerdotalism, which the Christian Scriptures had denied them, they now drew arguments from the same source for persecution, as old Christian persecutors ever since have done.

The good and learned Jeremy Taylor in his 'Liberty of Prophesying,' feeling that "it is unnatural and unreasonable to persecute disagreeing opinions," labours to persuade himself and his readers that "the Church in her distinct and clerical capacity was against destroying or punishing difference in opinion, till the popes of Rome did superseminate and persuade the contrary." Yet he admits that "the bishops did persuade the emperors to make laws against heretics, and to punish disobedient persons with fines and imprisonment, with death and banishment respectively." So that even, according to the good bishop's admission, little more can be pleaded in defence of the earlier Church than may with equal justice be pleaded for the "Popes of Rome." In fact the Church of Rome, in all the horrible persecutions with which it glutted itself, as long as it had the power, carried out—to a prodigious extent, it is true, but still only carried out—the very principles and practices which had come down from the fourth and fifth centuries.

What those principles and practices were, in accordance with which the Church authorities in the fourth century endeavoured to crush those, whom, however unjustly, they denounced as heretics, is sufficiently indicated by the treatment of Jovinian by the Italian bishops, amongst whom were Siricius Bishop of Rome, and Ambrose of Milan. Jovinian had ventured to protest against some of the gross errors of the Church, especially its extravagant doctrines on the subject of asceticism and celibacy. For this he was condemned and excommunicated by Siricius, and afterwards by Ambrose; and subsequently the Italian bishops prevailed upon the emperor Honorius to have him seized and scourged, with his abettors and attendants; after which, Jovinian himself was banished to the island of Boa, a wretched rock off the Illyrian coast, where he ended his days. The ecclesiastical historian, Fleury, says that Jovinian was scourged with thongs loaded with lead, "*battu de lanières plombées;*" and that he was banished to the island of Boa, where, he adds with malignant irony, "*on dit qu'il continua jusques à la mort sa vie voluptueuse.*"

enforcing ecclesiastical discipline, or what may be regarded as the *moral* aspect of the Church; it remains to be noticed that the laity held an influential position also in what may be contradistinguished as the *religious* aspect of the body, in questions, that is, of faith and doctrine which required any formal or authoritative decision. Strange to say, the apostolic practice in this respect seems to have been in many quarters so long and effectually ignored, that not only in times of hierarchal tyranny, but in our own Church at this present time, it is not unfrequently regarded as an undoubted, axiomatic, truth that the laity have no authority in questions of Christian doctrine, and ought to have no voice in their discussion or decision. Laymen, it is sometimes admitted, may be allowed to take a certain part in Church government, order, and discipline; but the clergy alone, it is contended, are entitled to judge matters of faith and creed; as if to them exclusively by some divine appointment such judgment had been indisputably assigned; and the only privilege of the laity was "to hear and to obey."

Yet so far from this being the case, it is evident from the New Testament that questions of dogmatic theology are to be considered by the lay members of the Church, as well as by the clergy; and that no Christian man is to resign his reason, or apprehension of religious truth, any more than his conscience, to the judgment of his pastor.

1. Thus doctrines as well as moral precepts are in the

apostolic Epistles addressed to the whole body of believers, and not handed over to the presbyters alone; as is obvious in those which, like the Epistles to the Romans and Galatians, dwell much on dogmatic truths.

2. All Church members are called upon to form an opinion on doctrinal questions, and to judge whether what they are taught is true or false. The Berœans are commended for testing the truth of St. Paul's own teaching. The Galatians are exhorted "to stand fast in the liberty wherewith Christ had made them free, and not to be entangled again with the yoke of bondage," which erring teachers would lay upon them. The Thessalonians were to "prove all things and to hold fast that which is good." And St. John addresses to all Christians, "Beloved, believe not every spirit, but try the spirits whether they be of God."

3. And the New Testament clearly shows that Christian ministers would sometimes teach false doctrine; as when St. Paul warns the Presbyters of Ephesus that "some would arise from among themselves speaking perverse things;" and St. Peter declares that there would be false teachers in the Church, even as there had been false prophets among the people of old. And when this should be so, it would necessarily be the duty of every Christian to refuse their teaching.

4. But besides these general notices of Christian responsibility which relate to the common course of ordinary Church life, it is manifest from a clear and decisive example of apostolic practice that the whole

body of the Church, and not its ministers only, was regarded by the Apostles as the guardian and expositor of Christian truth; and that in any doubt or question as to what this truth required, when put into the dogmatic form of a Church doctrine to be received by the faithful, not the clergy only but the whole community, laic as well as clerical, were to be consulted, and according to there deliberate judgment to decide. For when the dispute had arisen as to the obligation of the Gentile believers to observe the Jewish law, involving so important an alternative of doctrine as the justification of the Christian by his faith, or his justification by his legal observances, and it was felt to be so grave a crisis as to demand a special assembly or council of the Apostles to consider it—not the Apostles only, nor the Apostles and elders, but the whole Church with them—the Apostles, elders, and brethren formed the assembly, discussed the question, pronounced the decision, and issued the decree to the Church at Antioch in their united names.

Now in this case the Apostles, as the inspired and divinely commissioned founders and teachers of the Church, might justly have considered the question, and pronounced the decree, by themselves. Whatsoever they bound or loosed on earth was ratified in heaven. It was *their* voice and judgment which gave the decree its decisive authority, and which we still regard as the final settlement of the dispute; nor without this apostolic voice and judgment would the Church at Jerusalem have had any just pretension to legislate for the Church at Antioch, or in other places.

Yet, as an example to all future times, when no living apostolic voice, nor any other infallible human guide, would remain in the Church, they associated with themselves "the elders and the brethren," in order that every Christian community in all ages might learn after the same similitude to decide in similar emergencies; and that we might see that, while the Scriptures are the only treasure-house of all Christian doctrine, the responsibility of embodying such doctrine, when necessary, in Church forms, or dogmatic articles of belief, rests with the members of the Church at large, and ought not to be by them declined, or from them taken away.[1]

[1] It is not without some show of reason and probability that the "Council of Jerusalem" has been viewed in a different light from that given above. The twelve Apostles, it has been said, were a representation of the *twelve tribes, i. e.* of the people of God, the true Israel, taken as a whole. Thus M. de Pressensé remarks, "Les Apôtres sont la représentation idéale du veritable Israel, et comme ses ancêtres spirituels semblable aux douze fils de Jacob. Ils ne figurent évidemment pas la tribu sacerdotale, mais bien les douze tribus, c'est à dire le peuple de Dieu."—'Hist. de l'Eglise Chrét.' vol. i. p. 376.)

And then, this being so, the Apostles, elders, and brethren assembled on this occasion at Jerusalem, have been regarded as the true Israel of the New Covenant, met together, not so much to enact a theological decree, as to express their fraternization with the Gentile portion of God's people, and to hold out to them the right hand of fellowship; and so, for this purpose, the presence of the brethren —the people in general—as well as the Apostles and elders, was most appropriate and requisite.

If this were conclusively established, the meeting at Jerusalem would obviously have no single point of resemblance to a Church council of the later type. But this view is hardly consistent with the fact that Paul and Barnabas went up to Jerusalem for the express purpose of obtaining—not an acknowledgment of the Gentile Churches—but a decision upon the

Unfortunately in after ages, while the wholesome lesson, which this "first council" teaches, was quite neglected, the very point in which it could not be an example to post-apostolic times, but must ever stand alone in its authority, was perversely seized on by the misguided Church; and while laymen were gradually excluded from ecclesiastical synods, and all the clergy also, except the bishops, these councils arrogantly claimed for themselves the language which was exclusively appropriate to the Apostles, and, as if they were successors to *their* supernatural power and inspiration, published their decrees as the decisions of the Holy Ghost.[1]

If from the public and formal action of the Church in grave questions of order, discipline, and doctrine we now turn to its less prominent and official operations, and enquire what influences, if any, affected the domestic or individual life, and whether any practices or customs sanctioned, if not commanded, by apostolic authority prevailed in the Christian society of that time; although no full and precise information of this nature is given in the New Testament, yet enough is found in the way of incidental allusions, illustrated a. they are by the more formal developments of the following ages, to furnish us with at least some partial conception of the social aspect of primitive Christianity.

question of enforced Jewish observances; which very question was debated and decided upon by this meeting.

[1] For some account of the nature and authority of Church councils, see Appendix B.

The earliest views that are presented to us in this department of the Church's action, arose immediately from that striking characteristic of original Christianity already alluded to; its unselfish, broad, outflowing spirit of equality or kindly fellowship, which exhibited itself in a loving care for the temporal no less than the spiritual wants of all its members. Taking up, as we may perhaps infer, the injunctions implied in the Saviour's words recorded in Matt. xxv., and rejoicing to serve and honour Christ in the persons of His suffering brethren, the primitive Church exerted itself from the very first in relieving and comforting the poor and afflicted, the widows and fatherless. And soon afterwards to support and educate destitute or deserted children, to receive and assist strangers and foreigners,—and, in times of persecution to visit and encourage martyrs or confessors,—were special objects of its ministrations. And that this sympathizing spirit was generally prevalent in all the Churches, and that it was considered by the Apostles most desirable to keep it in lively action, is evidenced by the frequent directions scattered throughout the epistolary portion of the New Testament, "to remember the poor," "to minister to the necessities of the saints," "not to forget to entertain strangers," "to visit the fatherless and widows in their affliction."

The funds requisite for carrying out such benevolent purposes, as well as for the partial or entire support of the clergy, were supplied by the money which liberal contributors "laid at the Apostles' feet,"—by collections gathered generally throughout the several Churches,—by contributions made at the celebration of the Lord's Supper corresponding with the offertory among ourselves,—and at a later period by certain monthly [1] subscriptions or gifts which were customary in some Churches, and by special donations or legacies of money or other property. But pecuniary gifts, however liberal, were not in the earliest times deemed a sufficient discharge of Christian obligations. Personal services and labours were also required, and where possible were freely given. In such works of faith and self-denying kindness Christian women were especially distinguished: and several of these are honourably mentioned by name in St. Paul's Epistles as "having been succourers of many," or "labouring much in the Lord."

Such works of loving-kindness soon assumed, as might have been expected, certain definite forms; and regulations were made for their more orderly or effectual operation. Thus in the very earliest years of the Church the

[1] The following is Tertullian's account of these monthly subscriptions. "Modicam unusquisque stipem *menstrua die*, vel quum velit, et si modo velit, et si modo possit, apponit; nam nemo compellitur, sed sponte confert. Hæc quasi deposita pietatis sunt, nam inde non epulis, non potaculis, nec ingratis voratrinis, despensatur, sed egenis alendis, humandisque, et pueris ac puellis re ac parentibus destitutis, jamque domesticis senibus, et si qui in metallis," &c. —'Apol.' i. 39.

From the circumstance of these contributions being made *monthly*, a monthly distribution also among the presbyters seems to have been made in some places, and is alluded to by Cyprian, "cæterum presbyterii honorem designasse nos illis jam sciatis, ut et sportulis iisdem cum presbyteris honorentur, et *divisiones mensurnas* æquatis quantitatibus partiantur."—'Ep.' 34—end.

practice was begun at Jerusalem of providing a dinner or supper every day for Christian widows, including no doubt orphans and other destitute persons; and seven ecclesiastical officers were specially appointed for the orderly superintendence of these "daily ministrations." This custom, however, was apparently only for a time, since it is not elsewhere alluded to; and it was probably found better in general "to visit the fatherless and widows" at their own homes, rather than to assemble them together into one place for this purpose.

By the time that St. Paul wrote his first Epistle to Timothy the charitable operations of Christian Churches had received, in one respect at least, a still more definite organization; since associations of widows had been formed, who were supported by the funds of the Church, and who were expected to devote their time to the visitation of the sick and suffering, and under the superintendence of the ordained ministry to assist in carrying out the different works of Christian benevolence.

Of these ecclesiastical widows some probably became deaconesses[1] of their respective Churches; and the rest

---

[1] In the post-apostolic Church the widows here mentioned were sometimes supposed to have been in all cases deaconesses; and the same opinion has been held in modern times. On the other hand, the very opposite opinion has been entertained, that they were persons charged with no active service, 'who, as suited their age and condition, were removed from all occupation with earthly concerns, and dedicated their few remaining days to devotion and prayer." Thus Neander ('Hist. of Planting the Christian Church,' iii. 5): "We must imagine such women to be among those widows, who, after presenting a model in discharging their duties as Christian wives and

appear to have very much resembled the District Visitors and Bible Women of modern days: and to have had their several districts or number of houses assigned to them for their particular ministrations.[1] That these visitors then, as well as now, did not always perform their duties judiciously is evident from St. Paul's severe

mothers, would now obtain repose and a place of honour in the bosom of the Church, where alone they could find a refuge in their loneliness; and, by their devotional spiritual life set an edifying example to other women.....Hence, it would naturally be an occasion of scandal, if such persons quitted a life of retirement and devotion, and showed a fondness for habits that were inconsistent with their matronly character."

It does not appear to me that either of these views is altogether correct. St. Paul's account is hardly, I think, consistent with the supposition that all these widows were deaconesses, though deaconesses may have been sometimes taken from their number. Still less is it consistent with the opposite opinion that they had no active employment. The expression in 1 Tim. v. 5, "continueth in supplications and prayers night and day," has perhaps helped to lead to this latter supposition; but the words, *προσμένει ταῖς δεήσεσι καὶ ταῖς προσευχαῖς*, will naturally mean attends regularly the public devotions of the Church; in describing which, the same words, *δεήσεις* and *προσευχαί*, are used in chapter ii. 1, of this Epistle. And if there is any force in the meaning which I have ascribed to *περιερχόμεναι τὰς οἰκίας* (see the next Note), it follows that they must have had some active duties assigned to them. Consider, also, what is said about the duties of aged women in Titus ii. And it is further to be noticed, that this institution of Church widows was not, in its original intention, confined to elderly women, who would be unfit for active employment.

[1] The words in 1 Tim. v. 13, seem to me, when duly considered, to justify the view which I have given above. *Περιερχόμεναι τὰς οἰκίας* cannot mean, as in our English version, "wandering about from house to house," but must signify, "going round," or, according to a common idiom of the Greek participle, "while going round, to *the* houses." The article *τὰς* necessarily *particularizes* the houses spoken of. What then are the particular houses? I answer, the houses specially assigned to them, which it was their duty to visit; something in the manner of modern "district visitors.

reproof of those widows who made their visits occasions of tattling and idle curiosity, instead of opportunities of Christian kindness and encouragement in well-doing. And such abuses probably formed one reason why St. Paul directed that more tried and experienced women, not under sixty years of age, should alone be placed upon the Church List.[1]

It is to be observed that it was considered right for those only, who were destitute, and had no near relatives to support them, to be thus maintained and officially employed by the Church; and that consequently they were required on their admission to undertake not to marry again, in order that the Church funds might not be spent unnecessarily, or upon those who might not be

[1] The words of St. Paul in 1 Tim. v. 12, γαμεῖν θέλουσιν, ἔχουσαι κρῖμα, ὅτι τὴν πρώτην πίστιν ἠθέτησαν, have been variously interpreted; and our English version has increased the difficulty of the passage by rendering the word κρῖμα "damnation."

It appears to me not at all likely that πίστιν ἠθέτησαν should mean "casting off their Christian faith," or apostatizing; the expressions used for this in the New Testament are, "to *deny* the faith;" as τὴν πίστιν ἤρνηται in this very chapter, and οὐκ ἠρνήσω τὴν πίστιν μου, Rev. ii. 13; or else, "to *depart* from the faith;" as ἀποστήσονταί τινες τῆς πίστεως, 1 Tim. iv. 1.

I think that πίστιν here must mean the *assurance* or *promise* which the widows gave, on their admission, that they would remain unmarried; and which they, therefore, "set at nought," or "made of no effect," ἠθέτησαν, by marrying. This πίστις, or promise, was an engagement made to the Church, and not a "vow," or a devoting of themselves by an engagement to God, the word for which in the New Testament is εὐχή. By breaking this promise, they justly incurred the censure of the Church, and so were ἔχουσαι κρῖμα, having "judgment" passed upon them.

It would further appear that young widows having been at first admitted on the Church List, some scandals had ensued, to prevent the recurrence of which candidates were in future required to be at least sixty years of age.

able to render any service in return. But this affords no ground for the supposition, afterwards entertained, that a second marriage was considered an unhallowed thing; still less did it give any sanction or encouragement to the practice, which will be noticed more at length below, of inciting young women to make vows of celibacy and to devote themselves to the life of nuns, under the supposition that they thereby acquired an amount of holiness not attainable in the virtues of a Christian family.

It may be further remarked that the services of these Church widows were not designed to supersede or disparage similar ministrations on the part of others; for the widows were not to be admitted into the number, unless they had already been voluntarily engaged in the very same works of kindness as they would, after their admission, be required to perform officially. It was the usual practice commencing with, but continuing far beyond, the apostolic age, that every Christian woman, as far as she had opportunity, engaged in such ministrations; and Tertullian shows that in his time it was expected that Christian women would, as a matter of course, attend to the sick, go round to the houses of the poor, relieve the needy, and visit imprisoned martyrs; and he gives it as one reason why a Christian woman should not marry a pagan, that she would not then be able without let or hindrance to engage in such occupations.[1]

[1] "Quis enim sinat conjugem suam visitandorum fratrum gratia vicatim aliena et quidem pauperiora quæque tuguria circuire?....

It is evident that in the apostolic and sub-apostolic age, Christian women performed these works of charity and mercy without forming themselves into Sisterhoods, or making any vows, or wearing an unusual dress, or calling themselves by fantastic names, or in any way relinquishing their ordinary, simple, natural, and therefore most Christian, position in the family circle and household life.

This excellent spirit of brotherly kindness, so conspicuous in the earliest age, continued in its effects to be one of the most notable features of the new religion, attracting the admiration or envy even of those who rejected its doctrinal truths. In the fourth century, especially, when the Church, delivered from persecution, was free to extend and display its influences without restraint or fear, the new names of *Hospitals* or *Infirmaries*, of *Almshouses* for the aged, *Orphanages*, *Foundling-hospitals*, and *Strangers'-homes*, became words in common use. Yet, as Augustin remarks, it was the *names* only of some of these that then were new; the things themselves having existed with less publicity and prominence long before.[1]

Nor was the benevolence of the several Churches confined to the indigent of their own respective congregations; but foreign Churches were included in their

........Quis in carcerem ad osculanda vincula martyris reptare patietur?.....Si cui largiendum erit horreum, proma præclusa sunt."—Tertull. 'ad Uxorem,' ii. § 4.

[1] Such names were *νοσοκομεῖα* or *valetudinaria*, *γηροκομεῖα* *ὀρφανοτροφεῖα*, *βρεφοτροφεῖα*, *ξενοδοχεῖα*.

sympathies, and aided by their means. The collections made for the Christians at Jerusalem by the Churches of Antioch, and throughout the Roman provinces of Macedonia and Achaia, are well known instances in the apostolic period; and succeeding centuries followed the example.

With respect to the customs and habits of domestic and social life, the Christianity of the New Testament made no abrupt or sudden change, except in those things which necessarily and in themselves were sinful. It was to be the salt of the earth by gradually interpenetrating the corrupted and corrupting mass of heathen civilization, and not by shrinking from all contact with it. The Christian, therefore, was enjoined to cast off the vilenesses and abominations which heathenism produced or palliated; but he was neither commanded nor recommended to renounce the society or friendship of his heathen neighbours. He was to separate himself from sin, not from the sinful; to be not of the world, yet in it.

Thus he was utterly to forsake idolatry, but he was not forbidden to sit down with idolaters in social festivity; and the only reason why he was dissuaded from joining in a sacrificial feast in an idol's temple was—not that he must thereby incur any pollution in himself—but a consideration for the scruples of weaker brethren. He was to avoid all the intemperance and excess, the "drunkenness and revellings," so common then at festive meetings; but he might accept invitations to dinner or supper at a heathen neighbour's house, and mix with freedom and courtesy in such social gatherings. The Bacchanalian and Aphrodisian songs so prevalent in heathen companies were to have no countenance from him; but music and singing were by no means forbidden; on the contrary, both heart and voice alike might rejoice in inoffensive or sacred melodies. This, indeed, seems to have been an abundant source of recreation in Christian families, and Christian songs and hymns soon multiplied greatly, by which at meal times, and all family or friendly unions, they expressed their habitual faith, and hope, and joy.

Thus St. Paul sums up the whole duty of Christians in such particulars in one broad and comprehensive principle, "All things are lawful, but all things are not expedient." The Christian's liberty is wide and unconfined; but he must consider faithfulness to Christ before all things;—he must consider others as well as himself, and must abstain from acts which would wound the conscience of a brother, or encourage a sinner in his sin.

It is not surprising that this wise and liberal simplicity was not, and, perhaps, could not be, always observed in the following centuries, when the Church was brought into such trying and deadly collisions with heathenism and heathen powers, making at the same time promiscuous friendly intercourse almost impossible, and a distinct avowal of the Christian profession more imperative than ever. Errors were then sometimes committed on the side of godly zeal, which led men to regard as unlawful, what Paul or Peter would have allowed; and in the fear of countenancing even a semblance of idolatry to abridge the liberty of Christ.[1] But it is easier to criticize the errors of such men than it is to imitate their faithfulness. Similar errors may sometimes now be seen in the conduct of godly men in their contact with the surrounding worldliness of nominal Christianity: but the opposite, and less excusable, and more fatal error, it is to be feared, is much more usual, when Christians act as if they were of the world, as well as in it—as if they had no religious principles to acknowledge and maintain.[2]

---

[1] The refusal of a Christian soldier to wear the crown of laurel on a military festival, which gave occasion to Tertullian's treatise 'De Corono Militis,' is an example of such mistaken conscientiousness. This crown had no connection with idolatry; but, as a badge of victory, was worn in honour of the emperor on days when he gave largesses to the soldiers. Tertullian, however, entirely approves of the soldier's conduct, having at that time, it is supposed, adopted the principles of Montanism.

With a similar scrupulosity, Lucian the Martyr is said to have chosen to die of hunger rather than eat things which had been offered to idols, when his persecutors would allow him no other food.

And when the Emperor Julian had all the meat in the butchers' shops at Constantinople sprinkled with idolatrous lustrations, the Christians there would eat nothing but bread; although, according to St. Paul's direction, they might have eaten, without scruple, whatever was sold in the shambles.

The Christians at Antioch, under the same circumstances, acted with more wisdom, and took no notice of the emperor's petty spite.

Valentinian, in his younger days, according to a story told by Theodoret, went as a captain of the guard with Julian to an idol's temple; and when a drop of the lustral water fell on his coat, he struck the man who carried it a blow in the face; for which he was banished by the emperor. Theodoret commends him!—See Bingham, xvi. 4, 14.

[2] It is almost impossible for us now to form an adequate idea of the innumerable difficulties and fearful trials which beset the Christian in the second and third century.

Tertullian gives us some account

And if from these social aspects of Christian life we look more closely within the domestic walls at the influences there at work in the Apostles' days, we may see enough to convince us that by no means the least of the triumphs of the doctrine of Christ were to be found in the Christian family. Family religion among the Jews indeed was not unknown; and pleasing features had

---

of these difficulties, in his treatise on Idolatry, which had mixed itself up with and polluted the whole course and framework of civil and social life.

A Christian had to give up or avoid all the many trades and arts which were connected with idols and idol worship, the numerous festivals of false deities, invitations to idolatrous sacrifices, some civil and military offices, some common expressions and forms of speech.

The relation in which he stood to the emperor, who was the universal deity of the paganism of the Roman empire, and whose statue was everywhere worshipped, afforded another source of difficulty and danger.

But greater, and more pressing, and more unavoidable than these, were the trials and dangers which beset Christian life from the gross demoralization and fanaticism of the masses of the population. The pagan religion, which had sunk into contempt in the first century, and seemed to be dying out, burst out afresh with renewed vigour in the second and third. The old oracles, mysteries, and other superstitions, were revived in great force. And this revival in the masses—the rudest and most ignorant parts of the population—by its violence and fury carried away with it the better educated, who had previously laughed at the popular creed. In the Augustan age, it was the upper classes who were corrupt; but in the second century the whole lower population had become grossly demoralized, as well as fanatical.

Apuleius gives a dreadful account of the state of things at that time. See also the graphic narrative of Pressensé—Series ii. vol. II. p. 1—25.

What must have been the condition of Christian families living in the midst of such abominations! It is no marvel that they sometimes made mistakes. The marvel is that they held fast their Christian integrity, and were not swallowed up in the deluge of debauchery and superstition. Nothing but the force of their divine religion, and the living power of the Divine Spirit in their hearts, could have kept them from year to year in the midst of such an ordeal.

once been seen in the domestic life of Pagan Rome, before the decay of the Republic and the establishment of the Empire brought in a flood of demoralizations in their train. But at the commencement of the Christian era, throughout the most important portions of the Roman dominions, there was in general very little within the family circle, especially among the upper classes, to relieve the debased condition of religion and morals which was visible outside it. It was here that a most happy change was at once begun, wherever the preaching of the Apostles was received and bore its fruit. And it is not unworthy of remark that the first apostolic proclamation of the Gospel in Europe by the visit of Paul and Silas to Philippi illustrates the planting and early growth of family religion in the Church. It was at Philippi that occurred the first recorded instances of whole families being Christianized, when Lydia "and her household," the Jailor "and all his," were baptized into the Christian faith. The effects of such a faith, with its earnest realization of divine truth, its unselfish spirit, its equalizing privileges combined with orderly submission, made each Christian household a little centre of light and purity in the midst of the corruption all around. And many passages from the Epistles of St. Paul and St. Peter show how highly they appreciated these effects, when we find them exhorting Christian men, women, and children, by the very highest considerations, to the due performance of all their home duties; and calling upon them as husbands and wives, as parents and children, as masters and servants, "to adorn the doctrine of God their Saviour" in all the occupations of their ordinary life. "Henceforth," it has been well observed, "the worship of the household plays an important part in the divine economy of the Church. As in primæval days the patriarch was the recognized priest of his clan, so in the Christian Church the father of the house is the divinely appointed centre of religious life to his own family. The family religion is the true starting point, the surest foundation, of the religion of cities and dioceses, of nations and empires." Lightfoot's 'Philippians,' p. 56.

It so happens also that the work of Paul and Silas at Philippi serves to indicate the two great social revolutions effected by the Gospel, to which the growth and maintenance of family religion were principally due. The case of the Slave-girl "possessed with the spirit of divination," and the fact that the first congregation addressed by Paul in that place consisted of women, and that Lydia was the first convert, exemplify the Christian influences which began at once to lead the way to the abolition of slavery and the elevation of woman to her proper place in the social system; and by means of these changes to alter the whole character of domestic life.

The abolition of slavery was brought about by the indirect and gradual operation of Christian principles, and not by any direct or violent denunciation of this nefarious but inveterate evil. Apostolic Christianity did not order the Christian master to emancipate his slaves, or bid the

Christian slave to rebel against his master. But besides the general lessons of caring for others as well as for ourselves, it taught both master and slave that in Christ they stood upon equal ground: the master, that he had a Lord over him in heaven with whom was no respect of persons; the slave, that he was Christ's freeman, however he might be in bonds on earth. And this immediately effected a marked amelioration in the slave's condition, relieving bondage from its most galling burdens, until its ultimate removal could be secured. The story of Onesimus, with the touching Epistle of Paul to Philemon, show how apostolic Christianity dealt with such questions, and with what marvellous tact and feeling an Apostle could respect the civil rights of a master, while securing freedom and brotherhood for a runaway slave.

The elevation of the female sex was a result which followed with more rapidity, wherever the religion of Jesus was received. The position of women among the Jews being much more honourable than in most Gentile nations, the Apostles had in this respect but little prejudice to overcome, when they began the formation of Christian Churches. And the devotion and loving faithfulness of the women who ministered to Jesus during His abode on earth,—the manner in which he received them as His disciples and friends,—the remembrance that He never uttered a reproach against the sex in general, or a word of severity to any individual woman, while to some He accorded the highest praise,—the knowledge that among His disciples no woman ever betrayed Him, denied Him, or forsook Him,—and that it was women who were the last at the cross and the earliest at the sepulchre,—must all have taught the Apostles, if they needed any such teaching, what position women were entitled to hold in the social economy of the Church.

Accordingly, in the very first meetings of the few faithful disciples between the Ascension and the day of Pentecost, the presence of "the women and Mary, the mother of Jesus," is expressly mentioned; the spiritual gifts in the primitive Church were bestowed upon women as well as men; the relief of widows was a special object of apostolic care; and wherever the name of Christ was preached, women were invited and welcomed into the Church,—were admitted equally with men to all Christian privileges, and showed themselves equally ready to receive religious truth,—equally faithful in obeying it,—equally self-denying in all good works,—equally courageous and patient in danger and tribulation. Hence in a Christian family the wife and mother occupied at once her destined place.

Nothing can surpass in simplicity and force, and in a just estimate of the relationship between the sexes,—nothing can more happily describe the place to which woman was restored in the apostolic Church,—than the short admonition of St. Peter, every expression of which is full of important meaning:—"Likewise, ye husbands, dwell with them according to knowledge, giving honour unto the wife as unto the weaker vessel, and as being heirs together of the grace of life; that your prayers be not hindered." And the conjugal union—the source of all other family relationships—being thus hallowed and honoured, communicated a happy Christianizing influence throughout the household.

And what views of Christian womanhood in the primitive time may be gained even from the scanty notices of female names contained in the New Testament! How much may be learnt by a thoughtful realization of what is implied, if not expressed, in the little narrative of Dorcas, "full of good works and almsdeeds which she did," and the incidental mention of "the house of Mary, the mother of John whose surname was Mark;"—how much from the glimpses given us of Christian women in Romans xvi., and of Euodia and Syntyche in the Epistle to the Philippians;[1]—how much especially from what is said of Priscilla, the wife of Aquila, a woman apparently superior in mental power and force of character to her husband, himself a man of note,[2] capable of instructing and convincing "an eloquent man and mighty in the Scriptures" like Apollos, being herself neither carried away by his eloquence,

[1] In Philippians iv. 2, both the names are feminine, and the first should be Euodia, not Euodias; and these two are the women mentioned in the following verse, which ought to be translated, "help them, since they laboured with me," συλλαμβάνου αὐταῖς, αἵτινες, &c.

[2] The manner in which Priscilla is always mentioned whenever Aquila's name occurs, her name being even put before his in Rom. xvi. 3; and the circumstance that she is described as taking a part in the interview with Apollos, and in all the Christian works and dangers of her husband, seem to justify this opinion of her character.

nor afraid of his learning, nor scornful of his mistaken views, and courageous together with her husband with a holy boldness even unto the danger of her life, to secure the safety of St. Paul; yet never stepping beyond her proper sphere, or giving occasion for any just reproach!

Such was the honour given by the Apostles to married life and family religion, and such its happy results.[1] And such results have always more or less obviously ensued whenever apostolic Christianity has been allowed to do its work. But what a strange and lamentable contrast is presented by the Church of the Nicene period in the principles and practices then advocated by the highest authorities, with reference to married life and Christian womanhood! At that time the delusive teachings of Gnosticism, though repelled by the Church as a formal heresy, had deeply infected all classes of Christians with some of the notions of its false philosophy. And one of

[1] St. Paul in 1 Cor. vii. gives a preference to a single life, especially in times of persecution and distress, provided that no violence be done to personal feelings; but he commends no vows of celibacy, nor attaches any special sanctity to that state. And, knowing what human nature is, he writes in this very chapter as a general rule, "Nevertheless, to avoid fornication, let every man have his own wife, and every woman have her own husband." And when some scandals had arisen at Ephesus, from young widows being admitted on the Church list, he directs that such candidates be in future refused, and that they should get married again instead: "I will, therefore, that the younger widows [τὰς νεωτέρας, not γυναῖκας, but the widows before spoken of] marry, bear children, guide the house, give none occasion to the adversary to speak reproachfully." 1 Tim. v. 14. But all this wise advice was before long utterly disregarded by the post-apostolic church.

the consequences of this was the exaltation of Asceticism in general, and of Virginity in particular, far, far above any holiness or virtue to be found in the married state. Without denying, as some Gnostic heretics did, that matrimony was a good and lawful estate for Christian men and women, celibacy was declared to be something infinitely higher and more holy, conferring a supernatural meritoriousness and perfection.

Young men were encouraged to devote themselves by irrevocable vows to a life of unmarried continence, not because of any "present distress," but because they would thereby be raised above all measures of earthly excellence, and would make themselves fit recipients of the highest spirituality and the most glorious sanctification. The eloquence of the greatest bishops and preachers of the time was exerted to persuade young women and girls to make vows of perpetual virginity,[1]

---

[1] It is said of Ambrose, Bishop of Milan, that he was pre-eminently zealous in extolling the glories of virginity; and that his burning eloquence persuaded so many hundreds of young girls to become nuns, that mothers forbade their daughters to go and hear him, for fear of their being induced to join the number.

"S. Ambroise recommandait avec un zêle tout particulier la virginité. Ses paroles ardentes retentirent jusqu' en Afrique et inspirèrent à des centaines de vierges la force de se consacrer au Seigneur. Les mères défendaient à leurs filles d'aller entendre les sermons d'Ambroise, tant elles craignaient qu'il ne les entraînât par son éloquence à préférer la virginité aux engagements de mariage."—'Dictionnaire Catholique.'

These remarks are fully borne out by the extant writings of Ambrose on this subject, abounding as they do with the most extravagant encomiums on the life and condition of nuns, and the exalted merit and glory of their devoting themselves to this angelic state.

by assuring them that a nun was in an ineffable manner the Bride of Christ, and was a being of superhuman holiness, of celestial perfection,—a very angel upon earth, to stand hereafter the very closest to the throne of God, and even now to be gazed upon with awe and trembling admiration by all beholders, as if one of the cherubim had come down from heaven! The success of such preaching was great; and was followed, as might be expected, with very dreadful results. A miserable substitution of a materialistic, factitious, unnatural sanctity for the pure and genuine holiness of apostolic Christianity generally prevailed: family religion was by comparison degraded in the common estimation of men; married men and women were regarded as a very inferior sort of Christians; and the *Nemesis* of the outraged laws of nature and of God came down, to its fearful dishonour, upon the Church. Examples of this state of things in the fourth century are given us by the best contemporary authority, even by one who, like all the rest, favoured and promoted the system, while declaiming against its natural effects. Under the very shadow of the Cathedral of Constantinople, within the sound of Chrysostom's fervid sermons, and subject to his episcopal supervision, the shameful and shameless conduct of monks and nuns, not then confined to cloisters and convents, became a public scandal in the Church.[1] In-

[1] This account of the institution of celibacy and its results is taken from the words of Chrysostom himself, contained in two addresses apparently delivered in his church, and entitled, πρὸς τοὺς ἔχοντας

deed, some of the worst moral and religious enormities of the monastic and conventual life, in the worst period of the Church of Rome, were equalled, if not surpassed, at Constantinople in the Church of the fourth century.

If the Nicene Church is to be held up to English Christians as their authority and guide, as many are now endeavouring to bring to pass, it will be well for its real teaching, with its necessary results, to be generally and correctly brought to light.

παρθένους συνεισακτούς, and περὶ τοῦ μὴ τὰς κανονικὰς συνοικεῖν ἀνδράσιν. They are in the first volume of his works in the Benedictine edition, and more than bear out all that has been stated. For some further information on this subject, see Appendix A.

LECTURE V.

PUBLIC WORSHIP.

V.

PUBLIC WORSHIP.

AMONG the manifestations of the outward life of the Christian Church a prominent position is necessarily occupied by the places, forms, and times of its public worship. Indeed, to the popular eye and mind, these are wont to appear as the very essence of a religion, —the religion itself. And, however superficial and defective such a view may be, it cannot be denied that the public worship of a Church deserves much attention, both as an effect and as a cause of its actual condition. The nature of its ritual, and the manner in which its united devotions are conducted, in any Christian community, when free to act without restraint, necessarily result from its hold and acceptance of religious truth or error, and furnish a fair criterion of the state of Christian doctrine prevalent in the body. But the administration of its ceremonial also re-acts with much force upon the religious opinions and creed of habitual worshippers, and becomes a cause, or at any rate a very efficient means, of producing and preserving among them the dogmatic theology which it most prominently exhibits. An unsound or questionable liturgy, and superstitious or unhealthy devotional practices, both imply and promote corresponding disorders in a Church's inner life; while liturgical purity, if it does not always preserve it from all departures from the faith, supplies a ready and wholesome instrument for its revival and recovery.[1]

A consideration therefore of the public worship of the apostolic Church will not be without its interest, even though we can gather from the New Testament no full account of its devotions; but only scattered notices, not sufficient to satisfy our curiosity, yet enough for our profitable instruction.

The absence, indeed, of numerous details of the public services in the apostolic Churches,—the omission of all record, even of regulations which the Apostles must have made for the guidance of Christian congregations in their religious exercises,—is not without its grave significance and beneficial results. It shows us, at any rate,

[1] It is a perfectly legitimate process of reasoning to infer from the contents of ancient liturgies now extant, that the doctrines involved in them were held and taught by the Churches where, and at the times when, these liturgies, as they stand, were used. Thus, the learned Dr. Neale, in his 'Tetralogia Liturgica,' undertakes to prove from ancient liturgies called by apostolic names, that certain doctrines contained in them were taught by the primitive Church; and if all the conditions of the argument were fulfilled, the conclusion would have been most fairly established. But in this he entirely fails. See further on this point, Note (2), p. 227.

that Churches are unfettered by any divine laws, but such as are of broad general principles, in their ritual observances and forms of worship. It has preserved us from possibly being entangled in a superstitious veneration for apostolic practices unsuitable to our times and people. It leaves us free to institute and cherish the reasonable service of spiritual devotion with such a ceremonial as may best exhibit and retain the simplicity of Christian truth, in accordance with the wants and feelings of our own place and generation.[1]

---

[1] "Why should not the Apostles or their followers have committed to paper, what we are sure must have been perpetually in their mouths, regular instructions to catechumens, articles of faith, prayers, and directions as to public worship and administration of the Sacraments?....Paul says to the Corinthians, 'The rest will I set in order when I come;' and so doubtless he did......Is it not strange then that these verbal directions should nowhere have been committed to writing?

"If the hymns and forms of prayer, the catechisms, the confessions of faith, and the ecclesiastical regulations, which the Apostles employed, had been recorded, these would all have been regarded as parts of *Scripture;* and even if they had been accompanied by the most express declarations of the lawfulness of altering or laying aside any of them, we cannot doubt that they would have been in practice most scrupulously retained, even when changes of manners, tastes, and local and temporary circumstances of every kind, rendered them no longer the most suitable. The Jewish ritual, designed for one nation and country, and intended to be of temporary duration, was fixed and accurately prescribed; the same divine wisdom from which both dispensations proceeded, having designed Christianity for all nations and ages, left Christians at large, in respect of those points in which variation might be desirable. But I think no *human* wisdom would have foreseen and provided for this. That a number of *Jews,* accustomed from their infancy to so strict a ritual, should, on introducing Christianity as the second part of the same dispensation, have abstained, not only from accurately prescribing for the use of all Christian Churches for ever the mode of divine worship, but even from recording what was actually

But while thus benefited by what has been omitted, we may notice with advantage what has been "written for our learning" on this subject, which will include a consideration of the places of worship,—the public worship itself,—and the religious times and seasons of the apostolic age.

I. *Places of Worship.*

Since the practice of Christians meeting together for united prayer and praise, as believers in Jesus Christ, began with the very beginning of the Christian Church, it is evident that several places of worship must have been required immediately after the day of Pentecost, when the three thousand converts joined themselves to the Apostles. And since there could not, for some considerable time at least, be any buildings expressly erected for this purpose, they must have used the most suitable rooms that they could procure. Possibly before long, at any rate at Jerusalem, some of the Jewish synagogues, whose congregations had become Christians, were used with some slight alterations for Christian services,—the *place*, as well as the government and orderly arrangements of the synagogue being adopted by the Church. (See Lect. III. p. 100.) But such cases would not be numerous, and the

---

in use under their own directions, does seem to me utterly incredible, unless we suppose them to have been restrained from doing this by special admonition of the Divine Spirit." — Archbishop Whately's 'Kingdom of Christ Delineated,' p. 290–292, and taken from his 'Essays on the Omissions of Holy Writ.'

Christians must in general have had places of assembly for themselves. Such places are indeed expressly named as early as in the second chapter of the Acts of the Apostles, and in connection with the very first formation of the apostolic Church. They are afterwards repeatedly mentioned in the New Testament, being always called by the same name (*οἶκος*), which became the ordinary term for a Christian place of worship; and in the Eastern Church continued long after the Apostles' time to be often used in the same sense, even when the place was a building expressly erected for the religious services of a Christian congregation.[1]

---

[1] *Οἰκία* and *Οἶκος*.

The two words *οἰκία* and *οἶκος* very frequently occur in the New Testament, and are in our version almost always translated indiscriminately "a house." But their meanings in the original are very distinct, and ought not to be confounded.

Οκiία is the *material house*—the actual building. It occurs 94 times in the New Testament; and only in four of these is it used to signify a *family*, according to the common metaphor, by which the name of a *place* is transferred to the *persons* who are in it. These four passages are in Matth. x. 13, xii. 25 (where Luke xi. 17 has *οἶκος*), Mark iii. 25, and 1 Cor. xvi. 1.

Οἶκος occurs 110 times in the New Testament, and only in *one* of these is it used to signify a material house like *οἰκία*; namely, in Luke xii. 39, "would not have suffered his house (*τὸν οἶκον αὐτοῦ*) to be broken through;" where Matth. xxiv. 43, has *οἰκίαν*; and even here the idea, intended by St. Luke to be conveyed by the word *οἶκος*, is probably not that of a mere house, but the house with all its contents,—"his house and goods;" just as it is used in Homer, *e. g.*,

Οὐ γὰρ ἔτ' ἀνσχετὰ ἔργα
τετεύχαται, οὐδ' ἔτι καλῶς
Οἶκος ἐμὸς διόλωλε.—'Odyss.' ii. 64, and elsewhere.

The general use of *οἶκος* in the New Testament exhibits two principal significations, under each of which some varying shades of meaning are found—

1. The most frequent meaning of *οἶκος* is "*a family*," or household, with a more or less distinct reference to the house as containing it; thus, in Matth. ix. 6, the first place

The meaning of this word is unfortunately lost to the English reader of the New Testament, from its being

in which the word occurs, ὕπαγε εἰς τὸν οἶκόν σου "go unto thine house," means, go to thy family and friends at home; which explanation is actually added in Mark v. 19, ὕπαγε εἰς τὸν οἶκόν σου, πρὸς τοὺς σούς. Hence the word is sometimes very properly translated "home," as in this place of St. Mark, "go home to thy friends," as also in 1 Cor. xi. 34, xiv. 35, and elsewhere.

From this meaning it followed that οἶκος was the word to signify "house," in the sense of a family of descendants, or a separate race; as, "the lost sheep of the house of Israel, οἴκου Ἰσραήλ." Matth. x. 6. "Of the house of David, ἐξ οἴκου Δαβίδ." Luke i. 27.

2. The second meaning of οἶκος nearly resembles that of the Latin word *ædes* in the singular number, and signifies an apartment, hall, or building appropriated to some special purpose, particularly a *sacred* purpose. Thus, in Luke xiv. 23, "that my house may be filled," where οἶκος is the hall or room in which the guests were assembled; in Matth. xi. 8, "in kings' houses"—ἐν τοῖς οἴκοις τῶν βασιλέων, in the halls or palaces of kings. So in Acts x. 30, Cornelius says, "I was praying in my house," meaning by ἐν τῷ οἴκῳ μου, the apartment to which doubtless he retired to pray.

Hence οἶκος is the word always used for "house" in a religious sense as applied to the Jewish Temple; as "My house shall be called the house of prayer," ὁ οἶκός μου οἶκος προσευχῆς κληθήσεται, Matth. xxi. 13. "My Father's house," τὸν οἶκον τοῦ πατρός μου, John ii. 16; while "in my Father's house," John xiv. 2, in a different sense, is ἐν τῇ οἰκίᾳ τοῦ πατρός μου. The same word οἶκος is also used in the Septuagint of the Temple, or any place in which the divine presence was especially acknowledged; as, in Gen. xxviii. 17, "the house of God," οἶκος Θεοῦ. And so also οἶκος is employed in speaking of the Christian Church under the similitude of a sacred building, or spiritual temple, as in 1 Tim. iii. 15, 1 Pet. ii 5.

Now this word οἶκος (never οἰκία) is the one always used in the New Testament as the common name of the places where Christians met for religious purposes. The "upper room" where the Apostles and their earliest adherents after the Ascension "continued with one accord in prayer and supplication," is probably meant by "the house (τὸν οἶκον) where they were sitting," in Acts ii. 2; and the word is afterwards indisputably applied to places of Christian worship in nine other passages. Acts ii. 46; v. 42; viii. 3; xx. 20; Rom. xvi. 5; 1 Cor. xvi. 19; Col. iv. 15; Tit. i. 11; Philem. 2.

translated, "a house;" whereby not only is the force of the original passage impaired, but in some cases a quite erroneous notion is necessarily suggested. As there is no one suitable English word exactly corresponding with it, it may in this connection be rendered "a worship-room;" and the substitution of this term for the word "house," in several passages in which it occurs, will greatly elucidate their meaning, while it will at the same time more clearly exhibit this early Christian usage. Thus in Acts ii. 46, the sacred historian informs us that the Apostles were in the habit of "breaking bread,"—not "from house to house"—as if they celebrated the Lord's Supper in private families one after another—but "at different worship-rooms," where religious assemblies were held by Christian congregations.[1] In Acts v. 42, it is related that "daily in the Temple," and—not "in every

---

Long after the apostolic age, the same word *οἶκος*, either alone or with some explanatory addition, continued to be used as one of the appellations of Christian churches, *i.e.*, places of worship; thus, in directions for building a church, *ὁ οἶκος ἔστω ἐπιμήκης καὶ κατ' ἀνατολὰς τετραμμένος*.—'Constitut. Apostol.' ii. 4.

Οἴκους ἐκκλησιῶν οἰκοδομεῖν.—Euseb. ix. 9.

Πρὸ θυρῶν τῶν οἰκῶν τῶν εὐκτηρίων.—Chrysost. 'Hom.' 24, de Verb. Apost.

Τὸν οἶκον τῆς προσευχῆς.—Basil, 'Epist.' 63, ad Neo. Cæsar.

Εὐκτηρίους οἴκους ᾠκοδόμησαν.—Sozomen, 'Hist. Eccl.' ii. 5.

[1] The words *κατ' οἶκον* in Acts ii. 46, could not mean "from house to house," whatever were the meaning of *οἶκος*; the words must signify "at different *οἶκοι*," and the use of the singular number, and without the article shows that, when St. Luke wrote his narrative, the custom of meeting in these worship-rooms for united devotions had become perfectly common and familiar; otherwise he would have written *κατὰ τοὺς οἴκους*. Just as we should say, "All the people in the city were *at church*," meaning in the different churches of the place; whereas a stranger, unused

house," as if the Apostles paid pastoral visits to every Christian family, but "in different worship-rooms, they ceased not to teach, and to preach Jesus as the Christ."[1]

When Saul "made havock of the Church," we are told in Acts viii. 3, that he entered,—not "into every house," which would not have answered his purpose,—but "into the different worship-rooms" at Jerusalem, where he might find Christians actually assembled and engaged in their religious services, and so might obtain positive proof against them. When St. Paul, in Rom. xvi., sends his salutation to Aquila and Priscilla, and "to the Church in their house," he does not mean, as the English reader is apt to imagine, the Christian members of their family, but the congregation of Roman Christians, who met in the worship-room, which they had provided. And the Judaizing teachers, whom Titus is warned against, are described in Tit. i. 11, as subverting by their erroneous doctrines,—not "whole houses" or families, though that would be bad enough,—but "whole worship-rooms" or congregations, whom they led astray. The false Christians, on the other hand, who did beguile the members of families, were said to "creep into houses"—εἰς τας οἰκίας, not οἴκους—2 Tim. iii. 6.

---

to this custom, would say "they were in the churches."

[1] The practice of the Apostles alluded to in Acts v. 42, corresponds exactly with that of zealous missionaries now. They addressed the general population in the Temple, and their converts in the worship-rooms; as the modern missionary appeals to men in the bazaar or other public place of resort; and as soon as he is able, assembles the native Christians in a room or church, for religious worship and instruction.

These places of religious assembly were probably at first those large upper rooms which are several times alluded to in the New Testament. And such a room is on one occasion expressly mentioned as used for Christian worship at Troas (Acts xx. 8), when St. Paul addressed the disciples there on his last journey to Jerusalem; besides the upper room noticed in the first chapter of the Acts. Probably also "the house of Mary, the mother of John, whose surname was Mark," mentioned in Acts xii. 12, "where many were gathered together praying," contained one of these worship-rooms well known to Peter, who went there immediately on his deliverance from the prison.

This apostolic practice of assembling in the rooms of private houses continued to nearly the end of the second century, as we may infer from Justin Martyr's description of Christian congregational worship in his time, and from the express declaration contained in the account of his martyrdom.[1]

[1] In Justin Martyr's account the *place* where Christians met has no name given to it; he merely describes it as "where the brethren were gathered together to engage in common prayers." Thus of a newly baptized convert, he says, ἐπι τοὺς λεγομένους ἀδελφοὺς ἄγομεν, ἔνθα συνηγμένοι εἰσὶ κοινὰς εὐχὰς ποιησόμενοι. And of the assembling for Sunday worship he merely writes, τῇ τοῦ ἡλίου λεγομένῃ ἡμέρᾳ πάντων κατὰ πόλεις ἢ ἀγροὺς μενόντων ἐπὶ τὸ αὐτὸ συνέλευσις γίγνεται.—'Apol.' i. 85, 87.

And in the account of his examination by the Prefect Rusticus, at Rome, before his martyrdom, it is mentioned, that in reply to the question as to where he assembled his disciples, he said that he neither had nor knew of any other place of assembling, except the upper room of the house where he lodged. ποῦ συνέρχεσθε; ἢ εἰς ποῖον τόπον ἀθροίζεις τοὺς μαθήτας σου;

At the end of this century or the beginning of the third appear the first indication of buildings specially appropriated to divine service; but these seem to have been of a simple and unpretending nature.[1] While

---

Answer. Ἐγὼ ἐπάνω μένω τινὸς Μαρτίνου τοῦ Τιμοτίνων βαλανίου, . . καὶ οὐ γιγνώσκω ἄλλην τινὰ συνέλευσιν, εἰ μὴ τὸν ἐκείνου. — 'Acta Martyrii Justini,' June 1.

[1] *The names given to Christian places of worship.* When places had been built expressly for Christian worshippers, they naturally acquired new names besides the original appellation of the simple οἶκος. The word Church (ἐκκλησία) is not used in the New Testament to signify a *place* of assembly. The passages sometimes alleged to prove this meaning, such as 1 Cor. xi. 18, 22; "When ye come together in the Church," and "despise ye the Church of God?" do not supply the requisite proof, notwithstanding their acceptance in this sense by such learned men as Joseph Mede in his 'Discourse on Churches.' The fact that this meaning *makes sense* in these passages, and accords with modern phraseology, is no proof that the word is so used. It is nothing better than a puerile delusion to suppose that the translation of a word must be correct, because it makes sense, and accords with our own usage. It is a much sounder principle to affirm that, when a word has been clearly seen, in a large number of examples, to have a certain definite meaning or meanings, we are not at liberty to assign to it (in the same authors) a different signification in some isolated passage, where, although the sense may admit of this translation, the ordinary rendering is perfectly intelligible.

Now the word ἐκκλησία occurs in the New Testament 115 times, and in all its acknowledged shades of meaning it signifies an assembly or body of *persons*, and not a *place;* therefore it is contrary to sound scholarship to assign to it a different meaning in the two solitary verses of 1 Cor. xi. when the established sense of a Christian congregation equally harmonizes with the context.

It is, of course, a very usual thing for the name of an assembly of *persons* to be applied to the *place* where they assemble, or *vice versâ;* but it so happens that there is no well authenticated instance of the word "Church" being used for a place of worship, before the third century, a passage from Clement of Alexandria (A. D. 204) being the earliest authority for this use. Οὐ νῦν τὸν τόπον, ἀλλὰ τὸ ἄθροισμα τῶν ἐκλεκτῶν, ἐκκλησίαν καλῶ.—'Strom.' Lib. vii.

Other ordinary names were ἐκ-

Christianity was in general an object of suspicion, and Christians were liable to be persecuted, either by popular violence or magisterial authority, it was obviously a matter of prudence, not to say necessity, on their part, not to make their places of assembly or any of their proceedings too conspicuous to the public eye. And in times of special persecution even rooms in private houses were too dangerous to be frequented. And then any retreat where two or three could assemble in the name of Christ became a Christian sanctuary.

But in the latter portion of the third century, and especially in the comparatively quiet times between the death of Cyprian and the persecution of Diocletian, more ample and spacious churches were erected. And in the reigns of Christian emperors sometimes the splendid public halls, called *Basilicæ*, were granted to the Church for Christian worship; sometimes magnificent churches were built and adorned by imperial munificence.

In the apostolic age, and during the time when Christian worshippers met in private rooms, or in edifices of a simple style, there was no distinction made between different portions of the building: men and women were not separated in the congregation;[1] neither was any

κλησιαστήριον, κυριακὸν, from whence our words "kirk" and "church," *προσευκτήριον, ναός*; and in the Western Church, *domus ecclesiæ*, *dominicum* (which also signified the Lord's Day, and the Lord's Supper), *templum*, and *titulus*.

[1] The custom of having separate places in a church for men and for women, and making them sit apart, prevailed in the fourth century; but this was not so in the beginning, as may probably be inferred from the short notice in Acts i. 14, and from the practices in the

form of consecration then used, or any particular sanctity or reverence attached to the place. The sanctity was in the worshippers, who met together in the Saviour's name; and the reverence was given to His spiritual presence, which had been promised to those who should be thus assembled. At a later period, coincident with the time when magnificent structures had superseded the simple worship-rooms, Christian churches were divided into the two—and later still into three—parts, which the ecclesiastical system in its progressive development required for duly carrying out its principles. For when, during the third century, the tide of sacerdotalism had set in, and Christian presbyters were looked upon as *priests*, who had a *sacrifice* to offer upon an *altar;* this imitation of the Jewish Temple in its officers and services was naturally followed by a further imitation of its material structure in the arrangements of Christian churches. Two parts separated from each other were now considered necessary for the ecclesiastical economy;—the *sanctuary* in which the "altar" stood, and which, being regarded as more holy than the rest of the building, was appropriated to the clergy alone, while the *body of the church,* marked off from it, was occupied by the general congregation.

Corinthian Church alluded to in 1 Cor. xi. Chrysostom, who says that the custom had been introduced on account of the bad behaviour of men and women when they sat together, adds, ὡς ἔγωγε ἀκούω τῶν πρεσβυτέρων, ὅτι τὸ παλαιὸν οὐδὲ ταῦτα ἦν τὰ τείχεια... καὶ ἐπὶ τῶν ἀποστόλων δὲ ὁμοῦ καὶ ἄνδρες καὶ γυναῖκες ἦσαν . . . οὐκ ἠκούσατε ὅτι ἦσαν συνηγμένοι ἄνδρες καὶ γυναῖκες ἐν τῷ ὑπερῴῳ.—'Hom. 74, in Matth.'

The architectural arrangement of a Basilica when converted into a church, required little or no change to accommodate it to this twofold division. For the apse at the end of the hall, which in its civic use had been the "tribunal" for administering justice, was made the sanctuary for the "altar," and the hall itself supplied an ample space for the lay portion of the congregation to assemble.

In the mean while another want was beginning to be felt; and it was subsequently thought right that the catechumens should have a separate part of the church area assigned to them, divided off from the baptized worshippers. From the end of the second century the catechumens had been a distinct and numerous class, kept a long time under instruction and preparatory discipline before they were baptized, and although they were allowed to be in church during the reading of the Scriptures and the sermon, they were dismissed before the prayers began. In all probability therefore, they sat by themselves; but there does not appear to have been a place actually separated for them from the congregation of the "Faithful," until the fifth or sixth century. When this was done churches were built with a triple division, and Basilicas sometimes then had a portion for the catechumens marked off at the lower part of the hall.[1]

---

[1] *The Form and Divisions of Churches.*

When churches were built expressly for Christian worship in the third century and onwards, they were usually of an oblong shape

With these changes in the places of worship, and in the nature of the ministrations performed in them, the custom of consecrating churches after the manner of

---

and turned towards the east, according to the direction, ὁ οἶκος ἐπιμήκης ἔστω κατ' ἀνατολὰς τετραμμένος.—'Constitut. Apost.' ii. 4.

Other forms, however, were sometimes observed. Thus, of three noted churches built by Constantine, one at Golgotha was *round*, another at Antioch *octagon*, and the third at Constantinople in the form of a *cross*. [See Bingham, or Guericke, 'Manual of Church Antiquities.']

Christians in Tertullian's time had adopted the custom of worshipping with their faces towards the east,—the east (ἀνατολή) being taken to be an emblem of Christ [Luke i. 78], and consequently churches were usually so placed; the Communion Table—then called the "altar"—being at the eastern end. But this rule was not always observed. The church at Antioch mentioned by Socrates ('H. E.' v. 22), had the "altar" at the west end. Ἐν Ἀντιοχείᾳ τῆς Συρίας ἡ ἐκκλησία ἀντίστροφον ἔχει τὴν θέασιν, οὐ γὰρ πρὸς ἀνατολὰς τὸ θυσιαστήριον ἀλλὰ πρὸς δύσιν ὁρᾷ.

With respect to the divisions of churches into different parts, Guericke in his 'Manual of Church Antiquities,' observes that, "The whole of the rectangular space of the splendid public buildings (*basilicæ*), which were transferred to ecclesiastical purposes, was usually divided into three portions with either a single, or with three, and sometimes even five naves. And this architectural arrangement of the basilicæ determined beforehand the character of the Christian churches." But this assertion must not be taken without some qualification. The plan of building churches with a curved apse at the east end, and with a central division and two, or occasionally four, side aisles, separated from it by columns, was no doubt borrowed from the *basilicæ;* but the triple division for the "altar," the faithful, and the catechumens, was not suggested by these civic halls, but by ideas and consequent arrangements which arose within the church itself. The *basilica,* too, was distinctly divided not into *three,* but *two* parts—the tribunal, and the body of the hall; as described by Vitruvius, to whom Guericke himself refers, and as appears still in some very ancient Italian churches, particularly at Ravenna, retaining the form of the Roman *basilica,* and dating possibly from the fourth or fifth century. The following is Vitruvius's description "of the basilica built in the Julian colony of Fano:"—

"The middle vault between the

the Jewish Temple easily followed, the buildings themselves were then deemed holy, and the sanctuary or

---

columns, is 120 feet long and 60 feet wide. The portico around it is 20 feet wide. The tribunal is in the shape of a segment of a circle, the front dimension of which is 46 feet, that of its depth 15 feet; and is so contrived that the merchants who are in the basilica may not interfere with those who have business before the magistrates."—Vitruvius, v. 1. translated by J. Gwilt, p. 127.

The three divisions when adopted in Churches were called—1. The νάρθηξ, or ante-temple, where penitents and catechumens stood, and to which heathens were admitted.

2. The ναός, or temple, where the "faithful," or communicants, were placed, and which was also called *aula laïcorum.* The word ναός was afterwards Latinized into *navis*, whence the English word "nave."

3. The βῆμα, or sanctuary, where the "altar" was placed. It was also called ἅγιον, ἱεράτειον, θυσιαστήριον; or in Latin, sanctuarium, sacrarium, sancta sanctorum, the Holy of Holies. It was separated by rails or lattice-work—*cancelli;* whence the modern name "chancel." The entrance to this was closed by gates or curtains, "partly to hide the prospect of this part of the church from the catechumens and unbelievers, and partly to cover the sacrifice of the Eucharist in the time of consecration."

Thus both the Jewish notion of a temple which none but priests might enter, and the heathen notion of sacred mysteries hidden from the uninitiated, were encouraged in the Church. None of these things have the least countenance in the Church system of the New Testament.

Morinus having declared that the ancient churches had no νάρθηξ, or special place for catechumens and unbelievers, for above 500 years, Bingham affirms that "in this he is evidently mistaken; for though the name, perhaps, is not very ancient, yet the thing itself is; for this was *always* a distinct and separate part of the church, as any one will easily imagine that considers the ancient use of it. For the Church, ever since she first divided her catechumens and penitents into distinct orders and classes, had also distinct places in the church for them."—viii. 4, 2. But Bingham gives no proof at all of this confident assertion of his. For his references to the 'Constitutiones Apostolicæ,' to Basil, and others, only prove that catechumens were required to withdraw from the church after the reading of the Scripture lessons and the sermon; from which it by no means necessarily follows that churches must have been always built with a distinct and separate part for their use.

chancel the most holy part of all; and men were taught to believe that their prayers were more efficacious in a consecrated building, and that the divine presence in an especial manner dwelt within its walls.[1]

There is not the slightest trace of any of these things

---

[1] The *consecration* of churches with formal solemnities, which were supposed to impart a sacredness to the place and building, does not appear until the fourth century. Before that time it was thought sufficient to "dedicate" a church by the first act of using it for public prayer, as had been the case also with the Jewish synagogues. And thus the word *dedico* is used by Cyprian in the sense of doing a sacred thing for the first time, when he says of Aurelius whom he had ordained as a reader, "Dominico legit interim nobis, id est auspicatus est precem, dum *dedicat lectionem.*" —Ep. 33 ad Clerum et Plebem. See the remarks of Selden and Dodwell on this subject, quoted by Vitringa.—'De Synag.' i. 3, 2.

But from the time of Constantine much more elaborate ceremonies were introduced. The sacerdotal notions, taken from the Jewish temple, were enhanced by an accession of mystery and awfulness; and, in particular, the place where the "altar" stood was regarded as "most holy," and hidden from the vulgar sight.

Then too *incense*, and *lighted lamps* in the day time, were used in the celebration of the Lord's Supper, although the latter, as a pagan custom, had been forbidden by the Council of Elvira at the beginning of this century. Both, however, are sanctioned by the 'Canones Apostolici,' which direct *μὴ ἐξὸν ἔστω προσάγεσθαί τι ἕτερον εἰς τὸ θυσιαστήριον, ἢ ἔλαιον εἰς τὴν λυχνίαν, καὶ θυμίαμα τῷ καίρῳ τῆς ἁγίας προσφορᾶς.*—Canon 3.

Crosses, sometimes of silver, were set up on the "altar," and *flowers* were placed on it; while, as Jerome approvingly observes in his panegyric on Nepotian, flowers, leaves, and vine-branches ornamented other parts of the church. "Basilicas ecclesiæ et martyrdum conciliabula diversis floribus, et arborum comis, vitiumque pampinis adumbravit."

Pictures were first introduced into churches at the end of the fourth century by Paulinus at Nola, in order to keep the people from disturbances and excess at the Church festivals! *Images* and *statues* came in later; but a superstitious reverence for the supposed relics of saints and martyrs, and the ascription of miraculous powers to them, were encouraged by Paulinus himself.

in the New Testament, or for a hundred years after the Apostles' time; and even in the fourth and following centuries thoughtful men could see that churches of architectural beauty, glittering with ornamentation, and invested with an artificial sacredness, lacked the true honour and simple dignity of the apostolic age, when the grace and spirituality of the congregation, and not the splendour of the building or the gorgeousness of priestly vestments, adorned the devotions of the Church. For us, who can now look back upon the history of the past, to choose for our imitation the florid display of the *later* time rather than the simplicity of the *first*, is surely a grave mistake, and one which ought not to be found in a Church in which the New Testament has been for more than 300 years in the hands of the people, and its supreme authority openly avowed.[1]

---

[1] Isidore of Pelusium, at the end of the fourth century, contrasting the times of the Apostles with his own, remarks, that *then* the congregation was adorned with spiritual gifts, and distinguished by an admirable social order, while the place in which they worshipped was unadorned; but in his own time the churches were decorated with an excess of ornamentation, and glittering with splendour, while the congregation, destitute of spiritual graces, was, to say the least, an object of reproach and ridicule. Ἐπὶ μὲν τῶν Ἀποστόλων, ὅτε ἡ ἐκκλησία ἐκόμα μὲν χαρίσμασι πνευματικοῖς, ἔβρυε δὲ πολιτείᾳ λαμπρᾷ ἐκκλησιαστήρια οὐκ ἦν. ἐπὶ δὲ ἡμῶν τὰ ἐκκλησιαστήρια πλέον τοῦ δέοντος κεκόσμηται, ἡ δὲ ἐκκλησία—ἀλλ' οὐδὲν βούλομαι δυσχερὲς εἰπεῖν—κωμῳδεῖται. Ἐγὼ γοῦν, εἴ γε αἵρεσίς μοι προύκειτο, εἱλόμην ἂν ἐν τοῖς καίροις ἐκείνοις γε γεγενῆσθαι, ἐν οἷς ἐκκλησιαστήρια μὲν οὕτω κεκοσμημένα οὐκ ἦν, ἐκκλησία δὲ θείοις καὶ οὐρανίοις χαρίσμασιν ἐστεμμένη, ἢ ἐν τούτοις, ἐν οἷς τὰ μὲν ἐκκλησιαστήρια παντοίοις κεκαλλώπισται μαρμάροις, ἡ δὲ ἐκκλησία

II. *Public Worship.*

From the places in which the early Christians met for their united devotions we are led next to enquire into the form and method of the devotions themselves ; and this enquiry is at once assisted by a scriptural account of the very earliest arrangement of Christian worship, commencing with the formation of the first Christian community. In Acts ii. 42, we are presented with an enumeration of the different parts which made up the religious services, instituted by the Apostles for the instruction and edification of the infant Church.

As the words indeed stand in our English Version, the information which they give is not very precise or clear, when we read of the new converts in this verse, that " they continued steadfastly in the Apostles' doctrine and fellowship, and in breaking of bread, and in prayers." But in the original it is evident that four distinct particulars are enumerated in such a manner as to show that, at the time when the account was written, they were well-known and customary portions of an established mode of procedure in the religious assemblies of the Church. To give the real meaning of the verse it may be translated, " They were constantly attending the Apostles' teaching, and the collection, or contribution

---

τῶν πνευματικῶν χαρισμάτων ἐκείνων ἐρήμη καὶ γυμνὴ καθέστηκεν.—Lib. ii. Ep. 246.

Chrysostom also very briefly expresses the same thoughts in an epigrammatic form, *τότε αἱ οἰκίαι ἐκκλησίαι ἦσαν, νῦν δὲ ἡ ἐκκλησία οἰκία γέγονεν.*—'Hom. 32 in Matth.'

(for the poor), and the breaking of the bread, and the prayers (of the congregation)."[1]

[1] It is necessary in this verse to mark the presence of the Article, repeated with each word, τῇ διδαχῇ τῶν Ἀποστόλων, καὶ τῇ κοινωνίᾳ, καὶ τῇ κλάσει τοῦ ἄρτου, καὶ ταῖς προσευχαῖς, which shows that every particular enumerated is a distinct and separate thing, and, consequently, that τῇ διδαχῇ τῶν Ἀποστόλων, καὶ τῇ κοινωνίᾳ cannot be "the Apostles' doctrine and fellowship;" and which shows besides that all these particulars were known and familiar objects, admitting of this precise and definite allusion.

The only possible doubt as to the meaning of the verse is connected with the word κοινωνία, which instead of "a contribution" *might* signify "a common participation"—that is, in this place, a partaking together of the Ἀγαπὴ, or Love Feast, which accompanied the celebration of the Lord's Supper in the earliest times. This is the opinion of Neander, in his 'History of the Planting and Training of the Christian Church,' where he says that κοινωνία here "means the daily meal of which believers partook as members of one family," and "in which they commemorated the last supper of the disciples with Christ, and their brotherly union with one another. At the close of the meal the president distributed bread and wine to the persons present, as a memorial of Christ's similar distribution to the disciples. Thus every meal was consecrated to the Lord, and at the same time was a meal of brotherly love. Hence, the designations afterwards chosen were δεῖπνον Κυρίου, and ἀγαπή."—B. i. 2.

Neander adds in a note, "Mosheim thinks, since everything else is mentioned that is found in later meetings of the Church, that the κοινωνία refers to the *collections* made on these occasions." And, besides Mosheim's reason, it may be noticed that κοινωνία is not elsewhere met with in the New Testament in the connection which Neander gives, nor in the sense of participation, without the object participated in being expressed; whereas it is several times used to signify a collection, or contribution.

Κοινωνία occurs nineteen times in the New Testament in the following senses:

I. *Fellowship*, or *communion*.

1. With a *person*, so as to share with him in his advantages, or work, &c. If the person is expressed, μετὰ, with a Gen., is put before it.

Δεξιὰς ἔδωκαν ἐμοὶ καὶ βαρνάβᾳ κοινωνίας, Gal. iii. 9, "they gave to me and Barnabas the right hands of fellowship," *i. e.* acknowledged us as having a share with them in their work.

Ἵνα καὶ ὑμεῖς κοινωνίαν ἔχητε μεθ' ἡμῶν· καὶ ἡ κοινωνία

"The Apostles' teaching" was the address or sermon delivered by them,—and afterwards by other ministers,

δὲ ἡμετέρα μετὰ τοῦ Πατρὸς, καὶ μετὰ τοῦ υἱοῦ αὐτοῦ, 1 John i. 3, a share with the Father and the Son in their blessings, &c.

So with ἐὰν εἴπωμεν ὅτι κοινωνίαν ἔχομεν μετ' αὐτοῦ, 1 John, i. 6; and κοινωνίαν ἔχομεν μετ' ἀλλήλων, 1 John i. 7.

2. Fellowship, or communion, in *a thing* (or Person) so as to share with others in the advantages, &c., which comes from it (or him).

Δὶ οὗ ἐκλήθητε εἰς κοινωνίαν τοῦ υἱοῦ αὐτοῦ, 1 Cor. i. 9, into a participation in His Son ; *i. e.* to be joint partakers in His blessings.

Τὸ ποτήριον τῆς εὐλογίας ὃ εὐλογοῦμεν, οὐχὶ κοινωνία τοῦ αἵματος τοῦ Χριστοῦ ἐστι; τὸν ἄρτον ὃν κλῶμεν, οὐχὶ κοινωνία τοῦ σώματος τοῦ Χριστοῦ ἔστιν; 1 Cor. x. 16, a participation in the blood—and the body.

Ἡ κοινωνία τοῦ ἁγίου Πνεύματος, 2 Cor. xiii. 13, the participation in the Holy Spirit.

Εἴ τις κοινωνία Πνεύματος, Phil. ii. 1, any participation in the Spirit.

So also with τίς ἡ κοινωνία τοῦ μυστηρίου, Eph. iii. 9 ; and τὴν κοινωνίαν τῶν παθημάτων αὐτοῦ, Phil. iii. 10.

II. *Communication*, or imparting a share of what we have to others. Hence—

1. A collection, or contribution.

Ἦσαν προσκαρτεροῦντες τῇ διδαχῇ τῶν ἀποστόλων, καὶ τῇ κοινωνίᾳ, Acts ii. 42, as given above.

Κοινωνίαν τινὰ ποιήσασθαι εἰς τοὺς πτωχοὺς, Rom. xv. 26, to make a certain collection for the poor.

Τὴν κοινωνίαν τῆς διακονίαν τῆς εἰς τοὺς ἁγίους, 2 Cor. viii. 4, the contribution of their service to the saints.

Καὶ ἁπλότητι τῆς κοινωνίας εἰς αὐτοὺς, 2 Cor. ix. 13, the liberality of their contribution for them.

Ἐπὶ τῇ κοινωνίᾳ ὑμῶν εἰς τὸ εὐαγγέλιον, Phil. i. 5, for your contribution to the Gospel ; *i. e.* the supplies which they had sent to St. Paul for the Gospel's sake.

2. A *communication*, or *distribution*.

Ὅπως ἡ κοινωνία τῆς πίστεως σου ἐνεργὴς γένηται, Philem. 6, that the communication of thy faith [to others] may prove effectual.

Τῆς δὲ εὐποιίας καὶ κοινωνίας μὴ ἐπιλανθάνεσθε, Heb. xiii. 16, "to do good, and to distribute, forget not."

The verb κοινωνέω occurs eight times in the New Testament, and signifies—

1. To *have a share* with others ; to *be partakers* with others, or in the things of others ; as in Rom. xv. 27 ; 1 Tim. v. 22 ; Heb. ii. 14 ; 1 Pet. iv. 13 ; 2 John 11. [2.

—to the assembled believers, accompanied no doubt with a reading of portions of the Jewish Scriptures, from which, as it evidently appears in the history of the Apostles' ministrations, so large a portion of their Christian preaching was more or less directly drawn.

"The collection or contribution" included probably those large and liberal gifts which are said to have been "laid at the Apostles' feet;" as well as the smaller donations of less wealthy Christians who were taught to give according to their means. And these together produced the fund which supplied the wants of the poorer brethren, and other ecclesiastical expenses, and which, being thus directly consecrated to the service of Christ, was invested with a religious or sacred character, so accordant with the devotional spirit of the apostolic Church.

"The breaking of the bread" was the celebration of the Lord's Supper, of which more will be said hereafter.

"The prayers" were the public supplications of the assembled people.

Taking then this original outline as a starting-point, we may trace allusions to one or another of these component parts of the primitive worship, scattered here and there throughout the New Testament. Thus in Acts xx. 7, we are informed that the Christians at Troas "on the first day of the week came together to break bread," and that St. Paul "preached to them." In 1 Cor. xi. and xiv. we have a fuller account of the religious meetings of the

2. To *give a share* to others; to *make* others *partakers* in the things which we have; as in Rom. xiii. 3; Gal. vi. 6; Phil. iv. 15.

Corinthian Christians, and of their prayers accompanied with singing,—their celebration of the Lord's Supper, and their prophesying, *i.e.* inculcating divine truths by the exposition of Scripture lessons, in what would now be termed Lectures or Sermons. In the Pastoral Epistles of St. Paul are found, as might be expected, several exhortations to Timothy and Titus to see that the religious services in their churches were duly performed. Thus he directs "that supplications, prayers, intercessions, and giving of thanks be made for all men." (1 Tim. ii. 1.) He desires Timothy "to attend to the reading" of the Scriptures in the congregations, and "to the exhortation and the instruction" addressed to them.[1] And since the teaching and admonitions of the ministers in any church must have a great influence on the faith and conduct of their congregations, he requires that a bishop, *i.e.* a presbyter having the oversight of a Church, should, among other qualifications, be "apt to teach," and able both to exhort Christian people by his sound instruction, and also to convince or refute opposers of the faith (Tit. i. 9). And he urges Timothy himself with all earnestness "to preach the word," "rightly to divide the word of truth," and "to take heed to himself and to his teaching."

The singing also of psalms and hymns, taken from the

[1] In Tim. iv. 13, *πρόσεχε τῇ ἀναγνώσει, τῇ παρακλήσει, τῇ διδασκαλίᾳ,* "the reading" having the Article prefixed, and being accompanied with the other words, must necessarily mean the public reading in the church.

Old Testament, or composed for Christian use, not only prevailed in Christian families, but was introduced in the very earliest times into the public services of the Church. It is mentioned by St. Paul in his directions to the Corinthians (1 Cor. xiv.); and it is with good reason believed that the words in Eph. v. 14, are a quotation from a Christian hymn.[1]

This apostolic mode of public worship was still continued in almost its original simplicity in the middle of the second century, as may be seen in the description of the Sunday services given by Justin Martyr, who enumerates the reading of lessons from the Gospels, or the prophetical Scriptures, followed by a sermon or address by the officiating minister,—after which the congregation stood up for their common prayers,—and the service concluded with the celebration of the Lord's Supper, which was immediately preceded by appropriate prayers and thanksgivings uttered by the minister, and responded to by the people with the word Amen; accompanied also with the voluntary contributions of the communicants.[2]

---

[1] The words in Eph. v. 14, form three lines of a hymn:

Ἔγειραι ὁ καθεύδων,
καὶ ἀνάστα ἐκ τῶν νεκρων,
και ἐπιφαύσει σοι ὁ Κριστός.

The quotation is introduced in a peculiar manner by *διὸ λέγει*, not *λέγει ἡ γραφὴ*, or *λέγεται*, or *γέγραπται*, but *λέγει* "one says"—in the Church service.

[2] The following is Justin's account of the Sunday service in his time: *Τῇ τοῦ ἡλίου λεγομένῃ ἡμέρᾳ πάντων κατὰ πόλεις ἢ ἀγροὺς μενόντων ἐπὶ τὸ αὐτὸ συνέλευσις γίνεται, καὶ τὰ ἀπομνημονεύματα τῶν ἀποστόλων ἢ τὰ συγγράμματα τῶν προφητῶν ἀναγινώσκεται μέχρις ἐγχωρεῖ· Εἶτα, παυσαμένου τοῦ ἀναγινώσκοντος, ὁ προεστὼς διὰ λόγου τὴν*

Notices of a similar kind are found in Tertullian,[1] and indeed throughout the third and fourth centuries and onwards; but little alteration is to be seen in the general form and outline of the public worship, except that the strongly marked distinction between believers and catechumens, and the tendency to deal with the Christian sacraments after the manner of the secret pagan mysteries led, in the third century, to a formal division of the Church services into two portions—subsequently called *Missa Catechumenorum* and *Missa Fidelium.* At first the former of these two divisions, to which all persons, whether Christians or not, were admissible, probably included the singing, Scripture lessons, and sermon; and the latter, at which Christians only were present, consisted of the common prayers of the people with the

---

νουθεσίαν καὶ πρόκλησιν τῆς τῶν καλῶν τούτων μιμήσεως ποιεῖται. Ἔπειτα ἀνιστάμεθα κοινῇ πάντες καὶ εὐχὰς πέμπομεν· καὶ ὡς προέφημεν, παυσαμενων ἡμῶν τῆς εὐχῆς, ἄρτος προσφέρεται καὶ οἶνος καὶ ὕδωρ, καὶ ὁ προεστὼς εὐχας ὁμοίως καὶ εὐχαριστίας, ὅση δύναμις αὐτῷ, ἀναπέμπει, καὶ ὁ λαὸς ἐπευφημεῖ λέγων τὸ Ἀμήν. καὶ ἡ διάδοσις καὶ ἡ μετάληψις ἀπὸ τῶν εὐχαριστηθεντων ἑκαστῳ γίνεται, καὶ τοῖς οὐ παροῦσι διὰ τῶν διακόνων πέμπεται. Οἱ εὐποροῦντες δὲ καὶ βουλόμενοι κατα προαίρεσιν ἕκαστος τὴν ἑαυτοῖ ὃ βούλεται δίδωσι, καὶ τὸ συλλεγόμενον παρὰ τῷ προεστῶτι ἀποτίθεται.—'Apol.' i. § 87.

Justin does not mention singing in this description; but it is evident that hymns were sung in the religious services of his time, from a remark which he makes in an earlier part of his 'Apology.' *πομπὰς καὶ ὕμνους πέμπομεν.*—§ 16.

[1] Tertullian, meaning apparently to enumerate with the greatest brevity the different parts of the Church service, says, "Jam vero prout Scripturæ leguntur, aut psalmi canuntur, aut allocutiones proferuntur, aut petitiones delegantur."—'De Anima,' § 9, ed. 1664.

usual devotions of the Eucharistic service; but in the fourth century a somewhat more complex arrangement was thought to be desirable.[1]

[1] As the Sunday morning service, as described by Justin Martyr, contained no other prayers but those which Christians offered together (κοιναὶ εὐχαί), and the prayers of the officiating minister immediately before the celebration of the Lord's Supper, the parts of the service which were suitable for non-Christians would be the singing, the Scripture lessons, and the sermon; and, consequently, a division would naturally be made there. In the fourth century, however, when catechumens were sufficiently numerous to form a distinct class, under a long course of instruction;—when Christians, who had committed grave offences, or had submitted to heathen compliances in times of persecution, had to be placed under a penitential discipline;—and when Christian worship attracted more attention in the pagan part of the population;—certain prayers were added to the 'Missa Catechumenorum;' and, at the same time, the latter portion of the service, or 'Missa Fidelium,' was also enlarged.

The accounts, however, which are given of these enlarged services do not exactly agree in all their details; and, probably, some difference was observable in this respect in different Churches.

Thus, with respect to the 'Missa Catechumenorum,' according to the directions of the Council of Laodicea (A. D. 360), the sermon was followed by a prayer for the catechumens, who then retired; after which came a prayer for the penitents, who also then withdrew from the church, the heathen part of the congregation, if any, having apparently departed at the end of the sermon. *Μετὰ τὰς ὁμιλίας τῶν ἐπισκόπων, καὶ τῶν κατηχουμένων εὐχὴν ἐπιτελεῖσθαι·—καὶ μετὰ τὸ ἐξελθεῖν τοὺς κατηχουμένους τῶν ἐν μετανοίᾳ τὴν εὐχὴν γίγνεσθαι, καὶ τούτων προσελθόντων ὑπὸ χεῖρα, καὶ ὑποχωρησάντων, οὕτως τῶν πιστῶν τὰς εὐχὰς γίγνεσθαι.*—'Conc. Laodic. Can.' 19; Labbé Conc.' vol. ii. p. 567.

But in the 'Canonica' of Basil (A. D. 370), the prayer for the penitents seems to have been the *only one* which followed the sermon, before the 'Missa Fidelium' began. For he there directs that a certain penitent should at first be shut out of the Church altogether: *μετὰ δὲ τὰ τέσσαρα ἔτη εἰς τοὺς ἀκροωμένους δεχθήσεται, καὶ ἐν πέντε ἔτεσι μετ' αὐτῶν ἐξελεύσεται,—ἐν ἑπτὰ ἔτεσι μετὰ τῶν ἐν ὑποπτώσει προσευχόμενος ἐξελεύσεται,—ἐν τέσσαρσι συστήσεται μόνον τοῖς πιστοῖς.*—Epist. 217; Can. 56; also Can. 75.

And then the directions given in

And thus the general outline of the Christian worship, instituted by the Apostles, "was maintained down to the Reformation, notwithstanding some variety of details, and the continual addition of ceremonies, intended to present its rites in an outward form, and with a symbolical pomp, calculated to strike and gratify the senses." And now, delivered from such excessive and superstitious accumulations, with which they had been overlaid, the four particulars mentioned in the original apostolic

---

the 'Constitutiones Apostolicæ' speak of no less than *four* distinct courses of prayer after the end of the sermon, and the departure of the unbelievers, namely, prayers (1) for the catechumens; (2) for the energumens, *i. e.* those who were possessed with evil spirits, *οἱ ἐνεργούμενοι ὑπὸ πνευμάτων ἀκαθάρτων;* (3) for those who were ready for baptism; (4) for the penitents; all these classes of persons leaving the church when their respective prayers were concluded—See 'Constit. Apost.' viii. 5—9.

In the 'Missa Fidelium,' between the prayers of the people, and the Eucharistic prayers of the officiating minister, mentioned by Justin, there are found in the fourth century *two other prayers* inserted. The former of these was a "Bidding Prayer," *εὐχὴ διὰ προσφωνήσεως*, pronounced by a deacon, and responded to by the people with some short ejaculations; and the latter was a prayer by the bishop, at the end of which they said, Amen. All these three prayers are mentioned in the directions of the Council of Laodicea, above referred to; and the two of later introduction are described in the 'Apostolic Constitutions,' viii. 9, 10.

The first and most ancient of these prayers was a "silent prayer," each member of the congregation praying mentally by and with himself. It is expressly so named by the Council of Laodicea, *εὐχὴ διὰ σιωπῆς*. And I cannot but think that it was a silent prayer in Justin's time, and, possibly, from a still earlier date. Thus, in Justin's narrative, the people said Amen only after the prayers and thanksgivings uttered by the minister; but of the "common prayers" before this, he says, "We all stand up together and send forth prayers," *ἀνιστάμεθα κοινῇ πάντες καὶ εὐχὰς πέμπομεν;* and "When we have ceased from our prayer," *παυσαμένων ἡμῶν τῆς εὐχῆς*, with no Amen, and no minister uttering the prayers before them; while there is no intimation that

worship are still exhibited in our own congregations, when our full morning service is performed, and when besides the common prayers of the assembled worshippers, "the breaking of bread" is continued in the Lord's Supper,—"the collection" is preserved in the offertory,—and "the Apostles' doctrine" is, or ought to be, heard in the sermon.

As it does not come within the scope of these lectures to dwell upon all the particulars which might be noticed in a treatise on Christian Antiquities, it will be sufficient to mention very briefly that the usual *postures* of prayer in the earliest Churches were in all probability "standing" and "kneeling." The latter alone is expressly named in the New Testament in connection with Christian worship; but standing was a posture used in prayer by the Jews; and Christians, even as early as Justin's time, stood up to pray in their Sunday congregations,—a custom afterwards very scrupulously observed.[1]

---

they were all uttering one common form of words. This therefore seems to have been "silent prayer."

Tertullian, too, can hardly mean anything but silent prayer, when he says in allusion to the public worship of Christians, "sine monitore quia de pectore oramus" ('Apol.' § 30), for a number of persons could not pray together aloud in this manner.

Indeed, the only prayers which the people seem to have uttered aloud were the Lord's Prayer, and certain short ejaculations in reply to words of the officiating minister.

It was in this "silent prayer" that the people *stood up;* in the others they knelt down.

[1] Justin, in his account of the Christian worship on Sundays, says, that they stood up to pray, *ἀνιστάμεθα κοινῇ παντες, καὶ εὐχὰς πέμπομεν.*—'Apol,' i. 87. Irenæus, half a century later, mentions the same practice, and says that it was done in token of the resurrection, and began from the times of the Apostles, *τὸ δὲ ἐν Κυριακῇ μὴ κλίνειν γόνυ σύμβολόν ἐστι τῆς ἀναστα-*

The practice of stretching out or lifting up the hands in praying, also of Jewish origin, is alluded to by St. Paul in 1 Tim. ii. 8, "I will therefore that men pray everywhere lifting up holy hands," but doubtless without the conceit of doing so in the form of a cross, as was the case in the third century.

There is in the New Testament no trace of Christian worshippers *turning to the east* in their prayers, or other parts of their service; though this practice appears at the beginning of the third century, and was probably begun much earlier.[1] Neither is the use of *incense* or of *lamps or candles*, as sacred or symbolical accompaniments in any Christian ceremony, to be found in the apostolic age; nor does it appear that Christian ministers then wore any *peculiar dress* or *official vestments* in any of

σεως. . . . ἐκ τῶν ἀποστολικῶν χρόνων τοιαυτὴ συνήθεια ἔλαβε τὴν ἀρχήν.—'Fragm. de Pasch.' And in Tertullian's time it was considered quite an unlawful thing to kneel at prayers on the Lord's Day, "Die Dominico jejunium nefas ducimus vel de geniculis adorare. Eadem immunitate a die Paschæ in Pentecosten usque gaudemus."—'De Cor. Mil.' 3.

In the fourth century, however, it seems to have been the custom for the people to stand up at one portion of the prayers, while in the others they knelt down. See Bingham, xv. 1, and 'Constit. Apost.' viii. 9; see also note (1) p. 211.

[1] The practice of turning to the east in the prayers of the church is first mentioned by Tertullian, who says, that Christians were on this account accused of worshipping the sun, "quod innotuerit nos ad Orientis regionem precari."—('Apol.' 16.) The words of Zechariah, iii. 8, "Behold I will bring forth my servant, the Branch," being translated in the Septuagint, ἰδοὺ ἐγω ἄγω τὸν δοῦλόν μου, Ἀνατολήν, Christians, at a very early period, looked upon the east as an emblem of Christ; thus Justin M. says, Χριστὸς ἀνατολὴ διὰ Ζαχαρίου κέκληται.—'Dial. c. Tryph.' § 126. And Tertullian, "Orientem Christi figuram."—'Adv. Valentin.' p. 284.

their ministrations. All these came in at a later period and were derived from Jewish or heathen practices, as the Church, having lost the freshness and fulness of apostolic truth, learned from such objectionable sources to affect a more elaborate ceremonial, and to court an exhibition of æsthetic display, quite foreign to the devout simplicity of the apostolic age.

There is, however, one part of this subject which demands more than a passing notice, from its connection with Church controversies of the past, and from the interest which it even now in some respects assumes in its bearing upon wants and difficulties in our own Church and time.

The controversies in the sixteenth and seventeenth centuries between the advocates of a fixed liturgy on the one hand, and of extemporaneous or at least unprescribed prayers in public worship on the other, necessarily gave importance to the question as to what was the rule or practice of the apostolic age in this matter; and what authority or deference the ancient liturgies, bearing apostolic or other venerated names, are justly entitled to receive.

The opponents in those times, too much influenced on both sides by personal and party feelings, appear to have satisfied themselves that the practice which they respectively preferred was the only lawful one; the other, unjustifiable,—not to say heretical. And even now particular views of Christian doctrine which men desire to advocate, or their individual preferences in matters ecclesiastical, seem to bias their minds unduly in the investigation of such questions.

But for those who acknowledge the sufficiency and supremacy of Scripture, and the independent authority of each particular Church in subordination to the written word, and who duly appreciate the force of the omissions in the New Testament, there can surely be no doubt that inasmuch as no forms of prayer of apostolic authority are given in the sacred record, nor any command from the Apostles as to the use or non-use of such forms, this is an open question to be decided by every Church for itself; each Church having a full right to act according to its discretion and deliberate judgment; but no right at all to condemn or disparage the opposite practice, which another Christian community may prefer. Nor in the decision of such questions can any Church with propriety or safety disregard the consideration of times, circumstances, and men's manners; the feelings and requirements of any given age.

But this general conclusion does not make it less interesting or instructive to consider the question of liturgical formularies in the ancient Church somewhat more widely, even though we do nothing more than take a brief notice of the most important of those particulars which the study of this subject presents to view.

Setting out then from the general position just mentioned, that there is no authority in the New Testament either for or against set forms of prayer; let us first enquire what was, in fact, the practice of the earliest Churches.

Since forms of prayer were in use in the Jewish Synagogues, and in some heathen religious services a scrupulous adherence to the words of a sacred formula was considered essential; the Churches, whether of Jewish or of Gentile Christians, could not have been unprepared for, or naturally averse to, prescribed and settled formularies of devotion for their own use. But did they, in fact, employ them?

There is no need to prove, nor for this question is there any advantage in proving, that the apostolic Churches used devotional forms, so far as to sing Old Testament Psalms and precomposed hymns; and that the Lord's prayer, as a well-known and honoured prescription of the Saviour, found a place in their religious services. Such might well be the case, even in Churches which allowed the fullest liberty to themselves and their officiating ministers in conducting their public devotions.

The only questions to be answered are such as these: Were the public *prayers* in the apostolic Churches set forms known beforehand, and repeated on every occasion, like our own?

When such forms first appeared, did they spring up gradually with a spontaneous growth, or were they at some given time imposed by authority, so as to supersede all extemporaneous or discretionary prayers?

When formal liturgies had been adopted, were they regarded as fixed and settled for future generations as well as for the one then present, so that to alter them would be thought a dangerous undertaking almost involving an ecclesiastical revolution? or was revision and alteration felt to be a natural, easy, necessary thing, requiring attention from time to time, and effected without danger or alarm?

Now, I think it is perfectly certain that in the earliest period of the apostolic age, a fixed and prescribed liturgy could not have been used, especially in the Gentile Churches, and during the time when the "Ministry of Gifts" prevailed. The remarks which St. Paul makes about the public worship of the Corinthian Christians, where "every one had a psalm, had a doctrine, had a tongue, had a revelation," and did not even observe due order and propriety in uttering them, and where the Apostle found it necessary to bid them not to pray or give thanks in a language which the congregation could not understand or respond to, are quite incompatible with the use of devotional formularies laid down beforehand, and known to all the worshippers. And when it is further noticed that St. Paul, though desiring to correct disorders, does not at all condemn or disapprove of this mode of worship, provided that all things were "done decently and in order;" and that he neither here, nor elsewhere,—nor any other of the Apostles, as far as we are informed,—recommended any forms of prayer to be used; it is scarcely possible that there should be any reasonable doubt as to what the practice was at that period.

In the course of time, and as the "Ministry of Orders" gradually superseded the "Ministry of Gifts," it might naturally be expected that without any marked or sudden change, and without any authoritative directions being given by the Apostles, some devotional utterances would by common use acquire certain definite forms of expression, conveniently employed on recurring occasions, and thus paving the way for more extensive changes in this direction, whenever the feeling or the circumstances of any Church should render them desirable. That this, in fact, did take place we are justified in concluding; and allusions to such familiar formulas are found here and there in the later portions of the New Testament, such as, "Hold fast the form of sound words" (2 Tim. i. 13); and, "The answer of a good conscience towards God" (1 Pet. iii. 21).[1]

Besides this in the administration of Baptism, and of the Lord's Supper, the words of Jesus were probably used from the first without variation, whatever religious service might be added to them. And the prayers made "for kings and all in authority," with others of a

[1] The expression in 2 Tim. i. 13, ὑποτύπωσιν ἔχε ὑγιαινόντων λόγων, cannot mean, on any sound principles of translation, "hold fast the form of sound words;" but among many explanations which have been suggested, it may possibly mean, "Have (or keep) an exemplar or formulary of sound words," for the instruction and guidance of Christians. In 1 Pet. iii. 21, συνειδήσεως ἀγαθῆς ἐπερώτημα may mean, as Alford gives it, "the enquiry of a good conscience;" but it is not impossible that those interpreters may be right who suppose that it means "the questions [with their answers] asked in Baptism," which, perhaps, even in the apostolic age were expressed in a well-known form of words.

similar kind, might naturally from their frequent use soon fall into a settled form of words; as would also be the case with short ejaculatory expressions and answers between the minister and the people, designed to keep alive a spirit of devotion; such as *Sursum corda*, "Lift up your hearts!" and *Habemus ad Dominum*, "We lift them up unto the Lord." But all this is very far from being a proof of the existence of precomposed liturgies; though it may be deemed a certain advance towards, and preparation for, their introduction. And thus all the evidence directly deducible from the New Testament is against the use of such formularies in the apostolic age.

Nor throughout the second century is any reliable testimony to be found indicative of any considerable alteration in this respect. On the contrary, the prayers of the Church, described by Justin Martyr, seem to have depended upon the ability and discretion[1] of the officiat-

[1] In his account of Christian worship, Justin Martyr relates that the officiating minister *εὐχὰς καὶ εὐχαριστίας, ὅση δύναμις αὐτῷ, ἀναπέμπει*, which words have very naturally been considered a proof that "liturgies, or set forms of prayer" were not then used, since the minister here is said to send up his prayers to the utmost of his ability. But this is controverted by those who are desirous to represent liturgies as of more ancient date. Thus Bingham affirms, "Some misconstrue this passage, and interpret the abilities of the minister officiating, as if they meant no more but his invention, expression, or the like;..... whereas, indeed, it signifies here quite a different thing, viz. that spiritual vigour, or intenseness and ardency of devotion with which the minister offered up the sacrifices of the Church of God."—Bing. vi. 3, 5.

But the fact is that *ὅση δύναμις* and other kindred expressions, such as *κατὰ δύναμιν, ὡς δύναται, ἐφ' ὅσον ἦν ἐν δυνατῷ*, are so common that there cannot be the least doubt as to their real meaning. They can signify nothing else but,

ing minister, as much as they did in the preceding century. And none of the passages sometimes cited from other patristic authors of this period are at all at variance with Justin's account.[1]

"as well as one can," or, "to the best of one's ability;" and the particular nature of the ability must depend upon the context with which the expression is joined in any given case. And as there is nothing else in Justin's words to indicate a set form of prayer, *ὅση δύναμις* cannot, in fairness, be taken to mean anything else than that the minister prayed in the best manner that he could.

The words *ὅση δύναμις* occur in two other places in Justin's 'Apology,' § 16, and § 72; and Lord King, in his 'Enquiry into the Constitution, &c. of the Primitive Church,' has collected a large number of examples from Origen and others; remarking, "I have not found one place wherein this phrase, *ὅση δύναμις*, doth not comprehend personal abilities."

Bingham, returning to the subject in Book xiii. 5, 5, repeats his assertion that *ὅση δύναμις* "relates to the ardency and intenseness of devotion," and adds, "And *so it is plain* the very same phrase is used by Nazianzen when he exhorts Christians to sing *ὅση δύναμις* 'with all their might' that triumphant hymn (upon the death of Julian) which the children of Israel sang when the Egyptians were drowned in the Red Sea." The passage in Nazianzen is, *φέρε, ὅση δύναμις ἁγνισάμενοι καὶ σώματα καὶ ψυχὰς, καὶ μίαν ἀναλαβόντες φωνὴν, ἑνὶ συναρμοσθέντες πνεύματι ᾄδωμεν*, &c., Greg. Naz. 'Orat.' iii., where, however, it is by no means *plain* that *ὅση δύναμις* is so used as the learned Antiquarian asserts; on the contrary, it most naturally connects itself with *ἁγνισάμενοι*, and the immediately following words, and means here, just as in other places, nothing else than "to the best of our ability."

It may be further remarked that, in the 'Constitutiones Apostolicæ,' where frequent exhortations to "ardency and intenseness of devotion" are found, the words employed for this purpose are not *ὅση δύναμις*, but such as *ἐκτενῶς*, or *συντόνως*.

[1] The following are all the evidences about liturgical forms in the second century which the diligence of the learned has been able to collect.

1. Pliny's celebrated letter to Trajan (x. 97), in which he relates that Christians were accustomed to meet, and "carmen Christo quasi Deo dicere secum invicem." The word "carmen," it is true, may mean any "formulary;" but "carmen dicere invicem," much more

It is not until the third century that any evidence, at all clear and conclusive, of the use of settled forms of

---

naturally means "singing" than "praying."

2. Ignatius is reported by Socrates, the ecclesiastical historian, to have introduced the practice of *alternate singing* into his Church at Antioch. But, besides that this is second-hand testimony, it mentions only "singing," which is nothing to the purpose.

3. Lucian, the pagan satirist, describing his coming into a religious assembly, says, "He heard there that prayer which began with the Father and ended with the hymn of many names!" Surely there is not much evidence to be extracted from this!

4. Justin Martyr, as already noticed before, says that Christians met together, κοινὰς εὐχὰς ποιησόμενοι, &c.; but it is acknowledged on all hands that this expression proves nothing in behalf of liturgies. Justin's words about the prayer of the officiating minister have been considered in the preceding note.

5. Irenæus shows that in his time the words "for ever and ever," εἰς αἰῶνας τῶν αἰώνων, were used in Christian worship—a very minute contribution towards a liturgy; especially as the words occur frequently in the New Testament, and might as well be employed in extemporaneous prayer, as in one previously composed.

6. Tertullian relates that psalms were sung in Christian worship; and he mentions the things which Christians prayed for, such as the peace and welfare of the emperor, &c., but he does not say that such prayers were expressed in a set form of words. On the contrary, the following passages, in which he refers to such prayers, shows that they were *not* in any prescribed form: "Illuc suspicientes Christiani manibus expansis, quia innocuis, capite nudo, quia non erubescimus; denique *sine monitore quia de pectore oramus*, precantus sumus semper pro omnibus Imperatoribus."—Tert. 'Apol.' § 33. Whatever part of the Christian service this may refer to, *sine monitore quia de pectore oramus*, must mean extemporaneous prayer.

7. Clement of Alexandria, according to Bingham, says, "that the congregation prostrated themselves in prayers, having, as it were, one common voice." The words of Clement are, ἐστὶ γοῦν τὸ παρ' ἡμῖν θυσιαστήριον ἐνταῦθα τὸ ἐπίγειον, τὸ ἄθροισμα τῶν ταῖς εὐχαῖς ἀνακειμένων, μίαν ὥσπερ ἔχον φωνὴν τὴν κοινὴν, καὶ μίαν γνώμην.—'Stromat.' vii. 6. And contrasting the Christian worship with the sacrifices and religious services of heathens to their gods, he says, "Our altar here on earth is the assembly of those who are offered up to God in prayers, having, as it

prayer in Christian Churches, is to be found in contemporary authorities. And even in that century, although the evidence *is* conclusive as far as it goes, it does not make it certain that other prayers suggested by particular circumstances or occasions were altogether excluded.

In the fourth century several distinct liturgies are found clearly established in different Churches, and, having been then committed to writing, some of the most celebrated of them are still preserved.

This, therefore, very briefly expressed, is the sum and substance of the contemporary patristic testimony; and it points us conclusively to the third and fourth centuries, and not to the apostolic age, for the distinct appearance and growth to maturity of formal liturgies in Christian Churches.

Another distinct consideration in the liturgical question, which confirms the conclusion just arrived at, is presented by the fact that no rules or forms were ever in the first centuries imposed upon a Church by any authority *from without.* The Apostles, as we have seen, left no commands on this subject; and after them nothing interfered with this general independence for three or four centuries at least. Every Church at the

were, one voice, their common utterance, and being of one mind." On which it is sufficient to observe that the *φωνὴν τὴν κοινὴν* cannot mean anything more liturgical than the *κοιναὶ εὐχαὶ* of Justin, which did not mean a precomposed form, but only that all were praying together.

Besides, the two last-mentioned authorities, Tertullian and Clement, belong to the third century rather than the second.

beginning arranged the details of its own public services according to its own discretion; and when the Episcopal form of government had been established, it was left to the prudence, choice, and judgment of each bishop to decide what words and ceremonies he would use in the devotions of his Church; and each one varied his petitions according to the existing circumstances and emergencies of his place and people. During this time prayers, originally extemporaneous or composed by individual bishops, were from their beauty or suitableness repeatedly used, and grew into a settled form, without being committed to writing, or having any authority beyond their own Church. And sometimes, in the third century, the liturgical arrangements made by some distinguished bishop were regarded with much veneration and continued long in use. Thus it is mentioned by Basil that the prayers and devotional rites of the Church at Neo-Cæsarea, which had been arranged for them by their Bishop Gregory (Thaumaturgus) in the middle of the third century, were still, a hundred years after his decease, scrupulously retained by them without any addition.[1]

At a later period "bishops agreed by common consent to conform their liturgies to the model of the metropolitan Churches of the province to which they belonged,"

---

[1] Basil, in his panegyric on Gregory of Neo-Cæsarea, says that the Church there had not chosen to add a single action, or word, or mystic symbol, to what he had left them, *οὐ πρᾶξίν τινα, οὐ λόγον, οὐ τύπον τινὰ μυστικὸν παρ' ὃν ἐκεῖνος κατέλιπε τῇ ἐκκλησίᾳ προσέθηκαν*.—'De Spirit. Sanct.' § 29.

the first intimation of which is given in the Council of Epone (A. D. 517).[1] And when the Roman empire was broken up into different nations, then national Churches and national liturgies began together; although even then different liturgical forms were sometimes used together in the same national Church, as was the case in our own country at the time of the Reformation.

A third source of argument in the questions about the worship of the primitive Church is found in the ancient liturgies themselves. Some of these which are in existence still, and from which many parts of our own formularies are derived, have the names of Apostles attached to them; and have naturally attracted much attention from their acknowledged antiquity, willingly supposed in many quarters to be greater than it really is.

In the Church of Rome some of these liturgies have been accepted as the genuine offspring of the Apostles, to whom they were popularly ascribed. And one of the latest of the learned Anglican writers on this subject, while he does not venture to claim for the most ancient liturgy an earlier date than the end of the second century, boldly assumes that "though not composed by the Apostles whose names they bear, they were the legitimate development of their unwritten tradition respecting the Christian sacrifice; the words probably in the most important parts, the general tenor in all portions de-

[1] The Council of Epone (A. D. 517) directs, "ad celebranda divina officia ordinem quem Metropolitani tenent provinciales eorum observare debebunt."—Can. 27.

scending unchanged from the apostolic authors."[1] But seeing that the Apostles left no *written* tradition whatever respecting "the Christian sacrifice," but what is altogether at variance with the teaching of these liturgies; and seeing that, in the entire absence of all contemporary testimony, it is utterly impossible to know what was their *unwritten* tradition, if any such ever existed; this claim of apostolic authority is nothing but a gratuitous, unsupported assumption of Dr. Neale's; and is only one of the numerous instances of the tendency of ecclesiastical writers in all ages to take for granted that whatever they approve of in the Church at any given time must have come from apostolic hands.

For it is acknowledged that these ancient liturgies as we have them now were gradually formed, and grew

---

[1] Neale's "History of the Holy Eastern Church," p. 319. A good specimen of the untrustworthy nature of the most confident assertions of learned men, when their minds are strongly biased in a particular direction, is seen in the manner in which Cardinal Bona speaks of these ancient liturgies.

He acknowledges, indeed, that the 'Liturgy of Peter' is not really his; and that the liturgies of Matthew and Mark are doubtful. But he declares that the 'liturgy of James' is proved to be the genuine production of the Apostle by Allatius, who "prolatis antiquorum testimoniis genuinum Jacobi fœtum esse demonstrat." But on turning to Allatius, all his "demonstrations" are found to be nothing earlier than a quotation from Proclus, a patriarch of Constantinople in the fifth century, and a reference to the Council of Trullo at the end of the seventh. Bona's own proofs are only such insufficient testimony, as (1) "perpetua Ecclesiæ Græcæ traditio;" (2) "exemplaria in vetustissimis codicibus exarata," with no date mentioned; (3) quotations from it by ancient Fathers, but no date or instance given; and (4) the Council of Trullo, A. D. 692.

up by slow degrees and various changes from the apostolic age to the middle of the fourth century; of which a singular proof (among others) is supplied by the remarks of Basil about the liturgy of the Church at Neo-Cæsarea, which, he says, was in many respects deficient and old-fashioned; because from reverence to the memory of their Bishop Gregory (Thaumaturgus) they had admitted no alterations since his time, and had not received any rites, prayers, or practices which had subsequently been introduced.[1] It was not until the middle of the fourth century that the earliest of these liturgies were committed to writing, necessarily in the form which they had then acquired.[2] And it is admitted that "the later additions are so interwoven with the older parts that they cannot be separated without destroying the liturgies altogether." From whence it follows that there can be no solid ground for asserting that any particular parts of them are even as old as the second century; much less the very words of the Apostles themselves, unless some external evidence can sufficiently attest their date. But all the external

[1] Basil, 'De Spiritu Sancto,' § 29: *Ταύτῃ τοι καὶ πολλὰ τῶν παρ' αὐτοῖς τελουμένων ἐλλειπῶς ἔχειν δοκεῖ, διὰ τὸ τῆς κατασ-τάσεως ἀρχαιότροπον· οὐδὲν γὰρ ἠνέσχοντο οἱ κατα διαδοχὴν τὰς ἐκκλησίας οἰκονομήσαντες τῶν μετ' ἐκεῖνον ἐφευρεθέντων παραδέξασθαι εἰς προσθήκην.*—See Note, p. 224.

[2] In the persecutions under Diocletian and his associates, a strict enquiry was made after the sacred books belonging to Christian Churches; but, although copies of the Scriptures were often discovered, books of ritual or of divine service appear never to have been found. As far as liturgies existed, they were not written until after that time.

evidence in this case proves that those parts, which Dr. Neale wishes to be the most ancient, cannot be earlier than the third century.[1]

---

[1] The object of Dr. Neale in his 'Tetralogia Liturgica' is, to establish the apostolic authority of the three doctrines of "the real presence," *i. e.* the actual objective change of the Eucharistic elements into the body and blood of Christ; a true and beneficial sacrifice offered to God in the Eucharist; and the duty and advantage of praying for the dead—or, in his own words, "oblationem mysticam vere et realiter in corpus et sanguinem Domini nostri transmutari; in Eucharistia verum et salutare sacrificium Deo offerri; preces pro defunctorum requie perutiles iis esse." And his method of proof—perfectly logical in *form*—is as follows:

As the ancient liturgies are of apostolic antiquity and authority, the doctrines contained in them are apostolic;

The three doctrines above-named are contained in the ancient liturgies; therefore—

The three doctrines above-named are apostolic.

Now, Dr. Neale most clearly shows that these doctrines are indisputably, and without any disguise, taught in the ancient liturgies; but he utterly fails to prove the apostolic antiquity and authority of the liturgies which teach them. The whole truth of the matter is, that these ancient liturgies, as they are, belong to the fourth century, and contain the doctrines which in that century prevailed.

The evidence of the New Testament, and of subsequent Christian writers down to the end of the second century, shows that the three doctrines in question had not at that time appeared, and proves that those parts of the liturgies which express them cannot be earlier than the third century.

Dr. Neale, in his 'Essays on Liturgiology,' endeavours to show that a considerable number of expressions in the Epistles of the New Testament are quotations from ancient liturgies—a very interesting subject of enquiry—and if this theory could have been established, it would have made it evident that *some* portions, at any rate, of these formularies were of the very earliest antiquity. But the enquiry does not issue in a proof. The quotation from a hymn in Eph. iv. 14, has been already noticed; and that hymns were sung in churches from the beginning is admitted on all hands. But of all the allegod quotations from prayers, only one instance has anything like an approach to satisfactory evidence in its favour, namely, *ἃ ὀφθαλμος οὐκ εἶδε* &c. in 1 Cor. ii. 9, which is found in the 'Anaphora of St. James.'

The evidence in this instance, to

These ancient documents, therefore, do not at all invalidate the conclusion derived from other testimony, that liturgical forms were at any rate not used until after the apostolic times.

But independently of such questions there is a very instructive lesson for us to learn from the liturgical history of the early centuries. For when liturgies had been compiled and were habitually used, they were not regarded as forms so fixed and rigid, that they were not afterwards to be revised or altered; or so sacred, that they could not be touched without irreverence and danger. The exceptional conduct of the Church at Neo-Cæsarea in this respect was an amiable weakness, which might be to a certain extent excused, but was not thought worthy of imitation. On the contrary the liturgies were continually receiving alterations, as times were changed, and new wants or thoughts arose: men being then wise enough to see that the liturgy was made for the Church, and not the Church for the

the effect that the words are quoted from the liturgy, and not *vice versâ*, amounts to this: St. Paul gives the words as a quotation, "As it is written;" but they are *not* found exactly in this form in the Old Testament, while they *are* in the liturgy. And, secondly, the words in the Epistle are an abbreviated sentence, requiring something to be supplied; but, in the liturgy, the sentence is complete.

But then, on the other hand, it is to be noticed, that St. Paul says that the words which he quotes "are *written*"—γέγραπται—which the liturgies at that time were not; that quotations from the Old Testament in the New are sometimes given without much regard to verbal accuracy; and, what is a stronger objection, no one of the patristic commentators on this text—Origen, Chrysostom, and Jerome—knew anything of its being a quotation from a liturgy, which they could hardly have failed to know, if such had been the case.

liturgy. So that it was deemed no disrespect to the memory of venerable names or cherished traditions to adapt their Prayer-book to the new manners or feelings of another age; nor any injury to a living Church, that there should also be life, and consequently change, in the forms of its habitual devotions. So entirely, indeed, in the early centuries were liturgical forms regarded as subordinate to the actual circumstances of any Christian community, that when a district was divided and a new bishoprick erected in what had been a portion of the older diocese, "the new Church was not obliged to follow the model and prescriptions of the old, but might frame to herself a form of divine service agreeable to her own circumstances and condition."

Are we more wise in this our day, when we have allowed more than two hundred years to pass,—years of immense changes in everything connected with the life of man; changes ecclesiastical, political, social, intellectual, and moral,—with scarcely an infinitesimal change in our Church Liturgy and laws? And when notwithstanding the fact that the last revision of our Prayer-book was effected under circumstances the most hostile to a sound and sober appreciation of truth and wisdom, good men are now possessed with so superstitious a veneration, or so unreasonable a timidity, that they cry out against the bare proposal of a liturgical revision, and the most temperate ecclesiastical reform?

The ancient Churches made their liturgies so flexible and impressible that they altered their ritual to suit errors in doctrine and practice, into which they fell; while we shrink from any alteration, even that with the New Testament in our hands we may make our religious services as far as possible conformable to the divine record of Christian truth. And with a singular contrariety to the spirit of antiquity which we profess to venerate, we press our Anglican Prayer-book and formularies upon all the Churches which missionary labours have gathered in foreign lands, without any sufficient consideration of the most widely different habits, climes, and races; just as if the Church of the English Reformation were the absolute and essential model of Christian perfection,—the one only visible body of Christ to which all Christians must belong.

III. The "times and seasons" observed as sacred in the apostolic Church will next demand a brief notice, to complete our view of its religious worship. And here it must be at once acknowledged that there is in the New Testament no trace whatever of any one of those annual days of hallowed commemoration which are now celebrated in Christian Churches.

However seemly, grateful, and edifying we may justly esteem it to mark the anniversaries of our Lord's birth, death, and resurrection, with other days of special import in the Christian year, they were not distinguished in the ecclesiastical arrangements of the primitive Church, but are of a later and unapostolic origin.

But the observance of the first day of the week, or

"Lord's Day," stands upon a different footing, and plainly belongs to the New Testament period; although no commandment is repeated there for its religious celebration, or much notice taken of its recurrence.

In the earliest existence of the Christian Church, when a holy enthusiasm was strong in all its members, and their whole life was felt to be consecrated and elevated in Christ, all distinction of secular and sacred seasons seemed out of place; every day was a day of united worship; every day was holy to the Lord. This, indeed, was always, and is still, an abiding principle of the Gospel life, that all our standing-ground of acceptance, safety, and privilege being complete in Christ, and our whole selves, our souls and bodies, being presented as a living sacrifice to Him, no outward ordinances are essential to this completeness, no observance of special days can be an adequate substitute for this self-surrender. But as a high state of spiritual elevation cannot in ordinary cases be long sustained; and man's complex nature needs some external ordinances, as well as a power within; and as, moreover, a large number of Christians must then, as now, have been unable to attend a daily religious assembly; the observance of certain recurring days was needful for general edification. A sacred day became a religious necessity for the Christian Church; and it is from this point that we have to view the question of the obligation of the Fourth Commandment.

The *Jewish* Sabbath was indeed of no obligation in the Gospel Church; and by Gentile Christians it was better avoided as a remnant of a discarded dispensation. But the Fourth Commandment is not Judaistic in its essential character, but, like all the rest of the decalogue, has in its very wording a broad application to human life. And in conformity with it, a Christian day of rest and of religious worship, equally with the Jewish Sabbath the *seventh day after six* according to the exact wording of the Law,[1] was established in the Church, as soon apparently as the peculiar circumstances of the case would admit of its general introduction.

In modern discussions on the nature and obligation of the Christian Sabbath, great weight has not unreasonably been attached to the manner in which St. Paul warns Gentile Christians against the observance of Jewish days (specially in Rom. xiv. 5, Gal. iv. 10, Col. ii. 15), without a single word about any Christian day more hallowed or sacred than the rest.[2] But a consideration

---

[1] In considering the Sabbath question it must not be forgotten that neither in the Fourth Commandment nor anywhere else in the Mosaic law is the seventh day *of the week* ordered to be kept. It is always the seventh day *after six;* and, consequently the observance of the first day of the week is just as conformable to this law, in the letter and the spirit, as the Jewish Sabbath day; nor was any divine authority required for changing the day in the Christian Church.

[2] The following valuable remarks from Dr. Eadie's 'Commentary on Galatians' show that there is something to be said in reply to the repudiators of a "Christian Sabbath," even on their own ground, and without going beyond the texts upon which they especially rely.

Such considerations greatly strengthen the conclusion which I have endeavoured to deduce from an historical view of the question.

"Gal. iv. 10, 'Ye observe days and months,' &c. Dean Alford adds, 'Notice how utterly such a verse is at variance with any and every theory of a Christian Sabbath, cutting at the root, as it does, of *all obligatory observation of times as such.*' ["But,"

of the history of Sabbath observances during the period of transition between Judaism and Christianity seems to show that this argument is not so conclusive as it might at first appear.

When the Israelites were brought out from Egypt, they passed through their transition state in the wilderness, separated from all other people, while they received their Law, and became accustomed to its most essential enactments. But Christianity had to spring up and develop its religious and moral system in the presence of older religions still in force, and coming in contact with it at every turn. In particular it had to work its way in the midst of Judaism, which was not brought abruptly to an end to make room for it, but continued

"But," says Dr. Eadie, "this generalization is far too sweeping; for—

"1. It makes assertion on a subject which is not before the mind of the Apostle at all. Nothing is further from his thoughts, or his course of rebuke and expostulation, than the Christian Sabbath and its theme—the resurrection of Christ.

"2. The Apostle is not condemning the obligatory observances 'of times as such;' but he is condemning the observance only of the times, which the Galatians, in their relapse into Judaism, kept as sacred; for their keeping of such Jewish festivals was the proof and result of their partial apostacy.

"3. Nor is it even Jewish festivals as such which he condemns; for both before and after this period he observed some of them himself. But, first he condemns the Galatian Gentiles for observing sacred Jewish seasons which, not being intended for them, had therefore no authority over them. The Gentile keeping of Jewish Sabbaths, or of Passovers, Pentecosts, New Moons, or Júbilees, was in itself a wrong thing —a perilous blunder then, as it would be a wretched anachronism now. And, secondly, he condemns the observance of these 'times,' because the Galatians regarded such observance as essential to salvation, and as supplementing faith in the atoning work of Christ. These limitations are plainly supplied by the context, and the true theory of a Christian Sabbath, or rather Lord's Day, is not in the least involved in the discussion."

for a time to overlap the new dispensation; and thus some peculiar and apparently anomalous results were produced which must necessarily be taken into consideration.

Hence it was that at the beginning of the Gospel the Jewish Christians continued to keep their original Sabbath, and therefore no other day of rest was ordered for them; yet immediately after the resurrection of Christ, the first day of the week was observed by His disciples as a day of special and religious interest (John xx. 19, 26).

When Gentile Christians were gathered into the Church, they were, of course, not commanded to keep the Jewish Sabbath. They were rather discouraged from doing so, lest they should make to themselves a mixed and mongrel religion of Judaism and Christianity, as some Gentile Churches in fact began to do. The great object in dealing with *them* was to raise their minds to the purity of the Christian faith out of the carnal, sensuous, formal religionism, which they saw in their own heathen rites, and in Judaism as then popularly held. Yet the first day of the week was kept by Gentile Churches; and it is to its observance among *them* that reference is made in the New Testament (Acts xx. 7; 1 Cor. xvi. 2).

If it be thought strange that no more than this is recorded, let it be remembered that before the Jewish polity was entirely broken up by the destruction of Jerusalem, it must have been impossible without some violent disruption to effect a complete change from the Jewish to the Christian day. But the Gospel in this, as in some other parts of Christian duty, was to work by slow but effectual influences, rather than by precise commands; to establish principles rather than enforce precepts. And while Christians were a small and feeble body in the midst of heathen populations, the hindrances to the observance of any Sabbath at all must have been so great, that the rule, "I will have mercy and not sacrifice," must have had a very wide application to their case. For a Sabbath in accordance with the Fourth Commandment is necessarily a *social* institution, and could not well have a place except in a religion which had to some considerable extent penetrated and coloured the general life of a community. It could not, therefore, have appeared at once as an ordinance in Gentile Churches, even had there been nothing else to hinder its observance.

With the downfall of the Jewish nation a new and distinct era in the Church began. Christianity became formally and fully, "the kingdom of God,"—"the vineyard of the Lord's planting;" and the Christian Sabbath relieved (so to speak) from the rivalry of the Jewish day, gained a more decided position in the piety and morals of the Church. To distinguish it from the Jewish day, and at the same time to commemorate our Lord's resurrection, the first day of the week was permanently adopted; and the manner in which St. John terms it "The Lord's Day," without a word of explanation or remark, seems to indicate that before the end of the apostolic age it had become a well-known and acknowledged institution in the Church.

In the second century distinct proofs of the observance of this day are found; and by the end of that period (and we know not how long before), to abstain from all but necessary work on the Lord's day was considered a religious duty.[1]

In the reign of Constantine Sunday was recognized by law as a sacred day, and all public business was ordered to be suspended.

The celebration of the Christian Sunday was specially marked from the very first by assemblies for divine

---

[1] In Pliny's celebrated epistle to Trajan [Ep. x. 96] he reports that the Christians were "soliti *stato die* ante lucem convenire, carmenque Christo quasi deo dicere secum invicem," without, however, naming the day.

In the Epistle of Barnabas [A. D. 120–140] it is said, *Διὸ καὶ ἄγομεν τὴν ἡμέραν τὴν ὀγδόην εἰς εὐφροσύνην ἐν ᾗ καὶ ὁ Ἰησοῦς ἀνέστη ἐκ νεκρῶν.*—§ 15.

Justin Martyr mentions *τὴν δὲ ἡλίου ἡμέραν κοινῇ πάντες τὴν συνέλευσιν ποιούμεθα, ἐπειδὰν πρώτη ἐστὶν ἡμέρα, ἐν ᾗ ὁ Θεὸς τὸ σκότος καὶ τὴν ὕλην τρέψας κόσμον ἐποίησε, καὶ Ἰησοῦς Χριστὸς ὁ ἡμέτερος σωτὴρ τῇ αὐτῇ ἡμέρᾳ ἐκ νεκρῶν ἀνέστη.*—'Apol,' i. 67. And again, *τῇ τοῦ ἡλίου λεγομένῃ ἡμέρᾳ πάντων κατὰ πόλεις ἢ ἀγροὺς μενόντων ἐπὶ τὸ αὐτὸ συνέλευσις γίγνεται.*—§ 87.

Irenæus says, *τὸ δὲ ἐν κυριακῇ μὴ κλίνειν γόνυ σύμβολόν ἐστι τῆς ἀναστάσεως.*—'Fragm. de Pasch.'

Tertullian not only mentions the observance of the Lord's day, but shows that it was kept as a Sabbath, or day of rest. "Die dominico resurrectionis non ab isto tantum (genu flectendo) sed omni anxietatis habitu et officio cavere debemus, differentes etiam negotia ne quem diabolo locum demus."—'De Orat.' 23.

After Tertullian's time the observance of Sunday by Christians is plain and distinct.

worship and religious instruction; and the notices of it, which we meet with beyond the limits of the New Testament, show that it was considered a day of joy, all fasting being then strictly prohibited.[1] A Jewish rigour in observing the Christian Sabbath was discouraged in the early Church.

Some lingering influences of the Jewish Sabbath continued to be felt even in the fourth century in the Eastern Church, where Saturday was regarded as a religious festival in commemoration of the creation of the world, as Sunday commemorated the resurrection of Christ. But in the West, the Saturday festival was altogether repudiated as an undesirable remnant of Judaism.

---

1 "Die dominico jejunium nefas ducimus, vel de geniculis adorare." —Tert. 'De Coron. Milit.' § 3.

Τὸ σάββατον μέντοι καὶ τὴν κυριακὴν ἑορτάζετε, ὅτι τὸ μὲν δημιουργίας ἐστὶν ὑπόμνημα, ἡ δὲ ἀναστάσεως. —'Constit. Apost.' vii. 23.

LECTURE VI.

CHRISTIAN BAPTISM.

VI.

CHRISTIAN BAPTISM.

THE religion of Jesus Christ is emphatically a dispensation of the Spirit. His kingdom is a spiritual kingdom. His Church in the truest sense—"the Church which is His body, the fulness of Him that filleth all in all"—consists of those who are united to Him by no mere outward forms or symbols of profession, but by a living faith within, by the power of the Divine Spirit raising them to the higher life of God's children, and to the position of citizens of heaven.

And even the visible Christian Church, as the outward form and exhibition of this spiritual kingdom, so far as it can be seen, in the world, partakes of this spiritual character; not only in that its genuine power and influence operate from within, and give a manifestation and organism to the Spirit's invisible presence, but also in the characteristic absence of divinely appointed rites and ceremonies, which distinguishes the Christian Church from the earlier dispensation out of which it grew.

It has been already noticed how striking is the contrast between the manner in which the Apostles acted as the legislators of the Christian Church, and the method adopted by Moses in his legislation for the people of Israel. And it may now be further observed that all the ceremonial and ritual laws of the Jews, including their priesthood, sacrifices, and purifications, having been fulfilled and realized in the life, death, and intercession of Christ, no religious rites whatever were substituted in their place. And no visible, tangible, ordinances at all of divine appointment are to be found in the Christian Church, except the two simple institutions bequeathed by Jesus to His disciples in all future time, which are now called the Christian Sacraments.

Simple and unobtrusive as these two sacred ordinances appear in their original institution, they would under any circumstances have demanded a marked and reverent attention from their exclusive dignity as the appointments of our Lord. But the manner in which they have been dealt with by different generations in the Church, beginning with very early, although not the earliest, times,—the errors and superstitions, which have been reared upon them, not wholly demolished and dissipated even in reformed Churches,—the great influence for good or evil which sound or unsound dogmatic teaching respecting them, and a consequent healthy or unhealthy use of them, has had on Christian communities and their several members,—and the peculiar tenacity with which false opinions of this nature seem to adhere to the minds of Christian men,—have imparted a sad and painful interest to the history of the two sacraments. And it is therefore all the more necessary to consider them with a careful and grave attention in a review of the Ecclesiastical Polity of the apostolic Church;—all the more necessary to go boldly to the New Testament; to the practice and authority of the Apostles; and with a devout but determined spirit to enquire from them what the sacraments of Christ really are to us; and to bid all inferior teachings and authorities give way before their instructions as mists before the mid-day sun.

The two sacraments are both alike in this, that they are outward signs of an inward state;—material symbols of spiritual operations;—visible means of representing the invisible blessings which result from union with Christ, and are bestowed by Him, as the head, upon His true disciples as members of His body. And in the intelligent and believing use of these outward signs, presented to the senses, the inward spiritual man has these invisible blessings assured and imparted to him. They serve, therefore, to indicate and seal to our consciences the promises of saving grace in Christ, and also to testify on our part our faith and dutiful obedience towards God.[1] Or, in the words of our twenty-fifth Article, they are

[1] Fr. Turretinus, professor of theology at Geneva in 1688, whose works deserve to be less forgotten than they are in these days, gives the following wholesome definition of the Christian sacraments, which he says are, "Signa et sigilia sacra visibilia divinitus instituta ad significandas et obsignandas conscientiis nostris promissiones gratiæ salutaris in Christo, et nostram vicissim fidem, et pietatem ac obsequium erga Deum contestandam."—Loc. xix. Qu. 1, 9.

"sure witnesses and effectual signs of grace and God's good will towards us, by the which He doth work invisibly in us, and doth not only quicken, but also strengthen and confirm our faith in Him. . . . . And in such only as worthily receive the same they have a wholesome effect or operation:"

But as with this general resemblance each one of these sacred ordinances has its own special character and distinctive meaning, they require to be noticed separately. And the nature and use of baptism, as it is seen in the Church of the Apostles, may be first considered.

The earliest distinct mention of Christian baptism is found in the commission given by our Lord to His Apostles, when not long before His Ascension he bade them "Go and make disciples of all nations, baptizing them in the name of the Father, and of the Son, and of the Holy Spirit, teaching them to observe all things, whatsoever I have commanded you." The words, indeed, which were spoken by Jesus in His conversation with Nicodemus in a much earlier part of His ministry, have been commonly supposed to refer to Christian baptism, when he said, "Except a man be born of water, and of the Spirit;" but such reference is by no means certain. The words probably allude to water as a common emblem of the Divine Spirit's operation in purifying the heart from sin; like the expression in the fifty-first Psalm: "Wash me, and I shall be whiter than snow;" and the emblematical washing of the Apostles' feet by Jesus at the last supper; and just as the somewhat similar form of words, "He shall baptize you with the Holy Ghost and with fire," refers to the common effects of that element as an illustration of the subduing, softening, kindling influences of the Spirit upon the naturally hardened heart of man.

The baptism of John, as the harbinger of Christ, was not Christian baptism, although some of those who had only been baptized by him seem many years afterwards to have ranked as Christians.

And even the baptism of some of the professed disciples of Jesus during His ministry on earth, and apparently under His immediate direction, could not have been a baptism of the same type and significance as that which the Apostles administered after His Ascension. Christian baptism, in the full meaning of the words, could not take place until the Apostles began to gather believers into the visible Church of Christ, and *that,* as before shown, was not and could not be done until Jesus had finished His work on earth, and the Divine Comforter had been given in His stead.

The words in which our Lord gave His Apostles their commission to baptize, and which may be regarded as the institution of this sacrament, express with great brevity, but with equal distinctness, its position in the Christian system. And after noticing this, a fuller explanation of the ordinance, in its administration, significance, efficacy, and special bearing on the Christian life, may be gathered from the manner in which it seems to have been used in the ministrations of the Apostles and early Evangelizers, and from the references which are made to it in the Epistolary portions of the New Testament.

It may be at once inferred from the words of the original institution that this sacrament was to be an initiatory rite in the Church.[1] It was to be administered to those who believed in the One God, the Father of all; who acknowledged Jesus as the Christ, the Son of God, the long-promised and now manifested Saviour; who accepted the doctrine that the Divine Spirit is the author of holiness in man, and would lead them to the knowledge and practice of the Christian life; and who with this amount of understanding and conviction were desirous to renounce the dominion and deeds of sin, to become obedient subjects of Christ's spiritual kingdom, and to join themselves to Him and to His Church. To such persons, their baptism was to be the sign and seal of their discipleship; and thus to be the formal evidence of their Christian profession,—their actual admission into the visible fellowship of the Church; —the symbol of their union with Christ and of their

---

[1] The force of Christ's commission in Matt. xxviii. 19 is somewhat obscured in our English version from the word μαθητεύσατε being translated "teach." It ought to be, "Go and *make-disciples-of* all the nations;" and then follows the mode or process by which such disciples were to be made; namely, first, "by baptizing them into the name of the Father, and of the Son, and of the Holy Spirit;" not, of course, without some intelligent apprehension of what the divine name, and the baptism into it, implied; and, secondly, by teaching those who had been baptized to observe all the commandments of Christ.

participation in the privileges which that union imparts. And having been thus admitted to this standing-ground in Christ, they were to make further progress in Christian knowledge and experience,—to be "taught to observe all things whatsoever He had commanded them."

And thus it was evident from the first that Christian baptism, though in its outward form one single act, represented no single, isolated, state or feeling,—but a spiritual transaction carried on in the spirit and conscience and then declaring itself externally,—a power and influence which, from the beginning, attested by the baptismal rite, was to go on to the end of the inward Christian life, and be diffused over the whole of it.

Accordingly, on examining the manner in which this sacrament was used, and the estimation in which it was held in the Church of the Apostles, we find in the accounts presented by the New Testament an ample confirmation of the foregoing general view, exhibited with a considerable variety of details and circumstances.

The Apostles in their preaching,—*i. e.*, in proclaiming Christ, as the heralds of His kingdom, and offering Him to the acceptance of men,—pressed home upon the consciences of their hearers the conviction of sin, a sense of moral and spiritual deficiency and need; holding out to them at the same time a confident assurance that God had sent a Saviour all-sufficient for the deliverance of man, by believing in whom their sins would be taken away; and that the sanctifying power of the Holy Spirit would be imparted to those by whom this Saviour was received. To the Jews they pointed out that "Jesus of Nazareth," whom many of them had known, whom some of them had persecuted and slain, was the very Christ of their ancient Scriptures,—the very desire and hope of their nation. To their Gentile hearers they appealed on the grounds of common sense, reason, experience, and natural conscience; and exhorted them to turn from their senseless and debasing idolatry to the one living God,—the God of nature and of revealed truth. But equally upon all they urged the necessity of a change of mind and thought respecting God and themselves, and of a new life of privilege and duty in Christ, "testifying both to the Jews and also to the Greeks repentance towards God, and faith towards our Lord Jesus Christ." And those who received their words, and voluntarily professed this repentance and faith, were baptizing in the divine name and received into Christian fellowship.

The New Testament records no office or religious service as having been used in the administration of baptism; nor any particular form of words for the Christian profession of those who were baptized. Although at least *nine* different instances of baptism are expressly related in the Acts of the Apostles, besides all the allusions in the Epistles, yet in none of them is the actual form or manner of the administration given. The historian seems to have been restrained from giving any such details, lest a superstitious use should afterwards be made of them. But although in the brevity of the narrative men are sometimes said to have been baptized "in the name of the Lord," or "in the name of the Lord Jesus," I can see in this no reason for supposing that the formula given by Jesus Himself in Matt. xxviii. 19, was ever omitted or abbreviated.[1]

The religious profession of those who were baptized seems to have been made at first in the simplest manner possible, and without any particular form of words. In the course of no long time, however, it would naturally come to pass, and would be found convenient, that there should be some acknowledged modes of expressing the requisite repentance and faith on the part of the baptized, though these modes might differ in different Churches. And it is not impossible that the "answer of a good conscience towards God," in 1 Pet. iii. 21, may show that the custom had already begun of asking the candidate for baptism certain questions, by his answers to which his profession was declared. At a later period the principal articles of the Christian faith received a definite expression under ecclesiastical authority, and were comprised in short and convenient summaries. Different Churches then had their respective creeds, expressing

[1] The notion that the formula of baptism in the name of the Father, Son, and Holy Spirit is not the oldest, but that there was a shorter form, more anciently employed, in the name of Christ alone, has been held by some modern authorities. [See Neander's 'Church History,' vol. i. p. 423; and 'Hist. of the Planting,' &c. vol. i. p. 222.] But this supposition appears to me to be destitute of all solid foundation. That such expressions as being baptized "in the name of the Lord Jesus" referred to no other formula than that in Matt. xxviii. is evident from the circumstances connected with those persons who had only received the "baptism of John," and, consequently, had not heard of the Holy Spirit. See Acts xix. 1–5.

the same truths in different words, until after the union of the Church with the Empire one acknowledged and authorized form was at length generally adopted.[1]

---

[1] As the Apostles authorized no summary of Christian doctrine, the creeds which afterwards appeared grew up by degrees, and additional articles were formularized according to the convenience and discretion of the Churches. Nothing, however, that can be called a creed appears in any author of the second century. In the third some traces or elements of creeds are seen; and Cyprian mentions (Ep. 76, ad Magnum), that Novatian professed to use the same creed as he himself did: *eodem symbolo, quo et nos, baptizare.* Creeds were then taught to catechumens in the form of questions and answers, which were used at their baptism; only one of these, however, is given by Cyprian: *Credis remissionem peccatorum, et vitam æternam, per sanctam ecclesiam.*

A creed, said to have been used by Gregory Thaumaturgus, Bishop of Neo-Cæsarea (A. D. 250), is the earliest recorded example of such a formula, if its date can be relied upon. It does not appear, however, until a hundred years later, when it is given by his biographer, Gregory Nyssen; who relates, in connection with it, a marvellous story, to the effect that Thaumaturgus was ordained, against his will, by Phædimus, Bishop of Amasæa, who *laid his words* upon him, *in his absence, instead of his hands, ἀντὶ χειρὸς ἐπάγει τῷ Γρηγορίῳ τὸν λόγον, ἀφιερώσας τῷ Θεῷ τὸν σωματικῶς οὐ παρόντα.* Gregory then considered himself ordained; but being at a loss to know what was the true Catholic faith, free from heretical errors, the Virgin Mary and the Apostle John appeared to him as he lay awake at night; when the Apostle, at her request, communicated to him this Creed, which he immediately wrote down and preserved.—Greg. Nyss. vol. iii. p. 546.

In the fourth century a number of different creeds are found, those of the eastern Churches nearly resembling the form of the Nicene Creed, while that of Rome, and other western Churches, was the same as our "Apostles' Creed;" the oldest form, however, omits the articles, "He descended into hell," and "the life everlasting," with some other words.

This Roman Creed not having been drawn up by any council, or having any precise date, gave occasion to legendary traditions respecting it. It was called the Apostles' Creed; then a tradition was invented that it had been composed by all the Apostles, who met together for that purpose: "Duodecim Apostolorum symbolo sancta fides concepta est, qui velut periti artifices in unum convenientes clavem suo consilio conflaverunt, clavem enim

Christian baptism being thus given upon a personal profession of repentance or renunciation of sin, of belief in Christ as the Saviour, and of a desire and determination to live the Christian life,—and being a solemn dedication of the baptized believer to God, as revealed in the person of Christ, and acting by His Spirit,—its obvious significance pointed out the free gift of Christian grace and blessing on the part of the Heavenly Father, and the full surrender of himself to the divine will and guidance on the part of the baptized. And, consequently, the fact that persons had been baptized is in the New Testament often referred to, both as indicating their privileged position, and as reminding them of their serious obligation to live in a manner not unworthy of it. All baptized persons are spoken of as true disciples of Christ, until the contrary is known to be the case. This, however, even in the New Testament Church, is only the judgment of charity,—the judgment of man. It does not appear that the earliest Evangelizers—not even the Apostles themselves, except on rare occasions—possessed any supernatural discernment of men's inner character, whereby they could infallibly distinguish a true from a false disciple, either before or after his baptism. They judged of converts as we must judge;

quandam ipsum symbolum dixerim, per quod reserantur diaboli tenebræ ut lux Christi adveniat."—Ambrose, vol. iii. Serm. 38. And then, further, it was divided into twelve articles, each one of which was ascribed to a particular Apostle, as his contribution to the Creed. "Petrus dixit, credo in Deum, patrem omnipotentem; Johannes dixit, creatorem cæli et terræ," &c. — Augustin, vol. x. 'Serm. de Temp.' 115.

at first by a credible profession, and afterwards by their life and conduct. Thus the three thousand on the day of Pentecost were admitted at once into the Church without any further probation, in reliance on the profession which they then made; and many other examples in the Acts of the Apostles testify to the same practice.[1] But when baptized and professing Christians proved themselves unworthy of their name, they were addressed in the plainest words of reproof or condemnation. They were told that "they had neither part nor lot in the matter;" they were denounced as "enemies of the cross of Christ;" and as those who were "drawing back into perdition."

[1] There is no trace in the apostolic age of the class of persons, afterwards called *Catechumens*, who were kept for a considerable time under Christian instruction and discipline before they were allowed to be baptized. Such a period of probation was less needed at the first, when the abundant effusion of the Spirit was at its height, and when the stigma which attached to the Christian name deterred unworthy and wavering professors. But, afterwards, when lower motives could easily prevail, and especially in times when persecution slept, or had lost its power, it might well be found expedient to test a convert's knowledge and sincerity before his admission into the Church.

Catechumens are first mentioned as a distinct class by Tertullian, who blames certain heretics for not clearly separating them from the "faithful," *i. e.* the baptized: "Quis *catechumenus*, quis fidelis, incertum est: pariter adeunt, pariter audiunt, pariter orant."—'De præscript." § 41. Tertullian also calls them "audientes."

In Origen's time the catechumens were divided into two classes, the *audientes* or ἀκροώμενοι, and the more advanced, or "catechumens proper," called also *genuflectentes*, as they were permitted to join in a portion of the prayers. Orig. 'C. Cels.' iii. § 51.

In the fourth century they were divided into *three*, or sometimes *four* classes, and were subjected to a course of discipline for *two* or *three* years—a discipline marked with a large amount of the mystery and superstition which abounded in the Church system of that century.

The *efficacy* of Christian baptism in the apostolic age, or the nature of the religious state and its consequent privileges into which the baptized were brought, may be fully learned from the various notices respecting it, which are scattered throughout the New Testament. Baptism is nowhere in the sacred record declared in express terms to be the Sacrament or sign of Regeneration;[1] yet there can be no reasonable doubt that such words as "the washing of regeneration" (Tit. iii. 5), imply this connection between baptism and the new spiritual life that is in Christ, as does also the assertion that "Christ loved the Church, and gave Himself for it, that He might sanctify it by cleansing it with the washing of the water by the word" (Eph. v. 26). Besides this, the same connection is clearly implied, though in a different form of words, in those passages which describe the baptized as thereby brought into union with Christ, the fountain and source of the new spiritual life; as we find in such texts as "Through faith ye are all the children of God in Christ Jesus; for as many of you as were baptized into Christ, put on Christ"[2] (Gal. iii. 27); and "buried with Him in your baptism, in which ye

[1] I do not give here the text, "Except a man be born of water and of the Spirit," because, as mentioned before, I do not think it at all certain that these words refer to baptism. Those who are convinced that they do will, of course, use them in that connection.

[2] The force of this, and some other verses of a similar kind, is partially lost in our English version from a mistranslation of the Greek tenses; *ὅσοι εἰς Χριστὸν ἐβαπτίσθητε, Χριστὸν ἐνεδύσασθε,* must mean, "as many of you as *were baptized* into Christ, *put on* Christ" at the time, and by the act, of your baptism.

were also raised up with Him, through your faith in the operation of God." (Col. ii. 12.) While in other passages particular blessings which follow from this union, and belong to the regenerate state, — such as the forgiveness of sins, the gift of the Holy Spirit, fellowship with the Church of Christ,—are spoken of as the direct results of the believer's baptism. Thus we read, "Repent and be baptized, every one of you, in the name of Jesus Christ, for the remission of sins, and ye shall receive the gift of the Holy Ghost" (Acts ii. 38); "Arise and be baptized, and wash away thy sins" (Acts xxii. 16); "By one Spirit we are all baptized into one body" (1 Cor. xii. 13). And we find the whole summed by St. Peter in one bold assertion, "That baptism doth save us." (1 Pet. iii. 21.)

And finally, even in what may be called the moral or practical application of the subject, in appeals to baptized persons to live the life of godliness, the same view of baptism is involved; as we see in St. Paul's forcible enquiry, "How shall we, who died to sin, live any longer therein? know ye not that so many of us as were baptized into Jesus Christ, were baptized into His death; that, like as Christ was raised from the dead by the glory of the Father, even so we also should walk in newness of life" (Rom. vi. 2).

If, therefore, those who repent and believe in Jesus are declared in Scripture to be by their baptism baptized into Christ, to put on Christ, to be buried and raised up with Him, to wash away their sins, to have the washing of regeneration, to receive the Holy Spirit, and to be saved, there is surely a sound and Scriptural sense in which we may speak of "Baptismal Regeneration," and call baptism the Sacrament of the New Birth in Christ.

But now having shown in what strong terms the New Testament speaks of Christian Baptism,—terms which some good men scarcely know how to receive as applicable to an ordinance of outward action and material elements,—it is necessary, in the cause of truth and for a right understanding of the subject, to consider under what circumstances, and with what qualifications, if any, such words were used. It is necessary to ask, How, or in what sense, does baptism save us? How can it be said to unite us to Christ, wash away our sins, and obtain for us those powers and privileges of the spiritual life which in Scripture language are connected with it?

And then it may be at once replied that all this is affirmed—

Because Christian Baptism is the visible symbol of the invisible operation of the Divine Spirit, who alone is the efficient cause and real author of the new life in the spirit of man.

And because his baptism is the outward exhibition of a believer's repentance, whereby he forsakes sin; and of his faith, whereby he lays hold on Christ, and on God's promises in Him.

Hence the ascribing to the baptismal ordinance all

that is ascribed to it in Holy Writ, is only a particular instance of the general fact that in Scripture language a single part of a complex action, and even that part which is the most obvious to the senses, is often mentioned for the whole of it; and thus in this case the whole of the solemn transaction is designated by the external symbol.[1]

Besides this, it should be distinctly marked, first, that whatever efficacy is ascribed to baptism as a divinely-appointed ordinance, the sacred writers are careful to make it plain, that it is by no power or virtue, natural or supernatural, in the water and its application, that the ascribed effects are produced. For if they assure us that "as many as were baptized into Christ, put on Christ," they omit not to declare that it is "*through faith*" that "all are the children of God in Christ Jesus," that it is "*by one Spirit*" that "we are baptized into one body." It is "*in the name of the Lord Jesus*," and "*by the Spirit of our God*," that sinful men "are washed, sanctified, and justified." The "washing of regeneration" is "the renewing of the Holy Ghost."

And, secondly, it should be distinctly marked that the persons, whom their baptism is said to have cleansed from sin, to have sanctified and saved, were those who gladly received the Gospel word, who confessed their

---

[1] In a similar manner, the whole ordinance of the other srcrament is expressed by simply naming the visible action of "breaking the bread;" and the whole transaction in the ordination of ministers is termed "the imposition of hands."

sins, and who believed in Christ. They were at any rate those who, as far as man could see, made an honest profession of repentance and faith; who consequently in the economy of the apostolic age, as in all subsequent times, were spoken of on this hypothesis, and so far as this hypothesis was realised, as being what they credibly professed to be, and who on the ground of such profession were received into the communion of the Church. And thus St. Peter in affirming that baptism saves us, immediately adds that it is not "the putting away of the filth of the flesh," —the mere application of water to the body,—" but the answer of a good conscience towards God;" the inward state of the baptized corresponding with the outward appearance; the belief of the heart with the profession of the lips. Thus, too, whatever the inspired writers affirm of the effects of baptism, they take care to make it plain that the *fruits of the Spirit* are the only certain proof of the Spirit's presence and exerted power; and that no act previously performed, no privileges once received, can be allowed as evidence, when these fruits are absent from those in whom they ought to appear. "As many as are *led by the Spirit of God,* they are the sons of God." "He that is born of God doth not commit sin,"—" believeth that Jesus is the Christ,"—and "overcometh the world."

And what still further shows that it was only as a visible symbol of invisible realities, that baptism is said to have had any power, is the complete omission in the New Testament of everything which could lead to the supposition that there was any virtue inherent in the rite itself, or the visible element which it employed. In the Churches of the Apostles there was *no consecration* of the baptismal water to intimate that some mystical power was imparted to it. A pool or stream in any place was a sufficient baptistery. Nor was there any thought of sacramental grace dependent on the act and office of the officiating minister, or of any power in him to impart it by his ministrations. The Apostles seem to have purposely guarded against all such notions; when even on the important occasion of the baptism of Cornelius, which formed a distinct epoch in the early history of the Church, Peter did not administer the ordinance himself; and when Paul informed the Corinthians that he had "not been sent to baptize, but to preach the Gospel," and considered it a cause of thankfulness that he had himself baptized very few of his converts in that city.

It only remains to be observed that baptism in the primitive Church was evidently administered by immersion of the body in the water,—a mode which added to the significance of the rite, and gave a peculiar force to some of the allusions to it. But in the absence of all commands on the subject, this mode of administration cannot justly be considered as essential to the ordinance, or a deviation from it as detrimental to its validity.

And thus on looking at the general bearing of this Sacrament upon the religious life of the apostolic times, we see that without savouring of formalism, or encouraging a vain reliance on the "bodily exercise" of ceremonial acts, it served to impress the minds of converts with a happy assurance of their union with Christ in the covenant of grace;—to teach them that they had not merely received a new creed, but had entered upon a *new life* under the guidance of the Holy Spirit; and to remind them continually that they had enlisted in Christ's spiritual army for a holy warfare against self and sin, and were to remain His faithful soldiers and servants unto their life's end.

And the simple grandeur of this view and use of Christian baptism, which marked the earliest age, reverently honouring the outward act as a divine appointment, without allowing it to overshadow, or take the place of, the inner spirit of the ordinance, continued to the middle of the second century with little alteration; except that even then there appears some slight tendency to dwell more strongly upon the outward rite, and to speak of it more positively as if it were in itself a direct cause of the inward and spiritual blessings sacramentally connected with it.

Thus Ignatius, in his short notice of baptism in his Epistle to Polycarp (§ 3), connects it immediately with the faith, love, and patience of the Christian; putting these Christian graces as the component parts, so to speak, of the baptism itself. His words are, *τὸ βάπτισμα ὑμῶν μενέτω ὡς ὅπλα, ἡ πίστις ὡς περικεφαλαία, ἡ ἀγάπη ὡς δόρυ, ἡ ὑπομονὴ ὡς πανοπλία.* Where having called baptism the Christian's armour, he enumerates, as different parts of that armour, his faith, love, and patience.

From Justin Martyr's account of the administration of baptism in his time we learn—

That there was still no special class of catechumens undergoing a long probation; but those who received the Christian doctrines, repented of their sins, and promised to live the Christian life, were thereupon baptized.

That the candidates for baptism were taught to pray for the forgiveness of their past transgressions, the Christians, into whose community they were to be admitted, joining with them in these devotions.

That they were then led to some water, in which they were baptized by immersion, without any consecration of the element, or any ceremony implying the existence of a mystical virtue in it.

That this baptism was distinctly called their regeneration. "They are brought," says Justin, "where there is water, and are regenerated in the same manner as we ourselves also were regenerated."

That the baptized were considered to have obtained the remission of sins and other spiritual blessings *in the water*, because there was invoked over them the name of God the Father and Lord of all things, and of Jesus Christ, who was crucified under Pontius Pilate, and of the Holy Spirit, who proclaimed beforehand by the prophets all the things concerning Jesus.

That this baptism was also called their "illumination,"

because those who learned the truths of Christianity had their minds thereby enlightened.

And that the newly-baptized persons were at once received into the Christian congregation, and were welcomed with the kiss of peace and brotherhood.[1]

But by the beginning of the third century a decided change had taken place both in the views which were entertained of this sacrament, and in the manner of its administration ;—a change which increased in intensity during that century, and in the course of the following age advanced so far, that the simple apostolic rite can

[1] Justin. 'Apolog.' i. *Ὅσοι ἂν πεισθῶσι καὶ πιστεύωσιν ἀληθῆ ταῦτα τὰ ὑφ' ἡμῶν διδασκόμενα καὶ λεγόμενα εἶναι, καὶ βιοῦν οὕτως δύνασθαι ὑπισχνῶνται, εὔχεσθαί τε καὶ αἰτεῖν νηστεύοντες παρὰ τοῦ Θεοῦ τῶν προημαρτημένων ἄφεσιν διδάσκονται, ἡμῶν συνευχομένων καὶ συννηστευόντων αὐτοῖς· ἔπειτα ἄγονται ὑφ' ἡμῶν ἔνθα ὕδωρ ἐστὶ, καὶ τρόπον ἀναγεννήσεως, ὃν καὶ ἡμεῖς αὐτοὶ ἀνεγεννήθημεν, ἀναγεννῶνται, ἐπ' ὀνόματος γὰρ τοῦ Πατρὸς τῶν ὅλων καὶ δεσπότου Θεοῦ, καὶ τοῦ Σωτῆρος ἡμῶν Ἰησοῦ Χριστοῦ, καὶ Πνεύματος ἁγίου, τὸ ἐν τῷ ὕδατι τότε λουτρὸν ποιοῦνται.*—§ 79.

Again, *Καλεῖται δὲ τοῦτο τὸ λουτρὸν φωτισμὸς, ὡς φωτιζομένων τὴν διάνοιαν τῶν ταῦτα μανθανόντων. καὶ ἐπ' ὀνόματος δὲ Ἰησοῦ Χριστοῦ τοῦ σταυρωθέντος ἐπὶ Ποντίου Πιλάτου, καὶ ἐπ' ὀνόματος Πνεύματος ἁγίου, ὃ διὰ τῶν προφητῶν προεκήρυξε τὰ κατὰ τὸν Ἰησοῦν πάντα, ὁ φωτιζόμενος λούεται.*—§ 80.

And, *Ἡμεῖς δὲ μετὰ τὸ οὕτως λοῦσαι τὸν πεπεισμένον καὶ συγκατατεθεμένον ἐπὶ τοὺς λεγομένους αδελφοὺς ἄγομεν, ἔνθα συνηγμένοι εἰσί κοινὰς εὐχὰς ποιησόμενοι ὑπέρ τε ἑαυτῶν καὶ τοῦ φωτισθέντος. . . Ἀλλήλους φιλήματι ἀσπαζόμεθα παυσάμενοι τῶν εὐχῶν.*—§ 85.

The term "enlightened," or "illuminated," as applied to the baptized, seems to be so far of apostolic authority, that it is used in the Epistle to the Hebrews of those who had become Christians, though their baptism is not there expressly mentioned : *ἅπαξ φωτισθέντας*—vi. 4; *ἐν αἷς φωτισθέντες*—x. 32.

scarcely be recognized in the elaborate ceremonial which then prevailed, and which more resembled the practices observed in heathen mysteries, than a hallowed ordinance in the Christian Church.

During this period, the Catechumenate was established as a distinct and acknowledged order in the Christian economy, with its several ranks or subdivisions; and candidates were introduced into it with a religious ceremony, which was said *to make them Christians*, although they had not yet been baptized, and had made no profession of the Christian faith.

In this order they usually continued for two years, or more,—passing through several stages of probationary discipline with numerous symbolical rites,—and receiving successive communications of Christian doctrines, gradually and somewhat mysteriously imparted to them.

Before their baptism, the candidates were anointed with a holy oil, which had been consecrated by a bishop, and which was supposed to have thereby had a supernatural power communicated to it to act as an exorcism, and to expel the evil spirit from the soul.[1]

---

[1] Catechumens were admitted by imposition of hands, the sign of the cross, and prayers; and this was said *to make them Christians*, though only in an inferior sense. Thus, the Council of Eliberis (A. D. 305) directed that, "Gentiles si in infirmitate desideraverint sibi manum imponi, si fuerit eorum ex aliqua parte vita honesta, placuit iis manum imponi et *fieri Christianos*."—Can. 39. And, again, with reference to a catechumen who might have indefinitely delayed his baptism, "Si eum de clero quisquam cognoverit esse *Christianum*."—Can. 65. And so, also, the Council of Constantinople (A. D. 381), speaking of the reception of heretics into the Church, says, *τηνπρώτην ἡμέραν ποιοῦμεν αὐτοὺς Χριστιάνους τὴν δε*

The baptism itself was performed with a dramatic ceremonial, made as imposing as possible, and every action invested with an esoteric meaning. And the immersion took place in a baptistery, where the water was solemnly consecrated by calling upon the Divine Spirit to descend into it, and by pouring upon it in the form of a cross some of the holy ointment, which like the anointing oil had received a spirit-imparting virtue from a bishop's hands. And the people were then taught that an actual objective change was thus wrought in the water itself—a change so distinctly acknowledged as to be called by the name of "transelementation,"[1] giving to

---

δευτέραν κατηχουμένους.—Can. 7.

After their admission, the catechumens were disciplined by exercises of fasting, abstinence, confession, and penitence. They were taught the words of some creed, and of the Lord's Prayer, and the answers which they were to make at their baptism.

They had performed upon them the symbolical ceremonies of veiling the head, breathing into the nostrils, touching the ears, signing with the cross, giving them salt to taste, and, lastly and especially, the anointing of the whole body with the holy oil, in order to drive out demons.

This anointing is not mentioned by Tertullian; and probably was not used in his time; but Cyril of Jerusalem (A. D. 350) describes it, and says that this holy oil was possessed of such power that it not only destroyed all traces of sins, but also drove out all the unseen powers of the evil one: *Εἶτα ἀποδυθέντες ἐλαίῳ ἠλείφεσθε ἐπορκιστῷ ἀπ' ἄκρων τριχῶν ἕως τῶν κάτω. . . . . τὸ ἐπορκιστὸν τοῦτο ἔλαιον ἐπικλήσει τοῦ Θεοῦ καὶ εὐχῇ δύναμιν τηλικαύτην λαμβάνει, ὥστε οὐ μόνον καῒον τὰ ἴχνη τῶν ἁμαρτημάτων ἀποκαθαίρει, ἀλλὰ καὶ πάσας ἀοράτους τοῦ πονήρου ἐκδιώκειν τὰς δυνάμεις.*—'Catech. Mystag.' ii. 3.

Just before they were baptized, they stood with outstretched hands in the porch of the church, and, turning to the west, renounced the devil and his works.

[1] The consecration of the baptismal water.

Tertullian says, "Aquæ sacramentum sanctificationis conse-

it a sanctifying power that by its own inherent efficacy it might wash away the sins of the baptized.

The due effect of the baptismal rite was further represented as depending upon the person who performed it. The visible orthodox Church, concentrated in its respective bishops, was the sole depository of spiritual life and blessing: and its ministers were priests possessed, as its delegates, of a sacerdotal power, and alone enabled thereby to confer divine grace through the medium of the sacraments.[1]

quuntur, invocato Deo, *supervenit enim statim Spiritus de cœlis et aquis superest, sanctificans eas de semet ipso;* et ita sanctificatæ *vim sanctificandi combibunt.*"—'De Bapt.' 4.

A form for this consecration is given in the 'Constit. Apostol.': *Κάτιδε ἐξ οὐρανοῦ, καὶ ἁγίασον τὸ ὕδωρ τοῦτο, δὸς δὲ χάριν καὶ δύναμιν* (give it grace and power) *ὥστε τὸν βαπτιζόμενον κατ' ἐντολὴν τοῦ Χριστοῦ σου, αὐτῷ συσταυρωθῆναι, καὶ συναποθανεῖν, καὶ συνταφῆναι, καὶ συναναστῆναι, εἰς υἱοθεσίαν.*—vii. 44.

The pouring of the ointment on the water in the form of a cross is mentioned by Dionysius (about the fourth century): *Διὸ καὶ ἡ τοῦ βαπτίσματος χάρις τελειοῦται διὰ τοῦ μύρου σταυροειδῶς ἐπιχεομένου τῷ βαπτιστηρίῳ παρὰ τοῦ Ἱεράρχου.*—'Eccles. Hierarch.' iv. 10.

The inherent power of the water thus consecrated to wash away sin is distinctly expressed in the above quotations from Tertullian, and the 'Constitutiones Apostolicæ.' Cyprian uses similar language: "Oportet mundari et sanctificari aquam prius a sacerdote, ut *possit baptismo suo peccata hominis,* qui baptizatur, *abluere.*"—Epist. 70 ad Janum.

The *transelementation* of the water is affirmed by Cyril of Alexandria (A. D 410): *Διὰ τῆς τοῦ Πνεύματος ἐνεργείας τὸ αἰσθητὸν ὕδωρ πρὸς θείαν τινὰ καὶ ἀπόρρητον μεταστοιχειοῦται δύναμιν, ἁγιάζει τε λοιπὸν τοὺς ἐν οἷς ἂν γένοιτο.*—'In Johann.' iii. 5.

[1] That a visible orthodox church, in communion with its regular bishop, alone possessed, and could through its ministers impart, spiritual grace in baptism, is distinctly declared and dwelt upon by Cyprian in his contests with Novatian and his followers; and also on the question about the rebaptiza-

Thus baptism, throughout its whole ceremonial, wore the appearance of an initiation into some of those secret mysteries, which were familiar to the pagan mind; nor was such an idea discouraged by the greatest teachers of the time. The highest spiritual blessings were supposed to be conferred not only *ex opere operato* by the outward rite, but even by the inherent virtue of the water, the power of the priest, and the gift of the Church. And being regarded on the one hand as absolutely necessary for the salvation of all, and on the other hand as a complete deliverance from, and obliteration of, all past sins, which could never afterwards be so effectually obtained, the whole ordinance was surrounded with an atmosphere of awe and superstitious reverence, encouraging the notion in some minds that they might come to it as a species of magic rites which could annihilate sin; and in others that it was better to defer their baptism as long

tion of heretics. Thus, "Quum dicunt, Credis remissionem peccatorum et vitam æternam *per sanctam ecclesiam*, mentiuntur in interrogatione, quando *non habeant sanctam ecclesiam*. Tunc deinde quum voce sua ipsi confitentur *remissionem peccatorum non dari nisi per sanctam ecclesiam posse*, quam non habent, ostendunt remitti illic peccata non posse."—Epist. 76, ad Magnum. Against the baptism of the Novationists. And on the necessity of not acknowledging heretical baptism, "Baptizandus est ut ovis fiat quia *una est aqua in Ecclesia sancta*, quæ oves faciat."—Ep. 71.

So far, indeed, does Cyprian carry his "High Churchism"—putting, in fact, his own visible community in the place of Christ himself,—that, notwithstanding the high estimation in which martyrdom was then held, as a merit which covered all other defects and sins, he affirms that those who died for the name of Christ were not at all benefited by it, unless they were in full communion with the orthodox Church, and that their death was no martyrdom at all. "An secum esse Christum quum collecti fuerint opinantur, *qui extra*

as possible, lest by subsequent sins its blessed effects might be irrevocably lost.[1]

The miserable demoralisation, produced by such doctrines and their natural consequences, scarcely needs to be pointed out.

These sad departures from apostolic practice are said to have arisen from the circumstance that the Christian sacraments and other religious services being originally so few and simple, with no imposing ceremonies, sacri-

---

Christi ecclesiam colliguntur. Tales *etiam si occisi in confessione nominis fuerint,* macula ista nec sanguine abluitur . . . . . *esse Martyr non potest,* qui *in ecclesia non est.*"—Cyp. 'de Unit. Eccles.'

The general opinion on this subject in the following century may be summed up in one line of Pacian's (A. D. 370), "Sic generat Christus in ecclesia per suos sacerdotes."—'Serm. de Bapt.'

1 "The custom, general as it became, of deferring baptism to the last hour, a custom so utterly opposed to the practice of the apostolic age, whence did it arise, but from the doctrine of the Church at the time? For the people estimating, if we may so speak, their chances of heaven, all things considered, concluded, and not unreasonably, that although in doing so they incurred the fearful risk of meeting death suddenly, or where the 'regenerating water' could not be obtained; yet inasmuch as a death-bed initiation, if it could but be had, would cover all defects; and, moreover, as *sin after baptism could be expiated, if at all, only in the precarious and painful methods of penance,* which expiatory process itself might be cut short by death, having no remedy whatever;—the safer course, though a perilous one, was to hold in reserve to the last, and trusting to good fortune, *that one remedy,* concerning the efficacy of which no doubt could be entertained. This course, moreover, had a further recommendation incidentally attached to it, namely, that with the sovereign remedy still untouched and at hand, a man might meantime live as he pleased; only let him be so fortunate at the last as to have a kind priest within call, and all would be right!

"In vain the great preachers of the Nicene age spent their eloquence in denouncing this impiety. Men coolly made their calculations, and chose to abide by what they felt to be their better chance."—'Ancient Christianity' (by Isaac Taylor) p. 247.

fices, and temples, the Christian teachers endeavoured to set them off by magnificent names,—by involving them in mystery,—and by adding to them as large a number of symbolical rites as possible, lest they should be despised for their simplicity and plainness ; for which reason also many things were hidden at first from the catechumens, in order to increase their veneration by the concealment, and to make even their curiosity a spur to their religion.

This doubtless in some cases was the truth ; but the causes of the change must be traced to a deeper source, and to principles of a wider operation. Arising out of the midst of Judaism and surrounded by pagan religions, Christianity was continually exposed to evil influences from them both. The former was constantly striving, as long as it had any power or life, to thrust or insinuate its observances into the Church, notwithstanding the unanimous sentence of the Apostles at Jerusalem. The latter was everywhere present, and while its grosser abominations were repudiated, some feelings and sentiments, which it produced or fostered, were not without their influence upon the Christian mind.

Now while Christianity, as established by the Apostles, was essentially a religion of the heart and spirit, exerting its power *within*, and acting *from within* so far as any outward display was needed ;—popular Judaism on the contrary, and all the denominations of paganism, were religions of *outward exhibition*, appealing to the bodily senses, and acting *from without* upon the inner man, so far as they acted inwardly at all. And then, as what is called the religious instinct in man tends naturally to make religion a thing of visible and sensuous forms;—neither Jewish nor Gentile converts could at once emancipate their minds from this inveterate tendency, but carried a portion of it with them into the Christian body, to spread and operate there; while the modes of thought outside the Church, if they had any influence at all, must have conduced to the same effect. After the departure of the Apostles, and when Christianity was extended more and more throughout the Roman Empire, this evil leaven spread itself more widely and with less restraint, although the vitality of the sound apostolic doctrine held out against it for a considerable time.

Then too, the rise and growth of the Gnostic philosophy, to which we have traced the pernicious and ungodly asceticism which so greatly prevailed in the Church, operated also on another side in strengthening these Jewish and pagan influences. For if Gnosticism by its notion that sin was especially connected with matter and animal life, led to the exaltation of the factitious holiness of bodily macerations,—its principles equally encouraged a belief that sin might be expelled by bodily appliances, and justified an exaggerated estimate of all material and palpable ceremonies. And these Gnostic principles, infecting as they did more or less perceptibly the heads and leaders of the Church,[1]

[1] "The ancient Church, coming as it did, suddenly and without the aid of any experience, into contact with the most prodigious evils, at

made them ready to encourage rather than to oppose the growing errors of the popular theology.

From these causes there was born and developed in the Christian body "*an undue estimation of externals.*" The conception of the Church, and of everything belonging to it, was *thrown outwards.* The whole current of ecclesiastial feeling, thought, and expression set strongly in the same direction; and the whole system was modified accordingly.

Hence the visible Church was advanced to an eminence not its own, and was almost deified. From it the communion of the Holy Spirit with all his gifts was declared to be first derived, and through its ministrations alone to be imparted to men.

Hence, instead of a Christian Ministry of the apostolic type and age, a priesthood after the Jewish or heathen

---

once *imparted* an impulse, and *admitted* an impulse. . . Did Christianity encounter the rigid, punctilious, and self-righteous pietism of the Jews? In the collision the Judaism of those who of the Hebrew race embraced the Gospel gave way to some extent, and was Christianised; and, in return, Christianity was Judaised. Or did it meet the vain philosophy and platonism of the speculative Greek and Gnostic? It did so; and platonism and Christianity thenceforward were intimately commingled. Did it impinge upon human society, then debauched in a most extraordinary degree? It did so; and with a violent revulsion it distorted its own principles of virtue in an equally extreme degree. Finally, did the religion of the New Testament, rational, spiritual, pure, confront the degrading superstitions of the pagan world? It did so, and on this ground, while it bore a clear testimony against the doctrine and the flagitious practice of polytheism, yet it merged itself in the boundless superstition of the times as a system of fear, spiritual servitude, formality, scrupulosity, visible magnificence of worship, mystery, artifice, and juggle."—'Ancient Christianity,' p. 130.

model was set up, and sacerdotal powers and functions were ascribed to it.

Hence the beautifully simple and spiritual ordinances of the sacraments were similarly dealt with; and baptism loaded with imposing ceremonies, was represented as having in its visible form and material elements a supernatural power imparted to them by the Church for regenerating the believer, and as being absolutely necessary for such regeneration.

So far the sacrament of baptism has been considered in connection "with a conscious entrance on Christian communion,"—as administered therefore only to *adults;* but it is now necessary to notice it also with reference to infants.

For myself I desire to express my entire assent to the words of our twenty-seventh Article, "The baptism of young children is in any wise to be retained in the Church, as most agreeable with the institution of Christ." But, at the same time, notwithstanding all that has been written by learned men upon this subject, it remains indisputable that infant-baptism is not mentioned in the New Testament. No instance of it is recorded there;—no allusion is made to its effects;—no directions are given for its administration.

However reasonably we may be convinced that we find in the Christian Scriptures "the fundamental idea from which infant-baptism was afterwards developed," and by which it may now be justified; it ought to be distinctly acknowledged that it is not an apostolic ordinance. Like modern Episcopacy, it is an ecclesiastical institution legitimately deduced by Church authority from apostolic principles, but not apostolic in its actual existence.

There is no trace of it until the last part of the second century, when a passage is found in Irenæus, which may possibly—and only possibly—refer to it. Nor is it anywhere distinctly mentioned before the time of Tertullian, who, while he testifies to the practice, was himself rather opposed to it.[1] As an established order of the Church, therefore, it belongs to the third century, when its use, and the mode of its administration, and the whole theory of it as a Christian ceremony, were necessarily moulded by the baptismal theology of the time. A circumstance which ought to be distinctly kept in view in every consideration of the subject.

The belief that baptism was absolutely necessary for

---

[1] Notwithstanding such valuable and learned works as 'Wall on Infant Baptism,' 'Hammond's Defence of Infant Baptism,' and others, the assertion of Suicer remains unrefuted, as far as any direct historical evidence is concerned, when he says, "Primis duobus sæculis nemo baptismum accipiebat, nisi qui in fide instructus et doctrina Christiana imbutus testari posset se credere, propter illa verba, Qui crediderit et baptizatus fuerit."

The passages put forward by Bingham and others from Clemens Romanus, Hermæ Pastor, Justin Martyr, and the "Author of the Recognitions," *say nothing about infant-baptism,* though some of them testify to the necessity of baptism in general.

The passage from Irenæus referred to is, "Omnes enim (Christus) venit per semet ipsum salvare; omnes, inquam, qui per eum renascuntur in Deum, infantes, et parvulos, et pueros, et juvenes, et seniores. Ideo per omnem venit ætatem, et infantibus infans factus, sanctificans infantes; et parvulis parvulus, sanctificans

all;[1] and that it conferred spiritual life by the inherent virtue of its material elements, and by the administra-

hanc ipsam habentes ætatem, et exemplum illis pietatis effectus." —ii. 22, 4.—a passage in which infant-baptism is not mentioned, and by no means necessarily implied.

[1] The belief in the absolute necessity of water baptism appears first in Tertullian, who also gives us the first distinct evidence of the practice of administering it to infants. His assertions, however, are not so definite and strong as are found at later periods. "Lex enim tingendi imposita est et forma præscripta; Ite, inquit, docete nationes tingentes eas in nomen Patris, et Filii, et Spiritus Sancti. Huic legi collata definitio illa, Nisi quis renatus fuerit ex aqua et Spiritu non intrabit in regnum cælorum, *obstrinxit fidem ad baptismi necessitatem.*"—Tert. 'de Bapt.' 13.

When this question of the necessity of baptism had connected itself expressly with the case of infants, a difference of opinion is at first observable respecting those who died unbaptized, which in process of time settled down into a most unqualified assertion of their hopeless condition. Thus Gregory Nazianzen thought that they were in an intermediate state, neither condemned nor blessed: *Τοὺς δὲ μήτε δοξασθήσεσθαι μήτε κολασθήσεσθαι παρὰ τοῦ δικαίου κριτοῦ, ὡς ἀσφραγίστους μὲν ἀπονήρους δέ, ἀλλὰ παθόντας μᾶλλον τὴν ζημίαν ἢ δράσαντας.*—Orat. 40.

But Augustin declares that they must be condemned, though with the lightest condemnation. "Potest proinde recte dici parvulos sine baptismo de corpore exeuntes in damnatione omnium mitissima futuros. Multum autem et fallitur, qui eos in damnatione prædicat non futuros, dicente Apostolo, judicium ex uno delicto in condemnationem."—'De Peccat. Merit. et Remiss.' i. 16.

So the author whose writings are subjoined to those of Augustin, "Nos dicimus eos [infantes] aliter salutem et vitam æternam non habituros, nisi baptizentur in Christo." Serm. 14, de Verb. Apost.

But Fulgentius, who lived a hundred years later than Augustin, asserts most positively of all men, "Firmissime tene et nullatenus dubites, exceptis illis qui pro nomine Christi suo sanguine baptizantur nullum hominem accepturum vitam æternam, qui non hic a malis suis fuerit per pœnitentiam, fidemque conversus, et per sacramentum fidei et pœnitentiæ, id est per baptismum liberatus. Parvulis vero. . . . . , ... sacramentum fidei et pœnitentiæ, quamdiu rationis ætas eorum capax esse non potest, sufficere ad salutem."—'De fide ad Petrum,' 30.

tion of a priest, led the Church to the conclusion, that infant-baptism was not merely justifiable, but *altogether necessary;* and also that its force and efficacy were *exactly the same* in the unconscious infant as in the believing man. This was nothing more than a simple and logical consequence of such an idea of this sacrament, and the infant having been placed on the same standing-ground as the adult, it was then unfortunately thought requisite to use, as far as possible, the same formula for both; and thus, as the adult by his own mouth professed the faith which he had,—the infant was by the mouth of another to profess the faith which he had not. Hence the introduction of baptismal sponsors to answer in the infant's stead;—an institution of very questionable propriety at the best, and one which at a later time was productive of superstitions, with which the Church of the Nicene period is certainly not chargeable,—though the germ of error was planted then, which has not altogether ceased to bear fruit, even amongst ourselves.

To admit infants to Christian baptism, as the children of believing parents, may be a wholesome development of Scripture truth and apostolic teaching; but it is quite a different thing, and by no means follows as a legitimate consequence, that such baptism should be exactly the same as in the adult believer. Still less was it wise or right to endeavour by an ecclesiastical fiction to exhibit an identity which did not exist, in such essentially different cases.

That even in very early times good men felt the objections which may be justly made to the sponsorial affirmations in infant-baptism,—and that no satisfactory answers could be given to such objections,—is made evident by the correspondence which took place between Boniface, Bishop of Rome, and Augustin on this subject; and by the miserable inconclusiveness of the only solutions which the latter could give of the difficulties which the former had presented to him.[1] It is no wonder therefore that the practice has been a stumbling-block, and a cause of disunion in the Church, even to the

[1] In Augustin's time the sponsors were asked "Does this child believe in God? Does he turn to God?" &c., and they answered, "He does." Upon which the worthy Bishop of Rome enquires, "How can it be said with truth that an infant believes, and repents, &c., when he has no thought or sense about such things?" And the only answer that Augustin gives him is, "That the infant is said to believe, because he receives the sacrament of faith and conversion. As the sacrament of the body of Christ is in a certain manner called His body, so the sacrament of faith is called faith; and he who has this sacrament, therefore, has faith; and consequently, an infant coming to be baptized may be said to have faith or to believe, because these questions and answers are a part of the celebration of the sacrament of faith." Sicut ergo secundum quendam modum sacramentum corporis Christi corpus Christi est, et sacramentum sanguinis Christi sanguis Christi est; ita sacramentum fidei fides est. Nihil est autem aliud credere, quam fidem habere. Ac per hoc quum respondetur parvulus credere, qui fidei nondum habet affectum, respondetur fidem habere propter fidei sacramentum, et convertere se ad Deum propter conversionis sacramentum, quia et ipsa responsio ad celebrationem pertinet sacramenti."—Epist. 23 ad Bonifacium.

Can anything be imagined more futile than such an explanation?—baptism is the sacrament of faith; therefore, he who has this sacrament has faith; therefore, an infant brought to be baptized may be said to have faith, *before the baptism has been administered*, because these questions and answers are a part of the administration!

This extreme absurdity is, at any rate, avoided in our baptismal service.

present day. Had our early Reformers been longer spared, with their earnest love of Scripture truth, and their candour and courage in setting forth the successive degrees of light which they themselves obtained, it may well be believed that in this, and in some other respects, our baptismal service would not have been left by them exactly as they did leave it. But since their day none like them have arisen in our Church ; and at the present time no one in authority seems to venture even to look such questions in the face.

There remains still one important particular to be noticed in the subject of infant-baptism, connected by different points of contact and of interest with apostolic practice, with the usages of the third and following centuries, and with those of our own Church.

It is evident from the New Testament that the Apostles had the power of conferring "spiritual gifts," (χαρίσματα) by the solemn imposition of hands and by prayer upon those who by baptism had been received into their communion. It is also evident that these spiritual gifts thus conferred were not personal graces requisite for the baptized believer's individual standing in Christ, or for his own faith and holiness of living; but were extraordinary powers granted for the general benefit and edification of the Christian community. And since none but the Apostles were able to bestow these gifts, they ceased to be given, when *they* departed from the world ; and consequently the ceremonial, which they used in this connection, was not to be continued as a permanent ordinance in the Church.

When, however, at the beginning of the third century Episcopal authority had been strongly developed in the Church system, and, when not long after, bishops called themselves successors of the Apostles, and inheritors of their spiritual authority, they professed to have, like them, the power of imparting the Holy Spirit,—though the gifts which followed upon the Apostles' imposition of hands, did not follow upon theirs. The exercise of this supposed power by the bishops, which was called affixing a "seal," or a "perfecting" of the baptized, and at a later period, "confirmation," was said to be after the example of the Apostles; but in reality in its use and intention it differed widely from the apostolic practice. Confirmation at this period was looked upon as a necessary adjunct to baptism, which, without this addition, was not considered perfect or complete.[1]

[1] Immediately after the actual baptism followed the ceremony of anointing the baptized with the holy ointment or *χρίσμα*, in order to impart the Holy Spirit. The practice was in use as early as the time of Tertullian, who says, "Non quod in aquis Spiritum Sanctum consequamur; sed in aqua emundati sub Angelo (by the priest), Spiritui Sancto præparamur." And, "Exinde egressi de lavacro perungimur benedicta unctione." And "Dehinc manus imponitur per benedictionem advocans et invitans Spiritum Sanctum."—'De Bapt.'—§§ 4, 7, 8.

Cyril of Jerusalem describes the power of this ointment: *τὸ ἅγιον τοῦτο μύρον οὐκέτι ψιλὸν, οὐδ' ὡς ἂν εἴποι τις κοινὸν, ἀλλὰ Χριστοῦ χάρισμα, καὶ Πνεύματος-τοῦ ἁγίου παρουσία τῆς αὐτοῦ θεότητος ἐνεργετικὸν γενόμενον.*—'Catech. Mystag.' iii. 3.

Pacian (A. D. 370) says expressly, that the baptismal water washes away sin, and the chrism gives the Holy Spirit; and so the regenera-

In accordance with the materialistic sentiments then prevalent in the Church, a sacred ointment, or *Chrism*, consecrated by a bishop, and thus (as it was believed), changed in its nature, and made able to impart the Divine Spirit, was applied, with the sign of the cross and imposition of hands to the baptized person immediately after his immersion if a bishop was present, by whom alone in ordinary cases this ceremony was to be performed. And thus, while the special virtue of the water was to wash away sins, the Chrism, with its equally marvellous efficacy, was to give the Holy Spirit; and then alone was the regeneration of the baptized completed, or at least so completed as to fit him for living the Christian life.

Such was the "confirmation" used in the third and fourth centuries;—an unauthorized and perverted application of an apostolic practice to an unapostolic purpose, and another example of the prevalent tendency to convert the Church into an outward system of mediation, and to confound together in a corrupt union the Old and New Testament dispensations.

Confirmation in the modern sense, as used in the

tion is complete: "Hæc compleri alias nequent, nisi lavacri, et chrismatis, et antistitis, sacramento. Lavacro enim peccata purgantur, chrismate Sanctus Spiritus superinfunditur; utraque vero ista manu et ore antistitis impetramus; atque ita totus homo renascitur et renovatur in Christo."—'Serm. de Bapt.'

In the Church of Rome, at the end of the fourth century, a presbyter was allowed to perform a *part* of the chrismation; thus, "Presbyteris chrismate baptizatos ungere licet, sed quod ab episcopo fuerit consecratum; non tamen frontem ex eodem oleo signare, *quod solis episcopis debetur* quum *tradunt Spiritum Sanctum* Paracletum."—Innocent I. Epist. I. ad Decent. § 3.

Church of England, is a very good and wholesome rite for those who have been baptized in their infancy, in order that they may solemnly make a personal and public profession of their Christian faith. And as infant baptism must necessarily be to a certain extent incomplete, such confirmation may well be called with Hooker, "A sacramental Complement." But it is not "after the example of the Apostles," who used no ceremony at all corresponding with it. Neither is it after the example of the Nicene Church above referred to; for *then* there was no profession made at the confirmation, either of adults or of infants, to whom it was alike applied, as an essential part of the baptismal ordinance. The direction in our rubric about the confirmation of those who have been baptized when "of riper years" was probably given from an erroneous supposition that we were following the practice of the early times; but it is quite inconsistent with the Anglican idea of confirmation. "The Order of Confirmation" in our Prayer-book is obviously intended for those who were baptized in their infancy; and there is no provision made for the confirmation of any others.[1]

[1] In the two Prayer-books of the reign of Edward VI., and in the Prayer-book which was issued at the beginning of Elizabeth's reign (A. D. 1559), a short preface was prefixed to the order of confirmation, containing the following sentence: "Secondly, for as much as confirmation is ministered to them that be baptized, that by imposition of hands and prayer they may receive strength and defence against all temptations to sin, and the assaults of the world and the devil; it is most meet to be ministered when children come to that age, that partly by the frailty of their own flesh, partly by the assaults of the world and the devil, they begin to be in danger to fall

But to return for a few moments to the confirmation of the early Church;—the Christian, by the application of the sacred ointment, being thus fully baptized, and strengthened, as he was taught to believe, with all spiritual grace and power, was clothed in white garments, delivered to him sometimes with a solemn charge;—he stood before the "altar" with a lighted taper in his hand;—the kiss of peace was given to him;—he tasted milk and honey in token of his new birth;—he said the Lord's prayer standing upright, as being now a free man, and a child of God;—and he was at once admitted to the Lord's Supper, which was commonly administered to newly baptized infants, as well as to those of riper years.

On reviewing the whole course of the baptismal ceremonial of that time, from the probationary discipline of the catechumen to his admission to the Lord's Table, it cannot be denied that this elaborate drama may have been very solemnly impressive. But how immeasurably different was it all from the baptism of the apostolic Church!

It may have been that the times and the people, with whom the Church then had to deal, demanded a somewhat different treatment in external things from that of

---

into sundry kinds of sin." This rubric indicates that the framers of those Anglican liturgies designed to retain to a certain extent the idea of confirmation which prevailed at the Nicene period. But the whole of this preface was omitted in A. D. 1578; and nothing at all corresponding with the above-quoted sentence appears in our Prayer-book now.

the apostolic period. It may have been that, when the high spiritual elevation and extraordinary gifts of the earliest time had passed away, a larger recourse to material and æsthetic appliances, for stimulating a needful energy in the Christian cause and life, was not altogether unreasonable. It may have been that a lower civilization in some parts of the Roman Empire required to be met with more striking appeals to the bodily senses and lower self-consciousness of the population. But nothing could justify the extremes to which the Church system was carried in this direction. Nothing could justify a Church of any time or people in thus burying the simple ordinance of Christ under a mass of sensational superstition.[1]

[1] Mr. Lecky, in his 'History of Rationalism,' among other monstrous assertions, utterly at variance with the facts of history, takes upon himself to affirm that "for 1500 years after the establishment of the Christian religion it was intellectually and morally impossible that any religion that was not material and superstitious could have reigned over Europe." And that "superstition is the inevitable, and therefore the legitimate condition of an early civilization."—Vol. ii. p. 227, 228.

When Christianity has come in contact with a people in a state of barbarism, or low civilization, *if it has not raised them out of this state so far as to enable them to apprehend its divine doctrines*, it has, of course, been debased by them and loaded with superstition. And the more surely so, if the teachers of the religion themselves have departed from the purity and truth of the Christian faith. But in the first century it was indisputably shown that a Christianity, not debased by idolatry and superstition, could be established in companies of men of all classes throughout the Roman empire ; and, therefore, there evidently was no intellectual or moral impossibility in the propagation of such a religion to any extent throughout the population. And if possible then, it was possible at any other time, if the same truths had been presented to men's hearts and minds.

The earliest and the latest annals of the Gospel distinctly show that the divine message of Christianity,

This *materialization* or *making-outward* of all spiritual acts grew up and flourished, when some of the fundamental inner principles of evangelic truth had been forgotten or obscured. It was strengthened and encouraged by the simultaneous growth of the hierarchical and sacerdotal pretensions with which it was closely allied. And it gained its height, when after its union with the imperial authority, the Church became more than ever a power of earth instead of heaven, and vainly thought to honour its heavenly Lord by an ambitious display of temporal magnificence.

We may admire whatever is admirable in the character of the good men of those days. We may acknowledge their piety, their zeal, their self-denial, their martyr-courage;—but to approve of the system which they upheld in the Church would be to prefer the delusions of man to the truth of God. And to attempt to revive that system now,—and to resuscitate, in an age so different from theirs, their dead and buried symbolisms and mysteries,—above all, to do this with the warnings of Church history sounding in our ears, and with the New Testament opened wide before our eyes,—would be a fatal anachronism indeed! It would seem to betoken a blindness which nothing could enlighten, an infatuation hopeless of a cure.

---

when faithfully proclaimed, is able to cope, not only with a low state of civilization, but with the barbarism of the negro, and the cannibalism of the New Zealander

LECTURE VII.

THE LORD'S SUPPER.

VII.

THE LORD'S SUPPER.

IN nothing perhaps has the tendency of human nature to pervert and corrupt the best gifts of God been more clearly and sadly shown than in the treatment which the Christian religion has received at the hands of Christian men. And in no part of that religion have the effects of such a tendency been more strikingly exhibited than in the Sacrament of the Lord's Supper.

In its original institution the most simple of all religious ordinances, it became in the hands of men a most awful mystery. In its apostolic use a pledge of soundness in the faith, it was made in the hands of men an example of gross superstition and idolatry. In its divine intention a bond of brotherly love and mutual kindness, it was changed in the hands of men into an occasion of the most cruel persecution.

Being instituted by Jesus just after his last participation in the most popular and attractive of the Jewish festivals, to the place of which this sacrament was in some measure to succeed,—and just before the last scenes of his death and passion, which it was especially intended to commemorate,—it forcibly appealed to the sympathies both of Hebrew and of Gentile Christians. And as it was not an ordinance, like baptism, for a single celebration at the beginning of the Christian life, but for frequent recurrence during the whole of it, for a continually renewed remembrance of the Saviour and his saving work, and for a sign and means of an unfailing perseverance in fellowship with him, it naturally became a central point round which were gathered the deepest feelings and devotions of the Church. And thus the whole spirit of Christian worship at any given period stamped itself upon the mode in which this sacrament was administered; and contrariwise the mode of its administration re-acted with a powerful influence upon the general character of the whole Christian worship.

In the early part of the apostolic period so simple was the manner in which this Christian ordinance was observed, that it hardly bore the appearance of a religious solemnity; except that every meeting of Christians at that time was marked with a strong outflowing of religious feeling, which solemnized their whole life, and almost made every action of it a religious service. The Lord's Supper, as then administered, was immediately preceded by the Agapé, or "feast of charity"[1] and

[1] The word Ἀγάπη in this sense of a feast or supper, in which *Christian love* was the most prominent feature, occurs in the Epistle of St. Jude (verse 12), ἐν ταῖς ἀγάπαις ὑμῶν, "in your feasts of charity."

Christian brotherhood, in which the distinctions of rank and social position were laid aside, and all met and sat down together with that free acknowledgment of equality in Christ, which has been before described. Immediately after this, and as a concluding part of it, bread and wine were laid on the table. And the bread was then broken and distributed with the wine among all the guests after Christ's example and appointment; the very words of thanksgiving and of presentation, which Jesus had originally used, being doubtless repeated by an Apostle, or whoever presided at the meeting. Hence the name of "The Lord's Supper," or the still more simple appellation of "The breaking of bread," was given to this ordinance, including apparently at first the whole social meal, the Agapé itself, as well as the sacramental celebration with which it closed. And this custom sufficiently accounts for the circumstance that among the first Christians at Jerusalem, who were so united as "to be together and to have all things common," and who were almost like one large family, the hallowed "breaking of bread" in the Lord's Supper seems to have taken place every evening; the principal

---

It is worthy of notice that this word ἀγάπη, which is used more than a hundred times in the New Testament, did not exist in the classical Greek language, though the kindred verb ἀγαπάω did. Neither of the Greek words, ἔρως and φιλία, were appropriate for expressing the holy love to God, and the disinterested love to man, which was to hold so preeminent a place in the Christian religion; a new word, therefore, was employed, which from the Latin *caritas*, has been often translated "charity" in our English Bible.

meal of each Christian company being eaten together, and concluded with this sacred rite.

That this practice of uniting the sacramental celebration with an actual supper was extended also to Gentile Churches is plainly evidenced by what occurred at Corinth in connection with it. For the disorders and profanation which St. Paul reproved there could not have happened, if an ordinary supper at which different classes met, and at which excess on the one hand and a deficiency of food on the other could take place, had not formed the commencement or introduction of the more strictly religious ceremony. These disorders, however, at Corinth, which arose from the mismanagement of the whole celebration, and which probably were not confined to that Church alone,—the increase in the numbers of Christian communities—and perhaps the suspicion with which their heathen neighbours regarded these evening meetings,—led afterwards to the separation of the sacramental supper from the "Feast of Charity." The former, as a more entirely religious act, was then attached to the principal public devotions of the Church, which took place in the morning; the Agapé being still held separately in the evening as had previously been the case.

This separation was possibly one of those things which St. Paul arranged among the other matters, which he promised "to set in order" on his next visit to Corinth after writing his Epistles to the Christians there. But as might be expected from no general authoritative order having been issued for this purpose, the change did not take effect in all places at once. Among the Christians in the Province of Pontus mentioned by Pliny[1] in his letter to Trajan, the older custom seems to have been still retained; but long before this, at the time when the second Epistle of St. Peter, and the Epistle of St. Jude, were written, the Agapé must have been already disunited from the Lord's Supper. For the disgraceful conduct of those who are so severely censured in these Epistles, though taking place at the "Feasts of Charity," does not appear to have had any connection with a profanation of the sacred ordinance.

In the time of Justin Martyr, in the middle of the second century, the separation had become an established practice, and the sacramental celebration formed a regular part of the usual Sunday morning services of the Church. Yet a reminiscence of the earlier custom survived even to the end of the fourth century in some churches, which seem to have kept the anniversary of

[1] Pliny's words are, "quod essent soliti stato die ante lucem convenire, carmenque Christo, quasi dèo, dicere secum invicem; seque sacramento non in scelus aliquod obstringere, sed ne furta, ne latrocinia, ne adulteria committerent, ne fidem fallerent, ne depositum appellati abnegarent, quibus peractis; morem sibi discedendi fuisse, *rursusque coeundi ad capiendum cibum*, promiscuum tamen, et innoxium."—Ep. x. 97.

If the Lord's Supper is alluded to in this account, I think it must be in the last part of the passage, when they met again later in the day *ad capiendum cibum;* which would hardly have been mentioned if it had not been a part of their religious worship. The use of the word *sacramento*, in connection with their early morning devotions, is no evidence that what we call a "sacrament" was added to their morning service. Pliny's whole account, however, is necessarily very imperfect and obscure.

the institution of this sacrament with an express imitation of the original supper of the Lord.[1]

The Agapé itself was evidently an apostolic institution; and was at first no doubt not only an evidence of the existence, but also a powerful means for the promotion, of a strong feeling of union and Christian brotherhood. Notwithstanding the irregularities above alluded to, it continued after its separation from the Lord's Supper to be observed not unprofitably by different Churches, though not so frequently as before. At the beginning of the third century, if Tertullian's account may be our guide, such social meetings, conducted with such excellent order, and so much piety and kindly feeling, as he describes, must have been productive of the best effects; and must have exhibited a very striking contrast to the ordinary pagan festivities. But these meetings, so excellent when well regulated, were from the beginning liable to abuse after they were separated from the Lord's Supper, as well as before. Such abuses are alluded to in the Epistle of St. Jude, as happening even in his time; and at a later period, when the early Christian fervour was diminished, discipline more relaxed, and the numbers of nominal Christians much increased, these abuses became more glaring. The original Ἀγάπη was of course held in the

---

[1] This custom appears to be alluded to in the canon of the Council of Carthage, A. D. 397, which was as follows: "Sacramenta altaris non nisi a jejunis hominibus celebrentur, *excepto uno die anniversario, quo cœna Domini celebratur.*"—Can. 29.

"worship-room," where Christian societies met for all religious purposes; and consequently it continued afterwards to take place in Churches; but when the festival became more secularized this custom was thought objectionable, and was ordered to be discontinued.[1] The

[1] According to Tertullian's account the object of the Agapé was the comfort and refreshment of the poor, as well as the promotion of cheerful piety. The eating and drinking was kept within the bounds of moderation, though sufficient to satisfy the wants of all; and being preceded by prayer, was followed by singing psalms or sacred songs; and prayer concluded.

"Cœna nostra de nomine rationem sui ostendit: vocatur enim Ἀγάπη, id quod dilectio penes Græcos est. Quantisque sumptibus constet, lucrum est pietatis nomine facere sumptum. Siquidem inopes quoque refrigerio isto juvamus. . . Si honesta causa est convivii, reliquum ordinem disciplinæ de causa estimate, quid sit de religionis officio. Non prius discumbitur quam oratio ad Deum prægustetur. Editur quantum esurientes capiunt; bibitur quantum pudicis est utile. Ita saturantur ut qui meminerint etiam per noctem adorandum Deum sibi esse; ita fabulantur, ut qui sciant Dominum audire. Post aquam manualem et lumina, ut quisque de Scripturis Sanctis, vel de proprio ingenio potest, provocatur in medium Deo canere. Hinc probatur quomodo biberit. Atque oratio convivium dirimit.—Tertul." 'Apol.' i. 39.

During the 3rd and 4th centuries the customs observed in connection with the "Feast of Charity" seem to have varied at different times and in different Churches.

In Tertullian's account given above the Agapé appears altogether disconnected from the Lord's Supper; but in Cyprian's time there seems to have been an evening feast, or supper, very much like an Agapé, which was regarded as a sequel of the sacrament administered in the morning. This, at any rate, appears to be implied in Cyprian's argument against the *Aquarii*—the *Teetotallers* of his time; though the passage (in Ep. 63, ad Cæcilium), is obscure.

In some places it was the custom, after the Eucharist was over, to have a common meal of the things which had been brought as offerings by the worshippers. And, in the fourth century, Chrysostom and others speak of feasts after the Sacramental Communion, without calling them "Agapæ:" and, according to these accounts the provisions on such occasions were not entirely what had been presented as offerings.

As the genuine Agapæ fell into disuse, their place was to some extent occupied by the festivals in honour of Martyrs, which were con-

genuine Agapé itself seems to have gradually fallen into disuse from the fourth century; Churches justly using their Christian liberty, and their legitimate authority as independent societies, to set aside at their discretion an apostolic ordinance which had not been expressly declared to be of perpetual obligation.

Since that time these "Feasts of Charity" have never to any extent been revived in Christian churches.[1] And it has continued to be usual for the public administration of the Lord's Supper to take place in the morn-

---

ducted on a similar plan, and which were apparently the originals of the more modern "Church-ales," wakes, and fairs, usually connected with Churches or their patron saints.

A consideration of what Augustin says in his answer to Faustus's objection, that the Christian festivals were derived from the heathen religious feasts and sacrifices, seems to show that what are there called Agapæ, were really Martyrs' festivals.—See Augustin 'Cont. Faust.' xx. 20, 21.

After what is recorded of Christian feasts, even in the apostolic age, we need not be surprised that drunkenness and other disorders sometimes disgraced these evening or night gatherings, giving just occasion for pagans to blaspheme; but Tertullian's violent abuse of them, after he became a Montanist,—so utterly at variance with what he had written in his 'Apology'—must, doubtless, not be taken *au pied de la lettre.* "Apud te Agape in cacabis fervet, fides in culinis calet, spes in ferculis jacet. Sed majoris est Agape, quia per hanc adolescentes tui cum sororibus dormiunt."—Tert. 'de Jejun.' 17.

Notwithstanding the decree of the Council of Laodicea, *Οὐ δεῖ ἐν τοῖς κυριακοῖς, ἢ ἐν ταῖς ἐκκλησίαις τὰς λεγομένας Ἀγάπας ποιεῖν, καὶ ἐν τῷ οἴκῳ τοῦ Θεοῦ ἐσθίειν καὶ ἀκκούβιτα στρωννύειν* (Can. 28); the custom of holding such feasts in Churches continued for a long time after in some places; and at the Council of Trullo (A. D. 692), it was found necessary to repeat the order.

[1] In modern times the Church of the Moravian Brethren have renewed a practice very similar to the ancient Agapé; and owing to their simple manners, and the vigilance which from the smallness of their numbers they are able to exercise, no offence, I believe, has arisen out of it.

ing; although there is no rule or direction of divine, or otherwise valid, authority restricting the celebration to that time; as there is evidently nothing in the ordinance itself, suggesting any obligation or propriety in such restriction. The custom of receiving this sacrament fasting seems to have prevailed even in Tertullian's time, who makes some allusion to it. But in the fourth century it had grown into a gross superstition; this tradition of the Church being then regarded as a divine command; and to administer or receive either of the two sacraments, after eating food on that day, being looked upon as a dreadful sin.[1]

The real nature, however, and true position of this

---

[1] Thus Augustin presumes to say that this custom was ordered by the Holy Spirit. "Et hoc placuit Spiritui Sancto ut in honorem tanti sacramenti in os Christiani prius Dominicum corpus intraret, quam cæteri cibi."—Ep. 118 ad Januarium, § 6.

And Chrysostom, being accused of transgressing this rule, protests his innocence with the most vehement asseverations, as if such an imputation implied a most awful degree of guilt. "If I have done this, let my name be wiped out of the catalogue of the bishops, and not be written in the book of the orthodox faith. If I have done any such thing, let Christ cast me out of His kingdom."

Λέγουσιν ὅτι τινὰς ἐκοινώνησα μετὰ τὸ φαγεῖν αὐτούς, καὶ εἰ μὲν τοῦτο ἐποίησα, ἐξαλειφθείη τὸ ὄνομά μου ἐκ τῆς βίβλου τῶν ἐπισκόπων, καὶ μὴ γραφείη ἐν τῇ βίβλῳ τῆς ὀρθοδόξου πίστεως· ὅτι ἴδου ἐὰν τοιοῦτον ἐγὼ ἔπραξα καὶ ἀποβαλεῖ με Χριστὸς ἐκ τῆς βασιλείας αὐτοῦ.—Chrysost. Ep. 125, ad Cyriacum.

There was the same superstition about baptism; and Chrysostom, being accused of having eaten something before he baptized, thinks it necessary to deny the charge with the same vehemence as before: *Λέγουσί μοι, ὅτι ἔφαγες καὶ ἐβάπτισας. Εἰ ἐποίησα τοῦτο, ἀνάθεμα ἔσομαι· μὴ ἀριθμηθείην εἰς ἐπισκόπων ῥίζαν, μὴ γένωμαι μετ' ἀγγέλων.*—Sermo antequam iret in exilium. (Doubtful whether it is Chrysostom's).

sacrament in the Christian system, and the light in which it ought to be regarded by Christian men, are questions of much more importance than any consideration of the time of administering it, or of its conjunction with other religious services. Such questions have at times violently agitated the Church, supplying cardinal subjects of debate in the gravest controversies, giving occasion to persecution and martyr deaths, and riveting or unbinding the fetters of superstition according as they were handled and resolved. Such questions are agitated still with no slight vehemence, and with no slight difference of thought and feeling. So different indeed are the views entertained respecting this sacrament, and prominently advocated in the present day by different sections in our Church; that the breadth of platform which can give standing-room for them all seems almost wide enough for Anglican and Roman Churchmen to find a place upon it together.

To consider this subject therefore as it is set forth in the New Testament, and as it appears in the ecclesiastical polity of the Apostles, is a task of very lively and serious interest. It is one which I would approach with all gravity, and with a desire to ascertain and to express the view which our Lord himself and His Apostles give us of this sacrament with as little as possible of any party spirit or personal prepossession.

The first step in the enquiry respecting the nature of the ordinance of the Lord's Supper is naturally to look at the circumstances and the language of its original institution. Our Lord Jesus Christ on the same night that He was betrayed, had joined with His Apostles in celebrating the Jewish Passover—that service of solemn joy, belonging to the promise made to Abraham rather than to the Sinaitic law—in which the lamb slain, and the sprinkled blood, were obvious types of Himself, and of what He was just going to accomplish for mankind. Taking some of the bread and of the wine which had been used in this sacrament of the Old Testament, He appointed them to be in future the outward symbols of a corresponding ordinance under the new dispensation of the Gospel covenant. Having pronounced a blessing, or thanksgiving, over them, He broke the bread, and gave it, and after it the cup of wine, to His disciples with those simple but solemn words, with which we are all familiar, bidding them henceforth to do this in remembrance of Him.

Whatever meaning Jesus *then* attached to His words, *that* is the meaning which we should desire to keep in all our thoughts upon this sacrament. In whatever sense His Apostles, taught by the Spirit, retained and applied the words in the administration of it, *that* is the sense in which we should desire still to receive and to apply them. And it may help us to do this aright, if we look first at some particulars of the Jewish ordinance out of which this Christian Passover was evolved.

1. At the celebration of this festival among the Jews the master of the house, or whoever presided at the supper, took some of the unleavened bread, and breaking

it blessed it, and gave thanks to God for all His mercies, and especially for the deliverance of their fathers from Egyptian bondage; and the cup of wine, which they drank immediately after eating the lamb, was called "the cup of blessing"—the very name which St. Paul gives to the wine of the Lord's Supper.[1] Thus our Lord took up some of the very ceremonies of the Passover, and applied them to His new institution; from whence we may conclude that they were to be understood as nearly as possible in the same sense as they had been in the older covenant. Now the Paschal Lamb with its blood of sprinkling was so eminently a representation of Christ and His atoning death, that we may well say that in the later ordinance the bread was to be Christ's body,

---

1 "The officiator at the Passover held up some of the unleavened bread, and said, 'This is the unleavened bread which we eat, because the dough of our fathers had not time to be leavened, before the Lord revealed himself, and redeemed them out of hand. Therefore are we bound to give thanks, to praise, to laud, to glorify, to extol, to honour, to magnify him, that hath done for our fathers and for us all these wonders; who hath brought us from bondage to freedom, from sorrow to rejoicing, from mourning to a good day, from darkness to a great light, from affliction to redemption. Therefore must we say before Him, Hallelujah, praise ye the Lord! praise, ye servants of the Lord,' &c. And so he said over Psalms cxiii. and cxiv., and concluded with this prayer, 'Blessed be Thou, O Lord our God, King everlasting, who hast redeemed us, and redeemed our fathers out of Egypt, and brought us to this night to eat unleavened bread and bitter herbs.'"—Lightfoot's 'Temple Service,' xiii. 6.

"At the Passover, the third cup (they drank four) was drunk after eating the Lamb, and was called the 'cup of blessing.' This is the cup which Jesus told his disciples to divide amongst themselves. The fourth cup—commonly called the cup of the Hallel, or hymn—was the one which he took and used for the institution of the Lord's Supper."—*Ibid.* xiii. 8.

just as the Paschal Lamb had been His body before: the wine was to be the New Testament in His blood, just as the sprinkled blood of the Paschal Lamb had been the Old Testament in His blood before. And as the lamb and its blood had been to the Israelites the body and blood of Christ by sacramental anticipation; so the bread and wine are in an exactly similar way the body and blood of Christ to us in a sacramental memorial of the past; there being in neither case any change whatever wrought out in the visible signs or figures by which the unseen realities were, and are, represented; nor in the later any more than in the earlier sacrament, any ground whatever for supposing that the things which are seen and used are transformed by some divine and mysterious action, into the invisible things which are represented by them.

2. The words also used by our Lord on this occasion, considered simply by themselves, lead to the same conclusion. "This cup," He said, "is the New Testament in my blood." Can these words mean anything else than that the cup with its wine, thus given to His Apostles, was to represent, or remind them of, the new Gospel covenant of mercy and blessing founded on and ratified by the shedding of His blood for the remission of sins? It is simply impossible in these words, with any regard to sense and intelligible meaning, to insist upon a literal acceptation of them, and to affirm that the cup is the New Testament, by some change miraculously effected in it, or that any other than a figurative or repre-

sentative character was imparted to it. And if this be so, then the words, "This is my body," applied to the bread, must have a similar meaning; and that element also of the supper must be equally a figure or representation.

3. Besides this there is an earlier chapter in the Gospel history, which without containing any expressed reference to this sacrament, supplies a most valuable explanation of the language of its institution. In John vi. the words used by our Lord, when He calls Himself the true bread from heaven, and asserts that without eating His flesh and drinking His blood we have no life in us, are declared by Him to be worthless, if taken in the literal and carnal sense, in which the multitude received them. His flesh and blood are here referred to, not as objects of sight or even of mental apprehension, as they were in themselves, but as being given for the salvation of man; and the declared necessity of eating and drinking them is only a striking lesson for the inner spiritual life deduced from the outward actions of the body. As bread in order to nourish the corporal life must be eaten, and not merely touched or seen; so Christ, the Son of God made man, and giving Himself for us to be the food and nourishment of our spiritual life, must not merely be known or heard of, but must be received within by the self-appropriating power of a personal assent to, and reliance upon, this Gospel truth. And any other meaning in this case is absolutely revolting and impossible. Moreover the words of Jesus in this chapter are all the more instructive, because the idea

of eating His flesh and drinking His blood is not here associated with any outward object, and is therefore the more unmistakably altogether a mental or spiritual act, a "feeding on Him in the heart by faith with thanksgiving." And hence it follows that the sacramental ordinance of the body and blood of Christ did nothing more than offer the same truth in another form; teaching us by visible objects and actions representing the unseen, what had been taught before by words; impressing the same doctrine upon our hearts by means of the sight and touch, which had been before imparted through the hearing of the ear. In both cases the saying is alike applicable, "Crede et manducasti." Believe in the Lord Jesus Christ, as having given His body, and shed His blood for thee, and then thou hast eaten and drunk, in the only way in which thou canst eat and drink, this spiritual food. And thus this sacrament, as it came from the Saviour's hands, appears as a sacred and significant action, exhibiting the faith, hope, and joy in Christ, and the communion with Him and with each other, which were to mark the profession and the life of His disciples.

The Apostles of Christ having received this ordinance from their Lord introduced it at once, under the divine guidance, into the ministrations of the Church. And while it is spoken of in the New Testament in the most simple terms, utterly avoiding the extravagant and sensational language which was afterwards so frequently employed; and while as an ecclesiastical rite it has no remarkable prominence given to it in the system of the apostolic Church; the following particulars may be distinctly gathered as taught and sanctioned by inspired authority.

1. That this sacrament is a divinely appointed ordinance, to be reverently used; and even when associated, as it was at first, with an ordinary supper, to be distinguished from it by its sacred character.

2. That it is to be celebrated as a memorial and representation of Christ, giving Himself to die for us; and is intended continually to declare or proclaim His death, and to remind Christians of what He did for them.

3. That by a due reception of this bread and wine in conformity with the Lord's appointment, the communicant has a participation in all the benefits of Christ's body given, and His blood shed, for us; and is thereby assured of God's love and goodness towards him, and of his spiritual union with the Saviour, and with the blessed company of all faithful people.

4. That being a service of this holy import, it should be attended, not without serious thought and self-examination; and that a careless or profane use of it, as if it differed not from some ordinary food, was an offence against the body and blood of Christ therein commemorated, and incurred the divine displeasure, instead of obtaining a blessing.[1]

[1] An unfortunate mistranslation and misunderstanding of two verses in 1 Cor. xi., have helped to occasion and keep up some erroneous views and superstitious scruples about the Lord's Supper. The words in verse 27, "Whosoever shall eat this bread and drink this

In the apostolic mode of administering this sacrament, it is more than probable that the only formulary observed was a repetition of the acts and words of the original institution.

Indeed, as the whole transaction of the Last Supper was reproduced in this service, the expressly sacramental portion of it would naturally be an imitation of what the Saviour had done and said; and the only form of consecration the blessing or thanksgiving such as He had used.[1]

In the middle of the second century, after the separa-

cup of the Lord unworthily *shall be guilty of the body and blood of the Lord,*" have led to a vague but alarming supposition, that a want of worthiness in the communicant makes him guilty of — putting Christ to death! But the words really mean that disorders such as those at Corinth—and, consequently, any other profane treatment of this holy ordinance — was an offence, not against good manners merely, or common propriety, but against the body and blood of Christ therein represented,—a desecration of a hallowed thing. The words, as they now stand in our Bible, have, strictly speaking, *no meaning*. A person may be guilty of a crime; and the expression "guilty of death," though incorrect in form, is obvious in sense; "but guilty of the body and blood" is, at any rate, in modern English, unintelligible: ἔνοχος ἔσται τοῦ σώματος should be translated, "Will be guilty *concerning* the body."

The words in verse 29, "Eateth and drinketh damnation to himself, not discerning the Lord's body," introduced also unfortunately into our Communion Service, have often alarmed scrupulous minds. The translation ought to be, "Eateth and drinketh (κρῖμα) judgment, or condemnation, to himself, from not distinguishing the Lord's body" from a common supper; such condemnation being immediately afterwards declared to have involved some affliction, sent to correct so grievous an error.

[1] The words of St. Paul in 1 Cor. x. 16, "the cup of blessing *which we bless,*" and "the bread *which we break,*" and his informing them in the following chapter, that he had received from the Lord and delivered unto the Corinthians, what Jesus did and said in the institution of this sacrament, seem to warrant this conclusion, independently of all other considerations.

tion of the Lord's Supper from the "Feast of Charity," a very similar usage was still observed. The bread and wine being placed before the presiding minister, he led the devotions of the congregation by ascribing praise and glory to God, and expressing at some length their thanksgivings for all His mercies, and especially for those more immediately associated with their present service. And so prominent a place did this giving of thanks then occupy in the minds of Christian worshippers, that the name of "The Eucharist," ἡ Εὐχαριστία, *i.e.*, the thanksgiving, was one of the common appellations by which this sacrament was at that time known. At the conclusion of the minister's prayer the congregation all expressed their assent by saying Amen, and the sacred elements were then distributed by the deacons of the Church. In this account thus given by Justin Martyr two practices are mentioned, which appear to have been usual at that period, though they are not found in the New Testament. Water was mixed with the sacramental wine, under the probably correct supposition that wine thus mixed, being used at the Jewish Passover, must have been given by Jesus at the first. And portions of the bread and wine were after the service taken by the deacons to members of the congregation, who from sickness or other causes were unavoidably absent, in token of the loving communion in which they also had a part.[1]

[1] The following is Justin's account: Ἔπειτα προσφέρεται τῷ προεστῶτι τῶν ἀδελφῶν ἄρτος καὶ ποτήριον ὕδατος καὶ κρά-

But in considering the apostolic use and administration of this ordinance it is particularly necessary, as in some other cases, to mark the *omissions* of the New Testament.

In the Sacred Record :—

1. There is not the slightest intimation that the validity of the sacrament depended upon any ministerial power or act; or that any Christian minister had the power of conferring sacramental grace through his administration of it. Indeed the analogy of the Jewish Passover, which this ordinance closely followed, will suggest that any Christian might preside at the Lord's table, although after a time, as a matter of order, it would naturally devolve upon a presbyter to conduct this as well as the other religious services.

2. There is not the slightest intimation that any change whatever was effected in the bread and wine; or that any power or virtue, natural or supernatural, was infused into them. They are not even said to be "consecrated," but only to have a blessing or thanksgiving offered over them.

ματος· καὶ οὗτος λαβὼν αἶνον καὶ δόξαν τῷ Πατρὶ τῶν ὅλων διὰ τοῦ ὀνόματος τοῦ υἱοῦ, καὶ τοῦ Πνεύματος ἁγίου ἀναπέμπει, καὶ εὐχαριστίαν ὑπὲρ τοῦ κατηξιῶσθαι τούτων παρ' αὐτοῦ ἐπὶ πολὺ ποιεῖται. Οὗ συντελέσαντος τὰς εὐχὰς καὶ τὴν εὐχαριστίαν, πᾶς ὁ παρὼν λαὸς ἐπευφημεῖ λέγων, Ἀμήν. Τὸ δὲ Ἀμὴν τῇ Ἑβραΐδι φωνῇ τὸ γένοιτο σημαίνει. Εὐχαριστήσαντος δὲ τοῦ προεστῶτος, καὶ ἐπευφημήσαντος παντὸς τοῦ λαοῦ, οἱ καλο μενοι παρ' ἡμῖν Διάκονοι, διδόασιν ἑκάστῳ τῶν παρόντων μεταλαβεῖν ἀπὸ τοῦ ευχαριστηθέντος ἄρτου καὶ οἴνου καὶ ὕδατος, καὶ τοῖς οὐ παροῦσιν ἀποφέρουσι. Καὶ ἡ τροφὴ αὕτη καλεῖται παρ' ἡμῖν, Εὐχαριστία.—'Apol.' i. § 85.

3. There is not the slightest intimation that our Lord Jesus Christ is in any sense present *in*, or *in conjunction with*, the consecrated elements; or that His presence in the believer's heart at this service is different in kind from His presence in him at prayer, or in any other spiritual communion.

4. There is not the slightest intimation that the Lord's Supper is a sacrifice, or that the sacramental elements are offered on an altar by a priest.

All these forms of sacramental doctrine, omitted in the New Testament, and unsupported by apostolic teaching, were afterwards introduced into the Church system, and grew in strength and hurtful power, as wider departures from divine truth took place. All these doctrines were more or less immediately connected with the sacerdotalism of those times. They are still favourite tenets with Churches and individual men, by whom such sacerdotalism is upheld. They fall to the ground when it is overthrown; and revive with the re-establishment of its power. For a priest must have a sacrifice;—the sacrifice in a Christian Church must be found in the Eucharistic elements;—these elements to be a sacrifice must become literally the body and blood of Christ, or must have Christ in them or with them;—and consequently some change, more subtle, or more gross, must be represented as effected in them by the official action and power of the priest. And thus the whole system is wrought out, and each part of it coheres with and supports another.

But it has been already pointed out, and, as I venture to think, distinctly proved, that according to the New Testament there is no priesthood in the Christian Church, but the eternal priesthood of our Lord Jesus Christ, and in a secondary sense the universal priesthood of all those who are in Him. And consequently, as a sacrifice requires a priest, there can be no sacrifices in the Christian dispensation, but the one great and all-sufficient sacrifice offered once for all in the Saviour's death; and the spiritual sacrifices which each Christian offers in virtue of his share in the universal priesthood,—the living sacrifice of himself,—the sacrifice of doing good, and communicating to others,—the sacrifice of praise and thanksgiving.

But it may be well further to remark that it is not by such an inference only that the idea of a sacrifice is excluded. It is excluded also by the fact that no word signifying a sacrifice, or an altar which implies a sacrifice, or anything akin to them, is ever in the New Testament used of the administration of the Lord's Supper, or of any other ministerial functions in the Christian Church.

In reply to this assertion, the words in the Epistle to the Hebrews, "We have an altar," are sometimes put forward to justify the notion of a Eucharistic sacrifice.

It is assumed that the "altar" here named is the Communion table, and consequently that the Lord's Supper is a sacrificial service, the officiating minister a sacrificing priest; and thus an attempt is made to bring in the whole sacerdotal system under cover of this scriptural authority.

But such an application of these words is inconsistent with the context, violates the principles of sound interpretation, and is at variance with the plain meaning of the words as they actually stand. For the context shows that the sin-offerings of the Jewish dispensation are here contrasted with the sacrifice of the death of Jesus as the sin-bearer for man, and therefore the "altar" must be the cross on which He died. And it is a mere makeshift to evade this meaning by thrusting the eleventh and the three following verses into a parenthesis, in order to disconnect them with the tenth.

It is also contrary to all legitimate interpretation to take this single expression, and without any internal necessity to give it a meaning, which will fasten upon the subject of the Lord's Supper a view quite at variance with all that is elsewhere plainly declared about it in the New Testament.[1]

---

[1] It may be laid down as an axiom in the theory and practice of hermeneutics, which must not be departed from in the interpretation of any author, and especially an inspired author, that, "when a subject has been clearly and distinctly spoken of in several passages, all consistently giving the same view of it, we are not at liberty to take some single expression, standing alone, and not necessarily referring to the subject at all, and from this to extract, according to our pleasure, quite a different view from that which was before given."

Now the subject of the Lord's Supper is repeatedly spoken of in the New Testament, and in every instance in which it is distinctly referred to, the words, and the ideas, of a *sacrifice* or an *altar*, are altogether excluded.

That this is so, is seen—

1. In the *terms of its institution:* where the attempt of Sacerdotalists to call "do this" τοῦτο ποιεῖτε, a sacrificial term, is sufficiently met by

And if we take the words, "we have an altar" just as they stand, and in their most literal acceptation, what do they affirm? That as the older dispensation had an altar, so *we*, in the Christian dispensation, *have an altar*. Yes! the Jewish Church had an altar, *one altar*, not an altar in every synagogue, but one, only, divinely sanctioned altar in the Temple, on which acceptable sacrifices were placed. And we, under the Christian covenant, have an altar, *one altar*, not an altar in every Church, but one, only, divinely sanctioned altar, the Cross of Christ, on which the one, full, perfect, and accepted sacrifice was offered for us once for all. It was a

---

observing that, among the nearly 600 times in which the word ποιέω occurs in the New Testament, there is no instance of its having this meaning, except that in such passages as these it suits their purpose to discover it.

2. In the *names* by which it is called—

"The breaking of bread."

"The Lord's Supper."

3. By the terms in which it is spoken of by St. Paul in 1 Cor. x. 16, &c., and 1 Cor. xi. 20, &c., where he dwells on the subject at some length. Notice especially in the former of these chapters, verses 20, 21: "The things which the Gentiles sacrifice they sacrifice to devils, and not to God; and I would not that ye should have fellowship with devils. Ye cannot drink the cup of the Lord, and the cup of devils; ye cannot be partakers of the Lord's table, and the table of devils." Where, if the Lord's Supper were a *sacrifice*, and the Lord's table an *altar*, it would have been more natural and forcible to say, "Ye cannot be partakers of the Lord's altar and the altar of devils." But though in the heathen worship there was *an altar and a table*, in the Christian churches there was a *table only*.

To call the Lord's table then "an altar," is to give quite a different view of the subject from that which is contained in all these passages, and to extract it from a solitary expression, which does not necessarily refer to that sacrament.

Therefore "we have an altar" cannot, by any just interpretation, be said to mean "we have the Lord's table."

criminal and superstitious will-worship, when the Jews multiplied altars in their land. What will it be in us, if we set up an altar in every parish church![1]

To trace in the history of post-apostolic thought and practice how the notion of a sacrifice in the Lord's Supper crept into the Church, and how with it the

---

1 Another interpretation of Heb. xiii. 10, which gives a very different view of the writer's meaning, but is supported with much ingenuity and sound argument, was put forward a few years ago by the Rev, J. Taylor, in his volume on 'The True Doctrine of the Holy Eucharist,' and deserves the serious consideration of theologians.

According to this view, the writer in this passage expresses himself as a Jew writing to Jews, and identifying himself with them, as St. Paul often does in other places; and the "altar" is the Jewish altar, or sacrifice, namely, the sin-offering, the blood of which was brought into the sanctuary, but the body was burned without the camp, no part of the flesh being eaten by those who attended in the Temple.

The following is accordingly Mr. Taylor's explanation of the whole passage. "Be not carried about with divers and strange doctrines; for it is a good thing that the heart be established with *grace*, not with *meats*, which have not profited those that have been occupied therein (those who have eaten). (Indeed, so far from *eating* being important,) we (Jewish people) have an altar (a sacrifice) whereof they have no right to eat who serve the tabernacle (whereof the priests themselves are not allowed to eat, which would never be, if *eating* were an essential part of the service). For (instance) the bodies of those beasts, whose blood is brought into the sanctuary by the high priest for sin, are *burned* without the camp, (and, therefore, could not be *eaten*, though this did not prevent the blessing being received by the faithful worshipper). Wherefore, Jesus also, that he might sanctify the people by (the sprinkling of) his own blood (and not by his flesh being carnally partaken of) suffered without the gate (as the sin-offering was always consumed there.)" For further details of Mr. Taylor's argument the reader is referred to pp. 116–122 of his book before-mentioned.

It is obvious that, if this be the true meaning of the passage, it only proves still more strongly the position which I have maintained, as to the absence of all sacerdotal terms in connection with the Christian ministry and its functions.

notion also of a change in the consecrated elements sprang up, and grew more and more, until these two together gave birth to the doctrines of transubstantiation, host-worship, and the offering of Christ himself upon an altar by a priest, with a train of gross superstitions which followed in the rear, would be an instructive though a saddening task. But I can here only with great brevity notice some of the different steps by which this progress of error marked its downward course.

1. As the spiritual sacrifice of praise and thanksgiving was intimately connected with the service of the Eucharist, to which it gave its name, it was a very slight departure from apostolic truth and language to call the whole solemnity in this sense a sacrifice. And of this some indications appear in the writings of Justin Martyr, who, although he does not use any such expressions in his account of the celebration of the Lord's Supper in his 'Apology;' yet when contrasting the Christian with the Jewish economy, he observes that the sacrifices, which Jesus Christ ordered, were those which Christians offered in the thanksgiving over the bread and wine; and again that prayers and thanksgivings are the only perfect and acceptable sacrifices, and that these alone are offered by Christians in their commemoration of the suffering of Christ.[1]

---

[1] The following are Justin's words: *πάσας οὖν διὰ τοῦ ὀνόματος τούτου θυσίας, ἃς παρέδωκεν Ἰησοῦς ὁ Χριστὸς γίνεσθαι, τουτέστιν ἐπὶ τῇ εὐχαριστίᾳ τοῦ ἄρτου καὶ τοῦ ποτηρίου, τὰς ἐν παντὶ τόπῳ τῆς γῆς γινομένας ὑπὸ τῶν Χριστιανῶν, προλαβὼν ὁ Θεὸς μαρτυρεῖ εὐαρέστους ὑπάρχειν αὐτῷ.*

And then just afterwards: *Ὅτι*

2. In the latter part of the second century, a little further advance had been made. It was customary at that time for all the members of a Church to give bread and wine from which the elements for the celebration of the Lord's Supper were taken. These, as we learn from Irenæus, were regarded as thank-offerings of gratitude to God, as the first-fruits of His creatures, and as a token that they consecrated to the Lord's use all that they possessed. Hence these were called a pure sacrifice, acceptable to God; just as St. Paul calls the supplies sent to him by the Philippians, "a sacrifice acceptable, well-pleasing to God." But that these oblations were still considered as spiritual sacrifices offered by all Christians, is evidenced by the remark of Irenæus, that these gifts were offered on "the altar in the heavens, to which all our prayers and oblations are directed." In this same author appears the first indication of the idea of a change of any kind effected in the elements by the prayer of consecration; although it has in Irenæus a somewhat vague and ill-defined expression.[1] But neither

---

μὲν οὖν καὶ εὐχαὶ καὶ εὐχαριστίαι ὑπὸ τῶν ἀξίων γινόμεναι τέλειαι μόναι καὶ εὐάρεστοί εἰσι τῷ Θεῷ θυσίαι, καὶ αὐτὸς φημι. Ταῦτα γὰρ μόνα καὶ Χριστιανοὶ παρέλαβον ποιεῖν· καὶ ἐπ' ἀναμνήσει δὲ τῆς τροφῆς αὐτῶν ξηρᾶς τε καὶ ὑγρᾶς, ἐν ᾗ καὶ τοῦ πάθους ὃ πέπονθε δι' αὐτοὺς ὁ υἱὸς τοῦ Θεοῦ, μέμνηνται.—'Dial. c. Tryph.' 117.

The idea of a sacrifice, thus connected with the Lord's Supper, differs but little from that which is expressed in our Communion Service, where, in one of the concluding prayers, we desire our heavenly Father, "to accept this our sacrifice of praise and thanksgiving."

[1] Irenæus about the sacrifice in the Lord's Supper, says, "Igitur Ecclesiæ oblatio quam Dominus

at this time, nor in the earlier view of Justin was there any reference to the sacrifice of *Christ* expressed or implied in such words, as if that was repeated in the Eucharistic service.

3. But in the third century, when the outward, materialized conception of spiritual things was already exerting a stronger influence, an influence extended and confirmed by the manner in which fellowship with Christ, instead of being regarded as flowing from a believing appropriation of the Saviour in the heart, was made to depend on the outward instrumentality and intervention of the visible Church;—when at the same time and in close

---

docuit offerri in universo mundo purum sacrificium reputatum est apud Deum et acceptum est ei. . . . . . . offerre igitur oportet Deo *primitias ejus creaturæ*, ut in quibus *gratus* exstitit homo, in his gratus ei deputatus, eum qui est ab eo percipiat honorem. . . . Et propter hoc illi quidem (the Jews compared to slaves) decimas suorum habebant consecratas, qui autem perceperunt libertatem (Christians) *omnia* quæ sunt ipsorum *ad Dominicos decernunt usus*, hilariter et libere dantes ea, non quæ sunt minora utpote majorem spem habentes, viduâ illâ et paupere hîc totum victum suum mittente in gazophylacium Dei. . . . . . Non igitur sacrificia sanctificant hominem; non enim sacrificio indiget Deus; sed conscientia ejus qui offert sanctificat sacrificium pura existens. . . . . . Quoniam igitur cum simplicitate Ecclesia offert, juste munus ejus purum sacrificium apud Deum deputatum est. Quemadmodum Paulus Philippensibus ait, &c. . . . . . Nos quoque offerre vult Deus munus ad altare frequenter sine intermissione. Est ergo altare in cælis; illuc enim preces nostræ et oblationes nostræ diriguntur.—'Adv. Hæres.' iv. 34.

The allusion of Irenæus to the idea of a change in the Eucharistic elements is found in the same chapter as the former quotation.

"Quemadmodum enim qui est e terra panis percipiens invocationem Dei, non jam communis panis est, sed eucharistia, ex duabus rebus constans terrena et cælesti; sic et corpora nostra percipientia eucharistiam jam non sunt corruptibilia, spem resurrectionis habentia."

connection with this view, the Christian ministry was represented as a priesthood after the Jewish model, and its ministrations conformed as far as might be to those of the Old Testament;—and when a desire to present Christianity in a form as attractive as possible to the pagan mind was felt by some of the best bishops of that age;—there inevitably resulted greater changes in the Church system with respect to the nature and administration of the Lord's Supper, as well as of the other sacrament, than any which had previously been made. And these changes, beginning with the third, gained force and emphasis in the following centuries, being recommended, encouraged, and insisted on, by the teaching of the most distinguished men who in those times adorned and misled the Church.

During that period, this once simple ordinance became in the general estimation of the Church a literal *sacrifice;* the Communion table, an *altar;* the officiating minister, a *priest.* The sacrifice was no longer now the spiritual sacrifice merely of praise and thanksgiving, or the thank-offerings of all the communicants; but it was the sacrifice of *Christ himself*, symbolically and representatively perhaps at first, but afterwards spoken of in language, which, however modern ingenuity may attempt to soften it down, could convey to ordinary hearers at the time no other meaning, but that a real sacrifice of Christ himself was repeated in this service;—that His body and blood objectively present in the elements were offered up by the priest;—and even that Christ himself lay upon the altar, surrounded by attendant angels to do Him honour, and sacrificed there for the benefit of man.[1]

The notion of a change in the bread and wine, of which a slight indication only had previously appeared, now necessarily assumed a very definite and literal shape. It was declared that the sacramental elements were transformed into the very body and blood of Christ by the priest, either through the divine power of the words of Christ which he repeated, or through the direct action of the Holy Spirit, whose descent upon the elements he invoked in his prayer. Communicants were accordingly taught that the priest took in his hand "the Lord of the universe," (*τοῦ κοινοῦ πάντων ἐφάπτηται δεσπότου*), and that they received into their hands their "king" (*τῇ δεξιᾷ ὡς μελλούσῃ βασιλέα δέχεσθαι*).

It is true that the patristic writers of this period sometimes use a more sober language; but even this is very far removed from that of the Apostles, and produced no effect upon the ordinary current of Church teaching, belief, and practice, when everything else which was said and done had a directly contrary tendency.

It is true also that the word "transubstantiation" was not then employed; on the contrary it was usually, though not always, declared that the *substance* or *nature* of the bread and wine was not changed;[2] yet it is equally

---

[1] The proofs of the statements contained in this and the following pages, being too long for a note, are placed in Appendix A.

[2] Sometimes the very *nature* was declared to be changed; as *μεταστοιχειώσας τῶν φαινομένων τὴν φυσιν*. Gregory Nyssen. 'Orat. Catech.' § 37.

insisted on that a *divine nature* was added to, and incorporated with, the material elements; that in them, as in the baptismal water, and in the ointment of the chrism, a change was made by which they were effectually altered in their *qualities*, and an inherent power imparted to them. And besides this the very explanations and modified statements, which were sometimes given, show what the common teaching of the Churches must have been, to render such modifications needful.

It is in vain that Protestant advocates have endeavoured to rescue the Nicene Church from the charge of gross superstition in their dealings with this sacred rite, and to fasten the doctrine of transubstantiation and its consequences upon the later Church of Rome alone. The doctrine of the earlier period differed from mediæval Romanism, on this point, in scarcely anything beyond the use of another and synonymous word. In the fourth century the change in the Eucharistic bread and wine was called, as in the case of the baptismal water, "transelementation." And is it possible to say what real or important distinction there is between the earlier and the later word? Is it possible to point out any practical difference between a change of *elements* or *qualities*, and a change of *substance?* seeing that we know nothing about the substance of anything, except from its qualities, and it is only through its qualities that the substance of anything can affect us.

Besides this, what the sacramental doctrines of those

times really were, may be safely inferred from various practices incidental to, or resultant from them.

With a superstitious reverence, quite alien to the Apostles' teaching, it was considered even in the time of Tertullian a distressing thing if a particle of the consecrated elements fell to the ground.

Minute directions for holding the hands in a particular way for receiving the bread into them, and for taking the cup, are given by Cyril of Jerusalem, mingled with expressions, which will accord only with the belief that the sacramental elements are the Lord himself.

Chrysostom repeatedly terms the Lord's Supper "a most awful sacrifice," at which "the very angels shuddered;"—shows, as before mentioned, that it was deemed a heinous sin for it to be given or received by one who had on that day previously taken food;—and declares that the sacred elements, when received into the body, did not pass through the processes of digestion and excretion like other food, but were in some miraculous way taken up into the human frame.

And, finally, the consecrated elements, as shown by Cyril of Jerusalem and Theodoret, were worshipped with an adoration, but little differing, if at all, from the mediæval host-worship of the Church of Rome.

In conformity with the same doctrine, this sacrament, like that of baptism, was thought to be absolutely necessary for the salvation of all, and to be possessed of an inherent supernatural virtue. It was consequently administered to infants, as well as to adults. Portions of the consecrated bread were "reserved" in the custody of the Church, to be ready for emergencies; and to be dropped into the mouth of the dying, as a *viaticum*, "to smooth their path from earth to heaven." It is no wonder therefore if some people went a little beyond the authorised superstitions, and gave this *viaticum* to the *dead*. Communicants even in the third century took home from Church some of the sacramental bread, and kept it in their houses, in order to eat a portion of it every morning by themselves for their soul's life and sustenance; and miraculous effects were even then ascribed to it. But in the following century it was usual for Christians to carry about portions of this bread with them in travels and voyages; and to have a small piece attached to the person was believed to be a sure preservative in the greatest dangers. Neither were such superstitions confined to the vulgar and ignorant; but were upheld by the highest authorities and lights of the Church.[1]

To complete our consideration of these sacramental doctrines and practices, which so strongly marked this notable period, it is necessary to observe how they affected the Christian remembrance of the dead. The communion of saints was not broken by death; and when the gifts of communicants were regarded as thank-offerings, similar oblations were presented in the name

---

1 See, for instance, Ambrose's account of his brother Satyrus being saved, when shipwrecked, by having a piece of the consecrated bread tied in a scarf round his neck.

of those who had fallen asleep, and especially of the martyrs of each community, to signify that they were still united together in the same bond of Christian fellowship. But this harmless custom soon degenerated; and the righteous dead were mentioned at this service in the belief that by the prayers and intercessions of departed prophets, apostles, and martyrs, the supplications of the Church were made more acceptable to God; and also that the offering up of the sacramental sacrifice in behalf of all dead Christians was of the greatest benefit to their souls. A little later in the same century the prayers and sacrifices of the Church were offered for all nominal Christians after their death, whether they were good or bad; and Augustin in particular expresses his approbation of the practice in terms which would fully justify the doctrine of Purgatory as held in the Church of Rome. Some of the grossest errors which darkened the mediæval Church before the dawn of the Reformation, were only these doctrines and practices of the third and fourth centuries a little more intensified, and mixed with a little more of ignorance and superstition.

At the Reformation it happened from various causes that the doctrines respecting the sacrament of the Lord's Supper became a very central point in the conflict with Rome. In this country, at any rate, in the transition period of this great movement, the question of alleged orthodoxy or heresy, of conformity or martyrdom, often rested on this ordinance, and gathered round it all the forces of the controversy. It was to some of our eminent and good men a question of actual life and death, demanding therefore their gravest consideration, and most careful judgment.

Before they had fully emancipated their minds from the trammels of human error which had so long bound the Church, our early Reformers had been enabled to grasp the great fundamental principle that the written word of God, and not ecclesiastical tradition, is the fountain of authority in religious doctrines; and with a truth-loving determination very rarely equalled, they resolved to seek *there* the solution of the Eucharistic question, and at all hazards to abide by it when found. In maintaining this resolution, they not only faced death in a dreadful form, rather than deny what they were convinced was true; but with a moral courage of a higher and more noble kind they preferred truth before every other consideration, before every opposing sentiment or opinion which had naturally preoccupied their minds. Deeply imbued as they were with patristic learning, the special study of their previous years, and accustomed as they had been to admire and venerate the Christian Fathers of the earlier centuries, and to derive from them their dogmatic theology and habits of religious thought; their love of truth outweighed all such prepossessions. They put aside all the teaching of the earlier and the later Church which they found to be inconsistent with that of the New Testament. And they went back to the pages of inspiration for the doctrines which they were to uphold, and to the purity of the apostolic age for the ceremonial in which these doctrines were to be set forth.

It is owing to this that we have now in our Prayer-book, in spite of some blemishes and unamended defects, so grandly simple and nearly primitive a Communion Service; with no teaching of transubstantiation or trans-elementation in it,—no change in the sacramental elements indicated or implied,—no exaggerated or materialized declaration of the presence of Christ,—the very word "altar" carefully excluded, with all notion of a sacrifice offered up in the service, except the spiritual sacrifices of praise and thanksgiving, of ourselves, our souls and bodies, and of communicating to those who are in need,—no prayers or offerings for the dead or trust in their intercession,—no adoration of the consecrated elements,—no directions for a fantastic or superstitious mode of receiving them,—no administration of them to infants,—no reserving of them for superstitious purposes,—no encouragement to a vain reliance on a formal use of them.

Every one of these unscriptural doctrines and practices our early Reformers had learned from the best Fathers of the third and fourth centuries, and found them almost all perpetuated and enforced in the Church of their own time. But they swept them all away from their own hearts, and from the Church of the Reformation, when they had discovered that they "were grounded upon no warranty of Scripture but were rather repugnant to the word of God." Oh! that we had more of their noble Berœan spirit to do the work which needs now to be done for the cause of Christian truth, and for the Church of Christ within our land.

LECTURE VIII.

APPLICATION AND CONCLUSION.

VIII.

APPLICATION AND CONCLUSION.

IN the foregoing lectures an attempt has been made,—not to give a full and comprehensive view of the apostolic Church as it appears in the records of the New Testament,—a subject too wide for our present limits,—but to select for consideration certain prominent points of special import, by which this divine institution is most strongly marked, and which, as it seems to me, are worthy of more attention, than at the present time they usually receive. And although many particulars have been left untouched, or noticed with great brevity; yet enough has at any rate been observed, to supply from its intrinsic importance materials for serious thought to Christian men in this our day; especially to those who reverence and love our national Church, who see its dangers, and who earnestly desire that its outward form, as well as its inner spirit, should be regulated, as far as possible, by divine truth and wisdom.

Most interesting has it been to me,—however I may

have failed to make it so to others,—most interesting, though not without its sadness, to trace the characteristic features of the Church of Christ in its primitive and apostolic state; and then to mark how its grand and spiritual simplicity, preserved awhile after the departure of the Apostles, began even in the earliest centuries to be marred by the doctrines and inventions of men, and to be overlaid with imposing but superstitious ceremonials. But it is not merely as an interesting historical study that I have desired to draw attention to the most ancient and only authoritative period of the Church. The lessons, which this history can teach us at the present time, are something more than an interesting study. They are, as it seems to me, the very lessons, which of all others it is most needful for us now to learn, that we may apply them to our own ecclesiastical polity and practice.

To put these lessons forward in a distinct and positive shape, and to say expressly, even in general terms, what ought consequently to be done, may be thought presumptuous in one who has no personal authority or official position, to command attention to his words. But in days like these, when long-established confidences are being overthrown, — when no mere reverence for antiquity can preserve any institution from the shaking of the time,—when in particular our national Church is in such a state, that men of all opinions are either wishing or fearing its speedy demolition,—it is well for every one, who sees the danger of its position, but does not despair of it, if only English Churchmen could be induced to consider what that position really is, and to act accordingly,—to speak out with all boldness, and to say, as far as he has opportunity to be heard by many or by few, what he believes the emergency requires. If it be God's pleasure the smallest instruments may produce the greatest effects; and strength may issue forth from weakness.

The original idea of an established or national Church unhappily grew up and shaped itself in Christendom from the false position assumed by the Christian body in the time of Constantine and subsequent Christian emperors. The Judaistic and semi-pagan tendencies, which before this had so strongly affected the Church system, unfortunately then carried the leading minds, and indeed the general feeling and convictions of the Church, to the Old Testament and the peculiarities of the Jewish polity, for their guidance in the change which had occurred in the posture of the civil power. Utterly forgetting the very essential distinction between the theocracy of the Jews with its politico-religious institutions of divine appointment,—and the religion of Christ, expressly declared to be not of this world, and to need not this world's weapons of defence,—they encouraged the employment of the civil sword to enforce the authority of the Church; until at last it became the settled and inveterate sentiment throughout Christendom, that it was the duty of kings and governments not only to establish Christianity as the religion of their dominions;

but to put down by force all deviations from the doctrines and practices of the Church thus established, and to maintain what it held to be Christian truth with the whole weight of their magisterial power.

This doctrine, though it attained its greatest height in the Church of Rome, and was associated with its most revolting tyranny, was too deeply rooted to be at once discarded by Protestant Churches, when they were freed from the Romish yoke. In our own Church religious toleration was long considered a national sin. The Puritans, with all their abhorrence of Romish doctrines, held as strongly as Rome itself that the persecution of dissentients, even to the death, was a religious duty. And the most earnest and devoted of the Scottish Churches at the present day still hold to nearly the same principles, but very partially modified by the opposing influence of modern thought.

The idea of a national Church entertained in England to the end of the Stuarts' dynasty, and since then only gradually and slowly put aside, was that the national Government was to choose *the true* religion,—*i.e.*, necessarily the religion which *it considered to be true;* to impose this chosen religion upon the people; to embody its forms and rules in the laws of the land; and to enforce them by civil penalties.[1] But at the present time, when reli-

[1] Jeremy Taylor, in his 'Liberty of Prophesying,' shows that he had some idea of the injustice and unreasonableness of religious persecution. He could write, "It is unnatural and unreasonable to persecute disagreeing opinions. Unnatural; for understanding being a thing wholly spiritual, cannot be restrained, and, therefore, neither

gious liberty has been at last secured, and the civil magistrate is no longer regarded as the highest authority in religious truth, our established Church stands on a very different footing,—must be looked upon in a very different light,—and must be maintained by very different means, from those which prevailed in the days of Queen Elizabeth, and in the seventeenth century.

For the security and permanence of our national Church it is necessary that it should be approved by the intelligence, and possess the affection, of the nation. The danger, therefore, of the Church of England at the present time may be measured by the extent to which it has lost its hold upon the mind and heart of the English people. Since, in a free country like this, where, if a popular conviction be real and strong, the popular voice

---

punished by corporal afflictions. It is in *aliena republica*, a matter of another world. You may as well cure the cholic by brushing a man's clothes, or fill a man's belly with a syllogism. . . . . And as it is unnatural, so it is unreasonable that Sempronius should force Caius to be of his opinion, because Sempronius is consul this year, and commands the lictors. As if he that can kill a man cannot but be infallible; and if he is not, why should I do violence to my conscience because he can do violence to my person?"—xiii. 10.

Yet in other passages of the same treatise, the worthy bishop is by no means so clear or satisfactory.

Locke, in his 'Letters on Toleration,' the first of which was published in 1689 is more decided and uncompromising in his opinions; and, as might be expected from him, enforces his conclusions with clear arguments, very forcibly expressed. But his sentiments were too much in advance of the age to produce much effect upon the minds even of the leading men.

King William III. seems to have had juster ideas, than any of our sovereigns before him, as to the duties of a civil government with respect to religion; but neither the parliament, nor the clergy, nor the country in general, were then able fully to appreciate them.

will be heard, and will prevail, the Church as a national institution could not long survive the loss of the national confidence. That our Church has lost this confidence to a considerable extent, and is, at any rate, approaching to a position which would render it no longer the Church of the English people, but one sect among others in the land, cannot, in the face of the most obvious facts, be with any truth denied, or with safety be ignored.

The causes, or essential symptoms, of this state of things, a consideration of which is necessary in order to appreciate, and if possible to apply, any remedies for their removal, are, I venture to submit, especially such as the following.

First, the felt unsuitableness of our Church system, in many respects, to the state of society, life, and thought amongst us. Some portions of its language, its formularies, and its regulations,—some of the things which it directs to be done, and some omissions of what might advantageously be ordered or allowed,—many of its processes, laws, and canons, whether cumbering the Church with their obsolete enactments like rusty weapons at once dangerous and useless, or else offending common sense and intelligence by their occasional and spasmodic enforcement,—its general stiffness and inflexibility in the midst of the great varieties of our actual circumstances,—have all operated to make it far less adapted to the present time, and far less capable of influencing the bulk of our population, than it is most desirable that a national Church should be. In all its outward points of contact with the nation's life, the Church for nearly the last three hundred years has, in fact, been almost standing still, while the people have been advancing in a movement, or rather a combination and succession of movements, which have wonderfully changed their whole condition; and have greatly altered their relation to the Church, and the feelings which they entertain towards it.

That great national institutions should shift and change with every breath of popular opinion, or with the ebb and flow of popular feelings, would indeed be a great evil even in secular affairs, and much more in those of religion: neither do I at all question the truth of Richard Hooker's words, that the alteration of long-established laws and customs, "though it be from worse to better, hath in it inconveniences and those weighty." Yet, on the other hand, it is no less certain that, while the divinely-revealed truths of Christian doctrine continue unchanged from age to age, and must always be unchangeably maintained, the forms, and ordinances, and prescribed practices, in which man's authority and Church discretion must exhibit those truths, may and ought to vary with the marked variations of human life and civilization. And a Church which does not allow this, must become in effect more and more dead and obsolete, and may expect to be left at last by the receding tide a stranded vessel upon a deserted shore.

A second cause of danger to our national Church arises from *internal dissension*,—from the great and irreconcilable differences of doctrine and of practice within its pale,—and the connection of these differences with our ecclesiastical system. That a national Church should embrace very considerable differences of religious opinion,—not requiring or expecting all it members, or even all its clergy, to look at the entire body of Christian truth with exactly the same eyes, or from the same point of view,—and that it should not insist on the very same outward forms and observances in every diocese, or in every congregation,—would not in itself be a cause of weakness and danger, but rather of strength and security. But that there should be, as there are in our case, doctrinal and ritualistic differences so strongly opposed to each other among the clergy of a Church, which still requires from them all the most exact agreement of doctrine and ritual, and which is supposed to bind down every beneficed clergyman to a rigid uniformity in his ministrations, as far as a solemn declaration can bind his conscience and his practice; and that there should be withal no discipline worthy of the name to prevent this scandal, nor any great attempt or care to alter the prescribed restrictions, the very strictness of which makes them so unavailing;[1] seems to me to be as

[1] Unreasonably stringent restrictions applied to a large body of men for any length of time will always be evaded or rendered practically worthless by many of those who are supposed to be bound by them, such result being often accompanied with demoralising effects. A memorable example of this has been exhibited in the history of the "Act of Uniformity," which was bound upon the Church of England at the "Restoration."

dangerous a symptom of decadence and disruption as can well be imagined in a Christian community.

Under such circumstances the different schools of religious thought and practice, as they are sometimes called, are not like the differences of opinion which mark a wholesome state of religious liberty, and intelligent faith; for they are necessarily stamped with more or less of a demoralized and dishonest character, which injuriously affects the clergy themselves, however they may succeed in satisfying their own consciences; and which tends to weaken their moral influence with the people at large,—to dissociate in the popular mind the ideas of religious profession and of honest truthfulness,—and so to undermine the general confidence in a Church which admits of so anomalous and unsatisfactory a condition.

The gravest evils might be expected to result from such a state of things, independently of any question as to the soundness or unsoundness of the doctrines which are held and taught by any of the different parties in the Church. But when to this is added the fact that an active, zealous, and influential body among the clergy, well organized and closely united within their own ranks, not over-scrupulous as to the use of means, and encouraged by a large measure of success, are endeavouring to bring us back to the doctrines and practices of the fourth and fifth centuries and through them to Rome,—the danger to the Church appears still more imminent. For although this Romeward movement will doubtless never succeed in persuading the English nation to submit again to the yoke of papal bondage,—it may succeed in producing a large amount of superstition and infidelity ;—it may succeed in creating such a feeling of disgust and indignation against the Church, as must ensure its overthrow,—its disestablishment and disendowment as a national institution,—its existence only as an opposing power against all the sense and intelligence of the nation.[1]

A third source of danger, and one in some respects more formidable than the others in its immediate bearing upon the security and permanence of our national Church, is *the want of union and consolidation* between ourselves

[1] The following remarks of Mr. Froude at the end of his 'History of the Reign of Queen Elizabeth,' should be carefully considered by all honest and patriotic churchmen. "To the countries which rejected the Reformation, freedom never offered itself again in the dress of a purer religion. It returned upon them as Revolution, as the negation of all religion. In Austria, in Spain, in France, in Italy, the Church has been stripped step by step of its wealth, of its power, even of control over the education of the people. Practical life has become secularized, and culture and intelligence have ceased to interest themselves in a creed which they no longer believe. Doctrine may be piled upon doctrine ; the laity are contemptuously indifferent, and leave the priests in possession of the field, in which reasonable men have ceased to expect any good thing to grow. . . . . If the same phenomena are beginning to be visible in England, they have appeared as yet in a less aggravated form. *They are manifesting themselves at present coincident with the repudiation by the clergy of the principles of the Reformation ;* and if the clergy are permitted to carry through their Catholic 'revival,' the divorce between intelligence and Christianity will be as complete among ourselves as it is elsewhere ; but we have been exempted hitherto by the efforts of those brave men, whose perseverance and victory it has been my privilege in these pages to describe ; and unless we are unworthy or degenerate, it is not yet too late for us to save ourselves."—Vol. vi. p. 534.

and other Christian bodies in our own country; and the want of a close alliance, and even of friendly communion, with Churches in other lands.

A desire for union with some other Churches has indeed of late years been increasingly felt in several quarters amongst us; and Eirenicons in word and act have been held forth, if haply either the Greek or the Roman portion of Christendom might be drawn nearer to us, and we to them. If such a union could be effected on the basis of acknowledged truth, and with a compromise only on such non-essential questions as are left undecided in the New Testament, to be ordered by the discretion of each Christian community, it would be a happy consummation, indeed. But as there seems at present no prospect of such a consummation, nor even any perceptible shadow of it appearing in the far distance, it will be wise to attempt an easier and more promising task, and to endeavour to unite ourselves with Churches, which hold the same great doctrinal truths as our own, and differ only, if at all, in outward form and government.

A union or close alliance with the Presbyterian Churches in Scotland, and with other orthodox Protestant bodies, Episcopal or Presbyterian, on the Continent, and in other parts, would necessarily strengthen our hands as well as theirs, and would greatly further the cause of apostolic Christianity throughout the world. And looking nearer home at the bodies of Christian men in England itself, as sound in the faith as we are, and holding all or almost all the Articles of our Church, but unfortunately separated altogether from us into different sects and denominations, it is impossible to doubt that, if they could be united with us in one religious community, it would prove an immense accession of strength to the Church, comprehending as it would within its borders almost the whole of the nation's religious life.

It is perfectly obvious that one of the greatest dangers which threaten the Established Church, is caused by the co-existence with it of large and powerful bodies of nonconformists, commanding respect by their numbers, intelligence, learning, and piety; and occupying a position necessarily more or less antagonistic to it. These dissenting Churches are growing stronger year by year; and how great is their influence on the national mind and will is but too painfully evidenced by the recurrence of "Religious Difficulties," which from time to time impede or utterly prevent important measures, of which all approve, but which can be accomplished only, if at all, with maimed and curtailed effect, from the antagonism existing between churchmanship and dissent.

Ever since the firm settlement of the reformed religion in this kingdom in the reign of Queen Elizabeth, it has been the desire of the wisest statesmen and of the most enlightened well-wishers to the country and the Church to consolidate the religious profession of the nation. And repeated attempts were made by them,—first, to prevent the extension of non-conformity, and afterwards to comprehend the great body of Protestant dissenters within the pale of the Church, by judicious alterations in its formularies. These laudable efforts were unfortunately frustrated by the obstinacy of the sovereign,—the reactionary violence of party feeling,—or the power and short-sightedness of the clergy. And since the failure of the "Comprehension Act"[1] nearly two hundred years ago, things have been allowed to take their course without any sustained and vigorous efforts to remedy the increasing evil.

In the presence of these dangers, all of which are still

---

[1] A grand opportunity was lost, and turned into a source of ruinous mischief, by the obstinacy of Queen Elizabeth in refusing all concession to the large, influential, and loyal portion of her subjects, who desired the principles of the Reformation to be legitimately carried out. And a similar policy on the part of the crown, under the influence of the Romanizing and tyrannical Laud, issued in the violent outbreak of Puritanism, and in the overthrow of the Church and throne.

At the Restoration much good might have been effected, if the violent reaction against the Presbyterian and Puritan party had not miserably blinded those who had the power.

The last golden time for consolidating the sound religious faith and feeling of the nation was lost in the reign of William III., when his wisest ministers, supported by the king's enlightened sentiments, endeavoured in vain to pass the "Comprehension Act."

"Those distinguished statesmen did, however, make a noble, and in some respects a successful, struggle for the rights of conscience. Their wish was to bring the great body of the Protestant Dissenters within the pale of the Church by judicious alterations in the liturgy and the articles; and to grant to those who still remained without that pale the most ample toleration. They framed a plan of comprehension which would have satisfied a great majority of the seceders; and they proposed the complete abolition of that absurd and odious test, which after having been during a century and a half a scandal to the pious, and a laughing-stock to the profane, was at length removed in our own time. The immense power of the clergy, and of the Tory gentry, frustrated these excellent designs."—'Macaulay's Essays;' 'History of the Revolution,' by Sir J. Mackintosh.

advancing with greater force as time goes on, it is surely the best policy to realize our actual position, to look the dangers in the face, and hopefully to adopt the best available means for averting them. And the path of policy is here the path of duty. For it is the duty of a national Church to extend its legitimate influence as widely as possible,—to hold forth divine truth in the clearest manner and to the greatest number,—and, as far as the manifestation of the truth can do it, to root itself in the affections of the people.

A grave and temperate, but at the same time courageous and comprehensive, revision of our liturgy and our whole ecclesiastical system, with a view to wise and conservative reforms, and such changes as are necessary for re-invigorating our Church life, seems therefore to be now imperatively demanded. Such a revision is required, not to gratify the wishes of this or that religious school or party in the Church, but in order to meet the real wants and circumstances of the present age,—to secure a less cumbrous and more real and reasonable discipline,—to strengthen the foundations of the Church in the national mind and conscience,—to enlarge its basis in conformity with a truly Christian and apostolic liberality,—and what is the greatest thing of all, to exhibit in the most distinct and impressive manner the great Christian truths which have been committed to its trust;—and thus as far as possible to draw together into a compact and healthy union the religious faith and life of the nation.

In attempting this great and needful work, it is not to the third and fourth centuries, or any subsequent period of ecclesiastical history, that we must look for our authorities and guides. The Church of England is not dependent on, or subject to, any other Church, or the Church of any other times. Nor is it an unnecessary thing emphatically to affirm this independence, since practices alien to our Church have often of late been introduced, and defended, on the ground of such presumed subjection; and the canons of ancient councils have been held forth, as if we were altogether bound to obey them. We have wisely retained good rules and customs of the earlier Church, as we have adopted many laws of imperial Rome; but we owe no more allegiance to the councils of the one, than we do to the civil edicts of the other.

The authority, to which alone we should appeal, is that of the Divine Head of the whole Church, as it may be gathered from the words and actions of his inspired Apostles. The one safe and legitimate course in all our Church reforms is to go to the New Testament as our guide. The one great object of our desire should be to exhibit apostolic truth, as far as possible, in its apostolic form; and never willingly to depart from the great *principles* of the Apostle's teaching, when we may justly feel that we have full Christian liberty to deviate from their regulations, or to regulate what they left unruled.

This course would be a noble following out of what was done by the noblest fathers of the English Reformation. With their determination to set forth clearly in the Church the truth of Christ, as far as they themselves could see and apprehend it, they wished no other consideration to interfere. And as further light and knowledge were gained by them from the Scriptures, they did not hesitate to revise and alter what they had authorized at first. But, entangled as they necessarily were with fond notions about the ancient Church, from which it was scarcely possible that, without a miracle, they should have altogether cleared their minds, they bequeathed to their Church some difficulties and inconsistencies for those who came after them to remove. The truest honour which we can pay to their memory is to complete what they so auspiciously began, and in the same spirit as that in which they served their generation, to endeavour to benefit our own.

Such a course avowedly adopted and honestly carried out is not only right in itself, whatever its results might be; but it is one, which more than any other possible alternative, would approve itself to the intelligence of the English people, win back their confidence, and restore their waning affection to the Church. The people of this country have not lost their love and reverence for the Scriptures; and reforms made in acknowledged conformity with Scripture teaching, with the express intention of bringing out that teaching more distinctly before the people, and not for state purposes, or to gratify political or religious party-spirit, would confirm instead of unsettling the best sentiments of the popular mind, and would have, at the very least, a most wholesome effect upon the nation at large.

In those things which no divine or apostolic authority has determined for us, which yet must be determined in some way in the practice of the Church, as also in numberless details, which have necessarily been left to the judgment of each Christian community, a consideration of, though not a submission to, what our own, or other Churches in former times decreed, will be wise and needful. Christianity is a religion of facts and history, not of philosophic dogmas or abstract truths. And every modern Church has links connecting it with the past. Yet the history of ancient Churches is much more useful in holding out beacons to warn us of their errors, than in lighting up safe paths for us to follow in their steps.

It is especially in non-essentials of this nature that times and circumstances—the ordinary feelings, habits, and social and intellectual conditions of our own age—should be considered; and the Church should endeavour to meet the people upon their own ground, and to bring its ministrations into close contact and friendly sympathy with the national life. In these things also it is no wisdom, but the contrary, to require a strict and unvarying uniformity, which secures no useful object, and hinders rather than helps the general edification.

But above all, sound practical common sense and honest truthfulness should be allowed full scope in ecclesiastical laws and regulations. The continuance of shams and unrealities in dealing with sacred things, whatever excuses may be made for them, has necessarily a demoralising effect, and tends to make all religion be regarded as nothing but a cunningly devised fable.

On looking then to the apostolic Church of the New Testament for direction in the religious and ecclesiastical questions, which it will be necessary to consider, two great primary lessons are at once presented to us by the ecclesiastical polity of the Apostles, and may take precedence of all the rest. These two important lessons relate to the ministry and the sacraments of the Church; and they teach us that

Sacerdotalism and *Sacramentalism*

had no place in the Apostles' practice, or encouragement from their authority. And consequently a return to the purity of the primitive Church will lead to the exclusion of these post-apostolic errors.

Sacerdotalism.—With regard to the first of these, it was shown in a former lecture that the Christian ministry as instituted by the Apostles was certainly not a priesthood:—that sacerdotalism appeared at the beginning of the third century, and in the progress of its development brought in all the kindred notions of a priestly caste, a material altar, and a material sacrifice, which opened a wide gate to a flood of superstitions; but all this had no foundation at all in the New Testament or in the teaching and practice of the apostolic Church:—that the ordination of ministers by the

Apostles and by others in their time did not confer a spiritual power, but an ecclesiastical authority :—and that there is no intimation whatever in the New Testament, that ministerial power or authority was to be exclusively transmitted through any particular line or succession of ordinations; or that the validity of the sacraments is in any way derived from the fact of their being administered by one who has been so ordained; or that there is any such thing as "the grace of absolution" to be obtained exclusively or with any special effect from ministerial lips and hands;—the doctrines of the special confession of sins to a priest, and of penance imposed and absolution given by him, being unknown to the Church of the Apostles, and invented in a later age.

When compared with the apostolic view of the Christian ministry, the formularies of our Church in their exhibition of the ministerial office, display an inconsistency or incompleteness which ought not to have remained so long uncorrected.[1]

[1] The inconsistencies in our Prayer-book are principally owing to the fact that the Prayer-book of Queen Elizabeth's reign, which is substantially the same as that now in use, was the result of a *compromise*. The policy of the queen, both from personal and from political motives, was to conciliate Papists, without herself submitting to the Pope. The commission appointed to prepare the book were ordered "to favour the *first* Prayer-book of Edward VI.;" and besides this, in opposition to their recommendations, many important changes were introduced by the queen and her council, before the book was submitted to Parliament. This compromise so far succeeded that "the book was made so passable amongst the Papists, that for ten years they generally repaired to their parish churches without doubt or scruple."—(Heylin, 'Hist. of Ref.' ii. p. 286.)

"The reluctant commission of divines," says Bishop Burnet,

"Altars" having even in the reign of Edward VI. given way to "honest tables" in our Churches, while the word "altar" itself has been carefully expunged from our Prayer-book,—and the idea of a material sacrifice having been removed from all the prescribed acts of our officiating ministers,—it needs only a completion of this good work to remove also whatever encourages the thought that a Christian presbyter is a priest, and as such possesses the power of granting priestly absolution, of offering sacrifices, or of performing any other mediatorial work for Christian men.[1]

And when the idea of a priesthood is eliminated from the ministry of our Church, it will the more readily be seen that it is a thing which cannot be justified by any principle or practice of the primitive Church, that in our Ordination Service the words of Christ's commission to His Apostles should be addressed to a presbyter, telling him at that solemn time, "whose sins thou dost forgive, they are forgiven; and whose sins thou dost retain, they are retained;" a form of words never applied in the New

"reckoned that if that generation could have been on any terms separated from the Papacy, though with *allowances for many other superstitious conceits*, it would once unite them all, and in the next age none of those should any more remain."

The next age came, and the next reign, but every petition for relief from those "who sought it neither as factious men, nor as schismatics aiming at the dissolution of the state ecclesiastical, but as faithful servants of Christ, desiring and longing for the redress of divers abuses of the Church," was met with refusal and persecution. In the mean while, as remarked by Bishop Pilkington "pious persons lamented, atheists laughed, and the Papists blew the coals."

[1] The insufficiency of the plea that the word "priest" now means only Christian minister is shown in Lecture iii.

Testament to any but those who received their authority immediately from Christ himself; never used in Ordinations for many centuries after the Apostles' time; and whatever meaning the forgiveness and retention of sins may be supposed to bear, appropriate only to men endued with infallible knowledge and unerring judgment through the special inspiration of the Holy Spirit.[1]

[1] It is remarkable that those, who from Richard Hooker to the present time, have undertaken to defend the use of these words in the ordination of a presbyter, almost invariably miss the really gravest point of objection against them ; and satisfy themselves with explaining how the forgiveness of sins may, in some lawful sense, be included in the ministerial office. Even Archbishop Whately, usually so clear-sighted in an argument, falls into this error; and thinks it enough to remark that, in forgiving sins *as against* God, the Apostles did so by proclaiming the good tidings of forgiveness to all who should accept the Gospel invitation, and admitting to baptism the attentive and professedly repentant and believing hearers ; and, consequently, that Christian ministers may in that sense forgive sins now. "While," he continues, "offences *as against a Community* may, it is plain, be pardoned, or pardon for them be withheld, by that community, or by those its officers who duly represent it."—'Kingdom of Christ Delineated,' p. 98–101.

But although it is at any rate very undesirable that words requiring so much explanation, and liable, as experience proves, to so much abuse, should be used in so solemn a service, the insuperable objection to them does not lie in any particular meaning of the word "forgive," but in the *grant of infallibility* contained in the emphatic words, *Whosesoever* sins ye forgive, *they are forgiven.* The Apostles, it is true, did not infallibly know the state of every man's heart, but they *did infallibly know,* and *unerringly declare,* the terms of forgiveness. They were empowered to announce, *as by the word of God,* and without the possibility of mistake or the right of appeal, what men "must do to be saved ;" and to say to those, who heartily received their word, that God had forgiven their sins. In their case, therefore, it might be truly said, "Whosesoever sins ye remit, they are remitted unto them." But this cannot be so said of Christian ministers now. They are not divinely inspired to teach infallibly what men must do to obtain God's forgiveness. They can and do make mistakes in their teaching, even on

These words moreover but ill accord with the rest of the service, in which the work and duty of a Christian presbyter are excellently described with much truth and feeling, and in admirable conformity with what, as far as we can judge, were the work and duty of presbyters under the Apostles, and in the time which immediately succeeded them.

This office, so solemn and responsible, requires the continual gift of divine grace, to teach, strengthen, guide, and animate those who are appointed to it. None but God, it has been truly said, can make a true minister of the New Testament. Nothing but His Spirit can give the requisite powers for such ministrations. To remind men of this with touching earnestness at their ordination is good indeed. Good and needful too it is that earnest and united prayer should then ask for an out-giving of

---

the most important points. We may appeal against their declaration to the judgment of the Scriptures. The words, therefore, cannot truly be said *to them*, as they were to the Apostles. They cannot truly be said to them, without introducing *another condition* which essentially alters their meaning; namely, that the minister shall remit sins, or proclaim the terms of forgiveness, *in exact accordance with God's written word.*

Even with regard to *ecclesiastical* forgiveness, or retention of sin, a presbyter in our Church has no authority to forgive or retain, except in certain cases and under certain restrictions, in connection with the Lord's Supper. This is indeed what Hooker represents it mainly to consist in.

But what words are these to express so slight an exercise of ministerial authority! To use expressions capable of supporting the most lofty pretensions, and then by explanations to attempt to bring them down to the most innocent and humble claims, is a delusion and a snare, which never ought to be allowed a place in the hallowed ordinances of a pure religion.

heavenly grace for those who are admitted to such sacred duties. Such prayer was an apostolic practice; and was retained in the Church even after many errors and unapostolic notions had been associated with the idea of the ministry. And far better would it be to give a greater prominence to such prayer in our ordinal; instead of directing the bishop to use words,[1] which imply

[1] The use of these words has been felt to be a stumbling-block for the last three hundred years. Hooker writes respecting them, "A thing much stumbled at in the manner of giving orders, is our using those memorable words of our Lord and Saviour Christ, 'Receive ye the Holy Ghost'" ('Eccl. Pol.' v. § 77). And most unsatisfactory is his defence of our thus using them, and hardly consistent with itself.

Among the most recent defences of this formulary is the following, contained in Dr. Blakeney's valuable work, on the Book of Common Prayer.

"The third form, 'Receive ye the Holy Ghost,' is also novel in its use. There is, however, nothing objectionable in these words, as used in the English ordinal, when properly received. It consists of *a prayer, an address, and a charge.* 'Receive ye the Holy Ghost for the office of a priest in the Church of God, now committed unto thee by the imposition of our hands,' *is a prayer.* Such was the description given of it by Whitgift, who must have known well the views of Archbishop Parker and the other bishops. He says, 'To use these words, "Receive ye the Holy Ghost," in ordering of ministers, which Christ himself used in appointing his Apostles, is no more ridiculous and blasphemous than it is to use the words that he used in the Supper; but it is blasphemy thus outrageously to speak of the words of Christ. The bishop, by speaking these words, *doth not take upon him to give the Holy Ghost,* no more than he doth to remit sins, when he pronounceth the remission of sins; but by speaking these words of Christ, "Receive the Holy Ghost; whose sins soever ye remit they are remitted," &c., he doth show the principal duty of a minister, and assureth him of the assistance of God's Holy Spirit, if he labour in the same accordingly.'"—Works of Whitgift, p. 489, vol. i. P. S.

Of this and all other similar explanations it is sufficient to remark, that they really involve a *condemnation* of that which they are designed to defend. Interpretations savouring so much of a non-natural sense, show what sort of language ought

the giving of the Holy Spirit by his own power, when he lays his hands on those who are ordained; and which authorise them in consequence of this gift to forgive or retain the sins of men.

As long as such words continue to be so employed, it must be impossible to prevent the practice of the confessional in our Church, with any amount of its abominations, that individual presbyters may, in their discretion—or their indiscretion—think proper to introduce; or indeed, to prevent the whole sacerdotalism of the Church of Rome from following with it. For he who is directed to forgive sins, or to withhold forgiveness, may reasonably urge the consequent necessity of individual confession to himself, or as it is commonly called, "auricular confession;" and he who is expressly declared to be a priest, cannot by any explanations be prevented from making for himself an altar, and a sacrifice, though none is provided for him in the Church. It must be in vain to expect that our Prayer-book, framed for the express purpose of including Romanists, should now be able without alteration to exclude Romanizers.[1]

---

to be used, instead of justifying the present use. If a prayer is intended, why is there not a prayer actually used, which would need no elaborate explanation? A very excellent prayer might be selected with scarcely any alteration, from the 'Constitutiones Apostolicæ,' and to adopt it would be to return to a practice much more ancient than the use of our present formula.

[1] Such inconsistencies as the form of absolution in "The Visitation of the Sick," evidently introduced there to serve a temporary purpose in the transition time of the Reformation, will necessarily be removed, whenever a Scriptural revision of the Ordination Service is allowed to take effect.

Sacramentalism.—There has been at all times a close connection between the estimation and use of the Christian sacraments, and the views entertained of the Christian ministry. Wherever a right understanding and Scriptural estimate of the ministerial office prevails, *Sacramentalism*, or an excessive, unscriptural, and therefore superstitious exaltation of the sacraments, cannot easily supersede the simple and healthy practice of the earliest Church.

In that Church the baptism of those who repented of sin, and believed in Jesus as the divine Saviour, was regarded as being to them, "the washing of regeneration," the beginning of a new spiritual life, and an imparting of all the privileges of Christ's disciples. While at the same time no virtue was believed to be inherent in the rite itself; no consecration of the water was made, as if to infuse into it some mystical power; no sacramental grace was supposed to pass forth through it from the minister who performed the service; neither is any instance of infant baptism recorded in the New Testament, nor any directions given respecting it.

But from and after the beginning of the third century this sacrament was overloaded with a burden of ceremonies before unknown, all tending but too surely to produce the belief that a special virtue was conveyed into the water, and that it washed away sin by a supernatural efficacy of its own.

The application of the consecrated ointment with other imposing rites still further encouraged in ordinary minds the notion that the Church possessed a species of magic, by which those who joined it could have their sins annihilated, and a spiritual power *ex opere operato* imparted to them.

In like manner the sacrament of the Lord's Supper was the most simple of all ordinances in the apostolic Church. No idea of a sacrifice was attached to its celebration; no change was supposed to take place in the sacred elements; no virtue to be imparted to them or through them by the administrator; no presence of Christ *in* them, or *with* them, in any especial or peculiar manner. But in the post-apostolic Church all this was gradually changed, until at last the service was represented as a sacrifice offered upon an altar by a priest, the elements were spoken of and worshipped, as if they were Christ himself; and other gross superstitions naturally ensued.

Through all these accumulations of error and delusion the Reformation had to clear its way, and if the heroic men who first undertook the work left some portions of the Herculean task unfinished, which those who followed neglected to complete, it becomes us, who still enjoy the fruits of their labours, not to shrink from a lighter labour of our own, that we may finish what they so happily began.

The circumstances have been already noticed which led our early Church Reformers to examine and test the then prevalent doctrines and practices of the Eucharistic service with more depth and earnestness than any other subject. And the happy results of their honest and courageous search for the truth have so far survived the compromising efforts of later hands, that but little is found in our Communion liturgy, which a Scriptural revision would mark with disapprobation.

Here and there a few words would be corrected which from an apparent misunderstanding of certain texts are calculated to mislead the minds of ordinary hearers, and to give birth to unhealthy feelings of awe and dread, instead of a wholesome reverence and sacred joy. And the expressions which are sometimes represented as inculcating the Romish doctrines of the confessional and priestly absolution, though they cannot justly bear all that has been built upon them, should be freed from the ambiguity, which now attaches to them, and thus gives some apparent sanction to the assumption of sacerdotal powers.

In dealing with the other sacrament the original framers of our baptismal formulary were not under the same urgent necessity to search the Scriptures for the solution of all questions connected with it, inasmuch as that ordinance had not been so cardinal a point of vital controversy, as that of the Lord's Supper. And, consequently, they did not give us in every part so good an exposition of primitive doctrine and practice, as they did in their Communion service.

They were, it is true, too well acquainted with the New Testament not to mark numerous unauthorized and superstitious ceremonies, which had been added to the ordinance of baptism since the Apostles' days. And their reverence for patristic antiquity did not prevent them from sweeping these away, in spite of the authority of the early Church. And this very circumstance plainly shows that they would have made further alterations besides these, if they had seen that there were still some things in their baptismal service not sufficiently conformed to the written word of truth.

The defects, which I venture to believe an unfettered and courageous appeal to apostolic authority, such as was made in the case of the other sacrament, would have removed, are particularly the consecration of the fontal water,—the taking for granted that the baptism of unconscious infants must be in all respects the same as that of believing adults,—and the ecclesiastical fiction of the sponsorial promises.

1. The prayer of consecration, "Sanctify this water to the mystical washing away of sin," encourages the old superstitious belief that a mysterious change is effected in the element, by means of which the sins of the baptized are removed; and it is altogether unauthorized by the practice of the primitive Church. There is nothing of this objectionable nature in the Communion service. What is there called the prayer of consecration does not contain a single word indicative of any change in the bread and wine corresponding with this presumed change in the baptismal water.

The explanation that these words in our administration of baptism only mean "that the water is separated from common use to a holy purpose," is one of those interpretations which only show that the words are very inappropriate to the meaning which ought to be expressed.

2. The baptism of the children of believing parents, deriving its plea and justification from a reasonable application of apostolic authority, and Scripture promises, to the circumstances of later times, requires no unwarranted assertions or assumptions for its wholesome administration. The language used in the New Testament, when speaking of the baptism of *believing men*, does not justify the use of the very same terms in the baptism of *unconscious infants*. Words of dedication, of prayer, and of hope, may be lawful; but positive affirmation can hardly be justifiable, when it has no positive information or authority whereon to rest. Nor can it be right, in a solemn religious ceremony, any more than in secular transactions of common life, to assert that to be a fact, which we do not know to be so.

The conduct of the churchmen of those times, when infant baptism is first known to have prevailed, was at any rate in this matter consistent with their creed. They believed baptism to be absolutely necessary for salvation, so that infants, dying without it, could not be saved—and they accordingly baptized them. They believed that through the consecrating and transforming power of certain sacerdotal acts, the baptismal water with its holy oil and the sacred chrism were able, by their own inherent virtue, to convey the pardon of sin and the gift of the Spirit;—and they accordingly asserted that these same effects were produced in infants and in adults. But if we do not believe, as they did, that infants dying unbaptized must certainly perish, we cannot consistently regard infant baptism exactly as they regarded it. And if we do believe, as they did not, that the sacraments "are not physical but moral instruments of salvation," and do not take effect from "any natural or supernatural quality in them,"—we cannot have the same reason as they had for supposing that the effect of baptism must be exactly the same in children as in men. As a *moral* instrument it must necessarily be imperfect in the infant recipient; and it ought therefore to be so regarded, and the service for its administration should be framed accordingly.

3. The use of sponsors, to make declarations in the infant's name, probably originated at first, and has been since retained, from laudable motives; yet it is not only destitute of all scriptural authority direct or inferred,—but the fiction, which it introduces, gives an appearance of unreality to the whole transaction, and has been followed to a large extent by a demoralizing effect. The more so, since, by a strange perversity, the parents, who are the most fitted by their position to answer for the baptized child, were, by our ecclesiastical laws, until very lately, excluded from the office. If infant baptism were in itself unlawful, the addition of the sponsorial promises could not make it right. If it be most agree-

able with the institution of Christ, it needs not this addition to give it validity.

Most right and proper would it be that parents should be called upon to undertake that children, presented for baptism, should be brought up "in all virtue and godliness of living;" and far better adapted would such a practice be to secure a healthy reverence for the sacred ordinance, and to promote a godly use of it in our population at large, than is now found to be the case with our present service.[1]

[1] Baptism is now very often regarded by our upper and middle classes as a ceremony which it is the right thing to have performed; —to be made an occasion for some family festivity; for the giving of presents; or for securing, through godfathers and godmothers, connections which may be useful to the child's pecuniary interests: and by the lower classes, as a ceremony for giving the child a name, and a title to decent burial, if it should die; or, at the best, as an unintelligible mysterious method of making the child a Christian; while sponsors are sought for at random, to meet the ecclesiastical demand, without any regard to the engagements which they have to assume.

Although the direct assertion that unbaptized children must perish, which appeared in the Articles of 1536, has been removed from our formularies, yet an idea of a similar kind, all the more superstitious from its vagueness, is kept up in our population, (1) by the Rubric, which affirms that, "It is certain by God's word that children which are baptized, dying before they commit actual sin, are undoubtedly saved;" though, by the way, God's word says nothing whatever upon the subject; (2) by parents being instructed that, in case of illness baptism should be administered privately in houses, and in any way rather than not at all; (3) by unbaptized children being excluded from Church burial.

If parents were plainly taught that baptism is not a charm to be administered to dying infants, but a sacrament for those who are to live the Christian life; and that, when they bring their children to be baptized, they are themselves undertaking a Christian responsibility,—there might be a better hope that this sacred ordinance would be more duly appreciated, and made more beneficial than it now is.

A Christian Church is doubtless at liberty to institute rites and ceremonies on its own authority, provided that nothing be enacted contrary to God's word. Yet within this limit many different degrees of wisdom, and unwisdom, may find a place; even if in the present instance it can be justly said that this limit has not been exceeded.

With infant baptism administered as an ordinance of prayer and hope for the solemn dedication of the children of Christians to that Saviour, who suffered little children to come unto Him, and forbade them not;—and with confirmation afterwards, as a "Sacramental Complement," made a service for a real profession of personal repentance, faith, and godly obedience, of those who had been baptized in childhood;—our Church might secure all, and more than all, that can be gained by our present system, without any of the stumbling-blocks, which now often give occasion for disingenuous or non-natural interpretations,—perplexities for tender consciences,—and disunion between those who ought to be united in Christian brotherhood.

The most important lessons then, which may be learned from the apostolic Church for our own ecclesiastical polity, are these which immediately relate to the ministry and the sacraments. But there are many others to be gathered from the same source, secondary only to these in their importance, and worthy of our serious consideration. Of these I desire especially to notice *two*, which are particularly applicable to some of the wants of the present time; and which relate to our *public worship*, and to the *position of the laity* in our Church.

As there is no command in the New Testament respecting the use of extemporaneous prayers, or of the set forms of a prescribed liturgy, in public worship,—but both these modes have the sanction of antiquity, and every Church is left without the least restriction in this matter,—it is remarkable that within the compass of this island two national Churches should not only have made a different choice in these alternatives, but with a determined and blind partiality should have long adhered each to one of these two modes of worship exclusively, and have looked with positive abhorrence upon the other. Though either method has its own advantages, and its own defects, free prayer in the North, and a rigid unchangeable liturgy in the South, have been regarded almost as objects of vital and essential faith by their respective communities.

In our own Church the evils resulting from an undeviating adherence to an inflexible form of prayer have long been felt, and have of late years sometimes been even in high places openly acknowledged. They have been aggravated in our case by the circumstance that our liturgy, however excellent, was compiled, and all its regulations and arrangements ordered, in a state of society and national life altogether different from the present; while a revision, which might make it more capable of meeting the requirements of modern times, has hitherto been effectually prevented, and seems to be regarded by some good men as if it were something sacrilegious and profane.

The opposite defects of the system, which entirely excludes prescribed forms of prayer, have also of late been to some extent acknowledged in the Churches of Scotland; and a desire is beginning to be felt for a partial use of devotional formularies, where hitherto they had been looked upon as abominations.[1] If such deep rooted prejudices are giving way, where they might have been the least expected to do so, will it be too much to hope that the Church of England, with its more liberal spirit, may be led to see that some degree of choice and freedom may be granted to its ministers and congregations in our public worship, without deviating from the earliest precedents,—without contravening any apostolic rule,—

---

1 'Church Tendencies in Scotland':—

"Accustomed to popularity and influence, and possessing considerable flexibility of constitution, Presbyterianism has seldom shown itself unwilling or unable to retain the popular attachment by meeting the popular wants. And in the present instance, there are many tokens that Presbyterianism is seeking to adapt itself to the demand that has arisen for a larger infusion of life and beauty into its ritual. To the late Dr. Robert Lee belongs the credit of having first, and most clearly, seen what was wanted here, and of having set himself in the most effectual manner to supply it. His aim was, while retaining the vigour and thoroughness of the Scotch ideal of preaching, to borrow from Episcopalianism the best elements of its liturgical method, while correcting some of its obvious faults. The protracted and somewhat angry controversy, which arose upon the introduction of his reforms, has issued substantially in the success of his ideas. The movement for the improvement of the Presbyterian ritual, instead of being extinguished, has been confirmed."—Essay, by Rev. R. Wallace, D.D., in 'Recess Studies.'

and with manifest advantage to general usefulness? There is at any rate no ground of objection, either in the Scriptures, or in reason, against a system, which would combine the advantages of both methods, without losing the time-honoured and beautiful prayers which we have inherited from the Church of old.

The position of the laity in our Church, including their relations to the clerical order,—the duties incumbent on them,—the authority or influence which they ought to exercise,—and the aid which they may justly be expected to afford for the general welfare of the Christian community,—has begun at last here and there to excite attention, and to engage some of the thoughts of earnest men.[1] One of the most distinctive features of the apostolic Church was the great importance of the part assigned to the lay members of it. In the first century, and for several centuries beyond it, they elected, or at least freely expressed their approval or disapproval of

[1] "It cannot be necessary to dwell at any length on the circumstances of the times which are bringing into the foreground this question of the place of the laity in Church government. Some persons are attracted towards it from one direction, some from another; but the thoughts of very many seem to converge towards the same point. Is it too much to say that it is the great Church question of the day?"

"The old machinery of the Establishment is perceived to be very much out of gear. Those who are most anxious for the retention of the great blessing of the union of 'Church and State,' are also those who are looking about most anxiously for some means of re-adjusting the relations which subsist between the two bodies, now more than ever distinct and separate. It is in the introduction of the Church laity in some form or other that they are beginning to see a way out of their difficulties."—Essay IV. in 'The Church and the Age,' on 'The Place of the Laity in Church Government.'

those who were ordained to minister among them; and they appear at first to have exercised the power of deposing offending presbyters. In the maintenance also of Church discipline in all its several forms, and in questions of faith and doctrine requiring any dogmatic decision, the laity in the New Testament period held an influential position, and were called upon to give their voice and sanction to all ecclesiastical proceedings. Besides this their mutual sympathies and kindly fellowship, kept up by the *Agapæ*, or other Christian meetings, —the words of exhortation, warning, and encouragement, which they did not shrink from addressing to each other, —and their constant and ready help in all works of charity and kindness,—were powerful means in the early Church for strengthening and cherishing the religious life.

In our Church, on the other hand, a great cause of weakness and of failure has been the almost utter absence of lay influence and work. The general tendency of our system, in its actual working at any rate, has been to place each clergyman alone as the only motive power of Godliness in his parish; and to assign nothing to the parishioners to do.[1] His public ministrations in the parish Church, and his visits from house to house to the sick and the whole within his cure, were all that seems to have been looked upon as needful; and anything

[1] The office of Churchwardens, whatever it may once have been, is now quite powerless for anything beyond what relates to the material fabric and furniture of the Church. The system to which they belong, if it ever was effectual for much good, has now, at any rate, become obsolete.

beyond this was until lately by our ecclesiastical authorities discouraged, if not forbidden. It is no wonder that such a course of action has greatly failed to reach the masses of our population; and that not only much spiritual destitution, but much rampant irreligion, prevails in our parishes. Praiseworthy efforts have been made by good men to remedy this lamented state of things. By additional Churches and clergy, Scripture readers, Bible women, and other similar means, something has been done to encounter the most glaring symptoms of this our English heathenism. And cottage lectures, Bible classes, and communicants' meetings, are sometimes used to supplement the necessarily imperfect instructions of the Prayer-book and the pulpit. But all these are at the best but partial, and are more or less spasmodic in their action and effects.

I venture to think that something more systematic is needed; and that a return, as far as may be practicable, to the apostolic plan, by giving the laity a more prominent place in our Church,—by showing them that they have Christian work to do, and by encouraging them to take an interest in doing it,—is what our present condition most especially requires. And without pretending here to trace the details of such a reform, or to assert that it could immediately be brought into full operation; some good might be done at once by giving congregations a voice in the appointment of their ministers; some good might be done by reviving the practice of frequently assembling together the earnest Christians in our parishes under the direction and superintendence of their clergy, so that they might have some amount of real Christian fellowship with each other, a thing now entirely banished from our Church system.

Each assembly of this kind would be the really visible Church,—the ἐκκλησία,—in every place, spreading its Christian influence all around it. The several members would have opportunities of mutual exhortation and counsel. Unity would be promoted. They would learn to know and care more for each other, to sympathise with each others' trials, and to assist each other in temporal and spiritual things. The clergyman also would know more of his people and they of him. He would be better able to direct his ministrations among them. All useful plans and machinery for religious instruction, edification, and general benevolence, could thus be carried out, and kept in operation without his being overburdened, or obliged to leave the work half-done. And by the force of a healthy public opinion created through the instrumentality of this assembly, or local Church, immorality and ungodliness might be put to shame, and a considerable amount of Christian discipline might be exercised, even without the intervention and enforcement of any ecclesiastical laws. The great obstacles to the useful working of any such plan, which are presented by the artificial state of modern society, and by the utter want of discipline which has so long prevailed in our Church, might, it is to be hoped, be overcome by tact and patience. But a broad, liberal, and scriptural reform of our Church laws and formularies would be essential to its success.[1]

But finally, in dealing with such questions and all others of a similar nature, it is needful to bear in mind one great principle of constant application in everything connected with our religion,—a principle which ought to influence the whole course of our ecclesiastical polity, all regulations of the Church, and every administration of its ordinances; yes, and to influence all the members of any Christian community in their use of their Church's ministrations.

This principle is the great master-truth, that the *true Church of Christ*,—the body of which he is the head,—"the fulness of him who filleth all in all,"—to which alone all the promises and blessings of the kingdom of God belong,—is *an invisible society*, consisting of all those who are really united to Christ, and who, from union

---

[1] Dr. Owen, on Heb. x. 25, "Not forsaking the assembling of yourselves together," remarks,—

"These assemblies were of two sorts: 1. Stated, on the Lord's Day, or first day of the week. 2. Occasional, as the duties or occasions of the Church did require (1 Cor. v. 4). The end of these assemblies was twofold. 1st. The due performance of all solemn, stated, orderly, evangelical worship in prayer, preaching of the word, singing of psalms, and the administration of the sacraments. 2nd. The exercise of discipline, or the watch of the Church over its members, with respect to their walking and conversation, that in all things it be such as becomes the gospel, and giving no offence. So to admonish, exhort, and provoke one another to love and good works; to comfort, establish and encourage them that were afflicted, or persecuted; to relieve the poor, &c. Such assemblies were constantly observed in the first Churches; how they came to be lost is not unknown, though how they may and ought to be revived, is difficult."—Owen's 'Works,' vol. xxvii.

with Him as the head, are living members of His mystical body; and further, that the visible Catholic Church of professing Christians, or any particular branch and portion of it, can be called Christ's body only in a secondary, inferior, and imperfect sense; this name describing only its professed intention, and not the reality of its actual being.

The fundamental mistake of confounding the visible and invisible together in thought and word,—and thus regarding any particular Church as being to all within its sphere the very body of Christ, out of which there is no safety or Christian privilege,—was an error into which, as we have seen, the Church began to fall towards the end of the second century, and which all the tendencies of that time gradually deepened and extended. This error, which manifested itself in the throwing outward of the whole conception of the Church, helped greatly to encourage the notion of a priesthood, and to give a false view of the Christian sacraments, and of the general relation of the Church's office and work to those who were within and without its pale. And such false views strengthened in their turn the original misapprehension; and thus intertwined with each other in the growth of error, they have continued to act and re-act upon one another ever since.

Most desirable and necessary is it therefore that, in all attempts at ecclesiastical improvement, it should be distinctly kept in view, and distinctly displayed to view, that Christ, and not the Church, is the author of spiritual life; and therefore, that it is not our being members of the Church which unites us with Christ, but our being united with Christ makes us true members of His Church; —that every visible Church on earth is necessarily a mixed body of real and nominal Christians;—that outward admission to it and communion with it is of no spiritual profit, without the inward union with Christ himself;—and that separation from it involves no spiritual loss, if the inward union with Christ is still preserved.

It follows from this, that the highest function of any Church is to bring those to Christ, who have not yet been united to Him; and to edify and encourage those, who are in Him, to adorn His doctrine in their lives: —that the ministers of a Church, as its representative officers, can have no more power than the community, which they represent, itself possesses, and consequently have no force or virtue in their office, except so far as they hold forth the Saviour to men, and so far as the Saviour thus held forth is received, as the immediate source of spiritual life and strength, by those for whom their ministrations are performed:—and that the sacraments also, administered in and by the Church at Christ's commandment, derive all their efficacy from Him, and that too from their being means of spiritual communication with Him, and not from any virtue imparted to them, or through them, by the Church office-bearers, by whom they are administered.

When these truths are clearly apprehended, the New Testament account of the Clerical order and its ministrations is seen to be consistent with them, and shows that they were admirably adapted for maintaining in the visible Christian communities, an abiding sense of the work assigned to them in the divine economy of the Gospel dispensation. And then warned by the lamentable errors, which grew up and strengthened themselves in after times from this apostolic theory of the Church being obscured and lost, we shall all the more readily turn back again to the primitive times, and endeavour to regain our true position.

Not only then will our Church office-bearers be no longer regarded as priests usurping the place of Christ, with unauthorised imitations of his mediatorial work; but all the deceptive adjuncts and consequences of sacerdotalism, will also be easily discarded, or even fall off of themselves. The notions that Episcopacy is essentially necessary for a Church, and that a mysterious power, transmitted through an unbroken chain of Episcopal ordinations, can alone make men Christian ministers, will be unable to hold their ground. The use of æsthetic stimulants to devotion, appealing to the senses and imagination by means of architectural ornamentation, pictures, images, processions, crosses, and other symbolical objects, or of histrionic displays of ministerial acts with vestments, incense, artificial lights, prostrations, and fantastic gestures, and with the whole array of priestcraft, which now, as in more ancient times, beguile the ignorant and unwary,—will be seen to be not only no aids to Christian doctrine and devotion, but positive hindrances to them. Since in proportion as such things answer the purpose for which they are intended, and engage the attention and affect the feelings, to the same extent do they shut out Gospel truth, and hide Christ from the spirit of the worshipper.

Not only then will the grosser sacramentalism of mediæval Christianity, with its materialized views of Christ's spiritual ordinances, be no longer possible among us, but there will be less danger of our trusting to sacraments instead of Christ,—of our putting baptism with water for regeneration by the Spirit,—and the Eucharistic elements received into our hands and mouths for the Saviour received into our hearts; less danger of our shrinking from the Lord's Table with a superstitious dread, or with equally superstitious confidence trusting to coming to it in vain.

Then it may be hoped that the artificial sanctity of consecrated places, and the excellence or antiquity of a form of prayer, will not be thought to make a heartless worship acceptable, or to be necessary for that which is sincere; and that the separation between the clerical and lay portions of the Church being found to be less wide and deep, than the theory of a priesthood suggests, both portions will be enabled to co-operate together, without detracting from the respect due to the one, or assigning a false position to the other.

And then, too, will less difficulty be felt in effecting a friendly union with orthodox foreign Churches, whether episcopal or otherwise; and should our attempts at "comprehension" in our own land not succeed so far as to bring back and consolidate with ourselves large bodies of non-conformists,—there will be nothing at any rate to prevent relations of a most friendly nature between us and our dissenting Churches which "hold the head" as firmly as we do, instead of the present antagonism and unchristian estrangement.[1]

I have thus endeavoured to trace, though very imperfectly, the visible features of the Church as it appears in the New Testament; and to point out some of the lessons which we may learn from them for ourselves. If in this dangerous time, when the truth of Christ has so many assailants on all sides, and when our beloved Church, which ought to be, under the divine blessing, a tower of strength against them for the nation at large,

---

[1] Even within the Church of Rome there is rising in the minds of learned and moderate men a desire to hold out a friendly hand to other Churches than their own, and to join with them in the warfare against sin and error under the banner of Christ, instead of anathematizing them as heretics. How much more may we be willing to co-operate with those with whom we have no cause of difference, but some points of a non-essential character, and who are already associated with us in the ties of citizenship and close vicinity. The words with which the distinguished Romanist Döllinger concludes his treatise on "The Church and the Churches," read to us a wholesome lesson. "Tendons la main à toutes les sectes qui croient au Christ, pour soutenir avec elles une lutte défensive contre toutes les tendances subversives de notre époque. Ainsi que l'a dit M. de Radowitz ; nous voyons les esprits se ranger sous deux drapeaux, dont l'un porte le nom du Christ, fils de Dieu, tandis que l'autre réunit autour de lui tous ceux qui regardent ce nom comme un scandale ou une folie."—French translation by L'Abbé A. Bayle.

seems itself to be tottering and ready to fall from its national position,—I may have been able to suggest some useful thought, or to stir any hearts and hands to some hopeful exertion for the religious welfare of our country,——but if not, I could not refrain from saying what I have said; and with whatever feebleness and whatever failure, *liberavi animam meam.*

APPENDICES.

APPENDIX A.

SOME PRACTICES AND DOCTRINES COMMONLY CONSIDERED ROMANISTIC, BUT IN REALITY SUCH AS EXISTED IN THE EARLY POST-APOSTOLIC CHURCH, AND WERE ONLY RETAINED AND CONTINUED IN THE CHURCH OF ROME.

MANY doctrines and practices, unscriptural, dangerous, and superstitious, are commonly supposed by Protestant Christians to be characteristic of Romanism, while in reality they existed in the Church before or at the end of the fourth century; and were by the Church of Rome only retained,—sometimes, it is true, with the principles involved in them rather more fully developed,—but in some instances, on the other hand, with their attendant evils moderated and partially corrected.

To speak distinctly, my allegation is, that the Church system of the Nicene period, *i.e.*, in the third and fourth centuries, or before the death of Augustin, Chrysostom, Jerome, and other contemporary Fathers, was in all essential respects the same as that of the more modern Romanism; and hence that in all consistency, if we protest against the one, we must protest against the other; if we denounce the one as having departed from the faith once delivered to the saints, and having overlaid the formal orthodoxy of the acknowledged creeds with a mass of superstition, our denunciation must extend equally to the other. And, contrariwise, if the earlier system is admired and accepted, the same admiration and acceptance cannot be justly withheld from its later counterpart.

To substantiate this allegation, I shall enumerate some of the principal doctrines or practices which marked the Church of the earlier time; giving under each of them one or two proofs from the best contemporary authorities; proofs which might in almost all the cases be indefinitely multiplied in a wider space; but which even in the narrow limits of an Appendix will sufficiently establish what they are adduced to prove.

I. *The mixed chalice* and *the sign of the cross.*—I will refer in the first place to certain practices innocent and indifferent enough in themselves, and when they were first introduced, but afterwards associated with superstition; and of these I will instance the "mixed chalice" and the "sign of the cross."

(*a.*) The custom of mixing water with the wine at the celebration of the Lord's Supper is alluded to by Justin Martyr (A.D. 150), without any comment, and in a manner which seems to show that it was then no novelty. His words are, *οἱ καλούμενοι παρ' ἡμῖν διάκονοι διδόασιν ἑκάστῳ τῶν παρόντων μεταλαβεῖν ἀπὸ τοῦ εὐχαρισθέντος ἄρτου, καὶ οἴνου καὶ ὕδατος.* 'Apol.' i. 85. And again, *Ἄρτος προσφέρεται, καὶ οἶνος καὶ ὕδωρ.* 'Apol.' i. 87.

This custom probably arose from the circumstance that in those times, and particularly in the East, it was a usual thing to drink wine mixed with water; and as such mixed wine was drunk at the Passover, it was reasonably concluded that at the original institution of this sacrament mingled wine had been used. This simple and natural explanation however seemed too trivial in the following century, when a taste for higher mystical interpretations prevailed; and the mixing of the water with the wine was then said to denote, or even to *effect*, the union of the communicants with Christ; so that without the water the efficacy of the sacrament *would be seriously impaired.* Thus an innocent custom was turned into a superstition, encouraging a low, materialistic conception of this spiritual service.

Cyprian (A.D. 250) says, "Videmus in aqua populum intelligi, in vino vero sanguinem Christi. Quando autem in calice vino aqua miscetur, *Christo populus adunatur*, et *credentium plebs ei*, in quem credidit, *copulatur et conjungitur*. . . . Sic in sanctificando calice Domini offerri aqua sola non potest, quo modo *nec vinum solum potest.* Nam si vinum tantum quis offerat, *sanguis Christi incipit esse sine nobis.*" *Epist.* 63, *ad Cæcilium.*

(*b.*) The sign of the cross, at first perhaps a simple emblem of the Christian faith (as it is used by us in the administration of baptism), and a symbol of recognition among Christians, had become in Tertullian's time (A.D. 200) a perpetually repeated, and consequently almost unmeaning, ceremony in the Christian *family* life. On getting up or going to bed, on putting on their clothes or their shoes, on walking out or sitting down, at table or at the bath, in short in every act or movement, they made the sign of the cross upon their forehead. "Ad omnem progressum atque promotum, ad vestitum et calceatum, ad lavacra, ad mensas, ad lumina, ad cubilia, ad sedilia, quæcunque nos conversatio exercet, *frontem crucis signaculo terimus.*" *De Corona Militis*, § 3.

In the following century it appears conspicuously in all the *public* ceremonies of the Church, to the efficacy of which it was supposed greatly to contribute. Thus even the consecrated ointment which was poured upon the baptismal water in the font must be made to form this sign. *Διὸ καὶ ἡ τοῦ βαπτίσματος χάρις τελειοῦται διὰ τοῦ μύρου σταυροειδῶς ἐπιχεομένου τῷ βαπτιστηρίῳ παρὰ τοῦ Ἱεράρχου.* Dionysius, 'Eccles. Hierarch.,' iv. 10. And Chrysostom informs us that all the sacred acts were accomplished by means of it, whether in our regeneration, in our nourishment by the mystic food of the Eucharist, in Ordination, or any other hallowed rite. πάντα δι' αὐτοῦ τελεῖται τὰ καθ' ἡμᾶς· κἂν ἀναγεννηθῆναι δέῃ, σταυρὸς παραγίνεται· κἂν τραφῆναι τὴν μυστικὴν ἐκείνην τροφήν· κἂν χειροτονηθῆναι, κἂν ὁτιοῦν ἕτερον ποιῆσαι, τοῦτο τῆς νίκης ἡμῖν παρίσταται σύμβολον. Hom. 55, in Matt. And in the same homily, Chrysostom assures his hearers that this sign, devoutly made upon the face, is most efficacious in private use for driving away unclean spirits, no one of which will dare to come near when it sees this token of Christ's victory. Οὐδὲ γὰρ ἁπλῶς τῷ δακτύλῳ ἐγχαράττειν αὐτὸν δεῖ· ἀλλὰ πρότερον τῇ προαιρέσει μετὰ πολλῆς τῆς πίστεως· κἂν οὕτως ἐντυπώσῃς αὐτὸν τῇ ὄψει, οὐδεὶς ἐγγύς σου στῆναι δυνήσεται τῶν ἀκαθάρτων δαιμόνων, ὁρῶν τὴν μάχαιραν ἐν ᾗ τὴν πληγὴν ἔλαβεν. And this continued to be one great use of the sign all through the middle ages.

II. *Sacerdotalism.*—There is no indication in the New Testament that the Christian ministry was in the apostolic age regarded as a *priesthood*, either in name or in office; nor are there any traces of such an opinion in the Fathers of the second century. But from and after the beginning of the third century a great change is seen. The ministers of the Church were then looked upon as priests, a mediating, sacrificing, and absolving order, as the priesthood is now in the Church of Rome.

The bishop was then a high-priest, ἀρχιερεὺς or *summus sacerdos;* the presbyter, a priest, ἱερεὺς or *sacerdos;* and the deacon, a Levite, λευίτης or *levita.* The Lord's table was turned into an *altar;* and the Lord's Supper became a *sacrifice*, an imitation or repetition of the sacrifice of Christ.

The first Christian writer who shows that this change had taken place is Tertullian (A.D. 200). Thus, "Dandi baptismum quidem habet jus *summus sacerdos*, qui est episcopus." '*De Bapt.*' § 17. And, "Nonne solennior erit statio tua, si ad *aram* Dei steteris? utrumque salvum est, et participatio *sacrificii*, et executio officii." '*De Orat.*' § 14.

After Tertullian every patristic author abounds with evidence of the establishment of this sacerdotal system, and of the manner in which it operated in the Church. The work of the Christian ministry became a *priestcraft*. The priest was a *mediator* between God and the Christian laity, who were taught that he stood to them in the place of Christ,—was His representative and vicegerent,—and performed his office upon earth. Thus *Cyprian* (A.D. 250), "Neque enim aliunde hæreses obortæ sunt, aut nata sunt schismata, quam inde quod Sacerdoti Dei non obtemperatur, nec unus in ecclesia ad tempus sacerdos et ad tempus judex *vice Christi* cogitatur." *Epist.* 65, *ad Cornelium*. And again, "Utique ille sacerdos *vice Christi vere fungitur*, qui id quod Christus fecit imitatur." *Epist.* 63, *ad Cæcilium*. *Ambrose* (A.D. 370), "In ecclesia propter reverentiam Episcopalem non habeat caput liberum, sed velamine tectum, nec habeat potestatum loquendi, quia Episcopus *personam habet Christi*. Quasi ergo ante judicem sic ante Episcopum, quia *vicarius Domini est*, propter reatûs originem subjecta debet videri." *Com. in* 1 *Cor.* xi. 10.

Hence it was the priest, and the power of his office which, according to the teaching of the Nicene Church, gave effect to every Christian ordinance. It was the bishop as high-priest who consecrated the "holy oil," and gave it power to cast out devils from the catechumen; and who in a similar manner supplied the "mystic ointment" which helped to impart to the baptismal water its regenerating power, and which after baptism gave the Holy Spirit. It was the priest who regenerated men in baptism, who made the body and blood of Christ in the "awful sacrifice" of the Eucharist, and who acceptably offered up Christ upon the "altar" for the quick and dead. It was by the voice of the priests that the sentence of excommunication might be pronounced, and re-admission into Church communion be obtained. And even after death the priest's prayers and offerings were still effectual for good, and extended their power beyond the grave.

In one respect, however, the priestcraft of the Nicene age had not departed so far from apostolic truth, as did that of the Church of Rome at a later time. The practice of confession and absolution after the Romish manner had no existence in the third and fourth centuries. *See* Appendix C.

III. *Sacramentalism.*—The sacerdotalism of the third and fourth centuries was no mere question of words and names, but a deep and essential change introduced into the Church system; and one of its first effects was to graft upon the divine and simple religion of the New Testament an elaborate *sacramentalism* not surpassed in its superstitions by the darkest ages of the Papacy.

Both the sacraments were turned into awful mysteries. In both, the *opus operatum* doctrine was taught in the broadest and most unqualified manner. In both, the elements were affirmed to have an actual, objective, physical, miraculous change wrought in them through the Holy Spirit brought down into them by the power of the Church, and of the priest as its functionary; by which they produced their marvellous effects, and were regarded by people in general more as the instruments of magic rites, than the symbols of a religious service.

1. *Baptism.*—Thus in baptism, besides all the other complicated ceremonies, through which the catechumens had to pass, the holy ointment consecrated by a bishop, and so possessed of celestial virtues, was poured upon the water in the form of a cross, and this together with the prayer of the officiating priest produced, as it was affirmed, a change in its very nature which they called "transelementation," and gave the water an inherent power to wash away sin. Thus

Cyril of Alexandria (A.D. 412 says), ὅνπερ γὰρ τρόπον το ἐν τοῖς λέβησιν ἐκχεόμενον ὕδωρ, ταῖς τοῦ πυρὸς ὁμιλῆσαν ἀκμαῖς τὴν ἐξ αὐτοῦ δύναμιν ἀναμάττεται, οὕτω διὰ τῆς τοῦ Πνευματος ἐνεργείας, τὸ αἰσθητὸν ὕδωρ πρὸς θείαν τινὰ καὶ ἀπόρρητον μεταστοιχειοῦται δύναμιν, ἁγιάζει τε λοιπὸν τοὺς ἐν οἷς ἂν γένοιτο. Com. in Johan. iii. 5. For additional quotations, *see* Lecture VII.

2. *The Lord's Supper.*—In the Lord's Supper an actual, objective, physical change was said to be effected in the bread and wine; which, with much variety of expression, were declared to be no longer mere bread and wine, but to *be*, to *become*, to *be made*, to *be transformed into*, to *be transelemented into*, the body and blood of Christ. Thus,

Cyril of Jerusalem (A.D. 350) says, "the bread of the Eucharist is no longer mere bread, but the body of Christ," Ὁ ἄρτος τῆς εὐχαριστίας μετὰ τὴν ἐπίκλησιν τοῦ ἁγίου Πνεύματος οὐκέτι ἄρτος λιτὸς, ἀλλὰ σῶμα Χριστοῦ. 'Catech. Mystag.' iii. 3.

Ambrose (A.D. 370) says, "the bread *becomes* the flesh of Christ," Panis iste panis est ante verba sacramentorum; ubi accesserit consecratio, de pane *fit* caro Christi. *De Sacram.* iv. 4.

And Gregory Nyssen (A.D. 350), Ὁ ἄρτος πάλιν ἄρτος ἐστὶ τέως κοινὸς, ἀλλ' ὅταν τὸ μυστήριον ἱερουργήσῃ, σῶμα Χριστου λέγεται τε καὶ γίνεται. 'De Bapt. Christi,' vol. iii. 369.

Jerome (A.D. 370) says, that "by the prayers of the priests the body and blood of Christ *are made*." Quid patitur mensarum et viduarum minister, ut supra eos tumidus se efferat, ad quorum preces Christi corpus et sanguis *conficitur*. *Ep.* 85, *ad Evag.* And Cyril of Jerusalem says that "we pray God to send forth the Holy Spirit upon the elements that He may *make* them the body and blood of

Christ." Παρακαλοῦμεν τὸν φιλάνθρωπον Θεὸν τὸ ἅγιον Πνεῦμα ἐξαποστεῖλαι ἐπὶ τὰ προκείμενα, ἵνα ποιήσῃ τὸν μὲν ἄρτον σῶμα Χριστοῦ, τὸν δὲ οἶνον αἷμα Χριστοῦ. 'Catech. Mystag.' v.

Ambrose says that "the elements are *transformed* into flesh and blood." Quotiescunque sacramenta sumimus, quæ per sacræ orationis mysterium *in carnem transfigurantur et sanguinem*, mortem Domini annunciamus. *De Fide*, v.

Gregory Nyssen says, "Christ in this sacrament mingles Himself with the bodies of those who believe, in order that man may partake of immortality," and he then adds, ταῦτα δὲ δίδωσι τῇ τῆς εὐλογίας δυνάμει πρὸς ἐκεῖνο μεταστοιχειώσας τῶν φαινομένων τὴν φύσιν—"by *transelementing* the nature of the visible elements"—a *physical* change. '*Orat. Catech.*' § 37.

In connection with the belief that an actual change was effected in the nature or substance of the Eucharistic elements may be mentioned the declaration of Chrysostom that when taken into the body they did not undergo the same natural processes as took place with ordinary food— Μὴ ὅτι ἄρτος ἐστὶν ἴδῃς, he exclaims, μηδ' ὅτι οἶνος ἐστι νομίσῃς· οὐ γὰρ ὡς αἱ λοιπαὶ βρώσεις εἰς ἀφεδρῶνα χωρεῖ· ἄπαγε! μὴ τοῦτο νόει· ἀλλ' ὥσπερ κηρὸς πυρὶ προσομιλήσας οὐδὲν ἀπουσιάζει, οὐδὲν περισσεύει, οὕτω καὶ ὧδε νόμιζε συναναλίσκεσθαι τὰ μυστήρια τῇ τοῦ σωματος οὐσίᾳ. 'De Pœnitentia,' Hom. ix.

(*a.*) All the consequences and logical inferences which follow from the doctrine of transubstantiation were unhesitatingly adopted. Thus,

The body and blood of Christ were said *to lie upon the altar*, to be *carried in the sacred vessels*, to be *taken into the hands*, to be *tasted in the mouth* of the communicant.

Corpus Christi est in altari. *Ambrose*, 'De Sacram.' iv. 2.

Qui corpus Domini canistro vimineo, sanguinem portat in vitro. *Jerome*, Ep. ad Rustic.

Κοιλάνας τὴν παλάμην δέχου τὸ σῶμα τοῦ Χριστοῦ. Cyril of Jerusalem, 'Catech. Mystag.' v. 18.

Οὐκ ἄρτον κελεύονται γεύσασθαι, ἀλλ' ἀντιτύπου σώματος καὶ αἵματος τοῦ Χριστοῦ. Ibid. v. 17.

(*b.*) Further than this, they said that *Christ himself lay upon the altar,*—was *sacrificed,*—was *handled.* The service was called *a fearful mystery,* a *most awful sacrifice,* angels standing round with awe, &c.

Σὺ δὲ θυσίᾳ προσίων, ἣν καὶ ἄγγελοι φρίττουσι . . . ἐκφερομένης τῆς θυσίας, καὶ τοῦ Χριστοῦ τεθυμένου, . . . ὅταν ἴδῃς ἀνελκόμενα τὰ ἀμφίθυρα, τότε νόμισον διαστέλλεσθαι τὸν οὐρανὸν ἄνωθεν καὶ κατιέναι τοὺς ἀγγέλους. Chrysostom, Hom. 24, in 1 Cor.

Ὅταν δὲ καὶ τὸ Πνεῦμα τὸ ἅγιον καλῇ καὶ τὴν φρικωδεστάτην ἐπιτελῇ θυσίαν, καὶ τοῦ κοινοῦ πάντων συνεχῶς ἐφάπτηται δεσπότου (and takes in his hands the Lord of the universe !) . . . *τότε καὶ ἄγγελοι περιεστήκασι τῷ ἱερεῖ, καὶ ουρανίων δυνάμεων ἅπαν τάγμα βοᾷ, καὶ ὁ περὶ τὸ θυσιαστήριον πληροῦται τόπος εἰς τιμὴν τοῦ κειμένου.* Idem 'de Sacerdotio,' vi. 4. Could the most determined believer in transubstantiation say more than this?

(*c.*) *Adoration of the Host.*—Such words as those just quoted imply and justify the practice of *Host-worship ;* but such adoration is also expressly mentioned. Thus—

Cyril of Jerusalem in his directions to communicants as to the manner in which they should receive the bread and wine implies an adoration of them throughout, and then expressly says that they must take the cup bending down in a posture of *worship and adoration*—*μὴ ἀνατείνων τὰς χεῖρας, ἀλλὰ κύπτων καὶ τρόπῳ προσκυνήσεως καὶ σεβάσματος.* 'Catech. Mystag.' v. 18.

And Theodoret (A. D. 390-447) says of the bread and wine, "They are understood and believed to be the very things which they have become, and *are worshipped* as being the very things which they are believed to be." νοεῖται δε ἅπερ ἐγένετο καὶ πιστεύεται, καὶ προσκυνεῖται ὡς ἐκεῖνα ὄντα ἅπερ πιστεύεται.[1] 'Adv. Eutych. Dial.' p. 85.

(*d.*) Various superstitions naturally followed. Thus—

The vessels and veils, &c., used in the Communion service were *venerated as most holy*, and none but the sacred hands of priests or deacons were allowed to touch them. And Jerome says of them, Ex consortio corporis et sanguinis Domini eâdem quâ corpus ejus et sanguis majestate veneranda. *Ep. ad Theoph.*

It was considered a *dreadful thing* for a particle of the bread or a drop of the wine to fall; and a *crime* if this happened through negligence.

Calicis aut panis etiam nostri aliquid decuti in terram anxie patimur. *Tertullian*, 'De Cor. Milit.' § 3.

Reos enim vos creditis et recte creditis, si quid inde per negligentiam decidat. *Origen*, Hom. 13, in Exod.

Quanta sollicitudine observamus quando nobis corpus

---

[1] The following extract from the judgment of the Court of Arches, delivered July 23rd 1870, in the case of Sheppard *v.* Rev. W. J. E. Bennett, shows how modern High-churchmen receive the doctrine of the "Adoration of the Host." And if the teaching of the Nicene Church is to be our authority, their practice is the right one.

"By the expressions, 'the real, actual, and visible presence of the Lord upon the altars of our churches,' and, 'who myself adore and teach the people to adore the consecrated elements, believing Christ to be in them, believing that under their veil is the sacred body and blood of my Lord and Saviour Jesus Christ,' I have no doubt that Mr. Bennett has contravened the plain meaning and clear intent of the formularies of the Church."

But in a later edition of his book, Mr. Bennett substituted for the above expressions, — "The real, actual, presence of our Lord under the form of bread and wine upon the altars of our churches," and "who myself adore and teach the people to adore Christ present in the elements, under the form of bread and wine." And this amended form of Host-worship satisfied the Court of Arches, and Mr. Bennett was accordingly acquitted on this charge.

Christi ministratur, ut nihil ex ipso de nostris manibus in terram cadat. *Augustin*, Hom. 26 and 50.

The directions of Cyril (already referred to) for preventing this dreadful thing, and at the same time worshipping the elements, are those from which modern High-church clergymen take their instructions for communicants. They are as follows. "When you come forward [to receive the bread], do not come with your hands stretched out or your fingers separated from each other ; but make your left hand a throne for your right hand, which is going to receive your King ; and so making a cavity in your palm receive the body of Christ ; and after sanctifying your eyes by touching them with it, partake of the holy body, taking care not to lose any of it ; for if you were to do so, it would be as if you lost a portion of one of your own limbs. Then, after partaking of the body of Christ, come forward for the cup of His blood, not stretching your hands upwards, but bending down in the posture of worship and adoration, and be sanctified by partaking of the blood of Christ. And also sanctify your eyes, and forehead, and your other organs of sense by touching them with some of the moisture that is on your lips."

Προσιὼν σὺν μὴ τεταμένοις τοῖς τῶν χειρῶν καρποῖς προσέρχου, μηδὲ διηρημένοις τοῖς δακτύλοις ἀλλὰ τὴν ἀριστερὰν θρόνον ποιήσας τῇ δεξιᾷ, ὡς μελλούσῃ βασιλέα δέχεσθαι, καὶ κοιλάνας τὴν παλάμην δέχου τὸ σῶμα τοῦ Χριστοῦ, ἐπιλέγων τὸ Ἀμήν· μετ' ἀσφαλείας οὖν ἁγιάσας τοὺς ὀφθαλμοὺς τῇ ἐπαφῇ τοῦ ἁγίου σώματος μεταλάμβανε, προσέχων μὴ παραπολέσῃς ἐκ τούτου αὐτοῦ, ὅπερ γὰρ ἐὰν ἀπολέσῃς, τούτῳ ὡς ἀπὸ οἰκείου δηλονότι ἐζημιώθης μέλους. . . . Εἶτα μετὰ τὸ κοινωνῆσαί τι τοῦ σώματος Χριστοῦ, προσέρχου καὶ τῷ ποτηρίῳ τοῦ αἵματος, μὴ ἀνατείνων τὰς χεῖρας, ἀλλὰ κύπτων, καὶ τρόπῳ προσκυνήσεως καὶ σεβάσματος, λέγων τὸ Ἀμήν, ἁγιάζου καὶ ἐκ τοῦ αἵματος μεταλαμβάνων Χριστοῦ, ἔτι δὲ τῆς νοτίδος ἐνούσης τοῖς χείλεσί σου χερσὶν ἐπαφώμενος καὶ ὀφθαλμοὺς, καὶ μέτωπον, καὶ τὰ λοιπὰ ἁγίαζε αἰσθητήρια. 'Catech. Mystag.' v. 18.

(*e.*) But this was not the worst. The consecrated elements were "reserved," and used for the purposes of the grossest superstition, which was kept up by means of marvellous legends of pretended miracles recorded and propagated by the highest authorities in the Church.

A piece of the consecrated bread put into the mouth of the dying was a sure *viaticum,* or safe passport for the soul. See the story of Serapion, an old man who had lapsed in a time of persecution, and not yet been re-admitted into the Church. When at the point of death he sent a boy for the priest. The priest was ill, and could not come. But the boy brought back a piece of the "reserved" bread, and dropped it into the old man's mouth, who, having been up to that moment marvellously preserved in life, thereupon immediately died in peace. The story is mentioned, not as anything extraordinary or unusual, in a letter of Dionysius of Alexandria, given by Eusebius, 'H. E.' vi. 44.

It was only going a little beyond this, when people gave this sacrament to the *dead.* This was forbidden by the Council of Carthage (A. D. 397); and Chrysostom spoke against it. It was discountenanced therefore by the authorities; but the "orthodox" practice gave occasion for it.

Cyprian mentions with satisfaction that a woman who kept "the Lord's Sacrament" in a box for her daily use, joined in some idol-worship, whereupon, when she attempted afterwards to open the box, a fire burst out from it with such fury that she did not dare to touch it again.

Quum quædam mulier arcam suam in qua Domini sanctum fuit, &c. See his treatise 'De Lapsis;' where he also gives another marvellous story of an infant who had been taken by its nurse to a heathen sacrifice, and was then brought to Church to receive the Eucharist.

In the following century nothing was thought too gross to

be used in order to inculcate a belief in the magical or miraculous power of the consecrated elements. Thus Ambrose, in a solemn oration on the death of his brother Satyrus, triumphantly relates that Satyrus being shipwrecked in a storm at sea, had a piece of "the divine sacrament" *tied round his neck* in a priest's scarf, and having thus cast himself into the waves was thereby preserved, without needing so much as a plank to support him. Satyrus at that time had not been baptized, but convinced by this miracle, determined to be so. Divinum illud fidelium sacramentum . . . ligari fecit in orario et orarium involvit collo, atque ita se dejecit in mare, non requirens de navis compage resolutam tabulam cui supernatans juvaretur. Ambrose adds the obvious lesson to be learned from this, Qui tantum mysterii cælestis involuti in orario præsidium fuisset expertus, quantum arbitrabatur, si ore sumeret et toto pectoris hauriret arcano! '*De Excessu Satyri*,' § 43.

IV. *Prayers and offerings for the Dead.*—First mentioned by Tertullian, who speaks of a wife praying for her dead husband, and presenting offerings for him (in the Eucharist) on the anniversaries of his death. Pro anima ejus orat et refrigerium interim appostulat ei, et in prima resurrectione consortium, et offert annuis diebus dormitionis ejus. *De Monogam.*, § 10.

Cyprian mentions the same custom, and forbids the offering of "the sacrifice" for those who had committed certain offences ;—Si quis hoc fecisset non offerretur pro eo, nec sacrificium pro dormitione ejus celebraretur. *Ep.* 66. *Ad. Cler. et Pleb. Furnit.*

Arnobius (A.D. 300) says it was the custom in Churches to pray for the dead, as well as the living. Pax cunctis et venia postulatur, . . . et resolutis corporum vinctione. B. iv. end.

Cyril of Jerusalem declares such prayers and offerings to

be of the greatest benefit to the dead. *Ταύτην προσφέρομέν σοι θυσίαν . . . καὶ ὑπὲρ τῶν προκεκοιμημένων ἁγίων πατέρων καὶ ἐπισκόπων, καὶ πάντων ἅπλως τῶν ἐν ἡμῖν προκεκοιμημένων μεγίστην ὄνησιν πιστεύοντες ἔσεσθαι ταῖς ψυχαῖς, ὑπὲρ ὧν ἡ δέησις ἀναφέρεται τῆς ἁγίας καὶ φρικωδεστάτης προκειμένης θυσίας.* 'Catech. Mystag.' v. 6.

These prayers and sacrifices at first were for the righteous dead: afterwards for *all*, whether good or bad. Thus Epiphanius (A.D. 370) disputes at large against the opinions of Aerius, who objected to prayers for the dead; and says that such prayers were beneficial,—that they were offered for the just and for sinners, asking for God's mercy for the latter, &c., *ὠφελεῖ δὲ καὶ ἡ ὑπὲρ αὐτῶν γενομένη εὐχὴ, εἰ καὶ τὰ ὅλα τῶν αἰτιαμάτων μὴ ἀποκόπτει· ἀλλ' οὖν γε διὰ τὸ πολλάκις ἐν κόσμῳ ἡμᾶς ὄντας σφάλλεσθαι ἀκουσίως τε καὶ ἑκουσίως, ἵνα τὸ ἐντελέστερον σημανθῇ· καὶ γὰρ δικαίων ποιούμεθα τὴν μνήμην, καὶ ὑπὲρ ἁμαρτώλων· ὑπὲρ μὲν ἁμαρτώλων ὑπὲρ ἐλέους Θεοῦ δεόμενοι.* 'Hæres.' 75. Aerianos.

Augustin makes an elaborate declaration to show that the souls of the dead are benefited by the prayers and sacrifices of the living. "Neque negandum est defunctorum animas pietate suorum viventium relevari, quum pro illis sacrificium mediatoris offertur, vel eleemosynæ in ecclesia fiunt." He then divides professing Christians into three classes whom he call ,—

1. *Valde boni.* 2. *Non valde mali.* 3. *Valde mali.* And the prayers and sacrifices offered for them have a different effect accordingly. For the "very good," they are thanksgivings; for the "not very bad," they are propitiations, and either procure their entire pardon, or at any rate alleviate their condemnation; for the "very bad," even if they are of no benefit to the dead, they are a certain consolation to the living. "Quum ergo sacrificia sive altaris, sive qua rumcunque eleemosynarum pro baptizatis defunctis omnibus

offeruntur, provalde bonis gratiarum actiones sunt; pro non valde malis propitiationes sunt; pro valde malis, etiamsi nulla sunt adjumenta mortuorum, qualescunque vivorum consolationes sunt. Quibus autem prosunt, aut ad hoc prosunt, ut sit plena remissio, aut certe tolerabilior fiat ipsa damnatio." *Encheiridion,* § 110.

Here then was a distinct beginning of the doctrine of *Purgatory.*

The Gospel doctrine of pardon and justification by faith in Christ had now been lost in the Church. Justification was by baptism, which gave a perfect remission of all previous sins; but after this it was by *works; i.e.,* by *sinless obedience;* this failing, the sacrifice of the Eucharist, penance, and especially almsgiving, were remedies, either partial or complete.

Monks and nuns, who were true to their vows, might be considered *perfectly righteous;* but ordinary persons must need some *purgation* after their death. Thus Augustin prayed for the soul of his mother Monica, because he dared not say that from the time when she was regenerated by baptism, no word came out of her mouth contrary to God's commands.

Several of the Fathers also believed that there would be "a fire of purgation" at the Day of Judgment through which all must pass. Thus Origen says of this fire, "Ego puto quod et post resurrectionem e mortuis indigeamus sacramento eluente nos atque purgante." *Hom.* 14. *in Lucam.*

V. PARDON *of sin and* JUSTIFICATION *by* ALMSGIVING *and other good works.*—After baptism, by which all past sins were forgiven, men had to keep themselves in sinless perfection, or else to obtain the pardon of their sins, and justification in the sight of God, by their own works and doings; among which a very conspicuous place was assigned to almsgiving. Cyprian wrote a treatise, "De opere et eleemosynis," in which he declares in the broadest possible manner, supporting his assertions with quotations from the Apocrypha, that "*any kind of sin after baptism is washed away by almsgiving.*" Ut sordes postmodum quascunque contrahimus eleemosynis abluamus : that "prayer is good with fasting and almsgiving, because *almsgiving delivers from death*, and *purges away our sins.*" Bona est oratio cum jejunio et eleemosyna, quia eleemosyna a morte liberat et ipsa purgat peccata.

Chrysostom teaches the same doctrine in his more rhetorical style. "Almsgiving is the queen of virtues, the best advocate, quickly lifting men up to heaven."—"If you have *ever so many sins, with its advocacy, you need not fear;* it demands back a debt for you ; whatever are your sins it outweighs them." *ἐλεημοσύνην βασιλίδα τῶν ἀρετῶν, τὴν ταχέως ἀνάγουσαν εἰς τὰς ἀψῖδας τῶν οὐρανῶν τοὺς ἀνθρώπους, συνήγορον τὴν ἀρίστην. Κἂν πολλὰς ἔχῃς ἁμαρτίας, ἐλεημοσύνη δὲ ᾖ συνήγορος, μὴ φοβοῦ,—χρέος ἀπαιτεῖ,—ὅσας ἔχεις ἁμαρτίας ἡ ἐλεημοσύνη σου βαρεῖ τὰς ὅλας.* Serm. ii. on Repentance.

VI. Intercession *of Saints and* prayers *to them.*—Cyril of Jerusalem, describing the common practice of the Church, relates that at the "Eucharistic sacrifice" patriarchs, prophets, apostles, and martyrs, are mentioned, in order that *by their prayers and intercessions* God may receive our supplications. *Ταύτην προσφέρομέν σοι θυσίαν, ἵνα μνημονεύωμεν καὶ τῶν προκεκοιμημένων πρῶτον πατριαρχῶν, προφητῶν, ἀποστόλων, μαρτύρων, ὅπως ὁ Θεὸς εὐχαῖς αὐτῶν καὶ πρεσβείαις προσδέξηται ἡμῶν τὴν δέησιν.* 'Catech. Mystag.' v. 6.

Gregory Nazianzen (A.D. 370) in an Oration in praise of his dead father, delivered in the presence of Basil, says that his father can do more now for those, whom he has left behind, by his *intercession*, than he could before by his instructions. *Πείθομαι δε ὅτι καὶ τῇ πρεσβείᾳ νῦν μᾶλλον, ἢ πρότερον τῇ διδασκαλίᾳ, ὅσῳ καὶ μᾶλλον ἐγγίζει Θεῷ.* And he then addresses *a direct prayer to his dead father*, "Make known to us in what glory thou art, and what light surrounds thee. . . . Receive me speedily to the same abode as thou art in thyself; . . . and guide in safety the whole flock, and all the chief-priests—*i.e.*, bishops—whose father thou wert called, and especially me, who have been governed by thy fatherly and spiritual authority." *Γνώρισον ἡμῖν ποῦ ποτε εἶ δόξης, καὶ τὸ περὶ σὲ φῶς. . . . κἀμὲ ταῖς αὐταῖς δέξαι σκηναῖς, ἢ μηδὲν ἔτι, ἢ μικρὰ τῷ βίῳ τούτῳ κακοπαθήσοντα. . . . παὶ διεξάγοις ἀκινδύνως μάλιστα μὲν ἅπασαν ποίμνην καὶ παντας ἀρχιερεῖς, ὧν ἐκλήθης πατὴρ, ἐξαιρέτως δὲ τὸν ὑπὸ σοῦ βιασθέντα καὶ τυραννηθέντα πατρικῶς τε καὶ πνευματικῶς, ὡς ἂν μὴ πάντα σε μεμφοίμην τῆς τυραννίδος.* Orat. 19, § 44.

Paulinus of Nola, a man of great note, affords a marked example of saint-worship in the fourth century. He was present in A.D. 379 or 380 at a festival in honour of Saint Felix at Nola, and then dedicated his vows and heart to that saint—

"Ex quo solennibus istis
Coram vota tibi, coram mea corda dicavi."

In 394 he retired to Nola, the place of his patron saint, and devoted himself to a life of asceticism and almsgiving. His "Natales," poems written every year in honour of the martyrdom of Felix, most distinctly show that he worshipped this saint. Thus in Natalis i. he thus addresses him—

"Vectus in æthereum sine sanguine Martyr honorem,
O pater, O domine, indignis licet annue servis.
. . . .
Seu placeat telluris iter, comes aggere tuto
Esto tuis; seu magna tui fiducia longo
Suadeat ire mari, da currere mollibus undis,
Et famulis famulos a puppi surgere ventos."

See a further account of Paulinus in 'Vigilantius and his times,' by Dr. Gilly, who well remarks, "It is impossible by any sophistry, or by any form of words or artifice of interpretation to rescue the memory of Paulinus from the charge of saint-worship." P. 79.

VII. Mariolatry.—The actual worship of the Virgin Mary does not appear to have been *prevalent* until after the end of the fourth century; yet it *had begun* before that date. Some time before this it had become usual to speak of her in exaggerated terms; marvellous stories were related of her; such as that which is recorded by Gregory Nyssen in his life of Gregory Thaumaturgus, to whom, as he was lying awake by night, the Virgin Mary paid a visit, and desired the Apostle John, who accompanied her, to explain to him the true faith, about which he had been in doubt.

The extravagant notions which were then entertained respecting the exalted, angelic, holiness of virginity naturally led to the unscriptural belief that the mother of Jesus was *ἀεὶ παρθενος*, ever-virgin. And those who did not receive this dogma were denounced as heretics under the formidable name of "Antidicomarianites"—*i.e.*, adversaries of Mary. Epiphanius in writing against them ('Hæres.' 78), expresses with much rhetorical declamation, his amazement at their madness in uttering such blasphemous insults against her, as to assert that she was really the wife of Joseph and the mother of other children besides Jesus. In his desire to do her honour, he suggests, without positively affirming, that she *never died;* but obtained immortality without passing through death. *Οὐ πάντως ὁρίζομαι τοῦτο καὶ οὐ λέγω ὅτι ἀθάνατος ἔμεινεν· ἀλλ' οὔτε διαβεβαιοῦμαι εἰ τέθνηκεν.* Thus exhibiting the earliest form of the later Romish doctrine of the "Assumption."

There were some at this time who worshipped her *as a goddess*, and transferred to her the old Eastern worship of the "queen of heaven;" the women offering her cakes (*κολλυρίδες*), as mentioned in Jeremiah vii. 18 and xliv. 19, whence they were called "Collyridians."

Epiphanius, to do him justice, denounces this idolatry in strong terms; *ναὶ μὴν ἅγιον ἦν τὸ σῶμα τῆς Μαρίας,—οὐ μὴν θεός· καὶ δὴ πάρθενος ἦν ἡ Πάρθενος καὶ τετιμημένη, ἀλλ' οὐκ εἰς προσκύνησιν ἡμῖν δοθεῖσα.* 'Hæres.' 79, 4.

But notwithstanding this, actual worship was addressed to her, without calling her a goddess, as it was to other saints: and Gregory Nazianzen in his oration on Cyprian relates without any disapprobation that a nun, whom Cyprian in his youth pursued with violent attentions, effectually *prayed* for help to the Virgin Mary. *Τὴν πάρθενον Μαρίαν ἱκετεύουσα βοηθῆσαι παρθένῳ κινδυνευούσῃ.* Orat. 18.

VIII. *The worship of pictures and images, &c.*—The use of pictures in Churches as *helps to devotion* must have been attempted at or before the very beginning of the fourth century; since the practice is forbidden by the Council of Elvira (A.D. 305), for the very proper reason, lest objects of worship should be painted on the walls. Placuit picturas in ecclesia esse non debere, ne quod colitur et adoratur in parietibus depingatur. *Can.* 36. But at the end of the century, Paulinus had pictures painted on the walls of his Church at Nola; because, as he said, the rude multitude, who flocked to the festival of the martyr (Felix) required such helps to devotion, and might be thus drawn away from the rioting and drunkenness which were too apt to occur on such occasions. The introduction of images, and the direct worship of them and of pictures, were of a later date. But Paulinus enriched his shrine with relics, relics of the Apostles Andrew and Thomas, of John the Baptist, and St. Luke, and pieces of the bones of numerous martyrs, in which he believed great virtue to reside. In this case the beginnings only or germ of the Romish practices are seen.

IX. *Asceticism.*—The monstrous asceticism of monks and anchorites in the fourth century could not be surpassed, if it was ever equalled, by anything of this kind in the later Church of Rome. To renounce every tie and every duty of social life, and every trace of civilization and humanity, and to macerate the body with savage fasting, sleeplessness, or other tortures, was universally regarded at the Nicene period as the very height of holiness, the attainment of superhuman perfection.

To show in any detail what this much admired life was in which men were looked upon as *angels,* because they sunk themselves lower than *brute beasts,* would be impossible in this short space. I give three quotations, of which one suggests the false *principle* of asceticism, and the others exhibit small specimens of its practice.

Gregory Nazianzen says of the nun above mentioned, that she had recourse to fasting and lying on the ground, that she might destroy her beauty, and at the same time propitiate God; for *by nothing in the world is God so much conciliated as by maceration of the body.* *Οὐδενὶ γὰρ οὕτω πάντων ὡς κακοπαθείᾳ θεραπεύεται Θεός.* Orat. 18.

Chrysostom, describing the mode of life pursued by some monks who endeavoured honestly to keep their vows, says that they fled to the tops of mountains, and lived in solitary huts, with their body pent in bands of iron and clothed with sackcloth, passing their time in continual fasting, watching, and every kind of severe discipline, if haply they might by such means as these gain the victory over their natural feelings. *Πολλοὶ καὶ σιδήρῳ ἅπαν τὸ σῶμα καταδήσαντες, καὶ σάκκῳ περιβαλόντες, καὶ πρὸς τὰς ὀρῶν ἀναδραμόντες κορυφὰς, καὶ νηστείᾳ συζῶντες διηνέκει, καὶ παννυχίσι, καὶ ἀγρυπνίαις, καὶ πᾶσαν ἐπιδεικνύμενοι σκληραγωγίαν, και γυναιξὶν ἁπάσαις ἀπαγορεύσαντες ἐπιβαίνειν τοῦ δωματίου καὶ τῆς καλύβης τῆς ἑαυτῶν, καὶ τῷ τρόπῳ τούτῳ παιδαγωγοῦντες ἑαυτοὺς μόλις περιγίνονται τῆς κατὰ τὴν ἐπιθυμίαν μανίας.* Vol. i. p. 228. Ed. Benedict., entitled *πρὸς τοὺς ἔχοντας παρθένους συνεισάκτους.*

Basil describes the life of an anchorite with whom he was acquainted, and whose ascetic discipline he greatly admired. This man deserted his wife and home, and fled to Jerusalem, where he lived in solitude devoting himself to divine contemplation. He wore rough sackcloth next his skin, and bound his loins with so hard a girdle that it almost crushed his bones. He fasted to such an extent that he had the appearance of a skeleton, the soft parts of his body being dried up, and drawn in close to the back-bone, while his ribs projected over them like the roof of a house. In the mean time he passed his nights in confessing his sins to God, with streams of tears running down over his beard. *Σκυβαλίζων μέν σου τὴν πολυκίνδυνον περιουσίαν, οἴκου θεραπείαν καὶ συνοίκου ὁμιλίαν ἀπαρνούμενος . . . κατέδραμες ἐπὶ τὰ Ἱεροσόλυμα, ἔνθα σοι καὶ αὐτὸς συνδιατρίβων ἐμακάριζον τῶν ἀθλητικῶν πόνων, ὅτε ἑβδοματικοῖς κύκλοις νῆστις διατελῶν Θεῷ προσεφιλοσόφεις, . . . ἡσυχίαν καὶ μονοτροπίαν σεαυτῷ ἐφαρμόσας. . . . Σάκκῳ δὲ τραχεῖ τὸ σῶμά σου διανύττων, καὶ ζώνῃ σκληρᾷ τὴν ὀσφύν σου περισφίγγων καρτερικῶς τὰ ὀστᾶ σου διέθλιβες· λαγόνας δὲ ταῖς ἐνδείαις κοιλαίνων μέχρι τῶν νωτιαίων μερῶν ὑπεχαύνωσας. . . . ἔνδοθεν δὲ τὰς λαπάρας σικύας δίκην ὑφελκύσας τοῖς νεφριτικοῖς χωρίοις προσκολλᾶσθαι ἐβιάζου, ὅλην δὲ τὴν σαρκὸς πιμελὴν ἐκκενώσας τοὺς τῶν ὑπογαστρίων ὀχέτους γενναίως ἐξήρανας . . . τὰ πλευριτικὰ μέρη ὥσπερ τινὰ στέγης ἐξοχὴν τοῖς ὀμφάλου μέρεσιν ἐπεσκίαζες.—Κατα τὰς νυκτερινὰς ὥρας ἀνθομολογούμενος τῷ Θεῷ τοῖς τῶν δακρύων ὀχετοῖς τὴν γενειάδα ἔμβροχον καθωμάλιζες.* Ep. 45, ad Monachum.

"The extant information bearing on this subject is not

scanty, and it is furnished explicitly, or it is incidentally confirmed, by Eusebius, Socrates, Sozomen, Theodoret, Athanasius, Palladius, Sulpitius Severus, Cassian, Jerome, Chrysostom, Basil, Augustine, Isidore, Ephrem ; some of whom furnish the minutest details of the 'seraphic life,' and all speak of it in terms of wonder and admiration." 'Ancient Christianity,' p. 316.

X. *Celibacy and Virginity.*—Monks and nuns, bound by vows of celibacy, were considered the highest glory and greatest boast of the Church. "The Greeks," says Chrysostom, "conceded this honour to the Church, and allowed that virginity, as seen in it, was a perfection supernatural and superhuman."

The manner in which celibacy was extolled, and the practical effects of it, are exhibited at length in Chrysostom's three treatises or Sermons, which stand at the beginning of his works in the Benedictine edition, and are entitled, *Πρὸς τοὺς ἔχοντας παρθένους συνεισάκτους, Περὶ τοῦ μὴ κανονικὰς συνοικεῖν ἀνδράσιν, Περὶ παρθενείας*, and from these the following extracts are taken :—

"Nuns stand in the very highest place in the heavenly choir. They are like the most select troops who form a King's body-guard in an army. Nay, they are higher than the personal guards of a King ; for these only stand by the King's chariot ; but virgins are as it were the very celestial chariot itself of the Heavenly King, like the Cherubim ; as well as standing close to Him, like the Seraphim." *Περὶ τοῦ μὴ*, &c., § 6.

"A true nun is the very personification and ornament of Christian perfection ! When she walks abroad she strikes every one with amazement as if an angel had come down from heaven. If one of the cherubim appeared on earth he would attract the eyes of all men ; and so a nun should strike all beholders with awe and wonder at her holiness.

Her time should be occupied with exercises of devotion or meditation :—at Church sitting in the deepest silence and abstraction ;—at home having nothing to do with any domestic affairs, avoiding the sight of men, and even the company of women who are engaged in any of the affairs of life. Who will not stand amazed at seeing such an angelic life in the form of woman! What human being would venture to approach or touch so dazzling a soul! All, whether they will or no, will stand off aghast as if they saw a mass of gold all flaming and flashing with fire." Ibid. § 7.

Such was the theory of this celestial, angelic, state. In its practical working at Constantinople, in Chrysostom's time, it exhibited the most shameless contempt of decency and religion! Monks and nuns, not then confined to monasteries and convents, cohabited together with everything of marriage but its sanctity. Nuns were escorted into Church by their paramours, and delighted in receiving numerous attentions from them during the celebration of the "most awful mysteries." *Πρὸς τοὺς ἔχοντας*, &c., § 10.

And the remedy for this disgraceful scandal was—not an acknowledgment that this unscriptural and extravagant exaltation of celibacy was a violation of the laws of nature and of God, and a return to a true and healthy mode of thought and life—but it was nothing less than compelling the nuns,—those angelic beings of superhuman, dazzling, holiness,—to submit to a regulation exactly similar to that clause in the "Contagious Diseases Act," which has been thought by many persons to be too degrading and abominable even for the very worst and vilest to submit to! The following are Chrysostom's words :—*Δρόμος λοιπὸν ταῖς μαίαις καθ' ἑκάστην ἡμέραν ἐπὶ τὰς τῶν παρθένων οἰκίας, καθάπερ πρὸς τὰς ὠδινούσας, οὐχ ὥστε λοχεῦσαι τικτούσας,—γέγονε μὲν γὰρ καὶ ἐπὶ τινων καὶ τοῦτο,—ἀλλὰ ὥστε διαγνῶναι καθάπερ ἐπὶ τῶν ὠνουμένων θεραπαινίδων, τίς μὲν ἡ διεφθαρμένη, τίς δὲ ἡ ἀνέπαφος; καὶ ἡ μὲν ὑπήκουσε ῥαδίως τῇ δοκιμασίᾳ, ἡ δὲ ἀντεῖπε καὶ αὐτῷ τούτῳ καταισχυνθεῖσα ἀπῆλθεν εἰ καὶ μὴ διέφθαρτο, καὶ ἡ μὲν ἑάλω, ἡ δὲ καὶ οὐκ ἑάλω, καὶ αὐτὴ δὲ πάλιν οὐχ ἧττον ἐκείνης αἰσχύνεται μὴ συνηθεῖσα ἀπὸ τοῦ τρόπου φανῆναι, ἀλλὰ μαρτυρίας τῆς ἀπὸ τῆς ἐξετάσεως δεηθεῖσα. Περὶ τοῦ μὴ*, &c., § 2.

Let it not be supposed that this disgraceful and demoralized state of things at Constantinople was altogether exceptional and rare. It was the natural and necessary result of the pernicious system which disparaged family life and family religion, and distorted and outraged the feelings of man, and the laws of God. A hundred years before the time of Chrysostom the same sort of thing was going on in the African Church, and the same disgraceful remedy applied; as may be seen in Cyprian's Epistle to Pomponius.

The Church of Rome has at any rate in this point improved upon the Nicene period; and has introduced better regulations than were in force in Chrysostom's time.

XI. *Enforced celibacy of the clergy.*—The clergy were naturally expected to live *the holy life*, not only as an example to others, but as *priests* who had to touch "the awful mysteries." Therefore when celibacy was regarded as a state of angelic holiness, and matrimony only at the best an allowed but low condition of Christian living, the clergy were expected not to marry.

As early as the days of Tertullian for a presbyter to marry a second time was thought an abomination.

By the beginning of the fourth century people were inclined to refuse the ministrations of a married presbyter.

The Council of Gangra (A. D. 324) condemns this objection. *εἴ τις διακρίνοιτο παρὰ πρεσβυτέρου γεγαμηκότος, ὡς μὴ χρῆναι, λειτουργήσαντος αὐτοῦ, προσφορᾶς μεταλαμβάνειν, ἀνάθεμα ἔστω.* Can. 4. But twenty years before this the Council of Elvira (A. D. 305), in which the ascetic spirit was stronger, ordered that all the clergy should separate from their wives, or be deposed. Placuit in totum prohiberi episcopis, presbyteris, et diaconibus, vel omnibus clericis positis in ministerio, abstinere se a conjugibus suis, et non generare filios; quicunque vero fecerit ab honore clericatûs exterminetur. *Can.* 33.

There was in fact in the earlier part of this century some variety in different places respecting the enforced celibacy of the clergy. The popular feeling against "married priests" was strong; but Church authorities had not everywhere formally spoken.

The Council of Ancyra (A.D. 315), Can. 9, decided that if a deacon at the time of his ordination declared his intention of marrying, as being in his case a necessity, he should be allowed to do so, otherwise not.

At the Council of Nice (A.D. 325) it was *proposed* (as related by Socrates and Sozomen) that, *for the reformation of manners*, all bishops, presbyters, and deacons, who had married before their ordination, should withdraw from their wives; but owing to the energetic opposition of Paphnutius, himself an ascetic, the Council contented itself with enacting *the old rule*, τὴν ἀρχαιὰν παράδοσιν, that *no one should be allowed to marry after he had been ordained.*

But before the end of the fourth century it had become at any rate a consuetudinary law, that the clergy must either be unmarried, or, if they had married before their ordination, they must thenceforth separate from their wives. Thus

Jerome says, "Certe confiteris non *posse esse* Episcopum, qui in Episcopatu filios faciat; alioqui, si deprehensus fuerit, *quasi adulter* damnabitur." '*Adv. Jovin.*' i. And again, "Aut virgines clericos accipiunt, aut continentes; aut si uxores habuerint, *mariti esse desinunt.*" '*Adv. Vigilant.*'

Siricius, Bishop of Rome (A.D. 385), writes with abhorrence of certain presbyters and deacons, who had committed the crime of having children by their wives! "Sacerdotes Christi et Levitas *tam de conjugibus*, quam de turpi coïtu, sobolem procreasse." *Ad Himerium Ep.* I. These were to be allowed, on repentance and separation for the future, to continue in their office, but were never to be promoted. But if any of them insisted on the liberty of marriage, they were to be deposed, and never allowed to touch the sacred mysteries again. Siricius declares that such priests cannot please God; and that the Spirit of God cannot dwell except in *holy bodies, i.e.*, in those who abstain from marriage!

So utterly did Church tradition contradict the Word of God! But the predicted apostacy was then far advanced.

XII. LYING WONDERS, *Miracles, and the Efficacy of Relics, &c.* —A taste for the invention and narration of miraculous occurrences appears as early as the beginning of the third century; and, being encouraged by the countenance and support of the Church authorities, miracles continually increased in number and marvellousness. The object of all these miracles was to prop up some superstition,—such as prayers for the dead,—fanatical sacramentalism,—the asceticism of hermits, monks and nuns,—or the sanctity of martyrs' bones, and other relics.

Tertullian tells the story of a *dead* woman, who had not married again after the death of her husband, and whose hands lifted themselves up in the attitude of prayer while the presbyter was praying over her corpse; and when the prayer was finished the hands laid themselves down again, as they had been before. "Scio fœminam quandam vernaculam Ecclesiæ, forma et ætate integra functam, post unicum et breve matrimonium, quum in pace dormîsset, et morante adhuc sepultura, interim oratione Presbyteri componeretur, ad primum habitum orationis manus e lateribus dimotas in habitum supplicem conformâsse, rursumque condita pace, situi suo reddidisse." *De Anim.* 51.

Cyprian's narrative of miracles, connected with the Eucharistic elements, has already been referred to. See his 'De Lapsis.'

But in the fourth century miracles flourished in much greater abundance.

Gregory Nazianzen, in his Oration on Cyprian relates that after Cyprian had been beheaded, his body wonderfully disappeared, and was hidden for a long time in the house of some woman ; but at last it was in a marvellous manner brought to light, and *was able to work miracles;* such as overcoming demons, curing diseases, giving a foreknowledge of future events ; "all which things the very dust of Cyprian is able," he says, "to perform with the faith of his votaries, as those who have tried it know."—*Τὴν δαιμόνων καθαιρεσίαν, τὴν τῶν νόσων κατάλυσιν, τὴν τῶν μελλόντων πρόγνωσιν, ἃ πάντα δύναται Κυπριάνου καὶ ἡ κόνις μετὰ τῆς πίστεως, ὡς ἴσασιν οἱ πεπειράμενοι, καὶ τὸ θαῦμα μέχρις ἡμῶν παραπέμψαντες.* Orat. 18.

Ambrose, as related by his biographer Paulinus, in a similar manner countenanced the pretended miracles connected with the discovery of the remains of the martyr Nazarius, *whose blood*, when his grave was opened, *was found quite fresh*, as if it had just been shed,—a prototype of the liquefaction of St. Januarius's blood at Naples ;—and his head, which had been cut off, was quite sound and undecayed, with the hair and beard not at all disorded. "Vidimus autem in sepulcro, quo jacebat corpus martyris, sanguinem martyris ita recentem quasi eodem die fuisset effusus. Caput etiam ipsius, quod ab impiis fuerat abscissum, ita integrum atque incorruptum cum capillis capitis atque barba, ut nobis videretur eodem tempore quo levabatur lotum atque compositum in sepulcro." *Paulin. Vit. Ambros.*

Paulinus also mentions the miracles performed by the remains of the martyrs Protasius and Gervasius, who, he says, discovered their bones to a priest, qui se sacerdoti revelaverunt, by which a blind man recovered his sight, devils were cast out of the possessed, &c.

Ambrose himself in his funeral oration over his brother

Satyrus, congratulated himself that he would now have the benefit of his brother's ashes; and that he would now be more in favour with God, when lying on his brother's tomb. "Habeo quas complectar reliquias: habeo sepulcrum super quod jaceam, et commendabiliorem Deo futurum esse me credam, quod supra sancti corporis ossa requiescam." *Orat. de Excessu Satyri*, § 18.

But indeed in this century all sorts of pretended miracles took place at the shrines of martyrs everywhere, or were performed by the relics of saints, or by a piece of the true cross (*see* Paulinus, Natalis x.), or by the hands of the most ascetic of the monks and hermits. These miracles were recorded and countenanced by the highest Church authorities. See as a specimen the 'Life of St. Anthony,' by Jerome; or any other work of a similar kind belonging to this age.

Such things are called "lying impostures" in mediæval Rome. What were they in the hands of Ambrose or Jerome?

XIII. Church Despotism—the oppression or persecution of those who opposed, or objected to, prevailing superstitions.

Even at the very beginning of the third century the *principle* of Church despotism was avowed by Tertullian. He declares that Scripture is of God, but that *discipline, i.e.*, all the customs and usages of the Church, is of God also. He asserts that the Holy Spirit was given in order that this discipline might be brought to perfection; and therefore Church ordinances (which are often in reality only man's perversions of God's truth), are the administration of His divine wisdom. "Quum propterea Paracletum miserit Dominus, ut paulatim dirigeretur, et ordinaretur, et ad perfectum perduceretur disciplina ab illo vicario Domini Spiritu Sancto . . . Quæ ergo est Paracleti administratio nisi hæc, quod disciplina dirigitur, quod scripturæ revelantur, quod intellectus reformantur." '*De Veland. Virgin.*' § 1.

And this principle was acted upon, and carried out by those who followed. Augustin, a century and a half later, presumed to say that *the Holy Spirit ordered the Lord's Supper to be received fasting,* because this was then the custom of the Church. "Hoc enim placuit Spiritui Sancto ut in honorem tanti sacramenti in os Christiani prius Dominicum corpus intraret quam cæteri cibi." *Ep.* 118, *Januar.* § 6.

And so the visible Church with all its human laws and regulations, with all its accumulating superstitions, and departures from Christian truth, was declared to be the expression of the very mind and will, the presence and operation, of the divine Spirit; and those who ventured to dissent from anything in or of the Church, however corrupt, were branded as heretics, and, if possible, crushed. There were good and true men here and there in the fourth century, who attempted to raise their voices against the corruptions of that age; but as we see in the case of Vigilantius, Jovinian, and others, they were trampled upon by Jerome, Ambrose, and their "orthodox" contemporaries; and if they persisted in proclaiming Scriptural truth the secular arm was appealed to, to put them down. (See the case of Jovinian referred to in Lecture III. : and 'Vigilantius and his Times,' by Dr. Gilly, may be read with advantage.)

XIV. The Papacy, or the authority of the *Bishop of Rome.*—The authority of the Bishop of Rome over all Christendom was not of course fully established as early as the Nicene age. Plain instances of resistance to attempted dominion on the part of the Roman See occurred; as when the endeavour of Victor (A.D. 185) to force the Roman observance of Easter upon the Greek Churches was resolutely opposed. Yet even in the third century, and increasingly so in the fourth, traces of an incipient papal supremacy are found, and principles acknowledged which were naturally developed into it.

1. Thus Cyprian, though he maintained his own independence against Rome, considered that Peter had a *primacy* among the Apostles given to him. "He regards Peter as the representative of the One Church; whosoever therefore, according to him, forsakes the outward fellowship with the one visible Catholic Church, turns himself away from the representative of the unity of the Church connected by divine appointment with the person of the Apostle Peter."

2. Then *another step* was taken; and as there was a tradition, even in the time of Irenæus and Tertullian, that Peter and Paul were the founders of the Church of Rome, and as Rome was once the seat of the dominion of the world, men began to consider the Roman Church as the seat or see of Peter, *cathedra Petri*, and to apply to it, what had been said of the Apostle Peter, as the representative of Church unity. Hence Cyprian calls Rome, "Petri ecclesia, ecclesia principalis, unde unitas sacerdotalis exorta est." *Ep.* 55 *ad Cornel.* And again in the same Epistle, "Quum locus Petri, et gradus cathedræ sacerdotalis vacaret."

3. Thirdly, in the fourth century, and especially in the latter part of it, we find foreign bishops applying to Rome for direction in ecclesiastical matters, and the Bishop of Rome replying, not to give advice as an equal writing to one independent of him, but as if issuing *decrees* and *orders* with an acknowledged authority over other Churches. Thus Siricius (A.D. 385), in answer to Himerius, Bishop of Tarracona, who had written about some disorders in his Church, says, "De his vero non incongrue dilectio tua apostolicam sedem credidit consulendam. De quibus . . . id duximus *decernendum*." And again, "Has ergo impudicas detestabilesque personas . . . eliminandas esse *mandamus*;" and he speaks of persons who had been degraded, as "auctoritate apostolicæ sedis dejectors." In the same Epistle Siricius takes upon himself to lay down the law for all Churches, "Quid *universis* posthac *ecclesiis* sequendum sit, quid

vitandum generali pronuntiatione *decernimus*." '*Ep. ad Himer.*' § 9, 10. And no objection seems to have been made to these claims. Indeed, at this very time, Theodosius the Great had ordered all nations who were subject to his dominion, to receive the faith which had been delivered by St. Peter to the Romans. "Cunctos populos quos clementiæ nostræ regit temperamentum in tali volumus religione versari, quam divinum Petrum apostolum tradidisse Romanis religio usque nunc ab ipso insinuata declarat." '*Codex Theodos.*' xvi, 1, 2. And "Valentinian III. (A.D. 424) forbade the bishops both in Gaul and in other provinces to depart from ancient usages without the approbation of the venerable man, the Pope of the holy city." Ranke, 'History of the Popes,' vol. i. p. 12.

APPENDIX B.

ON THE AUTHORITY OF COUNCILS.

QUESTIONS about the action and influence of the Councils or Synods of the post-apostolic Church are not actually included within the scope of the ecclesiastical polity of the New Testament. Yet they are so far indirectly concerned with it or supplementary to it, that some notice of the true position and legitimate authority of such councils, seems to be required for the complete consideration of the subject. The more so, inasmuch as this authority and position have often been misrepresented not only by the extravagant assumptions of the councils themselves, but by many theological writers ever since; and even in our own Church such misconception seems still not to be uncommon, notwithstanding the clear and emphatic declaration of our Articles to the contrary.

It appears in many quarters to be taken for granted that, because each "Church has power to decree rites and ceremonies and authority in controversies of faith," therefore the whole Church Universal has a similar power and authority over all national and particular Churches. From an indistinct and erroneous idea of the unity of the Catholic Church, it is assumed that, being One, it is a *single community*, authorised and able to govern its component members, and having a divine commission to exercise such government.

Then, as nothing else can be found to answer the purpose, General Councils are assumed to be the judicial or legislative organs of this reigning Catholicity ; and their decrees and canons are represented as the authoritative utterances of the Universal Church, binding with a divine sanction upon Christian men and Churches at all times and in every place. So that on the whole we are landed in the conclusion that, while provincial synods had authority over their respective provinces, Œcumenical Councils demand the obedience of the whole of Christendom for ever.

But to all such representations it is sufficient to reply, First, that it is an inexorable fact that the Catholic Church on earth is not one community, but is One, just as the human race is one, though divided into separate and independent nations. It cannot, therefore, and never could, exercise the functions of government. It has no means or machinery for governing, even if it had any authority to govern. In the words of Archbishop Whately, "No Christian, and no particular Church owes obedience to the Universal Church of which it is a part. There is not, and there never was, since the Apostles' time, any such body existing as could claim such obedience. The Catholic Church on earth is not one society, but is one, just as the human race is one." ('*Kingdom of Christ Delineated,*' p. 181.)

Secondly, it is obvious that there were no General Councils during the first three centuries of the Church's history ; and therefore if these are the voice and expression of Catholic authority, Catholicity during all that time was dumb. During all that time of difficulty and danger both within and without, and often of fierce struggles for very life, Catholicity put forth no authoritative utterance—exercised no government at all! Was this a dereliction of duty,—or a natural and necessary consequence of its true position?

Thirdly, there is such a striking difference between the consultation of the Apostles at Jerusalem, and the General

Councils of the fourth and following centuries, that it may be affirmed that there is in the New Testament no example, as there is certainly no precept or command, for the holding of such assemblies, or for the exercise of any government at all by the Catholic Church.

A very short review of the origin and action of Church Councils in the early centuries will further elucidate this not unimportant subject; and a solution of the questions connected with it is to be found in the joint consideration of two things,—the *mutual independence of the Churches*, and the *force of public opinion*,—*i.e.* the opinion of Christians generally throughout the world.

During the first three centuries each Church with its bishop,—as soon as it had a bishop,—at its head, was independent, and carried on the government within its own diocese, or *παροικία*, without subjection to any foreign or superior authority. No one Church pretended to exercise a dominion over others; or when such attempts were made, they were resisted as an unlawful usurpation. Even the Church of Rome, though already receiving a certain degree of special respect and reverence as the supposed "See of Peter," was not permitted until the latter part of the fourth century, and not always then without remonstrance, to interfere with this Diocesan independence; as was seen, when Victor (A.D. 185) endeavoured to force the Eastern Churches to conform to the Roman mode of observing Easter; or when Zosimus and Celestinus in the early part of the fifth century took upon them to absolve persons excommunicated by Churches in Africa.

The only force which then bound the several Churches together, and preserved their unity,—that is to say, the only external power besides the divine truth and grace in the hearts of men,—was the general state of Christian feeling and opinion maintained amongst them all. The grand common objects of the Christians' faith and hope,—their deep consciousness of a community in blessings, and in brotherhood,—and their common position as small bodies of men in the midst of heathen populations,—all from the very first drew Christians together by the closest ties,—fostered a comprehensive unity among them,—and gave birth immediately to that undefined and unorganized, but vigorous and effective power, which is produced by the mutual sympathies of men acting and reacting on each other, and which the term Public Opinion is intended to describe.

This power is often appealed to in the New Testament, especially by St. Paul, who had to deal with so many Churches of different nations and localities. To this power he appealed, when he informed the Roman Christians as an inducement to avoid disunion and divisions, that "their obedience was come abroad unto all men;" — when he silenced the Corinthians with the final argument, "We have no such custom, neither the Churches of God;" or stimulated their zeal by relating to them the liberal contributions of the Macedonian Churches; and so in other epistles in words of similar effect. And this power lost none of its force in the ensuing centuries. The common sentiments, which kept it in healthy action, were themselves cherished and maintained by various means [1] which promoted a close and friendly

[1] Among these means were:—

Collections made for foreign Churches in times of distress; a practice begun in apostolic times, as mentioned in Acts xi. and 2 Cor. viii., ix.

Commendatory letters given to Christians who were going abroad, and who thereby obtained a hospitable and friendly reception from the brethren in distant lands; a practice also alluded to in the New Testament, as in Rom. xvi. 1; 2 Cor. iii.

Letters addressed to Churches by distant bishops, or persons in authority, on particular emergencies; such as the Epistle of Clement to the Corinthians, and of Polycarp to the Philippians.

A mutual consent on the part of every Church to acknowledge the validity of the ecclesiastical acts of all other Churches; and to join in communion with them, or their individual members, in divine worship and all holy offices, notwithstanding any difference in

union, and an interchange of thought and feeling between all the Churches.

Hence it naturally came to pass that neighbouring Churches often sought each other's counsel, and strengthened each other's hands. If a bishop of one Church had a perplexing case to deal with, or a difficult point to determine, he had recourse to another bishop, or to several others, for advice. Hence Provincial Synods, consisting of representatives from the different Churches in a province met from time to time, to consider matters of common interest or danger,—to express their opinions on some difficulty or prevailing error,—and to encourage united and harmonious action throughout the province. These provincial Synods were *voluntary assemblies, self-convened by their own choice and appointment;* and their decisions, however formally expressed, had no power or authority, except what came from voluntary submission to them, and from the operation of public opinion in the Church at large. This is plainly evidenced by such cases as that of Paul of Samosata, who when condemned and deposed from the see of Antioch, refused to submit, and kept possession of the Church-house and premises. And the Council was powerless in the matter, until they called in the aid of the pagan government, and prevailed upon the Emperor Aurelian to interfere.—*See* Eusebius, 'H. E.' vii. 30.

The deliberate judgments of a number of grave and respected men from different places necessarily carried with them great weight, and commended themselves to general acceptance. Those Churches who had joined in the decisions of course obeyed them. Those who disapproved of them might disregard them, if they chose; but they would be ex-

religious rites and forms, which they might severally prefer.

A practice, which however came somewhat later into use, that every bishop on his appointment sent circular letters to foreign Churches, to signify that he was in communion with them.

posed to the ill-opinion, and possibly the avoidance, of other Churches if they did so ; and individual Christians could hardly venture to stand aloof from the rest,—at least with any peace or safety to themselves. A very considerable amount of influence thus accrued to these Synods ; and they were at last looked upon as a sort of court of appeal for the redress of grievances, and the decision of ecclesiastical questions, both of doctrine and of discipline.[1]

The nature and position of the so called Œcumenical or General Councils, so far as they were ecclesiastical assemblies, differed not at all from the Provincial Synods, except that they gathered representatives from a wider field. Their authority in this respect stood upon exactly the same footing, and their decrees could claim nothing more than a voluntary submission. For, as it may be observed in the words of Jeremy Taylor, "That the authority of General Councils was never esteemed absolute, infallible, and unlimited appears in this, that before they were obliging it was necessary that each particular Church respectively should accept them, concurrente universali totius ecclesiæ consensu, &c., in declaratione veritatum quæ credendæ

---

[1] Provincial synods appear to have been first commenced in the provinces of Greece, where at the end of the second century they seem to have been already established as regular institutions, meeting at stated seasons. The familiarity of the Greeks with representative assemblies, such as their Amphictyonic Council, and the meetings of the Achæan and the Ætolian League, perhaps led the Churches in those districts to be the first to adopt a similar practice for themselves. Tertullian thus alludes to these synods. "Aguntur per Græcias illa certis in locis concilia ex universis ecclesiis, per quæ et altiora quæque in commune tractantur, et ipsa repræsentatio totius nominis Christiani magna veneratione celebratur."—'*De Jejun.*' § 13.

"By the middle of the third century, the annual provincial synods appear to have been universal, if we may judge from the fact that we find them observed at the same time in parts of the Church so widely remote from each other as Northern Africa and Cappadocia."—Neander 'Church Hist.', vol i. 281.

sunt. That is the way of making the decrees of Councils become authentic and be turned into a law, as Gerson observes; and till they did, their decrees were but a dead letter. And therefore it is that these later popes have so laboured that the Council of Trent should be received in France; and Carolus Molineus, a great lawyer and of the Roman communion, disputed against the reception. And this is a known condition in the Canon Law; but it proves plainly that the decrees of councils have their authority from the voluntary submission of the particular Churches, not from the prime sanction and constitution of the Council. . . . And as there was never any Council so general, but it might have been more general; for in respect of the whole Church even Nice itself was but a small assembly, so there is no decree so well constituted, but it may be proved by an argument higher than the authority of the Council; and therefore General Councils, and national, and provincial, in their several degrees, are excellent guides for the prophets and directions and instructions for their prophesyings; but not of weight and authority to restrain their liberty so wholly, but that they may dissent, when they see a reason strong enough so to persuade them, as to be willing upon the confidence of that reason and their own sincerity to answer to God for such their modesty and peaceable, but, as they believe, their necessary, disagreeing."—'*Liberty of Prophesying*,' *Sect.* vi. *end.*

Hence it follows that our Church is bound only by those General Councils whose authority it has accepted, and only so far as it has accepted their decisions.

But besides this there is another consideration which must not be overlooked. The General Councils which were held in the earlier centuries of the Church, and which are the most commonly held up now for our submission, were not simply ecclesiastical assemblies. They partook of the nature, and had a share in the power, of a civil institution. For they never came into existence until after the accession of Constantine, when Christianity had become to a certain extent the established religion of the Roman Empire, and was in alliance with the State. They were convened by the emperor's edict : they held their sittings under his sanction : their decrees were enforced by the imperial authority ; and in some cases civil penalties were inflicted on those who disobeyed them. The decrees therefore of such General Councils were in reality constitutions or regulations of the Imperial Church as then existing ; and they can have no more authority over other Churches, than the laws of the Imperial State have over other nations. The Canons of the Council of Nice have as such no more claim upon our obedience as English Christians, than the civil edicts of Constantine have upon our obedience as English citizens.

Nor is it superfluous even in these days, and in our own Church, to assert our Christian liberty in this very thing ; and to speak plainly about the supposed authority of General Councils over us. On a late occasion a learned bishop of the Church of England, and others with him, asserted, "That an Archbishop *by the law of the Church,* had only the power of consecration in association with his Suffragans ;" and maintained, "that the Archbishop would not be acting in accordance *with the law of the Church,* if he should consecrate a Bishop in the face of a protest from his Suffragans ;" the only proof of the existence of such a law being a reference to Canon IV. of the first Council of Nice, and Canon XIX. of the Council of Antioch (A.D. 341) ; just as if the Canons of these Councils were *ipso facto* undoubted laws of the Church of England!

And in accordance with modern practice this theology was published in 'The Times' newspaper, Dec. 22, 1869.

APPENDIX C.

CONFESSION, ABSOLUTION, AND PENANCE.

THE gross moral and religious evils of the Confessional and of priestly Absolution, which polluted the Church of Rome in the Middle Ages, and which still to a certain extent adhere to its system, are not, like many others of the Romish errors, to be laid to the charge of the Nicene Fathers. Even after the flood of Sacerdotalism had set in strongly upon the Church in the third and fourth centuries, the practice of Confession and Absolution continued to be remarkably free from the infection of priestcraft; even while the loss of apostolic truth in other respects caused the acts of penitence, or penance, which were enjoined by Church authority, to be mingled with lamentable errors.

I. *Confession.*—1. Public Confession in the presence of a Christian congregation,—called even in the Latin Churches by the Greek name *Exomologesis,*—was at first the only mode in use; and it was either *obligatory* or *voluntary.*

(*a*) Confession was obligatory in the case of great offenders, who had been excommunicated, and were required to make a public acknowledgment of their transgressions, before they were re-admitted to Church communion.

(*b*) Persons who had sinned more secretly, and had not been excommunicated, sometimes voluntarily made this public confession, before they ventured to come to the Lord's Supper.

This public confession seems to have been the only kind known to Tertullian, and after him to Cyprian. The former in his treatise 'De pœnitentia,' and the latter in his 'De Lapsis,' give full expression to their sentiments on this subject; and they exhort those who had committed any grievous sin in secret to confess it publicly before the Church,—a duty which apparently was sometimes very reluctantly performed.

2. *Private Confession.*—During the third century, and first in the Eastern Church, the increasing reluctance felt by Christians to make a public confession of their sins, and the occurrence of some difficulties connected with this practice, caused the introduction of private confession for voluntary penitents. Origen mentions both the public and the private mode as used for voluntary confessions in his time; and he recommends those who feared publicity to choose some prudent and friendly Presbyter, and to confess to him in private; and then to be guided by his advice, as to whether a public confession should afterwards be resorted to or not. "Circumspice diligentius cui debeas confiteri peccatum tuum: proba prius medicum cui debeas causam languoris exponere . . . . . si intellexerit et perviderit talem esse languorem tuum, ut in conventu totius ecclesiæ exponi debeat et curari, ex quo fortassis et cæteri ædificari poterunt, et tu ipse facile sanari, multa hoc deliberatione, et satis perito medici illius consilio, procurandum est."—*De Psalm.* 37. Hom. 2.

In some Churches, however, and in particular at Constantinople, a Presbyter was specially appointed to act as a Penitentiary, or Confessor,—ὁ ἐπὶ τῆς μετανοίας,—to hear private confession; and the practice of thus confessing became general in the East. In the Latin Church the public voluntary confession appears still to have held a place; since Leo I., Bishop of Rome, issued a direction for its discontinuance in A.D. 459, to the following effect. "Ne de singulorum peccatorum genere libellis scripta professio publice recitetur, quum reatus conscientiarum sufficiat solis sacerdotibus indicare confessione secreta; . . . sufficiat enim illa confessio quæ primum Deo offertur, tum etiam sacerdoti, qui pro delictis precator attendit."—*Labbé* '*Concil.*' vol. vi. p. 410.

The confession of secret sins, whether publicly before the Church, or privately to a Presbyter, during all this time was *voluntary*. But persons were exhorted to have recourse to it, and the practice was greatly promoted by the prevalence of exaggerated notions about the Lord's Supper, —by the belief that Christian ministers could release them from the guilt of their transgressions, and were priests who could make their peace with God for them—and by ignorance of the way of safety and of pardon in Christ.

Auricular confession to a priest was ordered and made obligatory in the Church of Rome by the Fourth Lateran Council, A.D. 1215, in the following decree:—"Omnis utriusque sexus fidelis postquam ad annos discretionis pervenerit, omnia sua solus peccata confiteatur fideliter, saltem semel in anno, proprio sacerdoti, et injunctam sibi pœnitentiam studeat pro viribus adimplere."—*Labbé* '*Concil.*' vol. xxiii. p. 1008. This entirely altered the whole character of the Confessional, not merely because what was before voluntary was now compulsory, but because now *every* sin was to be confessed, and consequently in many cases *extorted* by the priest, whereas before only those sins which were felt to be a burden upon the conscience were disclosed, and then only so far as the penitent himself thought necessary or expedient.

At Constantinople, in the middle of the fourth century, on account of certain scandals in which a Deacon was involved in connection with private confession, the Bishop Nectarius, the predecessor of Chrysostom, was induced to abolish the office of Penitentiary, and men were directed to confess their sins to God; all Christians, being then allowed to come to the Lord's Table according to their own judgment and conscience, unless they were under censures publicly pronounced upon them by the Church authorities. Ὑπὸ τὸν αὐτὸν χρόνον ἔδοξε καὶ τοὺς ἐπὶ τῆς μετανοίας περιελεῖν πρεσβυτέρους τῶν ἐκκλησιῶν. . . . . συγχωρῆσαι δὲ ἕκαστον τῷ ἰδίῳ συνειδότι τῶν μυστηρίων μετέχειν.—Socrat. 'Hist. Eccl.' v. 19.

This was a wise return to the apostolic doctrine and practice. And it is a further testimony to the soundness of the Church at Constantinople in this respect, however erroneous in others, that many exhortations conceived in a similar spirit are found in the Homilies of Chrysostom.

The abolition of this mode of private confession, as an acknowledged Church ordinance, could not of course prevent those, who wished to do so, from relieving a burdened conscience by opening their griefs or perplexities to a Christian friend, whether Presbyter or Layman.

II. *Absolution.*—Absolution like Confession was either *public* or *private*. 1. Public absolution consisted of a declaration of God's forgiveness of the sins which had been repented of and confessed, accompanied with the imposition of the hands of the Bishop and Presbyters, and the prayers of the congregation. If Church censures had been imposed they were then formally removed; and the absolved person was admitted to Church communion, and to a participation in the Lord's Supper, exclusion from, and admission to, which was especially connected with confession and absolution.

This ministerial absolution was called "Remission of sins," —*remissio facta per sacerdotes,*—and was regarded as a matter of great importance. It was in giving and refusing this that the "priests" exercised the power of loosing and binding, which the Church claimed for them; as Ambrose says, when writing against the tenets of the Novatianists, "Qui solvere non potest peccatum, non habet Spiritum Sanctum. Munus Spiritus Sancti est officium sacerdotis; jus autem Spiritus Sancti in solvendis ligandisque criminibus est."—*De pœnitentia,* i. 5. Yet Cyprian, who entertained very high notions of the power of the Christian "priesthood," declares that none can forgive sins but God. "Solus Deus misereri potest veniam peccatis, quæ in ipsum commissa sunt, solus potest ille largiri, qui peccata nostra portavit." So that the ministerial action, however exalted and necessary in the estimation of those times, was strictly speaking regarded as *declaratory* only. Unfortunately this was not always kept in view in the Church's teaching, or in the popular theology.

2. Private absolution was a much less solemn act, amounting to little more than a permission given by the Presbyter to come to the Holy Communion, and a declaration of God's forgiveness, which he seems to have expressed in the form of a prayer; if we may judge so from the words in the quotation cited above, "qui pro delictis *precator* attendit."

III. *Penance* or *penitence,*—pœnitentia.—Before absolution was given it was requisite that the Church, acting through its Bishop and other ministers,—or the individual Presbyter in the case of private absolution,—should be satisfied of the reality of the repentance of those who sought to be absolved. Hence those, who by great sins had incurred the public censures of the Church, were required to go through a course of penitence, longer or shorter, more or less severe, according to the nature of the offence. This was called in the Greek Church by the general term *μετανοεῖν* or *μεταμέλεσθαι;* but in Latin "agere pœnitentiam," whence the English expression "to do penance."

Tertullian includes the whole course of this humiliation

under the name of *exomologesis*, and he requires a person by way of penitence, during the time of his exclusion from Church communion, "to lie in sackcloth and ashes, to defile his body with filth, and cast down his spirit with grief, to eat and drink nothing pleasant, to strengthen his prayers with fasting, to groan, weep, and moan aloud by night and day to God, to roll on the ground before the presbyters, to kneel to the favourites of heaven, to entreat all the brethren to pray and intercede for him."

"Exomologesis prosternendi et humilificandi hominis disciplina est, conversationem injungens misericordiæ illicem. De ipso quoque habitu atque victu mandat, sacco et cineri incubare, corpus sordibus obscurare, animum mœroribus dejicere, illa quæ peccavit tristi tractatione mutare. Cæterum pastum et potum pura nosse, non ventris scilicet sed animæ causa; plerumque vero jejuniis preces alere, ingemiscere, lacrimari et mugire noctes diesque ad Dominum Deum tuum, presbyteris advolvi, et caris Dei adgeniculari, omnibus fratribus legationes deprecationis suæ injungere."—'*De pœnit.*' § 9.

Cyprian's recommendations are very similar to those of Tertullian, adding only an injunction to the penitent "to devote himself to good works, *by which sins are taken away,* and to almsgiving, *by which souls are delivered from death.*" Orare oportet impensius et rogare, diem luctu transigere, vigiliis noctes ac fletibus ducere, tempus omne lacrimosis lamentationibus occupare, stratos solo adhærere, in cinere et cilicio et sordibus volutari, post indumentum Christi perditum nullum jam malle vestitum, post diaboli cibum malle jejunium, justis operibus incumbere *quibus peccata purgantur*, eleemosynis frequenter insistere *quibus a morte animæ liberantur.*—'De Lapsis.'

The object of all this was declared to be *to make satisfaction* to God,—to appease his anger,—to win his compassion by self-inflicted suffering,—to expiate the sins committed,

—to purchase pardon and deliver the soul from death. This is the doctrine taught by Tertullian, and still more distinctly by Cyprian, whose treatise, *De Lapsis*, abounds with such expressions as "Deo satisfacere,—satisfactionem facere,—Dominus satisfactione placandus est,—Illi mœstitia satisfacere,—expiare delicta,—Dei iram et offensam jejuniis, fletibus, planctibus placare,—pœnitentia crimine minor non sit; putasne tu Dominum cito posse placari;"—and, as we saw above, the necessity of purchasing the divine forgiveness by almsgiving and other good works.

Similar ideas and similar practices prevailed also in the following century, especially in the Western Church. Thus Ambrose, in his 'De pœnitentia,' while powerfully urging against the Novatianists the duty of receiving returning penitents, and while expressing many excellent thoughts on the subject of repentance and forgiveness,—yet equally with Tertullian and Cyprian requires the most abject outward humiliation on the part of those who sought re-admission into the Church. "Volo veniam reus speret; petat eam lacrimis, petat gemitibus, petat populi totius fletibus; ut ignoscatur et obsecret; et quum secundo et tertio fuerit dilata ejus communio, credat remissius se supplicasse, fletus augeat miserabilior, postea revertatur, teneat pedes brachiis, osculetur osculis, lavet fletibus, nec dimittat, ut de ipso dicat Dominus Jesus, Remissa sunt peccata ejus multa, quoniam dilexit multum. Cognovi quosdam in pœnitentia sulcasse vultum lacrimis, exarasse continuis fletibus genas, stravisse corpus suum calcandum omnibus, jejuno ore semper et pallido mortis speciem spiranti in corpore prætulisse." *De pœnit.* i. 16.

All this is clearly accounted for by the fact that the whole view taken by the Church of the third and fourth centuries, on the subject of repentance and forgiveness, was of necessity very much affected by two false principles then almost universally prevalent. The one—that self-inflicted suffering and bodily maceration were especially pleasing to the Almighty, and most effectual for obtaining his favour. The other—that almsgiving, or bestowing one's property upon the Church, was a sovereign remedy for sins, and cancelled a sinner's guilt.—*See* Appendix A, Nos. v. and ix.

In the fourth century the course of penitence prescribed for grave offences of a moral character appears more distinctly formalized than it had previously been ; the period of exclusion for different degrees of guilt was more clearly defined ; and penitents had to pass through three or four successive stages of partial admission into the Church, before they were received into full communion. *Ten, twelve,* or even *twenty* years were sometimes occupied with this discipline. The following is Ambrose's account of one of these periods of humiliation.—"After the guilty man has come to sense of his sin let him stand for three years weeping at the door of the house of prayer, and begging the people as they enter to make earnest and sympathizing prayers for him. After this let him for three years be received inside the Church as a hearer only, and be turned out after the Scripture Lessons and the Sermon, without being allowed to stay during the prayers. Then if he has sought it with tears, and fallen down before the Lord [the Bishop?] with contrition of heart and deep humiliation, let him be allowed for another space of three years to kneel down during the prayers. And so, when he has thus displayed the fitting fruits of repentance, let him be received in the tenth year at the prayers of the faithful [the *missa fidelium*], but without partaking in the Eucharistic sacrifice ; and lastly, when two years more have passed, let him be deemed worthy of the communion."—*Basil. Canon.* 75.

"It is to this system of penance and confession that in the Roman Church there has attached itself an immense and most singular mass of superstition and abuses."—*Guericke* iv. 19.

APPENDIX D.

THE APOSTOLICAL SUCCESSION.

OUR review of the office and position of the Christian ministry would hardly be complete without some notice of what has been called, "The Apostolical Succession," inasmuch as the doctrine designated by this expression claims a direct connection with the Apostles and the exercise of their authority.

The idea which forms the foundation of this dogma appeared in some slight form as early as the beginning of the third century; when it supplied Tertullian with one of his weapons against some heretical Churches. But it was matured and put forth most distinctly in more modern times. At the Reformation sharp disputes about the validity of our Protestant Orders originated from it. It furnishes still to Romanists a ground of attack against all Churches who have protested against Romish errors; and the spiritual authority and position of our clergy are by some amongst ourselves supposed to rest upon a foundation which it supplies.

The doctrine of the Apostolic Succession of the Ministry, according to those who hold it, "means that all men who have a right to be considered duly appointed ministers of Christ have received from Him a commission to minister in His name, conveyed in an outward and visible manner in a direct line from the holy Apostles." That is to say, that Christ gave his Apostles a certain spiritual authority and power, which they by His direction transferred to their successors; and these again to others after them, and so on in a perpetual line of successive transmissions. The authority and power which have been thus transmitted are specially those of ordaining priests, and giving them the power of duly administering the sacraments,—bestowing the grace of absolution,—or doing other priestly acts. And the successors, to and through whom alone this authority and power have been transmitted, are bishops. According to this theory the whole virtue, force, and efficacy of the Christian ministry from the Apostles to the present time have been in and by this succession. Those who have been ordained by bishops, descended in an unbroken line of this succession from the Apostles, are alone lawful Christian ministers; since any break in the links of this ecclesiastical chain invalidates the whole standing of an individual functionary, or of a Church, by cutting off, as it were, the flow of essential energy and divine power, by the uninterrupted communication of which the true ministerial life is enabled to act and move. So that there can be no true Christian ministry, no true Church, and no validity in the sacraments, except where there are ministers duly ordained by bishops who have received their episcopal authority and power by this uninterrupted transmission from the Apostles. All others, therefore, who minister in any congregation, are regarded as usurpers, schismatics, or heretics,—intruding into an office which is not theirs,—the Korah, Dathan, and Abiram, of modern days,—without lawful authority, powerless of all good, and constituting with their people a band of revolters from Christ, instead of a branch of His Church.

But what solid resting-ground of conviction is there in all this imaginative theory, when examined by the light of Scripture and of truth? It is true that a restricted succession something like this was in force for the priesthood of the Jewish Church, and the services of their Temple ; but the Christian ministry, as we have seen, is not a priesthood, nor was it taken from the Temple services, so as to suggest any argument of analogy from that source, except an argument altogether *against* this theory and entirely subversive of such a doctrine. But what is of much more weight, and forms *an absolutely conclusive refutation of this dogma*, is the following consideration. The succession of the Jewish priests was distinctly laid down by divine authority from the beginning ; and reiterated commands, enforced by the severest judgments, emphatically declared, that no one who was not of the seed of Aaron might officiate at the altar of God. Nothing but a divine command expressly given could ever make such a regulation imperatively exclusive. Nothing but a direct and positive ordinance of the New Testament could justify the assertion of such a doctrine now. But in the Christian dispensation no such command was ever given ; nor is there in the New Testament the slightest intimation, much less an authoritative announcement, that such an apostolical succession is the only source of lawful ministerial authority. The subject, in fact, is not once mentioned or alluded to in the Christian Scriptures ; nor are the Apostles ever shown to have themselves received, or to have given to others, any such powers as this dogma asserts to have been transmitted.

The words of the New Testament, which are sometimes pressed into the service of this doctrine of the corrupted Church, are in reality destitute of all evidence in its favour ; whereas nothing short of the most explicit declaration would be of any avail. When Jesus said to his Apostles, "Lo, I am with you alway, even unto the end of the world," he gave indeed a gracious promise to his ministering servants in all ages ;—but he spoke not a word about the virtue or necessity of any particular mode of their succession. When St. Paul wrote to Timothy to commit the truth which he had received "to faithful men who should be able to teach others also," he desired indeed a succession of sound doctrine, and of faithful men to teach it ;—but he did not declare that ministerial authority must be transmitted from himself through a chain of episcopally consecrated bishops, and must depend for its preservation and very existence upon that chain's unbroken continuity. The citation of such texts as these shows what an infinitesimal amount, or miserable pretence, of evidence is enough for those who have made up their minds without it ; and shows also what little countenance in the apostolic age was given to such theology.

If from the consideration of the conclusive argument, derived from the absence of all scriptural authority, we turn to matters of fact and historical experience, we may see some, who profess to have this apostolic succession, teaching vain traditions and gross errors instead of apostolic truth ; and some, who make no pretensions to it, and are not even episcopally ordained, altogether sound in doctrine and in practice, and with as true seals of their ministry among their people, as St. Paul had of his Apostleship among the Christians at Corinth.

The only answer that is or can be given for this is, that it is not the security of true teaching, but the power of imparting the grace of the sacraments, and of absolution, which the apostolic succession conveys. And this betrays the real character of the doctrine in question, and shows that it is only a fiction invented and propagated in the Church to bolster up sacerdotal superstitions.

Add to this the fact, that if this dogma were true, there is no Christian minister now living, who has ascertained, r could ascertain, whether he is lawfully exercising the duties of his office or not ; but he must remain in doubt as to the validity of his ordination and the position in which it has placed him.

Of an apostolic succession, which is not commanded by the Apostles, nor mentioned in the New Testament ;—which professes to transmit powers, never, as far as we know, by the Apostles either received or given ;—which secures no soundness in the faith, but lends itself to error, as readily as to truth ;—which can exclude the best as well as include the worst of ministers ;—and which would leave every Church in doubt about the validity of its ministrations and very existence ;—it is surely not too much to say that it "is a fond thing vainly invented, and grounded upon no warranty of Scripture, but rather repugnant to the word of God."

The authority of the Christian minister in any place is given to him by the Church in which, and for which, he acts : and this authority is *apostolic*, if his teaching is sound in apostolic truth ; this authority is from *Christ*, if His Church is a legitimate Christian community formed in obedience to Christ's command.

The doctrine of the apostolical succession, though it sometimes unduly alarmed our early Reformers not yet entirely disentangled from the errors of the ancient Church ;—though clung to since their time by some respected names in our communion ;—though now strongly maintained, and insisted on, by advanced Anglicans not yet drawn to Rome ;—is *not the doctrine of the Church of England*, as the following proofs distinctly testify.

1. A doctrine, so important and fundamental, if it is believed to be true, could not have been omitted, as it is, from our Articles and Prayer-book, if it had been held by our Church ; whereas it is not only omitted, but the wording of Art. XXIII. is quite incompatible with it.

2. The Statute of Queen Elizabeth, A. D. 1570, Anno xiii. Reginæ Elizabethæ c. 12, entituled "An Act for the Ministers of the Church to be of sound Religion," only requires

those, who had received Ordination in "any other form of Institution, Consecration or Ordering" than that of the Church of England, to subscribe to the "Articles of Religion" in order to hold Ecclesiastical preferment in this country; no objection at all being raised to the validity of such ordinations.

3. It is proved by a great variety and a long series of evidence, that during the first hundred years after the beginning of the English Reformation Presbyterian communities were recognised, and men who had only Presbyterian ordination were received, and obtained the highest preferments in the Church of England.

4. Hooker, the learned and revered champion of the English Church, whom no one will accuse of not knowing what its doctrines really were, while declaring Episcopacy to be the best and most desirable, says, nevertheless, "Whereas some do infer that no ordination can stand but such only as is made by Bishops, which have had their ordination likewise by other Bishops before them till we come to the very Apostles, ... to this we answer, that there may be sometimes very just and sufficient reason to allow ordination made without a Bishop,"—'*Eccl. Pol.*,' vii. 14, which gives up the whole question.

5. And even now the modern practice of not receiving men with Presbyterian orders, to minister in our Church, only points to the necessity of Episcopacy as a *form of ecclesiastical government*, and not to the *transmission of sacerdotal power* through Bishops. This, therefore, is not holding the "apostolical succession," which deals with Episcopacy not as a desirable mode of government, but as *a necessary channel of divine grace.*

Much valuable information on this subject is to be found in a pamphlet very recently published by Longmans, entituled, 'Apostolical Succession, not a doctrine of the Church of England.' It is written by an honest High-church Anglican clergyman who has joined the Church of Rome, and is addressed to another clergyman of the same school, who has not yet taken that step. He, of course, looks at the subject from the Romanist point of view ; but the historical and documentary evidence which he adduces is fairly dealt with, and clearly proves what the title of the book expresses.